the Adobe® Photoshop® Lightroom®2

book for digital photographers

Scott Kelby

AWARD-WINNING, BEST-SELLING AUTHOR OF
THE DIGITAL PHOTOGRAPHY BOOK, vols. 1 & 2

**The Adobe Photoshop Lightroom 2
Book for Digital Photographers Team**

CREATIVE DIRECTOR
Felix Nelson

TECHNICAL EDITORS
Cindy Snyder
Kim Doty

TRAFFIC DIRECTOR
Kim Gabriel

PRODUCTION MANAGER
Dave Damstra

DESIGNER
Jessica Maldonado

COVER PHOTOS
COURTESY OF
Scott Kelby

Published by **New Riders**

Copyright ©2009 by Scott Kelby

Composed in Cronos, Helvetica, Myriad Pro, and Blair ITC by Kelby Media Group, Inc.

Trademarks

All terms mentioned in this book that are known to be trademarks or service marks have been appropriately capitalized. New Riders cannot attest to the accuracy of this information. Use of a term in the book should not be regarded as affecting the validity of any trademark or service mark.

Photoshop Lightroom is a registered trademark of Adobe Systems, Inc.
Photoshop is a registered trademark of Adobe Systems, Inc.
Macintosh, Mac, and Mac OS X Leopard are registered trademarks of Apple Inc.
Windows is a registered trademark of Microsoft Corporation.

Warning and Disclaimer

This book is designed to provide information about Adobe Photoshop Lightroom for digital photographers. Every effort has been made to make this book as complete and as accurate as possible, but no warranty of fitness is implied.

The information is provided on an as-is basis. The author and New Riders shall have neither liability nor responsibility to any person or entity with respect to any loss or damages arising from the information contained in this book or from the use of the discs or programs that may accompany it.

THIS PRODUCT IS NOT ENDORSED OR SPONSORED BY ADOBE SYSTEMS INCORPORATED, PUBLISHER OF ADOBE PHOTOSHOP LIGHTROOM 2.

ISBN13: 978-0-321-55556-4
ISBN10:   0-321-55556-2

9 8 7 6 5 4 3 2 1

www.newriders.com
www.kelbytraining.com

For my Editor, Kim Doty.
You make writing books
an awful lot of fun, and
I just couldn't do it
without you.

ACKNOWLEDGMENTS

I start the acknowledgments for every book I've ever written the same way; I start by thanking my amazing wife, Kalebra. If you knew what an incredible woman she is, you'd totally understand why.

This is going to sound silly, but if we go grocery shopping together, and she sends me off to a different aisle to get milk, when I return with the milk and she sees me coming back down the aisle, she gives me the warmest, most wonderful smile. It's not because she's happy that I found the milk; I get that same smile every time I see her, even if we've only been apart for 60 seconds. It's a smile that says, "There's the man I love."

If you got that smile, dozens of times a day, for nearly 20 years of marriage, you'd feel like the luckiest guy in the world, and believe me—I do. To this day, just seeing her puts a song in my heart and makes it skip a beat. When you go through life like this, it makes you one incredibly happy and grateful guy, and I truly am.

So, thank you, my love. Thanks for your kindness, your hugs, your understanding, your advice, your patience, your generosity, and for being such a caring and compassionate mother and wife. I love you.

Secondly, a big thanks to my son, Jordan. I wrote my first book when my wife was pregnant with him (12 years ago), and he's literally grown up around my writing. Maybe that's why he's so patient as he waits for me to finish a page or two so we can go upstairs and play a quick game of Halo 3 (and much to his dismay, I've been surprisingly good at throwing plasma grenades, jacking a Scorpion Tank, and piloting a Hornet). He's such a great "little buddy" to me, and it's been a blast watching him grow up into such a wonderful young man, with his mother's tender and loving heart. (You're the greatest, little buddy!)

Thanks to our wonderful daughter, Kira, for being the answer to our prayers, for being such a blessing to your older brother, and for proving once again that miracles happen every day. You are a little clone of your mother, and believe me, there is no greater compliment I could give you. You're my little sweetie!

A special thanks to my big brother, Jeff. I have so much to be thankful for in my life, and having you as such a positive role model while I was growing up is one thing I'm particularly thankful for. You're the best brother any guy could ever have, and I've said it a million times before, but one more surely wouldn't hurt—I love you, man!

My heartfelt thanks go to my entire team at Kelby Media Group. I know everybody thinks their team is really special, but this one time—I'm right. I'm so proud to get to work with you all, and I'm still amazed at what you're able to accomplish day in, day out, and I'm constantly impressed with how much passion and pride you put into everything you do.

A warm word of thanks goes to my in-house Editor Kim Doty, to whom this book is dedicated (and who would be duly impressed that I used the word "whom"). It's her amazing attitude, passion, poise, and attention to detail that has kept me writing books. When you're writing a book like this, sometimes you can really feel like you're all alone, but she really makes me feel that I'm not alone—that we're a team. It often is her encouraging words or helpful ideas that keep me going when I've hit a wall, and I just can't thank her enough. Kim, you are "the best!"

I'm equally as lucky to have the immensely talented Jessica Maldonado working on the design of my books. I just love the way Jessica designs, and all the clever little things she adds to her layouts and cover designs. She's not just incredibly talented, and a joy to work with, she's a very smart designer and thinks five steps ahead in every layout she builds. I feel very, very fortunate to have her on my team.

Also, a big thanks to my in-house tech editor Cindy Snyder, who helps test all the techniques in the book (and makes sure I didn't leave out that one little step that would take the train off the tracks), and she catches lots of little things others would have missed.

Thanks to "Big Dave" Damstra, who does the layout work once the text and graphics start coming in, and he does such a great job, on such a tight deadline, yet still turns out books with a tight, clean layout that people love. You rock!

The guy leading this crew of creative superstars is none other than my friend (and Creative Director), Felix Nelson, whose limitless talent, creativity, input, and flat-out great ideas make every book we do that much better.

Thanks to my best buddy, Dave Moser. As I write this, Dave has just been blessed with twin baby girls who will have already turned this precision-oriented, dedicated, ex-military man into a bowl of mush. I love it (and I love him, too. Ya know, in the way a man loves Vermont).

Thanks to my friend and business partner, Jean A. Kendra, for her support and friendship all these years. You mean a lot to me, to Kalebra, and to our company.

A huge, huge thanks to my Executive Assistant, and general wonder woman, Kathy Siler. Without her fielding a lot of balls for me, and taking so much off my plate, I wouldn't have the time to write books in the first place. Each year I appreciate her more and more, and her amazing attitude, and MacGyver-like qualities make coming into the office an awful lot of fun. So much so, that I now actually root for the Redskins (unless, of course, they're playing the Bucs, in which case we're bitter mortal enemies for four quarters).

Thanks to my Editor Ted Waitt at Peachpit Press. Ted, I dig you (again, the Vermont thing), and like Kim Doty does in-house, you do outside by helping me feel connected to "the mothership." Thanks for all your hard work and dedication to making the kind of books that make a difference. Also, thanks to my Publisher Nancy Ruenzel, and her team, including Glenn Bisignani and Scott Cowlin. (Lest we forget Gary-Paul.)

Thanks to Lightroom Product Manager Tom Hogarty for answering all my late-night emails, and to Bryan Hughes for helping out in such an impactful way. My personal thanks to Kevin Connor at Adobe for his help, support, and for totally "getting "us.

I owe a special debt of gratitude to my buddy, Matt Kloskowski, for being such an excellent sounding board (and sometimes tech editor) during the development of this new version of the book. Your input made this book better than it would have been.

Thanks to my friends at Adobe Systems: Terry White, Addy Roff, Cari Gushiken, John Loiacono, Julieanne Kost, and Russell Preston Brown. Gone but not forgotten: Barbara Rice, Rye Livingston, Bryan Lamkin, and Karen Gauthier.

I want to thank all the talented and gifted photographers who've taught me so much over the years, including: Moose Peterson, Joe McNally, Bill Fortney, George Lepp, Anne Cahill, Vincent Versace, David Ziser, Jim DiVitale, Helene Glassman, and Monte Zucker.

Thanks to my mentors, whose wisdom and whip-cracking have helped me immeasurably, including John Graden, Jack Lee, Dave Gales, Judy Farmer, and Douglas Poole.

Most importantly, I want to thank God, and His son Jesus Christ, for leading me to the woman of my dreams, for blessing us with two amazing children, for allowing me to make a living doing something I truly love, for always being there when I need Him, for blessing me with a wonderful, fulfilling, and happy life, and such a warm, loving family to share it with.

OTHER BOOKS BY SCOTT KELBY

The Digital Photography Book, vols. 1 & 2

Scott Kelby's 7-Point System for Adobe Photoshop CS3

The iPod Book

The Photoshop CS3 Book for Digital Photographers

The Photoshop Channels Book

The iPhone Book

Photoshop Down & Dirty Tricks

Photoshop Killer Tips

Photoshop Classic Effects

The Mac OS X Leopard Book

Mac OS X Leopard Killer Tips

ABOUT THE AUTHOR

 Scott is Editor, Publisher, and co-founder of *Photoshop User* magazine, Editor-in-Chief of *Layers* magazine (the how-to magazine for everything Adobe), and is the host of the top-rated weekly video podcast *Photoshop User TV*.

He is President of the National Association of Photoshop Professionals (NAPP), the trade association for Adobe® Photoshop® users, and he's President of the training, education, and publishing firm, Kelby Media Group, Inc.

Scott is a photographer, designer, and award-winning author of more than 50 books, including *The Photoshop CS3 Book for Digital Photographers, Photoshop Down & Dirty Tricks, Scott Kelby's 7-Point System for Adobe Photoshop CS3, The Photoshop Channels Book, Photoshop Classic Effects, The iPhone Book, The iPod Book,* and *The Digital Photography Book,* vols. 1 & 2.

For four years straight, Scott has been honored with the distinction of being the world's #1 best-selling author of all computer and technology books, across all categories. His book, *The Digital Photography Book,* vol. 1, is now the best-selling book on digital photography in history.

His books have been translated into dozens of different languages, including Chinese, Russian, Spanish, Korean, Polish, Taiwanese, French, German, Italian, Japanese, Dutch, Swedish, Turkish, and Portuguese, among others, and he is a recipient of the prestigious Benjamin Franklin Award.

Scott is Training Director for the Adobe Photoshop Seminar Tour and Conference Technical Chair for the Photoshop World Conference & Expo. He's featured in a series of Adobe Photoshop training DVDs and online courses at KelbyTraining.com and has been training Adobe Photoshop users since 1993.

For more information on Scott, visit his daily blog, *Photoshop Insider,* at www.scottkelby.com.

TABLE OF CONTENTS

CHAPTER 1   1

▼ Importing
GETTING YOUR PHOTOS INTO PHOTOSHOP LIGHTROOM

Before You Do Anything, Choose Where to Store
Your Photos 2

Next, Do This: Set Up Your Folder Organization
(It's Really Important) 3

Getting Your Photos Into Lightroom 5

Shooting Tethered (Go Straight from Your Camera,
Right Into Lightroom) 20

Creating Your Own Custom File Naming
Templates 22

Choosing Your Preferences for Importing Photos . . 26

The Adobe DNG File Format Advantage 29

Creating Your Own Custom Metadata (Copyright)
Templates 30

Lightroom Quick Tips 32

Make Finding Your Photos Easier by Adding
Specific Keywords 60

Working with, and Adding to, Your
Photo's Metadata 67

If Your Camera Supports GPS, Prepare to Amaze
Your Friends 72

Finding Photos Fast! 74

Renaming Photos Already in Lightroom 80

Moving Photos and How to Use Folders 82

Working in Folders? Use Stacking to Keep
Things Organized 86

Creating and Using Multiple Catalogs 89

From Laptop to Desktop: Syncing Catalogs on Two
Computers 92

Backing Up Your Catalog (This Is VERY Important) . . 95

Relinking Missing Photos 97

Lightroom Quick Tips 99

CHAPTER 2   35

▼ Library
ORGANIZING YOUR PHOTOS

Four Things You'll Want to Know Now About
Working in Lightroom 36

Viewing Your Imported Photos 38

Using Lights Dim, Lights Out, and Other
Viewing Modes 40

Sorting Your Imported Photos Using Collections . . 42

Organizing Multiple Shoots Using Collection Sets . . 54

Using Smart Collections for Automatic
Organization 56

When to Use a Quick Collection Instead 58

CHAPTER 3   103

▼ Customizing
HOW TO SET UP THINGS YOUR WAY

Choosing What You See in Loupe View 104

Choosing What You See in Grid View 106

Choosing Lightroom's Background Color 110

Make Working with Panels Faster & Easier 111

Using Two Monitors with Lightroom 112

Adding Your Studio's Name or Logo for a
Custom Look 116

Choosing What the Filmstrip Displays 120

Naming Your Color Labels 121

Changing Those Ornaments Below the Last Panel . . 123

Lightroom Quick Tips 126

CHAPTER 4   129

▼ Editing Essentials
HOW TO DEVELOP YOUR PHOTOS

Setting the White Balance 130

How to Set Your Overall Exposure 135

Adding "Punch" to Your Images Using Clarity . . . 141

Making Your Colors More Vibrant 142

Using the Tone Curve to Add Contrast 143

Adjusting Individual Colors Using HSL. 148

Vignetting Effects and Post-Cropping Vignettes . . . 150

Getting That Trendy, Gritty Portrait Look 152

Virtual Copies—The "No Risk" Way
to Experiment 154

Applying Changes Made to One Photo to
Other Photos. 156

Fixing a Bunch of Photos Live, While Editing Just
One (Using Auto Sync) 158

Save Your Favorite Settings as One-Click Presets. . 159

Using the Library Module's Quick Develop Panel . 163

Lightroom Quick Tips 165

CHAPTER 5   169

▼ Local Adjustments
HOW TO EDIT JUST PART OF YOUR IMAGES

Dodging, Burning, and Adjusting Individual Areas
of Your Photo 170

Getting Creative with the Adjustment Brush. . . . 178

Retouching Portraits 180

Fixing Skies (and Other Stuff) with the
Gradient Filter 182

Lightroom Quick Tips 184

CHAPTER 6   187

▼ Problem Photos
CORRECTING DIGITAL CAMERA DILEMMAS

Undoing Changes Made in Lightroom. 188

Reducing Noise 190

Fixing Edge Vignetting. 191

Cropping Photos 192

The Ultimate Cropping View. 195

Straightening Crooked Photos 196

Great Trick for "Dust Spotting" Your Photos. . . . 198

Removing Spots and Other Nasty Junk 199

Removing Red Eye 203

Fixing Backlit Photos (Using Fill Light). 205

Sharpening Your Photos in Lightroom. 207

Fixing Chromatic Aberrations (a.k.a. That Annoying
Color Fringe) 212

Using Camera Profiles to Match the Look of the
Image on Your LCD. 213

Basic Camera Calibration in Lightroom 215

Lightroom Quick Tips 217

TABLE OF CONTENTS

CHAPTER 7   219

▼ **Exporting Images**
SAVING JPEGS, TIFFS, AND MORE

Saving Your Photos as JPEGs 220

Emailing Photos from Lightroom 226

Using Export Plug-Ins (Auto-Uploading to Flickr) . . 230

Exporting Your Original RAW Photo 232

Lightroom Quick Tips 234

CHAPTER 8   237

▼ **Jumping to Photoshop**
HOW AND WHEN TO DO IT

Choosing How Your Files Are Sent to Photoshop . . 238

How to Jump Over to Photoshop, and How
to Jump Back. 239

Adding Photoshop Automation to Your
Lightroom Workflow 247

Double-Processing by Opening Photos in
Photoshop as a Smart Object 253

Stitching Panoramas Using Photoshop 259

Merging HDR Images in Photoshop 262

Lightroom Quick Tips 268

CHAPTER 9   271

▼ **Gorgeous B&W**
CONVERTING FROM COLOR TO BLACK AND WHITE

Finding Out Which Photos Might Look Great
in Black & White 272

Better Black and White by Doing It Yourself 274

How to Tweak Individual Areas When You
Convert to Black and White 278

Adding a Split-Tone Effect to Your
Black-and-White Photos 282

Creating Duotones Using the Split Toning Panel. . .286

Lightroom Quick Tips 288

CHAPTER 10   291

▼ **Slideshow**
SHARING YOUR PHOTOS ONSCREEN

Creating a Quick, Basic Slide Show 292

Adding Opening and Closing Title Slides 296

Customizing the Look of Your Slides 298

Using a Photo as Your Slide Background. 306

Adding Background Music 308

Choosing Your Slide Show Preferences 311

Emailing Your Slide Show 312

Lightroom Quick Tips 314

CHAPTER 11   317

▼ **Print**
PRINTING YOUR PHOTOS

Setting Up Your Photos for Printing
(It All Starts Here). 318

Adding Text to Your Print Layouts 326

Printing Multiple Photos on One Page 328

Having Lightroom Remember Your Last
Printing Layouts 336

The Final Print and Color Management Settings . .339

Saving Your Page Layout as a JPEG 347

Adding Cool Frame Borders to Your Prints 349

Lightroom Quick Tips 353

Workflow Step Four: Tweaking the Picks 381

Workflow Step Five: Letting Your Clients Proof
on the Web 385

Workflow Step Six: Making the Final Tweaks
& Working with Photoshop 387

Workflow Step Seven: Delivering the
Finished Image 393

CHAPTER 12   355

▼ Web
GETTING YOUR PHOTOS ON THE WEB

Building a Quick, Simple, Online Photo Gallery . . .356

Adding an Email or Website Link to Your Gallery . .360

Customizing Your Gallery Layout 362

Changing the Colors of Your Gallery 366

Using Cooler Flash Templates 368

Putting Your New Gallery on the Web 370

Lightroom Quick Tips 372

CHAPTER 13   375

▼ Portrait Workflow
MY STEP-BY-STEP ON-LOCATION PORTRAIT
SHOOT PROCESS

Workflow Step One: It All Starts with the Shoot . . .376

Workflow Step Two: Right After the Shoot,
Do This First 378

Workflow Step Three: Finding the "Keepers"
& Making a Collection. 379

CHAPTER 14   399

▼ Travel Workflow
MY STEP-BY-STEP TRAVEL PHOTOGRAPHY PROCESS

Workflow Step One: Importing
and Organizing 400

Workflow Step Two: Editing Our Images
in Lightroom 2 404

Workflow Step Three: Creating a Slide Show 410

Workflow Step Four: Putting Up a Web Gallery . .414

Bonus Video: My Wedding
Photography Workflow 416

Where to Go Next for More Lightroom Learning . .417

INDEX   420

Seven Things You'll Wish You Had Known Before Reading This Book

I really want to make sure you get the absolute most out of reading this book, and if you take two minutes and read these seven things now, I promise it will make a big difference in your success with Lightroom 2, and with this book (plus, it will keep you from sending me an email asking something that everyone who skips this part will wind up doing). By the way, the captures shown below are just for looks. Hey, we're photographers—how things look really matters.

(1) First, go right now to www.kelby training.com/books/lightroom2 and watch the short video I made to explain these seven things in more detail. It's short, it's quick, and it will help you read this book in half the time (okay, the "half the time" thing is marketing hype, but you'll get a lot out of the video, so head over there first. I'll make it worth your while).

(2) You can download many of the key photos used here in the book, so you can follow along using the same images that I used, at **www.kelbytraining.com/ books/lightroom2**. See, this is one of those things I was talking about that you'd miss if you skipped over this and jumped right to Chapter 1. Then you'd send me an angry email about how I didn't tell you where to download the photos. You wouldn't be the first.

(3) If you've read my other books, you know they're usually "jump in anywhere" books, but with Lightroom, I wrote the book in the order you'll probably wind up using the program, so if you're new to Lightroom, I would really recommend you start with Chapter 1 and go through the book in order. But hey—it's your book—if you decide to just hollow out the insides and store your valuables in there, I'll never know.

(4) The official name of the software is "Adobe Photoshop Lightroom 2" because it's part of the Photoshop family, but if every time I referred to it throughout the book, I called it "Adobe Photoshop Lightroom 2," you'd eventually want to strangle me (or the person sitting nearest you), so from here on out, I usually just refer to it as "Lightroom" or "Lightroom 2." Just so you know.

(5) The intro page at the beginning of each chapter is designed to give you a quick mental break, and honestly, they have little to do with the chapter. In fact, they have little to do with anything, but writing these quirky chapter intros is kind of a tradition of mine (I do this in all my books), but if you're one of those really "serious" types, you can skip them, because they'll just get on your nerves.

(6) At the end of the book are two special bonus chapters where I share my own complete workflow, from beginning to end, starting with the shoot, working with the images in Lightroom, right through to the final output. However, don't read these until you've read the entire book first, because I put those last for a reason—you have to have read the rest of the book for them to make sense.

(7) There's a third bonus workflow for wedding photographers, but I did this one for you live on video. It was filmed on location at a church while I was shooting a formal bridal portrait. You see the lighting setup, the camera gear, a quick shoot, and then we go into Lightroom to process the photos step by step, all the way through to the final print. You can see this bonus video at...well, you have to wait until the end of the book, and I'll tell you where then. Hey, you're supposed to read the book first, then do the workflow chapters and watch the video, right? Right! Okay, turn the page and let's get to work.

Importing
getting your photos
into photoshop lightroom

Now, do we really need an entire chapter just on importing photos? Nope. We could just skip it, but then the book would start with Chapter 2, and you'd be sending emails to the book's publisher complaining that your book is missing Chapter 1. See, that's the key word there—missing. You wouldn't think I intentionally skipped it—you'd think that there must have been some mix-up at the printing plant, and your copy accidentally wound up without a Chapter 1. So, you'd take it back to the bookstore and you'd ask for a replacement copy. You'd get home and find out that, once again, Chapter 1 was missing. Then you'd start to think that this is no coincidence. It must be some sort of a printing conspiracy (orchestrated by a covert government agency), and that right now, somewhere in the Midwest,

there's an unmarked warehouse chock full of Chapter 1s. You'd then start to call me names. Unspeakable names. Names that would make you feel ashamed and dirty, but you'd do it anyway because you'd feel so certain that this was all part of a carefully crafted strategy designed to keep you from knowing the contents of Chapter 1. Obviously, there's something in Chapter 1 that "they" don't want you to know. Suddenly that missing Chapter 1 is worth fighting for. You deserve a Chapter 1, and to know exactly what's in it. So, because I care about you, my reader, the way I do, I stood up to "the man" on your behalf and demanded that this book have a Chapter 1, and that it would be on importing photos, because there's more to it than it first seems. See, it all makes perfect sense once you look at it calmly and logically.

Before You Do Anything, Choose Where to Store Your Photos

Before you dive into Photoshop Lightroom and start importing photos, you need to make a decision about where you're going to store your photo library. This isn't as easy a decision as you might think, because you have to consider how many photos you've taken so far (and want to manage with Lightroom), how many you think you might take in the next few years, and you need to make sure you have enough room to store thousands of photos, wherever you decide to store them—on your computer or on an external hard drive. Here's where to start:

For Desktop Computer Users:

Lightroom assumes you're going to store your photos on your computer's internal hard disk, so by default, it automatically chooses your Mac's or PC's Pictures (My Pictures in Windows XP) folder to store all your photos. So, unless you choose differently (in Lightroom's Import dialog, which you'll learn about in just a few minutes), it's going to always choose to save your photos in this folder. As long as you've got a lot of free hard disk space available on your computer (and I mean a lot!), then you're all set. (*Note:* If you're wondering how much is "a lot," consider this: if you shoot just once a week, and fill up nothing more than a single 4-GB card with each shoot, in one year alone, you'll eat up more than 200 GB of drive space. So when it comes to hard drive storage space, think big!) If you don't have enough free hard disk space on your computer, then you'll need to buy an external hard drive to store all your photos (don't worry, Lightroom will still manage all your images, you're just storing them on a separate hard drive. You'll learn how to set this all up in the next few pages).

For Laptop Users:

If you primarily use a laptop computer for editing your images, then I would definitely recommend using an external hard drive to store your photo library because of the limited hard disk space on most laptops. Think about it. You're going to need to manage literally thousands (or tens of thousands) of images, and your laptop is going to get really full, really fast (believe me, it gets there faster than you'd think), so using an external drive (they're surprisingly inexpensive these days) has become the choice for many photographers using Lightroom. (You can find around 500-GB external hard drives for less than $200 these days, but if you can spend a little more, go for the now popular 1-TB [terabyte] drives, which hold 1,000 GB.)

SCOTT KELBY

Lightroom can do a brilliant job of keeping you organized, as long as you start out being organized, and that means sticking to this one simple, but critical, rule: keep all your photos inside one main folder. It doesn't matter how many other folders you have inside it, just make sure all your photos reside within that main folder. This is the key ingredient to making everything work smoothly. If, instead, you import photos from folders in different locations all over your computer, you're headed for trouble. Here's how to set things up right from the start:

Next, Do This: Set Up Your Folder Organization (It's Really Important)

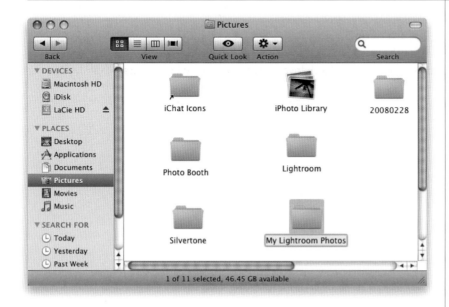

Step One:

As you read above, our goal is to get all our photos inside one main folder, right? Well, if you decided to store all your photos on your computer, then the rest is pretty easy. By default, Lightroom automatically chooses your Pictures (or My Pictures) folder as your main photo folder, and when you go to import photos from a memory card, it will automatically choose that folder for you. However, I'm going to recommend doing one extra thing now to make your life much easier: go inside your Pictures (or My Pictures) folder, create a new empty folder, and name it "My Lightroom Photos" (you don't have to name it that exactly, but just to make things consistent here in the book, that's what I've named my main folder). That way, when that day comes when you run out of hard disk space (and it will come way sooner than you might imagine), you can move, copy, or back up your entire photo library by simply moving one folder—your My Lightroom Photos folder. This is one of those things that if you do it now, there will come a day when it will save you not just hours, but literally days, worth of work.

Continued

Step Two:

If you already have folders full of photos on your computer, before you start importing them into Lightroom, you'll want to drag-and-drop those folders inside your My Lightroom Photos folder first. That way, all your photos reside inside that that one My Lightroom Photos folder before you import them into Lightroom. Although it doesn't seem like it now, again, it's amazing how this one little bit of organization will make your life that much easier down the road. If you chose to store your photos on an external hard drive, then you'll just have one extra step here, just this one time, at this setup stage (that's in the next step).

Step Three:

On your external hard drive, just create a new folder, name it My Lightroom Photos (or whatever you'd like), then drag-and-drop any photos on your computer that you want managed by Lightroom into that My Lightroom Photos folder on your external drive. Of course, keep them in their original folders when you drag-and-drop them over into your My Lightroom Photos folder (after all, you don't want to just drag-and-drop thousands of photos into one big empty folder). Do all this before you start importing them into Lightroom (which we'll talk about in detail on the next page, along with how to tell Lightroom how to use that new folder you created to store all your imported photos).

At its heart, Lightroom is a very slick photo database, and one of the coolest things about it is it keeps track of all the photos you import, even if they're not on your computer any longer. For example, if you imported photos that you keep on an external hard drive, even when you unplug that drive, their thumbnails are still in Lightroom's database, so you can still work with those photos, and when you reconnect the drive, it reconnects to the real photos. Not too shabby. But this all starts with getting your photos into Lightroom, so let's get to it.

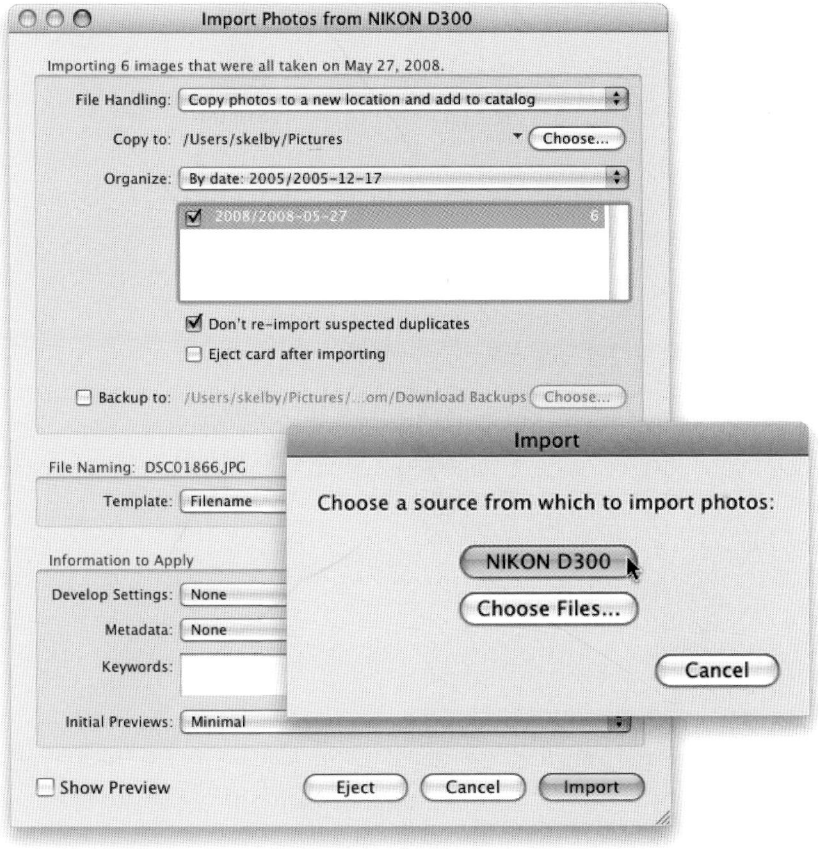

Getting Your Photos Into Lightroom

Import Photos from NIKON D300

Importing 6 images that were all taken on May 27, 2008.

File Handling: Copy photos to a new location and add to catalog

Copy to: /Users/skelby/Pictures   Choose...

Organize: By date: 2005/2005-12-17

☑ 2008/2008-05-27   6

☑ Don't re-import suspected duplicates
☐ Eject card after importing

☐ Backup to: /Users/skelby/Pictures/...om/Download Backups Choose...

File Naming: DSC01866.JPG

Template: Filename

Information to Apply

Develop Settings: None

Metadata: None

Keywords:

Initial Previews: Minimal

Import

Choose a source from which to import photos:

NIKON D300

Choose Files...

Cancel

☐ Show Preview   Eject   Cancel   Import

Step One:
The photos you bring into Lightroom are probably coming from either your camera (well, your camera's memory card), or they're already on your computer (everybody's got a bunch of photos already on their computer, right?). We'll start with importing photos from your camera's memory card. If you have Lightroom open, and you connect your camera or memory card reader to your computer, the Import Photos dialog you see here appears. (*Note:* If you don't actually want to import the photos from your memory card right now, just click the Cancel button and this dialog goes away. At the end of this chapter, I'll show you how to stop that Import Photos dialog from showing up automatically if it's driving you crazy.) If you cancel the Import Photos dialog, you can always get back to it by clicking on the Import button (found at the bottom of the left side Panels area in Lightroom's Library module). If your camera or memory card reader is still connected, the smaller Import dialog (shown here) appears. Click the button that lists your camera or memory card reader on it to import photos from your memory card, or click the bottom button if you want to choose files already on your computer. In our case, click the top button.

Continued

Step Two:

I recommend turning on the Show Preview checkbox at the bottom left of the Import Photos dialog so you can see a preview of the photos on your memory card. This way, you get to choose which photos you want to import (or you can import them all, but at least this way you'll have a choice, right?). When you turn on the Show Preview checkbox (shown circled here in red), a Preview section appears on the right side of the dialog (as seen here). The slider that appears below the right side of that Preview section controls the size of the preview thumbnails, so if you want to see these thumbnails larger, just drag that slider to the right.

TIP: Upgrading from Lightroom 1

If you're upgrading from Lightroom 1 (or versions 1.1, 1.2, 1.3, or 1.4, depending on how often you updated), when you launch Lightroom 2 for the first time, it will ask if you want to import any existing catalogs you're already working with from Lightroom 1. Of course, you could say "no" and start by creating a new, fresh catalog. However, if you decide later that you want to import one or more of your older catalogs, just go under Lightroom's File menu and choose Open Catalog. Navigate your way to the old catalog, click the Import button, and Lightroom 2 will update your old catalog to have it work with Lightroom 2.

Step Three:

By default, every photo in this Preview section is selected for import (that's why there's a marked checkbox in the top-left corner of every thumbnail). If you see one or more photos you don't want imported, just turn off their checkboxes. Now, what if you have 300+ photos on your memory card, but you only want a handful of these imported? You click the Uncheck All button at the bottom of the Preview section (which unchecks every photo), and Command-click (PC: Ctrl-click) on just the photos you want to import. Then, turn on the checkbox for any of these selected photos and all the selected photos become checked, and will be imported.

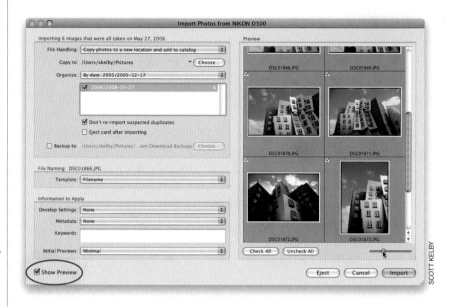

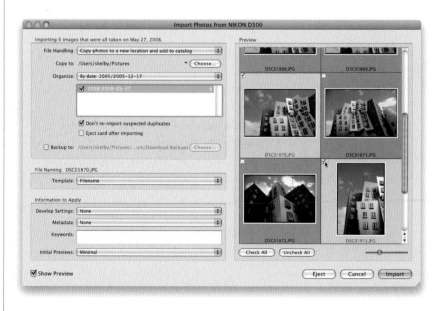

SCOTT KELBY

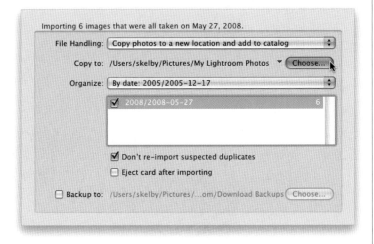

TIP: Selecting Multiple Photos
If the photos you want are contiguous, then click on the first photo, press-and-hold the Shift key, scroll down to the last photo, and click on it to select all the photos in between at once.

Step Four:
On the top left of this same Import Photos dialog, go to the File Handling pop-up menu (shown here) where you get to choose whether you want to just copy the photos from your memory card and import them into Lightroom as is, or to convert them into Adobe's DNG format as they're being imported (if you're not familiar with the advantages of Adobe's DNG file format, turn to page 29). Luckily, there's no wrong answer here, so if at this point you're unsure of what to do, for now just choose the default setting of Copy Photos to a New Location and Add to Catalog, which copies the images off the card onto your computer (or external drive) and imports them into Lightroom. Neither choice moves your originals off the card, it only copies them, so if there's a serious problem during import (hey, it happens), you still have the originals on the memory card.

Step Five:
Now we've come to the part where you tell Lightroom where to store the photos you're importing. You do this right below the File Handling pop-up menu, in the Copy To section. To the right of Copy To, it shows you the default location where Lightroom is going to save your imported photos, but you'll need to click the Choose button (as shown here) and navigate to your My Lightroom Photos folder (the one you made back on page 3, that is either on your computer or on an external hard drive connected to your computer). Click the Choose button in the Choose Folder dialog, and now your photos will be copied from your memory card into your My Lightroom Photos folder when you import them into Lightroom.

Continued

TIP: Converting Photos to DNG

If you didn't choose Copy Photos as Digital Negative (DNG) and Add to Catalog from the File Handling pop-up menu and want your imported photos saved in this file format, you can always convert any photo you've imported into Lightroom into a DNG by just clicking on the photo(s), going to Lightroom's Library menu, and choosing Convert Photo to DNG (although technically you can convert JPEGs and TIFFs into DNG format, converting them into DNG doesn't really offer any advantages, so I only convert RAW photos to DNG). This DNG replaces the RAW file you see in Lightroom, and the RAW file remains in the same folder on your computer (Lightroom, though, gives you the option of deleting the original RAW file when you make the conversion. This is what I choose, since the DNG includes the RAW photo within it).

Step Six:

Next you get to choose (from the Organize pop-up menu in the Import Photos dialog) how these images are organized as they're imported. If you click on the Organize pop-up menu, you'll see a list of different choices, and at first glance this might seem like a complicated list, but you really actually only have two choices: (1) If you choose Into One Folder, it tosses the photos loose into your My Lightroom Photos folder, and they're not organized within their own separate folder. So, I recommend that if you choose this option, that you turn on the Put in Subfolder checkbox (as shown here), and then name the folder. That way, it imports them into their own separate folder inside your My Lightroom Photos folder. Otherwise, things will get very messy, very quickly. I cover the second Organize choice in the next step.

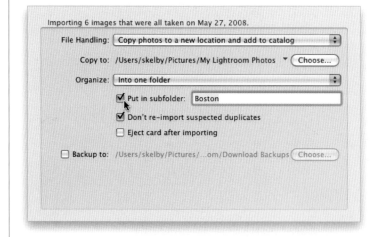

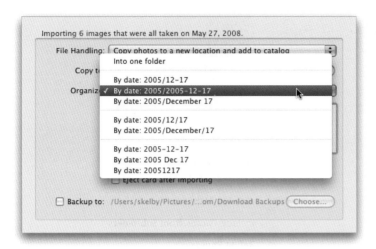

If you choose one of the options that has a forward slash after the year, it creates a year folder (like 2008) inside your My Lightroom Photos folder, then it creates another folder inside of that named with the month and day that the photos inside were taken (as seen above)

If, instead, you choose one of the options without a forward slash after the year, it creates just one folder with the date the photos were taken inside of your My Lightroom Photos folder

Step Seven:

Your second Organize choice is to have Lightroom organize your photos into folders by date. All the By Date choices you see in the pop-up menu let you choose which date format you like best. They all start by putting your photos inside a year folder. For example, if you took the photos in 2008, they'll automatically wind up in a folder (which Lightroom creates for you inside your My Lightroom Photos folder) named "2008." So, what you're really choosing from this list is the name of the folder that appears inside this new 2008 folder. Again, for example, if you took the photos you're importing on the 4th of August, you can choose to have this folder named "08-04" or "2008-08-04" or "August 04" and so on. If you look at the pop-up menu (shown here), if you choose a date option that has a forward slash in it, it means the folder inside your 2008 folder will be named what appears after the forward slash.

Step Eight:

If you choose a date option from the Organize pop-up menu that has no forward slash appearing after the year (one of the bottom three choices in the menu), it doesn't create a 2008 folder and then another folder with that month and day inside of it. Instead, it creates a new folder with the full date, and puts that inside your My Lightroom Photos folder, like any other folder. So, for example, if you choose the 2005 Dec 17 option from the pop-up menu, it would create a folder named "2008 Aug 04" inside your My Lightroom Photos folder (see how it skips creating that 2008 folder first?). There's no right or wrong choice here; it's just up to your personal preference of how you want the folders on your computer (or external drive) named and organized.

Continued

Step Nine:

If you're like me, you probably wind up having multiple shoots on the same memory card (for example, I often shoot one day and then shoot a few days later with the same memory card in my camera). If that's the case, then there's another advantage to using the Organize By Date feature, and that is it shows each of the shoots on your memory card by their date (as shown here). Only the shoots with a checkmark beside them will be imported into Lightroom, so if you only want to import shots from a particular date, you can turn off the checkbox beside the dates you don't want imported.

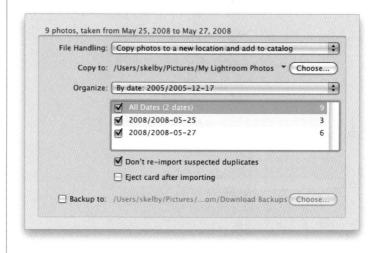

Step 10:

One last thing about the Organize By Date feature that might surprise you, and that's awfully darn handy, is that you can actually rename the folders so they're not imported by date, but by a custom name you create instead. Just double-click directly on a date in the list of shoots, and it highlights so you can type in a custom name. Press the Return (PC: Enter) key once you've typed in your custom name and now your shoot will appear in a separate folder, by name, inside your main My Lightroom Photos folder. This is the method I use in my own workflow when importing images from multiple shoots. There are two more options just below the shoots list, but they're pretty self-explanatory, and I always leave them both turned on because I don't want duplicates of photos imported, wasting extra hard drive space, and once my photos are imported, I want Lightroom to automatically eject my memory card.

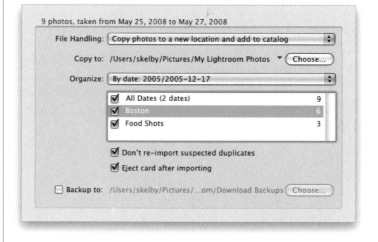

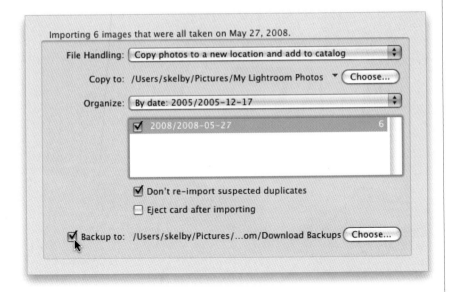

Step 11:

At the bottom of the File Handling section is the Backup To checkbox, and when you turn this on (and you absolutely, positively should), it automatically makes a backup copy of the photos you're importing (ideally, onto a separate hard drive), so you've always got an original backup of your photos. That way, you have a working set of photos on your computer (or external drive) that you can experiment with, change, and edit knowing that you have the untouched originals (the digital negatives) backed up. Only after I have two sets of copies (one on my computer [or external drive] and one on my backup drive) will I erase my camera's memory card.

Step 12:

For this backup feature to work properly, you've got to save the backup copies onto a separate external hard drive. You can't just back up your photos to a different folder on the same computer (or the external hard drive you are storing your photos on), because if your computer's hard drive (or your storage hard drive) crashes, then you lose both your working copies and the backup copies, too. That's why you've got to make sure the backups go to a completely separate external hard drive. So connect this separate drive, then click the Choose button to the right of the Backup To checkbox and in the Backup Folder dialog, select that drive (under Devices in Finder's sidebar on a Mac or under Computer on a PC) to back up to (don't forget to keep things simple—put your folders inside one main folder there, too).

Continued

Step 13:

Also, if you're already storing your original photos on an external hard drive, it means you now have two external hard drives—one for your working photos, and one for your backups. A lot of photographers buy two small stackable external hard drives (small hard drives that can stack one on top of the other), and then connect one with a FireWire cable (called an IEEE 1394 on a PC), and the other with a USB 2 cable (hey, I never said this was going to be cheap, but think of it this way: if one day you lost all your photos, you'd pay anything to get them back, right? Instead, just pay a fraction now for a backup hard drive—believe me, you'll sleep better at night).

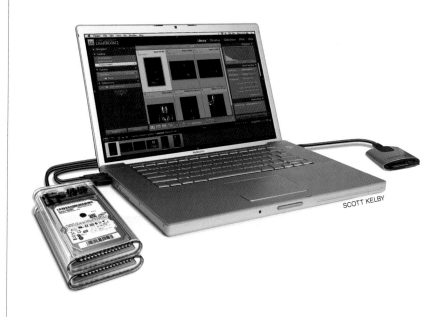

SCOTT KELBY

Step 14:

Before we go any further, what if you're not importing photos from a memory card, but importing photos already on your computer? It's much simpler and faster—you don't have to make many decisions, since the photos are already on your computer (if you followed the earlier instructions, they're in a folder inside your My Lightroom Photos folder). Go under Lightroom's File menu and choose Import Photos from Disk, or press **Command-Shift-I (PC: Ctrl-Shift-I)**. Select the photos you want to import and click Choose. In the Import Photos dialog, from the File Handling pop-up menu, choose Add Photos to Catalog Without Moving. The only option here is the checkbox at the bottom to not re-import photos that Lightroom thinks are duplicates. When you click Import, it doesn't copy or move any photos, it just adds them to Lightroom's catalog so you can manage, edit, and print them just like photos you import from a memory card.

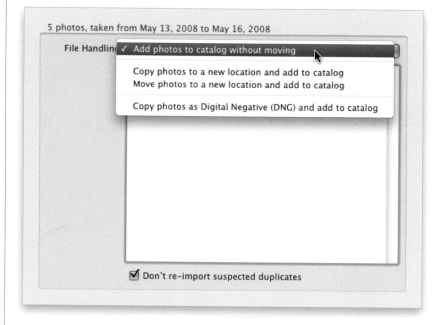

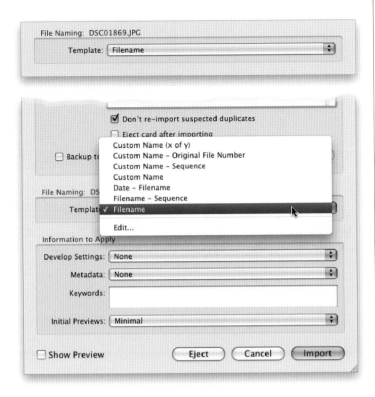

Step 15:

The next section down (in the Import Photos dialog) is the File Naming section. (*Note:* You'll only see this File Naming section when you're importing photos if you choose the copy or move options from the File Handling pop-up menu.) By default, Lightroom uses the photo's current filename, as shown here on top (in other words, it keeps the just-about-useless name assigned by your digital camera, like DSC01869.JPG. Is it just me or is that not a particularly descriptive name for a photo of a mountain stream?). Now, there are probably as many naming schemes out there today as there are photos on your memory card, and Lightroom has some of the more popular ones built right in, in the form of File Naming templates, so click on the Template pop-up menu to see the list (as shown here on the bottom).

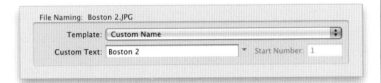

Step 16:

There is no "right" way to name your photos; it's really just a personal preference, so I rename the photos I'm importing with names that actually describe the shoot. For example, my images might be renamed something like Boston.JPG. That way, I have a searchable name and, without even seeing the image, I know that the photo was taken in Boston. If I might shoot there more than once, then I include the year first, making it 2008 Boston.JPG, or if I shot on multiple days, then I'd make it Boston 1.JPG and Boston 2.JPG. You do this by choosing Custom Name from the File Naming Template pop-up menu, and you type in the name you want in the Custom Text field (Lightroom automatically numbers the files for you, so the final rename would be Boston 2.JPG, Boston 2-1.JPG, Boston 2-2.JPG, and so on).

Continued

TIP: Multiple Cards from One Shoot

If you shot two or three memory cards of the same subject, you'll want to choose Custom Name – Sequence from the Template pop-up menu, which adds a Start Number field where you can type in which number you want to start with as you import each card, as shown here (rather than always starting with the number 1 like the Custom Name template). For example, if you imported 236 photos from your first card, you'd want the second card to start numbering with the number 237, so these shots of the same subject stay sequential. Once that card is imported (let's say you had 244 shots on that card), then you'd want the start number for the third card's photos to be 481. By the way, I don't do the math, I just look at the file number of the last photo I imported, and then add 1 to it in the Start Number field.

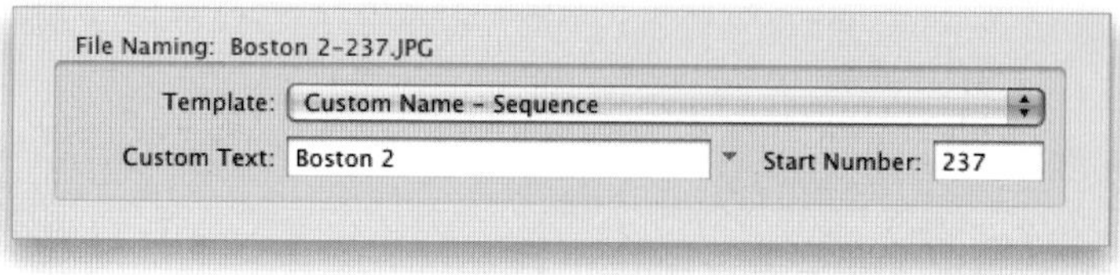

Step 17:

One last thing about file renaming: if you don't see a built-in File Naming template that you like, you can always create your own custom File Naming template, and when you're done, it will appear in the File Naming Template pop-up menu, just like the built-in ones. You do this by choosing Edit from the Template pop-up menu, which brings up the dialog you see here, where you create your template. *Note:* I included a step-by-step tutorial on how to create these templates later in this chapter, and if you just can't wait to create your own custom File Naming template, jump over to page 22. Once you save your new template, come right back here and we'll pick up where we left off. For the rest of us, just choose the built-in Custom Name template from the File Naming Template pop-up menu in the Import Photos dialog, and we'll move ahead from here.

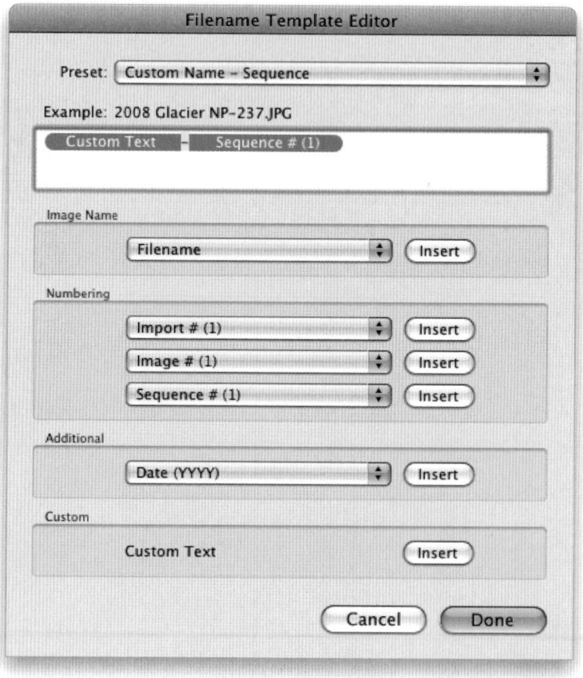

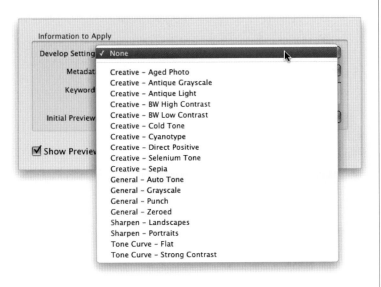

Step 18:

The next section down in the Import Photos dialog is Information to Apply, where you can choose to have up to three different settings automatically applied to your photos as they're imported. First is Develop Settings, which lets you apply preset tonal adjustments (either the built-in ones, or custom ones you create in the Develop module). For example, let's say your camera always makes photos a little too red for your taste, so you wind up always adjusting your photos so they have a little less red. You could create a preset that would automatically remove a little red from every photo imported from your camera. That way, once they appear in Lightroom, they've already had their red adjusted just the way you like it. It's pretty cool—I know. You'll learn how to use and create your own custom Develop presets in Chapter 4, so for now just leave the Develop Settings set to None.

Step 19:

The next pop-up menu down, Metadata, is where you can choose to embed your own personal copyright info, contact info, usage rights, captions, and loads of other information right into each file as it's imported. You do this by first entering all your copyright info, contact info, etc., into a template (called a Metadata template), and then when you save your template, it will appear in the Metadata pop-up menu (as shown here). You're also not limited to just one template; you can have different ones for different reasons. I show you step by step how to create Metadata templates on page 30 in this chapter, so go ahead and take two minutes to jump over there now and create your first template, then come right back here and choose your copyright template from this pop-up menu. Go ahead. I'll wait for you. Really, it's no bother.

Continued

Step 20:

Okay, welcome back (see, I told you that would be quick). The third option down in the Information to Apply section is a surprisingly important field—the Keywords field. Keywords are just search terms—words that Lightroom embeds directly into your photos as they're imported, so later you can search for (and actually find) them by using any one of these keywords. At this stage of the game, you'll want to use very generic keywords—words that would apply to every photo you're importing. For example, for these building photos, I clicked my cursor once in the Keywords field, and typed in generic keywords like Boston, buildings, and architecture. Put a comma between each search word or phrase, and just make sure the words you choose are generic enough to cover all the photos (in other words, don't use "brown buildings" because they're not all brown).

TIP: Choosing Keywords

Here's how I choose my keywords: I ask myself, "If months from now, I was trying to find these same photos, what words would I most likely type in the Find field?" Then I use those words. It works better than you'd think.

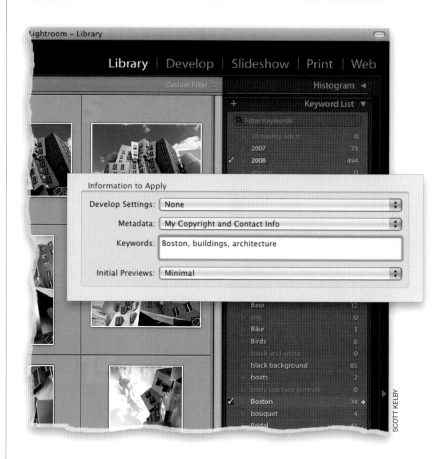

Step 21:

At the bottom of the Information to Apply section, there's an Initial Previews pop-up menu where you get to choose how quickly Lightroom displays the previews of your photos. You're really making a quality decision here, because the higher the quality of preview you choose, the longer it'll take for you to view them in Lightroom. You have four choices, and in the next steps, we'll look at the advantages and disadvantages of each.

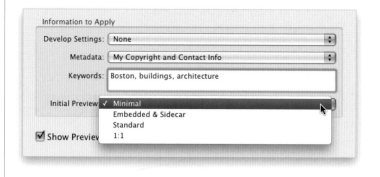

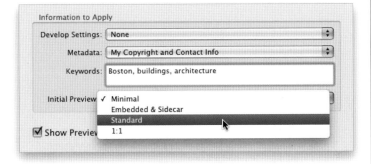

Step 22:

No matter which option you choose here, Lightroom first fetches a low-resolution JPEG preview from the photo as it's imported (the same preview that's displayed on the LCD screen on the back of your digital camera), and displays that in Lightroom as a small thumbnail (so, no matter which option you choose, your thumbnails all appear in the Library module at about the same speed, because they are all low-resolution previews). However, it's when you go to zoom in on one that makes the difference. For example, if you choose Embedded & Sidecar (which gives the fastest previews), when you double-click on a photo, you'll have to wait a few moments before the larger, higher-quality preview appears onscreen (you'll literally see a message appear onscreen that says "Rendering Preview"). If you zoom in closer, you'll have to wait a few moments more (the message will now read "Rendering: Higher Quality"). That's because it doesn't create a higher-quality preview until you try to zoom in.

Step 23:

Minimal is the next fastest, and it grabs the low-res JPEG thumbnails from your camera too, but once they load, it starts to load higher-resolution thumbnails that look more like what the higher-quality zoomed-in view will look like (even though the preview is still small). The Standard preview takes quite a bit longer because it renders a higher-resolution preview as soon as the low-res JPEG previews are imported, so you don't have to wait for it to render the first level of larger preview for any imported photo (so, if you double-click on any one, it zooms up to a Fit Screen view without having to wait for rendering). However, if you zoom in closer, you'll get that Rendering: Higher Quality message and you'll have to wait a few seconds.

Continued

Step 24:

The 1:1 (one-to-one) preview imports the photos, displays the low-res thumbnails, and then it starts rendering the highest-quality previews, so you can zoom in as much as you want with no waiting whatsoever. There are two downsides: (1) It's notoriously slow. Basically, you need to click the Import button, then walk away and go get a cup of coffee (maybe two), but when you come back, you can zoom in on any photo and never see a rendering message—it zooms right in. (2) These large, high-quality previews get stored in your Lightroom database, so your database file is going to get very large in file size. So much so that Lightroom lets you automatically delete these 1:1 previews after a certain amount of time (one day, one week, or even 30 days). So, if you haven't looked at a particular set of photos for 30 days, it figures you don't need the high-res previews, and it deletes them for you. You set this by going under the Lightroom menu (PC: Edit menu) and choosing Catalog Settings, then clicking on the File Handling tab and choosing your settings (as shown here).

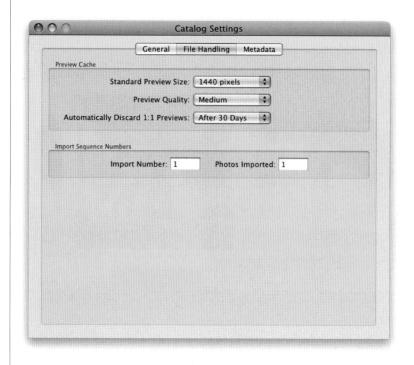

Step 25:

So which one do I use? I use Embedded & Sidecar, because I want to see my thumbnails appear, and start sorting my photos, as soon as possible. Then, if I click on a thumbnail, I do have to wait a moment or two while it renders the higher-resolution preview, but since I don't zoom in on every single photo (just the ones that I think might be good), I only have to wait for those photos I double-click on to render at a higher quality (an ideal workflow for people who want instant gratification—like me). However, if you charge by the hour, choose 1:1 previews—it will increase your billable hours. (You know I'm joking, right?)

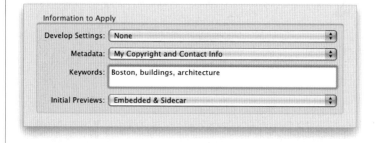

Step 26:

I ran a Lightroom preview time trial, importing just 14 RAW images off a memory card onto a laptop. Here's how long it took to import them and render their previews:

Embedded & Sidecar: 19 seconds
Minimal: 21 seconds
Standard: 1 minute, 15 seconds
1:1: 2 minutes, 14 seconds

You can see that the 1:1 preview took seven times as long as Embedded & Sidecar. That may not seem that bad with 14 photos, but what about 140 or 340 photos? Yikes! So, armed with that info, you can make a decision that fits your workflow. If you're the type of photographer that likes to zoom in tight on each and every photo to check focus and detail, then it might be worth it for you to wait for the 1:1 previews to render before working on your images. If you're like me, and want to quickly search through them, and just zoom in tight on the most likely keepers (maybe 15 or 20 images from an import), then Embedded & Sidecar makes sense. If you look at them mostly in full-screen view (but don't zoom in really tight that often), then Standard might work, and if you want thumbnails that more closely represent what your photo will look like when it is rendered at high quality, choose Minimal instead. Once you make your Initial Previews choice, click the Import button at the bottom right of the dialog. As your photos are imported, they will appear in the Library module's Grid view (as seen here). It took us 25 steps before we got to click the Import button here in the book, but in real life (once you've set up your metadata preset, file naming presets, etc.), you'll only spend literally about a minute in this dialog. But that minute will save you hours of time and loads of frustration down the road.

Shooting Tethered (Go Straight from Your Camera, Right Into Lightroom)

If you're working in a studio, I hope you'll consider trying this: shoot straight from your camera, bypassing your memory card, and send the photos directly into Lightroom. There are two advantages: (1) instead of just seeing your images on the tiny screen on the back of your camera, now you can see them full-screen size in Lightroom, and (2) when you see an image you think might work, you can tweak it right there in Lightroom and see the results live. Try it once; you'll love it!

Step One:

The first step is to create an empty folder in a convenient location on your computer that will act as your watched folder (I created mine on my desktop, so I wouldn't have to go digging around for it). Go ahead and create that new blank folder now (I named mine "Import Into Lightroom," just so it's clear at a glance what that folder is for).

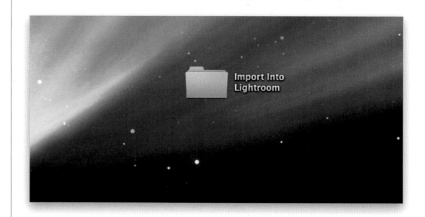

Step Two:

To connect your camera to your computer, you'll need software that acts as a go-between for your camera and Lightroom. For Nikon users, it's called Camera Control Pro 2 (if you don't have it, you can download a fully-working 30-day trial version from www.nikonusa.com). Once you launch it, go under the Camera Control Pro Tools menu and choose Download Options. At the top, where it asks which folder to place photos from the camera in, click on the Choose button (as shown here), and choose the Import Into Lightroom folder you created in Step One. Then, from the When a New Image Is Received from the Camera pop-up menu, choose Do Nothing. That's all you've got to do; now click OK. If you're a Canon shooter, your camera came with the software you need, called EOS Utility.

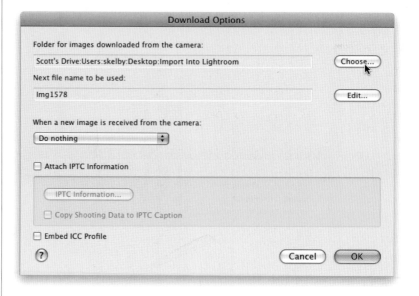

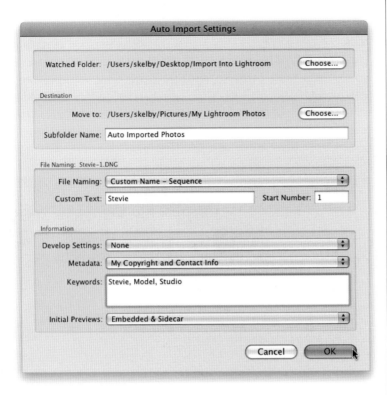

Step Three:

Back in Lightroom, go under the File menu, under Auto Import, and choose Auto Import Settings. This brings up the dialog you see here. The first thing you choose here is which folder you want to be your watched folder. So, click the Choose button to the right of Watched Folder, and choose your Import Into Lightroom folder. Next, under Destination, click the Choose button and choose where you want any auto-imported photos to be stored on your computer (here, choose your My Lightroom Photos folder). Right below this is a text field where you can name the subfolder where the images imported into Lightroom will be stored. The rest of this dialog is just like the standard Import Photos dialog, so here's what to do in the rest of the dialog: under File Naming, give your photos a descriptive name, then under Information, add your copyright metadata (well, if you created it already), then add some generic keywords to help make searching for these photos easier in the future, and choose your preview setting. Now that your settings are in place, you can click OK, but there's one more thing to do....

Step Four:

You've configured the Auto Import settings, but you haven't turned it on yet. You do that by going under the File menu, under Auto Import, and choosing Enable Auto Import (as shown here). That's it—now any photos you put in that folder will automatically be imported into Lightroom, with your copyright info and keywords already embedded.

TIP: Auto Import a Watched Folder

You can also use this Auto Import feature to have a watched folder on your desktop, where any photos you drop in that folder get automatically imported into Lightroom.

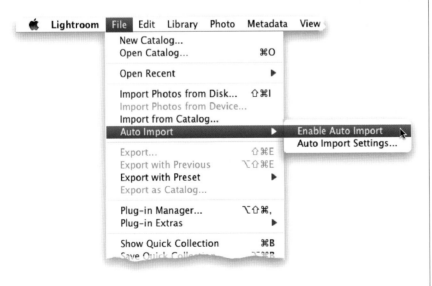

Creating Your Own Custom File Naming Templates

Staying organized is critical when you have thousands of photos, and because digital cameras generate the same set of names over and over, it's really important that you rename your photos with a unique name right during import. A popular strategy is to include the date of the shoot as part of the new name. Unfortunately, only one of Lightroom's import naming presets includes the date, and it makes you keep the camera's original filename along with it. Luckily, you can create your own custom file naming template just the way you want it. Here's how:

Step One:
Start in the Library module, and click on the Import button on the bottom-left side of the window (or use the keyboard short-cut **Command-Shift-I [PC: Ctrl-Shift-I]**). When the Import Photos dialog appears, from the File Handling pop-up menu at the top, choose Copy Photos to a New Location and Add to Catalog, and the File Naming section will appear. In that section, click on the Template pop-up menu and chose Edit (as shown here) to bring up the Filename Template Editor (shown below in Step Two).

Step Two:
At the top of the dialog, there is a pop-up menu where you can choose any of the built-in naming presets as a starting place. For example, if you choose Custom Name – Sequence, the field below shows two blue tokens (that's what Adobe calls them; on a PC, the info appears within braces) that make up that preset: the first represents the text, the second represents the auto numbering. To remove either token, click on it, then press the Delete (PC: Backspace) key on your keyboard. If you want to just start from scratch (as I'm going to do), delete both tokens, choose the options you want from the pop-up menus below, then click the Insert buttons to add them to the field.

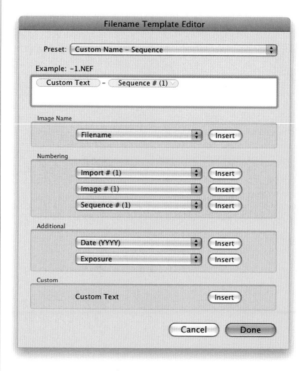

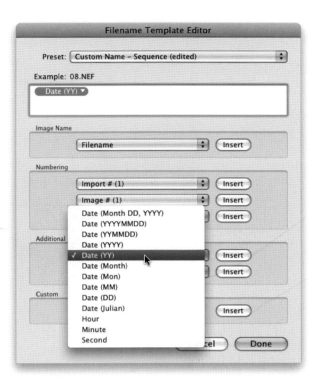

Step Three:

I'm going to show you the setup for a popular file naming system for photographers, but this is only an example—you can create a custom template later that fits your studio's needs. We'll start by adding the year first (this helps keep your filenames together when sorted by name). To keep your filenames from getting too long, I recommend using just the last two digits of the year. So go to the Additional section of the dialog, click on the first pop-up menu, and choose Date (YY), as shown here (the Y lets you know this is a year entry, the YY lets you know it's only going to display two digits). The Date (YY) token will appear in the naming field and if you look above the top-left side of it, you'll see a live example of the name template you're creating. At this point, my new filename is 08.NEF, as seen here.

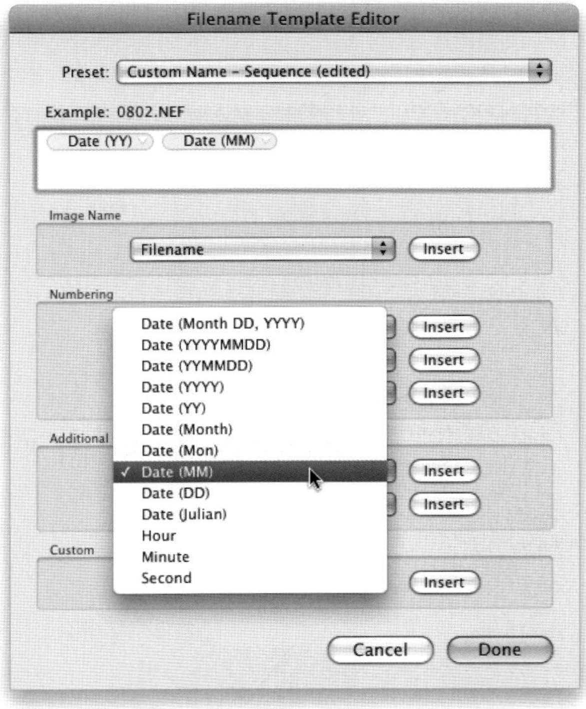

Step Four:

After the two-digit year, we add the two-digit month the photo was taken by going to the same pop-up menu, but this time choosing Date (MM), as shown here. (Both of these dates are drawn automatically from the metadata embedded into your photo by your digital camera at the moment the shot was taken.) By the way, if you had chosen Date (Month), it would display the entire month name, so your filename would have looked like this: 08February, rather than what we want, which is 0802.

Continued

Step Five:

Before we go any further, you should know there's a rule for file naming, and that's no spaces between words. However, if everything just runs together, it's really hard to read. So, after the date you're going to add a visual separator—a thin flat line called an underscore. To add one, just click your cursor right after the Date (MM) token, then press the Shift key and the Hyphen key to add an underscore (seen here). Now, here's where I differ from some of the other naming conventions: after the date, I include a custom name that describes what's in each shoot. This differs because some people choose to have the original camera-assigned filename appear there instead (personally, I like to have a name in there that makes sense to me without having to open the photo). So to do that, go to the Custom section of the dialog and to the right of Custom Text, click the Insert button (as shown here) to add a Custom Text token after your underscore (this lets you type in a one-word text description later), then add another underscore (so it looks like _Custom Text_. No text will appear in your example up top, though, until you add it).

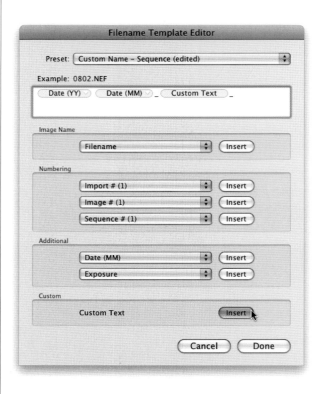

Step Six:

Now you're going to have Lightroom automatically number these photos sequentially. To do that, go to the Numbering section and choose your numbering sequence from the third pop-up menu down. Here I chose the Sequence # (001) token, which adds three-digit auto-numbering to the end of your filename (you can see the example above the naming field).

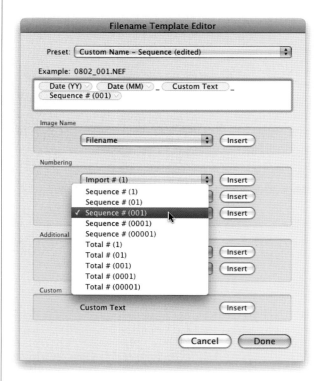

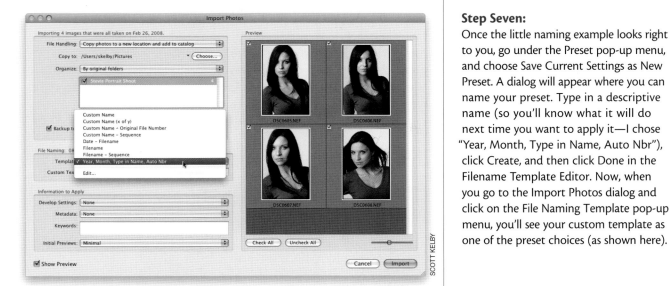

SCOTT KELBY

Step Seven:

Once the little naming example looks right to you, go under the Preset pop-up menu, and choose Save Current Settings as New Preset. A dialog will appear where you can name your preset. Type in a descriptive name (so you'll know what it will do next time you want to apply it—I chose "Year, Month, Type in Name, Auto Nbr"), click Create, and then click Done in the Filename Template Editor. Now, when you go to the Import Photos dialog and click on the File Naming Template pop-up menu, you'll see your custom template as one of the preset choices (as shown here).

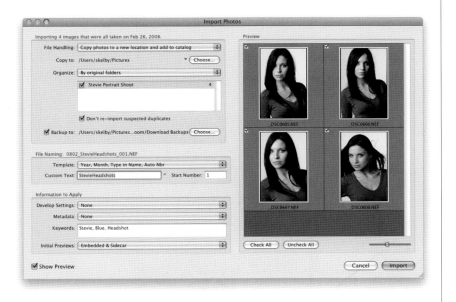

Step Eight:

Now, after you choose this new naming template from the Template pop-up menu, click below it in the Custom Text field (this is where that Custom Text token we added earlier comes into play) and type in the descriptive part of the name (in this case, I typed in "StevieHeadshots," all one word—no spaces between words). That custom text will appear between two underscores, giving you a visual separator so everything doesn't all run together (see, it all makes sense now). Once you click in another field, if you look at the File Naming example (right above the Template pop-up menu), you'll see a preview of how the photos will be renamed. Once you've chosen all your Information to Apply settings at the bottom of the dialog, you can click the Import button.

Choosing Your Preferences for Importing Photos

I put the import preferences near the end of the Importing chapter because I figured that, by now, you've imported some photos and you know enough about the importing process to know what you wish was different. That's what preferences are all about (and Lightroom has preference controls because it gives you lots of control over the way you want to work).

Step One:
The preferences for importing photos are found in a couple different places. First, to get to the Preferences dialog, go under the Lightroom menu on a Mac or the Edit menu on a PC, and choose Preferences (as shown here).

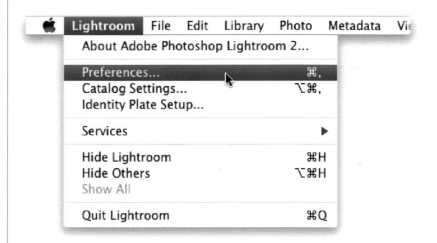

Step Two:
When the Preferences dialog appears, first click on the Import tab up top (shown highlighted here). The first preference lets you tell Lightroom how to react when you connect a memory card from your camera to your computer. By default, it opens the Import Photos dialog. However, if you'd prefer it didn't automatically open that dialog each time you plug in a camera or card reader, just turn off its checkbox (as shown here).

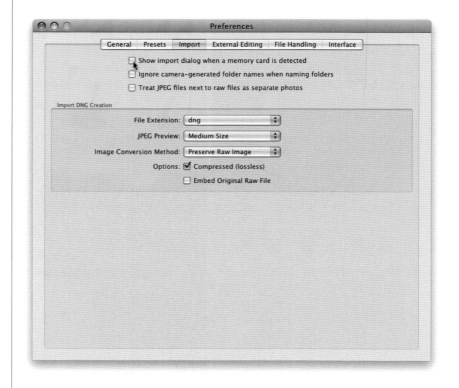

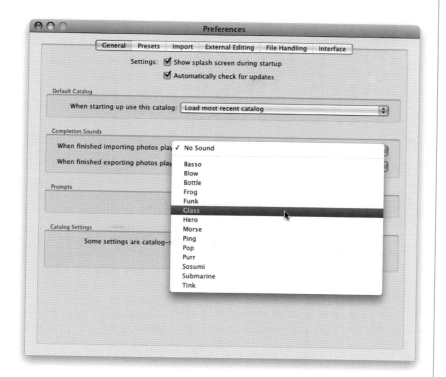

Step Three:

There are two other importing preference settings I'd like to mention, but they're found by clicking on the General tab up top (shown highlighted here). In the Completion Sounds section, you not only get to choose whether or not Lightroom plays an audible sound when it's done importing your photos, you also get to choose which sound (from the pop-up menu of system alert sounds already in your computer, as seen here).

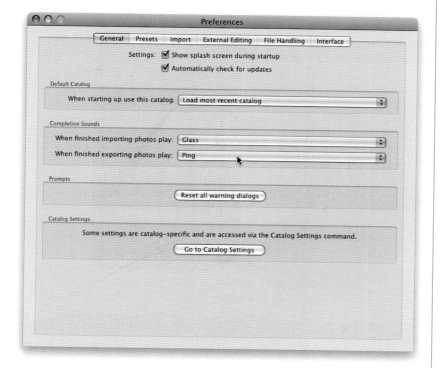

Step Four:

While you're right there, directly below the menu for choosing an "importing's done" sound is another pop-up menu for choosing a sound for when your exporting is done. I know, this isn't an importing preference, but since we're right there, I thought…what the heck. I'll talk more about some of the other preferences later in the book, but since this chapter is on importing, I thought I'd better tackle it here.

Continued

Step Five:

Now, at the bottom of the General tab, click the Go to Catalog Settings button (also found under the Lightroom [PC: Edit] menu). In the Catalog Settings dialog, click on the Metadata tab. Here you can determine whether you want to take the metadata you add to your photos (copyright, keywords, etc.) and have it written to a totally separate file, so then for each photo you'll have two files—one that contains the photo itself and a separate file (called an XMP sidecar) that contains that photo's metadata. You do this by turning on the Automatically Write Changes Into XMP Checkbox, but why would you ever want to do this? Well, normally Lightroom keeps track of all this metadata you add in its database file—it doesn't actually embed the info until your photo leaves Lightroom (by exporting a copy over to Photoshop, or exporting the file as a JPEG, TIFF, or PSD—all of which support having this metadata embedded right into the photo itself). However, some programs can't read embedded metadata, so they need a separate XMP sidecar file.

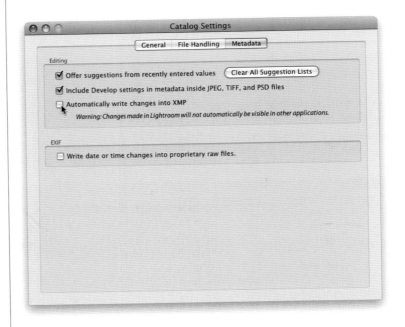

Step Six:

Now that I've shown you that Automatically Write Changes Into XMP checkbox, I don't actually recommend you turn it on, because writing all those XMP sidecars takes time, which slows Lightroom down. Instead, if you want to send a file to a friend or client and you want the metadata written to an XMP sidecar file, first go to the Library module and click on an image to select it, then press **Command-S (PC: Ctrl-S)**, which is the shortcut for Save Metadata to File (which is found under the Metadata menu). This writes any existing metadata to a separate XMP file (so you'll need to send both the photo and the XMP sidecar together).

I mentioned that you have the option of having your photos converted to DNG (Digital Negative) format as they're imported. DNG was created by Adobe because today each camera manufacturer has its own proprietary RAW file format, and Adobe is concerned that, one day, one or more manufacturers might abandon an older format for something new. With DNG, it's not proprietary—Adobe made it an open format, so anyone can write to that specification. While ensuring that your negatives could be opened in the future was the main goal, DNG brings other advantages, as well.

The Adobe DNG File Format Advantage

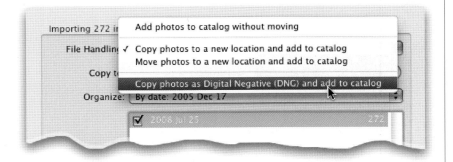

Setting Your DNG Preferences: Press **Command-, (comma; PC: Ctrl-,)** to bring up Lightroom's Preferences dialog, then click on the Import tab (as shown here). In the Import DNG Creation section, you see the settings I use for DNG conversion. Although you can embed the original proprietary RAW file, I don't (it adds to the file size, and pretty much kills Advantage #1 below). By the way, you choose Copy Photos as Digital Negative (DNG) and Add to Catalog from the File Handling menu in the Import Photos dialog (as shown below).

Advantage #1: DNG files are smaller
RAW files usually have a pretty large file size, so they eat up hard disk space pretty quickly, but when you convert a file to DNG, it's generally about 20% smaller.

Advantage #2: DNG files don't need a separate sidecar
When you edit a RAW file, that metadata is actually stored in a separate file called an XMP sidecar file. If you want to give someone your RAW file and have it include the metadata and changes you applied to it in Lightroom, you'd have to give them two files: (1) the RAW file itself, and (2) the XMP sidecar file, which holds the metadata and edit info. But with a DNG, that info is embedded right into the DNG file itself, so you only need the one file.

Creating Your Own Custom Metadata (Copyright) Templates

At the beginning of this chapter, I mentioned that you'll want to set up your own custom metadata template, so you can easily and automatically embed your own copyright and contact information right into your photos as they're imported into Lightroom. Well, here's how to do just that. Keep in mind that you can create more than one template, so if you create one with your full contact info (including your phone number), you might want to create one with just basic info, or one for when you're exporting images to be sent to a stock photo agency, etc.

Step One:

You can create a metadata template from right within the Import Photos dialog, so press **Command-Shift-I (PC: Ctrl-Shift-I)** to bring up the Import Photos dialog (first, you'll need to choose a folder, or memory card, of images to import—you don't actually have to import these images, but Lightroom wants you to choose a folder [or card] before it will bring up the dialog). Once it appears, in the Information to Apply section, choose New from the Metadata pop-up menu (as shown here). *Note:* You can also go to the Metadata panel in Lightroom's Library module, and from the Preset pop-up menu, choose Edit Presets.

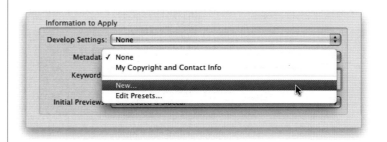

Step Two:

A blank New Metadata Preset dialog will appear. First, click the Check None button at the bottom of the dialog, as shown here (so no blank fields will appear when you view this metadata in Lightroom—only fields with data will be displayed).

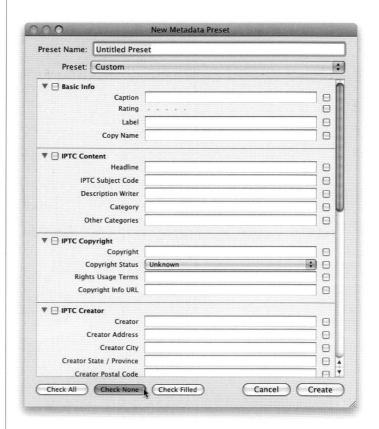

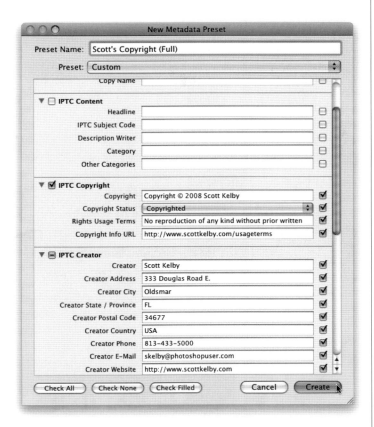

Step Three:

In the IPTC Copyright section, type in your copyright information (as shown here). Next, go to the IPTC Creator section and enter your contact info (after all, if someone goes by your website and downloads some of your images, you might want them to be able to contact you to arrange to license your photo). Now, you may feel that the Copyright Info URL (Web address) that you added in the previous section is enough contact info, and if that's the case, you can skip filling out the IPTC Creator info (after all, this metadata preset is to help make potential clients aware that your work is copyrighted, and how to get in contact with you). Once all the metadata info you want embedded in your photos is complete, go up to the top of the dialog, give your preset a name—I chose "Scott's Copyright (Full)"—and then click the Create button, as shown.

Step Four:

As easy as it is to create a metadata template, deleting one is a different story. You have to find the folder on your computer that contains your Lightroom metadata presets, and drag the preset you want to delete into the Trash (PC: Recycle Bin). On a Mac, start in your Home folder in Finder, then in your Library folder, go to Application Support. Inside that folder is an Adobe folder, and inside that, you'll find a Lightroom folder (you're almost there), and inside that folder, you'll see the Metadata Presets folder. (Whew! The path on my own computer is shown here.) On a PC: Start in your computer's C: drive in Windows Explorer. In XP, look in your Documents and Settings folder for the Application Data Folder, then the Adobe folder, and inside it, the Metadata Presets folder. In Vista, on the C: drive, look in the Users folder, then under your username, go in the AppData folder. In it, go under Roaming, and under Adobe to find the Lightroom folder that has the Metadata Presets folder in it.

Lightroom Quick Tips > >

▼ **Drag-and-Drop Straight Into Lightroom 2**

If you have photos on your desktop, or in a folder, that you want to import into Lightroom, you can drag-and-drop the photo (or a folder full of photos) right on the Lightroom icon (or the Dock icon if you're using a Mac), and it will launch Lightroom (if it's not already running), and bring up Lightroom's Import Photos dialog automatically.

▼ **Lightroom Won't Let You Import Duplicates**

If you go to import some photos, and some (or all) of them are already found in your Lightroom catalog (in other words, these are duplicates), it brings up a dialog letting you know which photos you're trying to import are already in Lightroom. If you click the Show in Library button, it closes the dialog and shows you those photos in the Library module's Grid view.

▼ **Using Separate Catalogs to Make Lightroom Faster**

Although I keep one single catalog for all the photos on my laptop, and just three catalogs for my entire collection in the studio, I have a friend who's a full-time wedding photographer who uses a different Lightroom catalog strategy that freaked me out when I first heard it, but really makes perfect sense (in fact, it may be just what you need). He creates a separate Lightroom catalog (go under the File menu and choose New Catalog) for every single wedding. At each wedding, he shoots more than a thousand shots, and often he has one to two other photographers shooting with him. His way, Lightroom really screams, because each catalog has only a thousand or

so photos (where for many folks, it's not unusual to have 30,000 or 40,000 images, which tends to slow Lightroom down a bit). Hey, if you're a high-volume shooter, it's worth considering.

▼ **When the Import Window Doesn't Appear Automatically**

If you connect a memory card reader to your computer, Lightroom's Import Photos dialog should appear automatically. If for some reason it doesn't, press **Command-, (comma; PC: Ctrl-,)** to bring up Lightroom's Preferences, then click the Import tab up top, and make sure the checkbox is turned on for Show Import Dialog When a Memory Card Is Detected.

▼ **Hard Drive Space an Issue? Convert to DNG on Import**

If you're working on a laptop, and you'd like to save between 15% and 20% (in most cases) of your hard drive space when importing RAW files, choose Copy Photos as Digital Negative (DNG) and Add to Catalog from the File Handling pop-up menu at the top left of the Import Photos dialog.

▼ **Fixing White Balance "On the Fly" When Shooting Tethered**

If you're shooting tethered, going from your camera straight into your computer (and then into Lightroom, as shown on page 20 in this chapter), here's a great tip for having your white balance look perfect as the images come into Lightroom. Shoot the first shot of your session with a gray card in the shot (either have your subject hold a gray card, or just place one clearly into the scene if it's a product shot). Then, when this photo comes into Lightroom, press **W** to get the White Balance

Selector tool, and click directly on that gray card to set your white balance. Now, go to the Presets panel in the Develop module's left side Panels area, and click on the + (plus sign) button to save that white balance setting as a new preset. Next, go under Lightroom's File menu, under Auto Import, and choose Auto Import Settings. When that dialog opens (it looks very similar to the regular Import Photos dialog), in the Information section, where it says Develop Settings, choose that preset you just created, and click OK. Now each photo that is imported from your shoot will automatically have the correct white balance applied to it, so when you see the photos large onscreen, the white balance looks right.

▼ **Why You Might Want to Wait to Rename Your Files**

As you saw in this chapter, you can rename your files as you import them into Lightroom (and I definitely think you should give your files descriptive names), but you might want to wait until after you've sorted your photos (and deleted any out-of-focus shots, or shots where the flash didn't fire, etc.), because Lightroom auto-numbers the files for you. Well, if you delete some of these files, then your numbering will be out of sequence (there will be numbers missing). This doesn't bother me at all, but I've learned that it drives some people crazy (you know who you are), so it's definitely something to consider.

Lightroom Quick Tips > >

▼ Getting Back to Your Last
    Imported Images

Lightroom keeps track of the last set
of images you imported, and you can
get back to those images anytime by
going to Catalog panel (in the Library
module's left side Panels area) and
clicking on Previous Import. However,
I think it's faster (and more convenient)
to go down to the filmstrip, and on the
left side, where you see the current
collection's name, click-and-hold, and
from the pop-up menu that appears,
choose Previous Import.

▼ Taking Advantage of Light-
    room Being 64-Bit

Lightroom 2 is the first version to be
64-bit capable, and if you're working on a
Mac, there's one thing you have to do to
turn this 64-bit mode on (which lets you
access as much RAM as you can jam into
your computer): go to the Applications
folder, click on the icon for Lightroom 2,
and press **Command-I** to bring up the
Get Info window, then turn off the Open
in 32 Bit Mode checkbox. That's it.
In Windows Vista 64-bit, by default,
only the 64-bit version of Lightroom is
installed, so there's nothing to turn on.
But, in Windows XP, you need to run the
setup64.exe file found in the Lightroom 2
folder (in your Program Files folder).

▼ Your Elements Library

If you're moving to Lightroom 2 from
the Windows version of Elements 5
or 6, you can have Lightroom import
your Elements catalog. Just go under
Lightroom's File menu, choose Upgrade
Photoshop Elements Catalog, and then
choose your Elements catalog from the
submenu. You may need to upgrade
your Elements catalog for Lightroom, so
just click Upgrade if prompted to. Lightroom will close and then reopen with
your Elements catalog imported.

Library
organizing your photos

The first module you wind up using in Adobe Photoshop Lightroom is usually the Library module—it's where you go to sort and organize your photos. Now, here's the thing: while what you're supposed to do here is organize your photos, very few people have the intestinal fortitude to actually do it—to actually go through all their images, and tag each and every one with keywords and custom metadata. My hat's off to these meticulous people (freaks), but I'm not one of them. That's because as soon as I import my photos, I take a quick look at 'em, separate the good from the bad, and then start messing with the good ones in the Develop, Slideshow, Print, and Web modules. Those are the party modules. That's where the fun is, so I hang out there (it's kind of like the

Rain® Nightclub in Vegas, only without all the celebrities, flashing lights, music, and liquor. Okay, there's some liquor, but not all that much). You know who uses the Library module to its fullest extent? People who have a metabolic predisposition to become serial killers—them and molecular biologists. I don't know why. Anyway, maybe I'm just speaking for myself here, because honestly, I couldn't keep track of all my photos if they had my name and phone number embedded in them with a microchip tracking device. I guess it's because I don't care about my bad photos. I only care about my good photos, so I don't want to waste my time tagging photos I'm probably never going to use for anything other than my work in molecular biology.

Four Things You'll Want to Know Now About Working in Lightroom

One of the things I love best about Photoshop Lightroom is how it can "get out of the way" and let you really focus on the photo (instead of being distracted by all the panels, and sliders, and numbers, etc.), and there are some tips about working with Lightroom's interface you're going to want to know about right up front that will make working in it much easier.

Step One:

When your imported photos appear in Lightroom, they always appear in the center of the Library module, which is where we do all our sorting, searching, keywording, etc. There are five different modules in Lightroom, and each does a different thing. The Develop module is where you go to do your photo editing (like changing the exposure, white balance, tweaking colors, etc.), and it's pretty obvious what the other three do (I'll spare you). You move from module to module by clicking on the module's name up in the taskbar across the top, or you can use the shortcuts **Command-Option-1** for Library, **Command-Option-2** for Develop, and so on (on a PC, it would be **Ctrl-Alt-1, Ctrl-Alt-2**, and so on).

Step Two:

There are five areas in the Lightroom interface overall: that taskbar on the top, the left and right side panels, and a filmstrip across the bottom (your photos always appear in the center Preview area). You can hide any panel (which makes the area where your photos are displayed larger) by clicking on the little gray triangle on the center of the panel. For example, go ahead and click on the little gray triangle at the top center of the screen, and you'll see it hides the taskbar. Click it again; it comes back.

Step Three:

The #1 complaint I hear from Lightroom users about working with panels is they hate the Auto Hide & Show feature (which is on by default). The idea behind it sounds great: if you've hidden a panel, and need it visible again to make an adjustment, you move your cursor over where the panel used to be, and it pops out. When you're done, you move your cursor away, and it automatically tucks back out of sight. Sounds great, right? The problem is it pops out anytime you move your cursor to the far right, left, top, or bottom of your screen. It really drives them nuts, and I've had people literally beg me to show them how to turn it off. You can turn Auto Hide & Show off by Control-clicking (PC: Right-clicking) on the little gray triangle for any panel. A contextual menu will appear (shown here) where you'll choose Manual, which turns the feature off. This works on a per-panel basis, so you'll have to do it to each of the four panels.

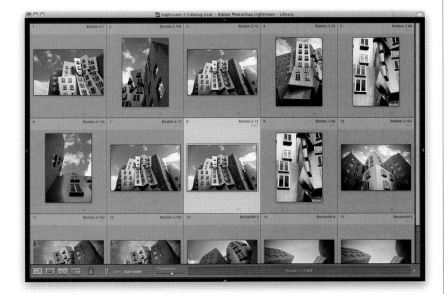

Step Four:

I use the Manual mode, so I can just open and close panels as I need them (you can also use the keyboard short-cuts: **F5** closes/opens the top taskbar, **F6** hides the filmstrip, **F7** hides the left side Panels area, and **F8** hides the right side). You can hide both side Panels areas by pressing the **Tab key**, but the one shortcut I probably use the most is **Shift-Tab**, because it hides everything— all the panels—and leaves just your photos visible (as shown here). Also, here's an insight into what is found where: the left side panels are used primarily for applying presets and templates, and showing you a preview of the photo, preset, or template you're working with. Everything else (all adjustments) is found on the right side. Okay, let's get to work.

Viewing Your Imported Photos

Although our main goal in this chapter is to sort our photos and separate the winners from the losers, learning the ins and outs of how Lightroom lets you work with and view your imported photos is important. Learning these viewing options now will really help you make the most informed decisions possible about which photos make it (and which ones don't).

Step One:

When your imported photos appear in Lightroom, they are displayed as small thumbnails in the center Preview area (as seen here). You can change the size of these thumbnails using the Thumbnails slider that appears in the toolbar (the dark gray horizontal bar that appears directly below the center Preview area). Drag it to the right, and they get bigger; drag to the left, and they get smaller (the slider is circled here).

Step Two:

To see any thumbnail at a larger size, just double-click on it, press the letter **E** on your keyboard, or press the **Spacebar**. This larger size is called Loupe view (as if you were looking at the photo through a loupe), and by default it zooms in so you can see your entire photo in the Preview area. This is called a Fit in Window view, but if you'd prefer that it zoomed in tighter, you can go up to the Navigator panel at the top left, and click on a different size, like Fill, and now when you double-click, it will zoom in until your photo literally fills the Preview area. Choosing 1:1 will zoom your photo in to a 100% actual size view when it's double-clicked, but I have to tell you, it's kind of awkward to go from a tiny thumbnail to a huge, tight zoom like that.

SCOTT KELBY

Step Three:

I leave my Navigator panel setting at Fit, so when I double-click I can see the entire photo fitting in the center Preview area, but if you want to get in closer to check sharpness, you'll notice that when you're in Loupe view, your cursor has changed into a magnifying glass. If you click it once on your photo, it jumps to a 1:1 view of the area where you clicked. To zoom back out, just click it again. To return to the thumbnail view (called Grid view), just press the letter **G** on your keyboard. This is one of the most important keyboard shortcuts to memorize (so far, the ones you really need to know are: **Shift-Tab** to hide all the panels, and now G to return to Grid view). This is a particularly handy shortcut, because when you're in any other module, pressing G brings you right back here to the Library module and your thumbnail grid.

The default cell view is called Expanded and gives you the most info

Step Four:

The area that surrounds your thumbnail is called a cell, and each cell displays information about the photo from the filename, to the file format, dimensions, etc.—you get to customize how much, or how little, it displays, as you'll see in Chapter 3. But in the meantime, here's another keyboard shortcut you'll want to know about: press the letter **J**. Each time you press it, it toggles you through the three different cell views, each of which displays different groups of info—an expanded cell with lots of info, a compact cell with just a little info, and the last one hides all that distracting stuff altogether (great for when you're showing thumbnails to clients). Also, you can hide (or show) the dark gray toolbar below the center Preview area by pressing **T**. If you press-and-hold T, it only hides it for as long as you have the T key held down.

The Compact view shrinks the size of the cell and amount of info, but numbers each cell

If you press J again, it hides all the info and just shows the photos

Using Lights Dim, Lights Out, and Other Viewing Modes

One of the things I love best about Lightroom is how it gets out of your way and lets your photo be the focus. That's why I love the Shift-Tab shortcut that hides all the panels. But if you want to really take things to the next level, after you hide those panels, you can dim everything around your photo, or literally "turn the lights out," so everything is blacked out but your photos. Here's how:

Step One:
Press the letter **L** on your keyboard to enter Lights Dim mode, in which everything but your photo(s) in the center Preview area is dimmed (kind of like you turned down a lighting dimmer). In this mode, a thin white border also appears around your thumbnails, so they really stand out. Perhaps the coolest thing about this dimmed mode is the fact that the panels, taskbar, and filmstrip all still work—you can still make adjustments (shown here in the right side Panels area), change photos, etc., just like when the "lights" are all on.

Step Two:
The next viewing mode is Lights Out (you get Lights Out by pressing **L** a second time), and this one really makes your photos the star of the show because everything else is totally blacked out, so there's nothing (and I mean nothing) but your photos onscreen (to return to regular Lights On mode, just press L again).

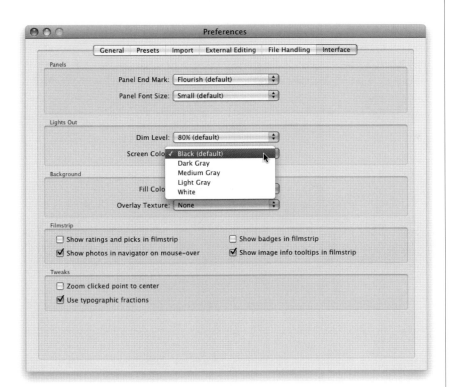

TIP: Controlling Lights Out Mode
You have more control over Lightroom's Lights Out mode than you might think: just go to Lightroom's preferences (under the Lightroom menu on a Mac or the Edit menu on a PC), click on the Interface tab, and you'll find pop-up menus that control both the Dim Level and the Screen Color when you're in full Lights Out mode.

Step Three:
If you want to view your grid of photos without distractions in the Lightroom window, press the **F** key on your keyboard twice. The first time you press F, it makes the Lightroom window fill your screen and hides the window's title bar (directly above the taskbar in Lightroom's interface). The second F actually hides the menu bar at the very top of your screen, so if you combine this with **Shift-Tab** to hide your panels, taskbar, and filmstrip, and **T** to hide the toolbar, you'll see just your photos on a solid top-to-bottom gray background. I know you might be thinking, "I don't know if I find those two thin bars at the top really that distracting." So, try hiding them once and see what you think. Luckily, there's an easy shortcut to jump to the "super-clean, distraction-free nirvana view" you see here: you press **Command-Shift-F (PC: Ctrl-Shift-F)**, then **T**. To return to regular view, use the same shortcut.

Sorting Your Imported Photos Using Collections

Sorting your images can be one of the most fun, or one of the most frustrating parts of the editing process—it just depends on how you go about it. Personally, this is one of the parts I enjoy the most, but I have to admit that I enjoy it more now than I used to, and that's mostly because I've come up with a workflow that's fast and efficient, and helps me get to the real goal of sorting, which is finding the best shots from your shoot—the "keepers"—the ones you'll actually show your client, or add to your portfolio, or print. Here's how I do it:

Step One:
Our goal is to find the best photos from our shoot (and Lightroom is pretty brilliant at helping you make the decision), but we also want to find the worst photos (those photos where the subject is totally out of focus, or you pressed the shutter by accident, or the flash didn't fire, etc.), because there's no sense in having photos that you'll never use taking up precious hard drive space, right? Lightroom gives you three ways to rate (or rank) your photos, the most popular being the 1-to-5-star rating system. To mark a photo with a star rating, just click on it and type the number on your keyboard. So, to mark a photo with a 3-star rating, you'd press the number **3**, and you'd see three stars appear under the photo (shown here). To change a star rating, type in a new number. To remove it altogether, press **0** (zero). The idea is that once you've got your 5-star photos marked, you can turn on a filter that displays only your 5-star photos. You can also use that filter to see just your 4-star, 3-star, etc., photos. Besides stars, you can also use color labels, so you could mark the worst photos with a red label, slightly better ones with yellow, and so on. Or, you could use these in conjunction with the stars to mark your best 5-star photo with a green label.

Step Two:

Now that I've mentioned star ratings and labels, I want to talk you out of using them. Here's why: they're way too slow. Think about it, your 5-star photos would be your very best shots, right? The only ones you'll show anybody. So your 4-star ones are good, but not good enough. Your 3-star ones are just so-so (nobody will ever see these). Your 2-star ones are bad shots—not so bad that you'll delete them, but bad, and your 1-star shots are out-of-focus, blurry, totally messed up shots you're going to delete. So what are you going to do with your 2- and 3-star photos? Nothing. What about your 4-star photos? Nothing. The 5-stars you keep, the 1-stars you delete, the rest you pretty much do nothing with, right? So, all we really care about are the best shots and the worst shots, right? The rest we ignore.

Step Three:

So instead, I hope you'll try flags. You mark the best shots as Picks and the really bad ones (the ones to be deleted) as Rejects. Lightroom will delete the Rejects for you when you're ready, leaving you with just your best shots and the ones you don't care about, but you don't waste time trying to decide if a particular photo you don't care about is a 3-star or a 2-star. I can't tell you how many times I've seen people sitting there saying out loud, "Now, is this a 2-star or a 3-star?" Who cares? It's not a 5-star; move on! To mark a photo as a Pick, just press the letter **P**. To mark a photo as a Reject, press the letter **X**. A little message will appear onscreen to tell you which flag you assigned to the photo, and a tiny flag icon will appear in that photo's grid cell. A white flag means it's marked as a Pick. A black flag means it's a Reject.

Continued

go about the process:
tos have been imported into
and they appear in the Library
module rid view, I double-click on the
first photo to jump to Loupe view so I
can get a closer look. I look at the photo,
and if I think it's one of the better shots
from the shoot, I press the letter **P** to
flag it as a Pick. If it's so bad that I want
to delete it, I press the letter **X** instead. If
it's just okay, I don't do anything; I just
move on to the next photo by pressing
the Right Arrow key on my keyboard. If I
make a mistake and mis-flag a photo (for
example, if I accidentally mark a photo
as a Reject when I didn't mean to), I just
press the letter **U** to un-flag it. That's
it—that's the process. You'll be amazed
at how quickly you can move through a
few hundred photos and mark the keepers and rejects. But you've still got some
things to do once you've done this first
essential part.

Step Five:
Once you've got your Picks and Rejects
flagged, let's get rid of the Rejects and
delete them from your computer (or your
external hard drive). Go under the Photo
menu and choose Delete Rejected Photos.
This displays just the photos you've
marked as Rejects, and a dialog appears
asking if you want to delete them from
your computer (your disk) or just remove
them from Lightroom. If these really are
all Rejects (none have been mis-flagged), I
always choose Delete from Disk, because
if they were bad enough for me to mark
them as Rejects, why would I want to
keep them? What could I possibly use
them for? So, if you feel the same way,
click the Delete from Disk button and it
returns you to the Grid view, where the
rest of your photos are still visible.

Step Six:

Now to see just your Picks, click on the word Attribute up in the Library Filter bar that appears at the top of the center Preview area, and a little Attribute bar pops down. Click on the white Picks flag, and now just your Picks are visible (as shown here).

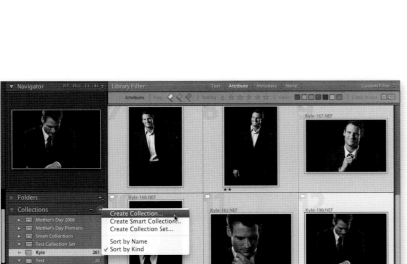

Step Seven:

What I do next is put these Picks into a collection. Collections are the key organizational tool we use, not just here in the sorting phase, but throughout the Lightroom workflow. You can think of a collection as an album of your favorite photos from this shoot, and once you put your Picks into their own collection, you'll always be just one click away from your keepers from this shoot. To get your Picks into a collection, press **Command-A (PC: Ctrl-A)** to select all the currently visible photos (your Picks), then go over to the Collections panel (in the left side Panels area), and click on the little + (plus sign) button on the right side of the panel header. A pop-up menu will appear, and from this menu, choose Create Collection (as shown here).

Continued

Step Eight:

This brings up the Create Collection dialog you see here, where you type in a name for this collection, and below it you can assign it to a set (we haven't talked about sets yet, or created any sets, or even admitted that they exist. So for now, leave the Set pop-up menu at None, but don't worry, sets are coming soon enough). In the Collection Options section, you want your collection to include the photos you selected (your Picks) in the previous step, and because you made a selection first, this checkbox is already turned on for you. For now, leave the Make New Virtual Copies checkbox turned off, then click the Create button.

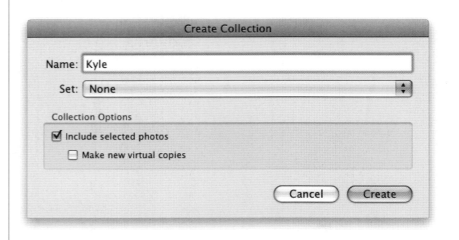

Step Nine:

Now you've got a collection of just your keepers from that shoot, and anytime you want to see these keepers, just go to the Collections panel and click on the collection named Kyle (as seen here). Just in case you were wondering, collections don't affect the actual photos on your computer—these are just "working collections" for our convenience, so we can delete photos from our collections and it doesn't affect the real photos (they're still in their folder on your computer, except for the Rejects we deleted earlier, before we created this collection). If you're an iPod owner, then you're familiar with Apple's iTunes software and how you create playlists of your favorite songs. When you remove a song from a playlist, it doesn't remove it from your iTunes Music Library, just from that playlist, right? Well, you can think of collections in Lightroom as kind of the same thing, but instead of songs, they're photos.

Step 10:
Now, from this point on, we'll just be working with the photos in our collection. Out of the 261 shots that were taken that day, 82 of them were good enough to be keepers, and that's how many wound up in a collection. But here are some questions: Are you going to print all 82 of these keepers? Are all 82 going in your portfolio, or are you going to email 82 shots to your client? Probably not, right? So, within our collection of keepers, there are some shots that really stand out—the best of the best, the ones you actually will want to email to the client, or print, or add to your portfolio. So, we need to refine our editing process a little more to find our best shots from this group of keepers—our "selects."

Step 11:
At this stage, there are three ways to go about viewing your photos to narrow things down. You already know the first method: double-click on a photo to jump to Loupe view, move through the photos using the Arrow keys on your keyboard, and when you see one that you know is one of the best of the bunch, you press the letter **P** to flag it as a Pick (when you created this collection, Lightroom removed the old Picks flags for you). The second view that you might find helpful is called Survey view, and I use this view when I have a number of shots that are very similar (like a number of shots of the same pose) and I'm trying to find the best ones from that group. You enter this view by first selecting the similar photos (click on one, then press-and-hold the Command [PC: Ctrl] key and click on the others, as shown here).

Continued

Step 12:

Now press the letter **N** to jump to Survey view (I don't know which is worse, this view being named Survey or using the letter N as its shortcut. Don't get me started). This puts your selected photos all onscreen, side by side, so you can easily compare them (as shown here). Also, anytime I enter this Survey view, I immediately press **Shift-Tab** to hide all the panels, which makes the photos as large as possible on my screen.

Step 13:

Now that my photos are displayed in Survey view, I start the process of elimination: I look for the weakest photo of the bunch and get rid of it first, then the next weakest, and the next, until I'm left with just the best two or three shots of that pose. To eliminate a photo, just move your cursor over the photo you want to remove from contention (the weakest photo of the bunch) and click on the small X that appears in the bottom-right corner of the image (as seen here), and it's hidden from view. It doesn't remove the photo from your collection, it just hides it to help with your process of elimination. Here, I removed one photo and the others automatically readjusted to fill in the free space. As you continue to eliminate images, the remaining images get larger and larger as they expand to take up the free space.

TIP: Changing Your Survey Order

While you're in Survey view, you can change the order of the images displayed onscreen by just dragging-and-dropping them into the order you want.

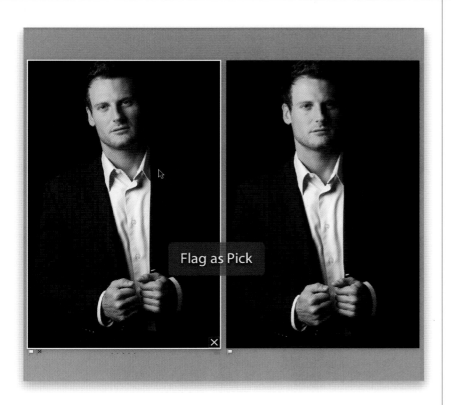

Step 14:

Once you get down to the ones you want to keep in this group, click one to select it, press the letter **P** to flag it as a Pick, then do the same to the other photo(s). (Notice how much larger the photos appear after you eliminated the other four photos?) Now that they're flagged, press **G** to return to the thumbnail Grid view, pick another group of photos that are similar, press **N** to jump to Survey view, and start the process of elimination on them. You can do this as many times as you need, until you've got the best shots from each set of similar shots tagged as Picks.

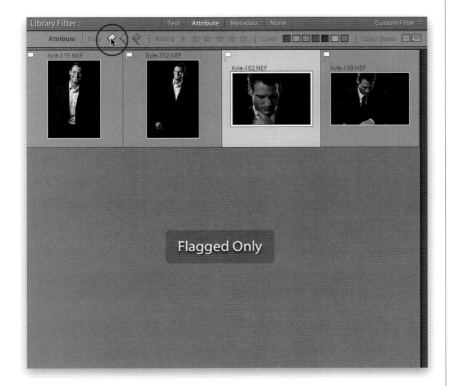

Step 15:

Now that you've found, and marked, the very best shots from the keepers collection, let's put just those "best of the best" in their own separate collection (this will make more sense in just a minute). At the top of the center Preview area, in the Library Filter bar, click on Attribute, and when the Attribute bar pops down, click on the white Picks flag (shown circled here in red) to display just the Picks from the keepers collection (as seen here).

Continued

Step 16:

Now press **Command-A (PC: Ctrl-A)** to select all the Picks displayed onscreen, and then press **Command-N (PC: Ctrl-N)**, which is the keyboard shortcut for New Collection. This brings up the Create Collection dialog. Here's a tip: Name this collection by starting with the name of your keepers collection, then add the word "Selects" (so in my case, I would name my new collection Kyle Selects). Collections appear listed in alphabetical order, so if you start with the same names, both collections will wind up together, which makes things easier for you in the next step (besides, you can always change the name later if you like).

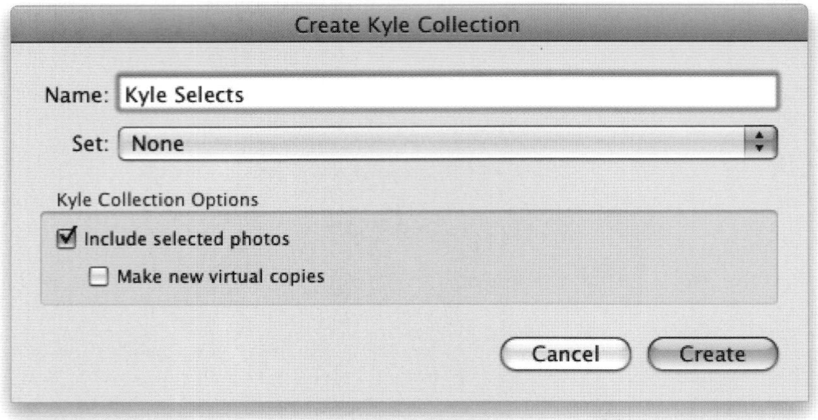

Step 17:

Just to recap, now you have two collections: one with your keepers from the shoot, and a Selects collection with only the very best images from the shoot. When you look in the Collections panel, you'll see your keepers collection with the Selects one right below (as shown here). Now, in the next tutorial, you'll also learn how to use collection sets (which are a little different than what we used here), and they are there to help you manage multiple collections and keep things from getting out of hand.

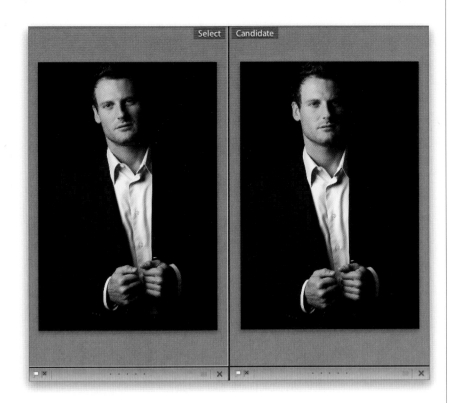

Step 18:
There's a third view of your images that can help you in situations where you need to find the one single, solitary, best shot from a shoot (for example, let's say you write a travel blog, and you need to find that one perfect shot from today's shoot to run with your article). That's when you go to Compare view. Now, of course, you still create your keepers collection just like usual, and once you've got that in place, select the first two photos in the collection (click on the first of the two photos you want to compare, then Command-click [PC: Ctrl-click] on the second image so they're both selected). Press the letter **C** to enter Compare view, where the two photos will appear side by side (as shown here), then press **Shift-Tab** to hide the panels and make the photos as large as possible.

Step 19:
So, here's how this works and this is a battle where only one photo can win: on the left is the current champion (called the Select), and on the right is the contender (called the Candidate). All you have to do is look at both photos, and then decide if the photo on the right is better than the photo on the left (in other words, does the photo on the right "beat the current champ?"). If it doesn't, then press the Right Arrow key on your keyboard and the next photo in your collection (the new contender) appears on the right to challenge the current champ on the left (as seen here, where a new photo has appeared on the right side).

Continued

Step 20:

If you press the Right Arrow key to bring up a new Candidate, and this new photo on the right actually does look better than the Select photo on the left, then click the Make Select button (the X|Y button with a single arrow, on the right side of the toolbar below the center Preview area, shown circled here in red). This makes the Candidate image become the Select image (it moves to the left side), and the battle starts again. So, to recap the process: You select two photos and press **C** to enter Compare view, then ask yourself the question, "Is the photo on the right better than the one on the left?" If it's not better, press the Right Arrow key on your keyboard. If it is better, click the Make Select button and continue the process. Once you've gone through all the photos in your keepers collection, whichever photo remains on the left (as the Select photo) is the best image from the shoot. When you're done, press the Done button on the right side of the toolbar.

Step 21:

Although I always use the Arrow keys on my keyboard to "do battle" in Compare view, you can also use the Previous and Next buttons in the toolbar at the bottom of the center Preview area. To the left of the Make Select button is the Swap button, which just swaps the two photos (making the Candidate the Select, and vice versa), but I haven't found a good reason to use this Swap button, and just stick to the Make Select button. So, which of the three views do you use when? Here's what I do: (1) the Loupe view is my main view when making Picks, (2) I use Survey view only when comparing a number of shots of a similar pose or scene, and (3) I use Compare view when I'm trying to find a single "best" image.

The Swap button (circled above) lets you swap the Candidate and Select images. I honestly haven't found a lot of use for this button

If you don't want to use the Left and Right Arrow keys on your keyboard, you can use the Previous and Next buttons in the toolbar to bring up the next Candidate or return to the previous one

Besides pressing C to enter Compare view, you can also click the Compare View button (circled here in red). The button to the right of it is the button to enter Survey view

When you're finished using Compare view, either click the Done button (circled above) to go to Loupe view, or click the Compare View button to return to the regular Grid view

Step 22:
One last thing about Compare view: once I've determined which photo is the single best photo from the shoot (which should be the image on the left side— what I call "the last photo standing"), I don't make a whole Selects collection for just this one photo. Instead, I mark this one photo on the left as the winner by pressing the number **6** on my keyboard. This assigns a Red label to this photo, and now anytime I want to find the single best photo out of these keepers, I can go to the Library module's Grid view, click on Attribute in the Library Filter bar, and then in the Attribute bar below it, I can click the Red label, and bang—there's my "Best of Show." So, that's the organizing process thus far, but we're not done. At this point, I go and add more specific keywords to the photos in my keepers collection, and we'll do that in just a few minutes, but before we get to that, I want to introduce you to two types of collections that are new in Lightroom 2: collection sets and Smart Collections.

Organizing Multiple Shoots Using Collection Sets

If you spent a week in New York and went out shooting every day, once you got all your shoots into Lightroom, you'd probably have collections with names like Times Square, Central Park, 5th Avenue, The Village, and so on. Because Lightroom automatically alphabetizes collections, these related shoots (they're all in New York, taken during the same trip) would be spread out throughout your list of collections. That's just one place where collection sets come in handy, because you could put all those shoots under one collection: New York.

Step One:
To create a collection set (which just acts like a folder to keep related collections organized together), click on the little + (plus sign) button on the right side of the Collections panel header (in the left side Panels area), and choose Create Collection Set, as shown here. This brings up the Collection Set dialog where you can name your set. In this example, we're going to use it to organize all the different shoots from a wedding, so name it "Stephenson Wedding," for Set choose None, and click the Create button.

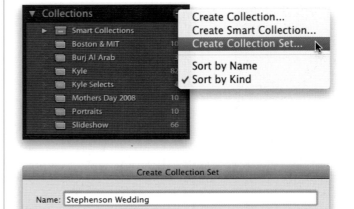

Step Two:
This empty collection set now appears in the Collections panel. When you go to create a new collection of shots from this wedding, before you choose Create Collection, just click once on the Stephenson Wedding set first, then choose Create Collection from the little + (plus sign) button's pop-up menu. What this does is brings up the Create Collection dialog with the Stephenson Wedding collection set already chosen (in the Set pop-up menu) as the set to save this collection into. If you forget to do this, it's no big deal, you can always just choose Stephenson Wedding from the Set pop-up menu.

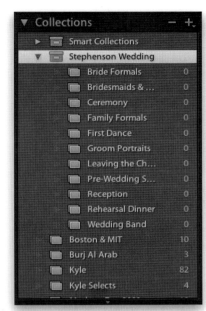

Here's the collection set expanded, so you can see all the collections you saved inside it

Here's the same collection set collapsed, and you can see how much shorter this makes your list of collections

Here, all your weddings are contained within one main Weddings collection set. If you want to see the individual collections inside a particular wedding, then you click on the triangle that appears before its name to reveal its contents

Step Three:
When you look in the Collections panel, you'll see the collections you've added to the Stephenson Wedding collection set appearing directly under it (well, they actually are grouped with it). With something like a wedding, where you might wind up creating a lot of separate collections for different parts of the wedding, you can see how keeping everything organized under one header like this really makes sense. Also, here we created the collection set first, but you don't have to—you can create one whenever you want, and then just drag-and-drop existing collections right onto that set in the Collections panel.

Step Four:
If you want to take things a step further, you can even create a collection set inside another collection set (that's why, back in Step One, when you created your first collection set, the Set pop-up menu appeared in that dialog—so you could put this new collection set inside an existing collection set). An example of why you might want to do this is so you can keep all your wedding shoots together. So, you'd have one collection set called Weddings (as shown here), and then inside of that you'd have separate collection sets for individual weddings. That way, anytime you want to see, or search through, all your wedding photos from all your weddings, you can click on that one Weddings collection set.

TIP: Collections from Lightroom 1
If you imported your old Lightroom catalog from Lightroom 1, and you had collections that had subcollections inside them, Lightroom 2 honors those subcollections. However, you can't add any more subcollections to that collection (instead, you have to create a collection set from scratch, and drag any new subcollections inside). You can drag old subcollections out of the old main collection, though.

Using Smart Collections for Automatic Organization

Let's say you wanted to put together a collection of nothing but your 5-star bridal portraits from the past three years using the Smart Collections feature (new in Lightroom 2). Lightroom can do the gathering for you, and in literally seconds, it's done. Or, how about having Lightroom automatically create a portfolio collection for you, by gathering nothing but your best Red-labeled images from the past year? Or maybe have it create a collection of nothing but photos you've taken with your fisheye lens? It can do all this, and much more. Here's how:

Step One:
Let's say you get a call from a local magazine, and they're doing a feature on weddings, and they're looking for a recent bridal image of yours to use with the story, but they need the image to be tall (rather than wide) to use in the story's opening spread. You can get your hands on all the images that fit those criteria using a Smart Collection. First, go to the Collections panel, click on the + (plus sign) button on the right side of the panel header and choose Create Smart Collection from the pop-up menu. This brings up the Create Smart Collection dialog (shown here). The default criterion is to create a collection based on the star rating, and you want nothing but your best photos, so click on the fifth dot to get five stars (as shown here).

Step Two:
Now let's add another criterion: click on the little + (plus sign) button to the far right of the star ratings, and another line of criteria appears. From the pop-up menu, choose Keywords, and then type in Bride (as shown here). If you clicked the Create button now, it would make a Smart Collection of all your 5-star photos that contain the keyword Bride, but we want to add a few more criteria before we create our Smart Collection.

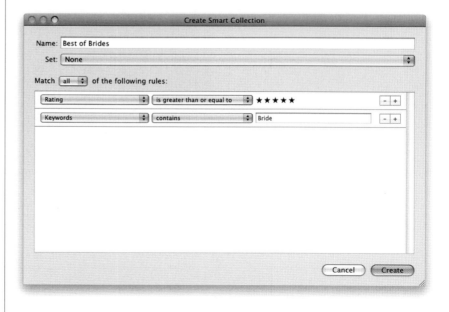

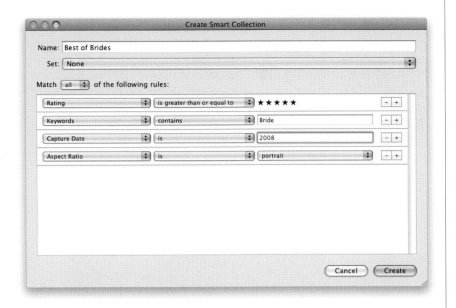

Step Three:
Click the + (plus sign) button again to add another line of criteria. Because they asked for recent photos, we're going to limit the search to photos taken just in 2008, so from the first pop-up menu, choose Capture Date, from the center pop-up menu, choose Is, then in the text field, type in 2008. Click the + (plus sign) button again, and in the next criteria field that appears, choose Aspect Ratio from the first pop-up menu, it will choose Is in the center pop-up menu for you, then choose Portrait.

Step Four:
Now you can click the Create button, and a new Smart Collection will be created of just your 5-star bridal images taken in 2008 that were shot with the camera vertical (tall), as shown here. Now, there are two very cool things you'll want to know about Smart Collections: (1) They're live. If you lower the rating of one of the photos in the collection (either here in the Smart Collection you created, or anywhere else within Lightroom), it will be removed from this Smart Collection automatically, because it no longer matches all the criteria. And, (2) you can edit the criteria for any existing Smart Collection by Control-clicking (PC: Right-clicking) on it in the Collections panel and choosing Edit Smart Collection from the contextual menu. This brings up the Edit Smart Collection dialog with your current criteria, where you can add additional criteria (by clicking the + [plus sign] button), delete criteria (by clicking the − [minus sign] button), or change the criteria in the pop-up menus.

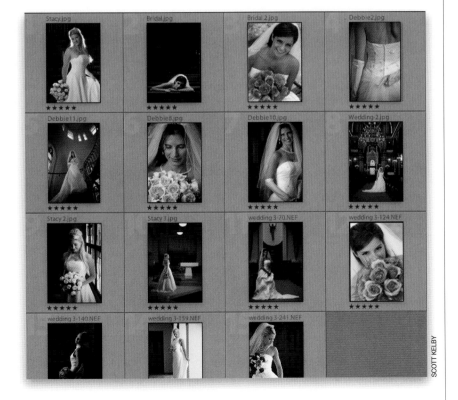

When to Use a Quick Collection Instead

When you create collections, they're a more permanent way of keeping your photos organized into separate albums (by permanent, I mean that when you relaunch Lightroom months later, your collections are still there—but of course, you can also choose to delete a collection, so they're never really that permanent). However, sometimes you want to just group a few photos temporarily, and you don't actually want to save these groupings long term. That's where Quick Collections can come in handy.

Step One:
There are a lot of reasons why you might want a temporary collection, but most of the time I use Quick Collections when I need to throw a quick slide show together, especially if I need to use images from a number of different collections. For example, let's say I get a call from a potential client who's doing a cookbook, and they want to see some examples of food I've shot. I'd go to a recent food shoot, click on its Selects collection, and then double-click to look at them in Loupe view. When I see one I want in my slide show, I just press the letter **B** to add it to my Quick Collection (you get a message onscreen to show you that it has been added).

Step Two:
Now I go to another food shoot collection and do the same thing—each time I see an image that I want in my slide show, I press **B** and it's added, so in no time I can whip through 10 or 15 "Best of" collections and mark the ones I want in my slide show as I go. (You can also add photos to your Quick Collection by clicking on the little gray dot that appears in the top-right corner of each thumbnail in the Grid view. You can hide the gray dot by pressing **Command-J [PC: Ctrl-J]**, clicking on the Grid View tab up top, then turning off the checkbox for Quick Collection Markers, as shown on the left here.)

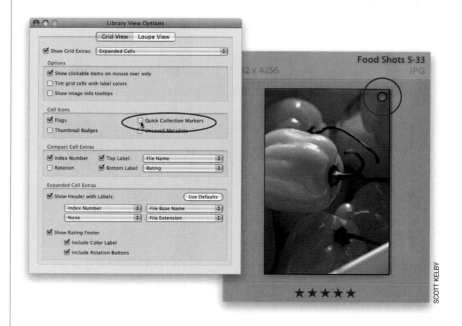

SCOTT KELBY

Step Three:
To see the photos you put in a Quick Collection, go to the Catalog panel (in the left side Panels area), and click on Quick Collection (as shown here). Now just those photos are visible, and if you like, you could do a quick impromptu slide show by pressing **Command-Return (PC: Ctrl-Enter)**. To remove a photo from your Quick Collection, just click on it and press the Delete (PC: Backspace) key on your keyboard (it doesn't delete the original, it just removes it from this temporary Quick Collection).

Step Four:
Now that my photos from all those different collections are in a Quick Collection, I can press **Command-Return (PC: Ctrl-Enter)** to start Lightroom's Impromptu Slideshow feature, which is a full-screen slide show (as shown here) of the photos in your Quick Collection, using the current settings in Lightroom's Slideshow module. So, if the last slide show you created in the Slideshow module had background music and a cool slide template, that's what you'll get now just by pressing those two keys. To stop the slide show, just press the Esc key.

TIP: Saving Your Quick Collection
If you decide you want your Quick Collection to be saved as a regular collection, just go to the Catalog panel, Control-click (PC: Right-click) on Quick Collection, choose Save Quick Collection from the contextual menu, and a dialog appears where you can give your new collection a name.

Make Finding Your Photos Easier by Adding Specific Keywords

When you first imported your photos into Lightroom, you added some generic keywords—search terms that applied to all the photos you were importing. But now that we've made a collection of our keepers, if you take just a few minutes, right now, and quickly go through and assign more specific keywords (search terms) that apply to each individual photo in your keepers set, you will have the fast, organized, super-searchable photo collection you've always dreamed of. It's easier and takes way less time than you'd think, as long as you do it now.

Step One:
Once you've imported your photos and put the keepers in a collection, it's time to add specific keywords, so you can narrow your searches and help yourself find the images you want fast. There are four ways to add these specific keywords, and we'll go through all four (there are different reasons why you might choose one way over another). In the right side Panels area is the Keywording panel, and if you click on a photo, it will list any keywords already assigned to that photo (we don't really use the word "assigned," we say they've been "tagged" with a keyword, as in, "It's tagged with the keyword Maine.")

SCOTT KELBY

Step Two:
For the photo highlighted in Step One, you can see in the Keywording panel that it has been tagged with three keywords: Kennebunkport, Maine, and Summer. If you wanted to add the keyword "Still Water" to this one photo, right below this keyword listing is a text field, and the field itself literally says, "Click here to add keywords." Just click in that field, and type in Still Water. If you want to add more keywords, put a comma between them. When you're done, press the Return (PC: Enter) key on your keyboard. Easy enough.

SCOTT KELBY

Step Three:
If you're just going to assign a specific keyword to one photo, that's not the most efficient way to do it. The method I just taught you really works best when you need to tag a much larger selection of photos. For example, in the shoot that I imported, a group of them were taken at dusk, so what I would do is click on the first dusk photo, press-and-hold the Shift key, then click on the last dusk photo taken in that shoot (holding the Shift key selects all the photos between the first one and the last one you clicked on). Now I would have 60 photos selected, and I'd click in that Click Here to Add Keywords field, type in "Dusk," and the moment I hit Return (PC: Enter), all 60 photos would be tagged with the keyword Dusk. So, I go to the Keywording panel first when I need to tag a lot of photos with the same keyword (or keywords, separated by a comma).

Step Four:
In Lightroom 2, Adobe added a pretty slick Keyword Suggestions feature to save you time (and brainpower) when it comes to creating keywords. Here's how it works: Let's say you add the keyword Maine to a photo. Lightroom instantly looks to see if you've tagged any previous photos with Maine, and if you did, it lists the other keywords you applied to that photo(s) in the Keyword Suggestions section of the Keywording panel for your current photo, and it puts these in a three-column row of buttons (as seen here). If you see a suggested keyword in the list that works for the photo (or selected photos) that you're keywording now, just click on it, and it adds that keyword (it even adds the comma for you). Plus, it's live; as you add more keywords, the suggestions update automatically. You'll love it.

Continued

Step Five:

Besides the new Keyword Suggestions feature in Lightroom 2, there are three other ways to put keywords one click away. If you click-and-hold on the Keyword Set pop-up menu (near the bottom of the Keywording panel), you'll see that you can: (1) choose to load a list of the most recent keywords you've applied (as shown here, at left), (2) load built-in sets of keywords for some common photo categories, like Outdoor Photography, Portrait Photography, or Wedding Photography (as shown here, at right), or (3) create and save your own custom sets with the keywords that fit what you shoot.

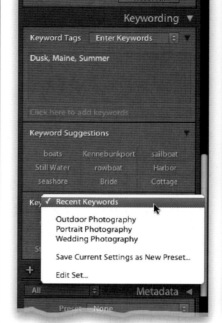

You can choose to load a set of the most recent keywords, so you can tag them to a photo with just one click

There are also built-in keyword sets for common subjects like weddings (shown above), outdoor, and portrait photography

Step Six:

If you decide that you want to create your own custom keyword set, choose Edit Set from the bottom of the Keyword Set pop-up menu to bring up the Edit Keyword Set dialog. There's a pop-up menu at the top that lets you load any of the existing sets, so you can use that as a starting place (if you'd like), and then you can just delete the ones you don't want and/or add to it. Just tab from field to field, typing in the keyword you'd like, and when you're done, choose Save Current Settings as New Preset from the Preset pop-up menu at the top of the dialog. Give your set a name, then click the Change button, and your new custom keyword set will be added to the Keyword Set pop-up menu (as shown here), so you can load it anytime.

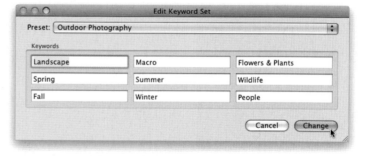

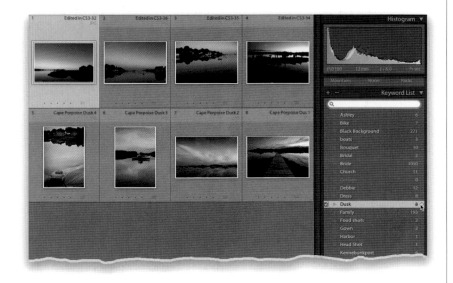

Step Seven:

Down below all this is the Keyword List panel (which used to be called the Keyword Tags panel, and lived in the left side Panels area back in Lightroom 1). The Keyword List panel is the master list of all the keywords you've created or that were already embedded into the photos you've imported into Lightroom. The number to the right of each keyword tells you how many photos are tagged with that particular keyword, and if you click on the arrow that appears to the far right of the keyword itself when you hover your cursor over it, it will instantly display just the photos with that keyword (in the example shown here, I clicked on the arrow for Dusk, and it brought up only the 8 photos in my entire catalog of photos tagged with the keyword Dusk). You're starting to see why keywords are so powerful, and why I urge you to add these more specific keywords as soon as you create your keepers collection.

Step Eight:

Even though it's called the Keyword List panel, it's more than just a list, it's another way to assign keywords, too. First, select all the photos you want to have a particular keyword. Now click on any of those selected photos, and drag-and-drop it onto a keyword in this list (just dragging one moves all the other selected photos at the same time, as a group), and that keyword is instantly assigned to all those photos at once. You can also do this in reverse: select a bunch of photos, and drag-and-drop the keyword (from the Keyword List panel) onto any one of the photos, and it assigns that keyword to all your selected photos. By the way, to remove a keyword, just click on it in the Keyword List panel and click the – (minus sign) button on the left side of the panel header.

Continued

Step Nine:

As you can imagine, it doesn't take very long for your list of keywords to get really long, but there are a couple of ways to deal with this. One is to create a keyword with sub-keywords (kind of like a collection set, but for keywords), so you'd create new keywords that wind up under a main keyword. The advantage of doing this is not just that your keyword list will be shorter and more organized (as shown here), but more importantly, it gives you more sorting power. For example, if you create the keyword Wedding and then create related sub-keywords like Groom, Reception, Ring, and Vows, here's how it helps: If you click on Wedding (the top-level keyword), it will show you every file in your entire library tagged with either Wedding, Groom, Reception, Ring, or Vows. But, if you click on Reception, it will show you only the files tagged with Reception. A huge time saver.

Step 10:

Here's how to set this all up: If you've already created a keyword that you want to appear as a sub-keyword, you can just drag-and-drop it on the keyword you want it to appear under. If you haven't created it yet, then start by Control-clicking (PC: Right-clicking) on the keyword you want as a top-level keyword. Then, from the contextual menu that appears, choose Create Keyword Tag Inside (as shown here). This will bring up a dialog where you can type in your new keyword. Click the Create button, and this new keyword will appear as a hierarchical keyword under your main keyword. The sub-keywords we added can be hidden from view by clicking on the gray triangle to the left of our main keyword. To see them again, just click that triangle again. So, they're there when you need them, tucked away when you don't.

Step 11:

Now, I mentioned there was a fourth way to assign keywords and I use it when I have just a few photos that might need a particular keyword (or keywords), but they're not all located right together. If they're together, it's usually easier to select them all, and either drag them onto a keyword in the Keyword List panel or drag a keyword onto any one of them. But, if you're going to scroll through your collection and assign a word here and there, there's nothing better than the Painter tool to let you spray keywords onto your photo (in Grid view, it's found down in the toolbar—it looks like a spray paint can). So, click on the Painter tool to select it (as shown here).

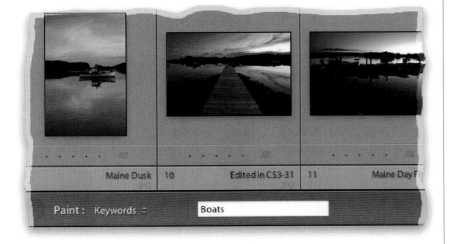

Step 12:

Once you click on the Painter tool, a pop-up menu appears next to it, asking what you want to paint with it. Choose Keywords from this menu, and a text field will appear to the right of that pop-up menu where you can type in the keyword (or keywords) you want to be able to spray onto photos (as seen here). For example, in our Maine collection there are nine shots that have boats in them, so type in the word "Boats," then press the Return (PC: Enter) key. Now that keyword is assigned to the Painter tool.

Continued

Step 13:

Now that you've got the Painter tool loaded with your keyword, click once directly on a photo in your collection that contains boats. When you do this, three things happen: (1) a message appears onscreen confirming that you've assigned the keyword Boats to it, as seen here; (2) your cursor turns into an eraser, so if you clicked the same photo again, it erases the keyword you just assigned; and (3) when this photo is selected, if you look at the Keywording panel in the right side Panels area, you'll see Boats appears as a keyword tagged to this photo, along with the keywords you assigned during import. Now just scroll through your images and each time you see one with a boat in it, click the Painter tool on it. If you click-and-hold, you can spray right over multiple photos.

TIP: Painting Multiple Keywords

To assign multiple keywords with the Painter tool, simply separate each word with a comma in the tool's text field in the toolbar.

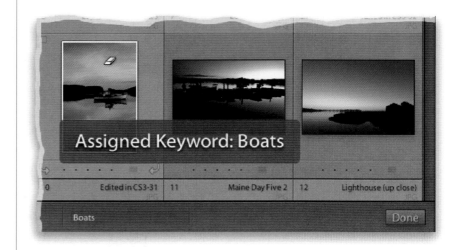

When you take a digital photo, the camera automatically embeds a host of information directly into the photo itself, including everything from the make and model of the camera it was taken with, to the type of lens that was on the camera at the time, to the time and date, and even whether your flash fired or not. That can be very handy stuff (and Lightroom can even search for photos based on this embedded information, called EXIF data). Beyond that, you can embed your own info into the file, and the ability to do that is more important than you might think.

Working with, and Adding to, Your Photo's Metadata

Step One:
In the Library module, to see a selected photo's metadata, go to the Metadata panel located in the right side Panels area (seen here). By default, Lightroom displays the selected photo's basic metadata, which includes the filename, dimensions, any titles or captions you've added (you'll learn how in a moment), any copyright data you added when the file was imported, any ratings, labels, when it was created, and the data embedded by your digital camera when you took the shot (called EXIF data) at the bottom.

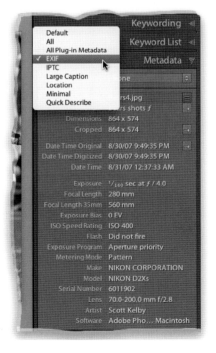

Step Two:
Although this is the default Metadata panel view, you can see more of the embedded data (or less if you feel this is info overload) by choosing different metadata views from the pop-up menu on the left side of the Metadata panel's header (as shown here). For example, choosing Minimal shows you just the filename, rating, caption, and copyright fields—that's it. But choosing All displays a long scrolling list of everything that's embedded, and every field where you can embed stuff, too. The EXIF view (shown here) just shows the info the camera embedded, and the IPTC view just shows the fields where you can enter your copyright, contact, and image info.

Continued

Step Three:

If you see an arrow to the right of any metadata field, that's a hot link to either more information or a search feature. For example, go to the Metadata panel's pop-up menu again, and choose EXIF to show just the info embedded by your camera. Now, hover your cursor over the arrow that appears to the right of Date Time Original for a few seconds and a little message will appear telling you what that arrow does (in this case, clicking that arrow would turn on a filter that would then display only photos taken on that date).

Step Four:

Now go and choose IPTC from the Metadata panel pop-up menu (in case you were wondering, IPTC stands for the International Press Telecommunications Council) to display just the section where you can add your own information to the file (outside the things you could have added during import using a metadata template—see page 30 for more on metadata templates). For example, one bit of metadata I like to add is the city, state, and country (if outside the U.S.) where the photo was taken (that way, I can search by city and instantly see all the photos taken in a particular city). To add this, just scroll down to the Image section, click anywhere inside the Location field to highlight it, and type in the location, then press the **Tab key** to move to the next field down to add the city, state, etc. It's the same process for any of the blank IPTC fields you see here—just click and type in whatever you'd like, and this information gets embedded right into the file.

Step Five:
If you have photos where you didn't apply your copyright metadata preset when you first imported the photos, it's not too late—you can apply it now. First, select all the photos you want to add this info to, then choose your template from the Preset pop-up menu at the top-right side of the Metadata panel (as shown here). That information is instantly added to every selected photo, and you can see the copyright and contact info now appears in the Metadata panel (as seen here).

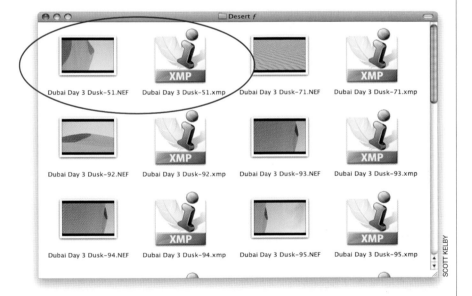

Step Six:
When you add metadata to a JPEG, TIFF, PSD, or DNG photo, that information is embedded directly into the file itself. However, RAW photos don't let you embed metadata directly into them (unless you convert them to DNG format, of course). So, with RAW files, any metadata you add (including copyright info, keywords, and even color correction edits to your photo) is either stored in Lightroom's catalog database, or you can choose to have it written to a separate file that lives right alongside your RAW file, called an XMP sidecar file. This is a separate file from your original RAW photo, and if you were to look at the RAW photo in its folder on your computer, you'd see your RAW file, then next to it, you'd see an XMP sidecar file with the same name, but with the XMP file extension (the two files are circled here in red). These two files need to stay together because one is the photo, and the other is that photo's metadata. So, if you back up this photo to a disc, or move it, or you want to give the RAW file to a friend or co-worker, be sure to grab both files.

Continued

Step Seven:

Although you do have to keep track of two files with RAW photos, there are some advantages: (1) Any color correction settings or sharpening you've applied, and all your embedded keywords, ratings, and cropping will be recognized by the latest versions of Adobe Bridge and Adobe Camera Raw (both are part of Photoshop). And, (2) if you share your RAW photos with other people, you'll be able to include your metadata. If you'd like to have your RAW photo metadata in separate XMP sidecar files, then press **Command-Option-, (comma; PC: Ctrl-Alt-,)** to open Lightroom's Catalog Settings dialog, click on the Metadata tab, and turn on the checkbox for Automatically Write Changes into XMP. Now, your changes to RAW photos (from edits, to cropping, to keywords, to ratings, etc.) will be written to a separate XMP sidecar file automatically.

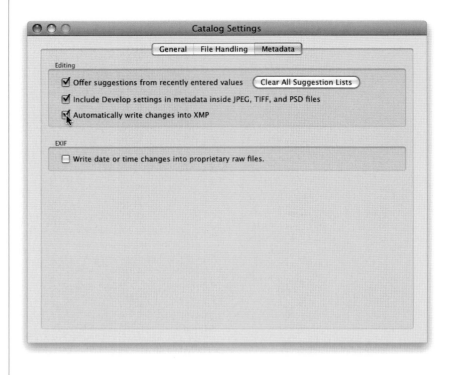

Step Eight:

The downside of always writing the metadata to XMP sidecars is a speed issue. Each time you make a change to a RAW file, Lightroom has to write that change into XMP, which slows things down a bit, so I leave the Automatically Write Changes into XMP checkbox turned off. Instead, when I need to send somebody a RAW file, at that point I go under the Metadata menu, and choose Save Metadata to File (as shown here). *Note:* Remember, this XMP sidecar issue only relates to RAW files, not JPEGs, TIFFs, PSDs, or DNGs, which all embed the metadata directly into the files themselves.

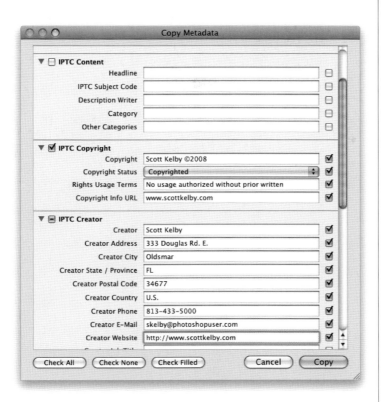

Step Nine:

Here's a tip that could really save you some time: if you manually entered some IPTC metadata for a photo, and you want to apply that same metadata to a different photo, you don't have to type it all in again—you can copy that metadata and paste it on another photo. Start by clicking on the photo where you entered your metadata, then go under the Metadata menu and choose Copy Metadata, or press **Command-Option-Shift-C (PC: Ctrl-Alt-Shift-C)**. This brings up the Copy Metadata dialog (shown here), where you can choose which lines of metadata you want to copy (just turn off the checkbox to the right of any data field you don't want).

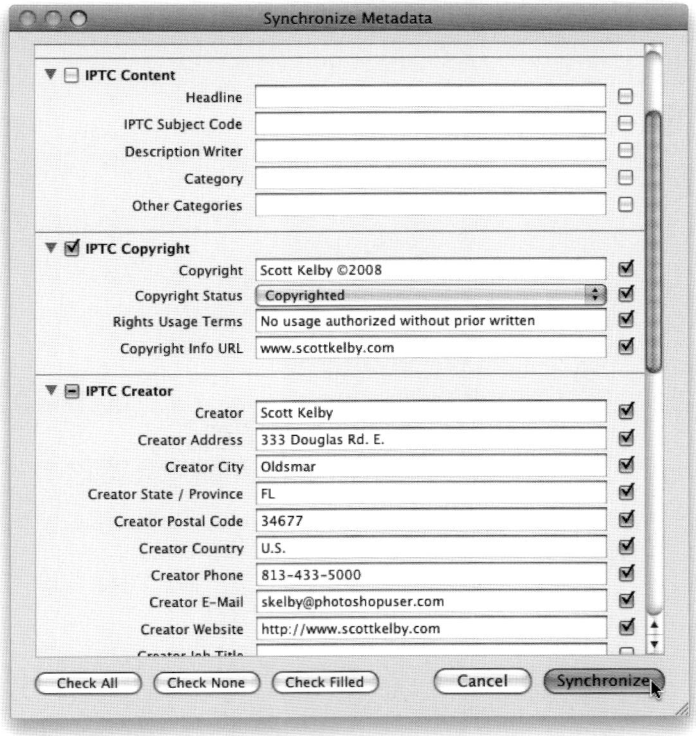

Step 10:

Click the Copy button and that info is stored into memory. Now select the photo(s) you want it applied to, go under the Metadata menu, and choose Paste Metadata. Better yet, that copied meta-data stays in Lightroom's memory, so you can paste it tomorrow, the next day, etc. (Basically, it stays there until you copy a different set of metadata.) If you don't need that long-term storage of metadata, then try this: Click on the photo that has the metadata you want, then Command-click (PC: Ctrl-click) on those other photos to select them. Now click the Sync Metadata button (at the bottom of the right side Panels area), which brings up the Synchronize Metadata dialog (shown here). It looks and works almost exactly like the Copy Metadata dialog. Turn off the checkboxes for any data you don't want synced, then click the Synchronize button to update those other photos.

If Your Camera Supports GPS, Prepare to Amaze Your Friends

Admittedly, this particular feature is more of a "Wow, that's cool!" feature than an incredibly useful feature, but…wow, is it cool! If your camera has built-in GPS (which automatically embeds into your photo the exact latitude and longitude of where the photo was shot), then gather your friends around Lightroom and prepare to blow them away, because it not only displays this GPS information, but one click will actually bring up a map and pinpoint the location where you took the photo. That way…well…well…I dunno—it's just really cool.

Step One:

Import a photo into Lightroom that was taken with a digital camera that has the built-in (or add-on) ability to record GPS data (camera companies like Ricoh make GPS-enabled digital cameras, and many Nikon dSLRs [like the D200, D2X, and D2Hs, for example] have a GPS-compatible connector port, which can make use of add-ons like Sony's GPS CS1KASP unit, with a street price of around $120 [at the time of writing]).

Step Two:

In the Library module, go to the Metadata panel in the right side Panels area. Near the bottom of the panel, if your photo has GPS info encoded, you'll see a meta-data field labeled GPS with the exact coordinates of where that shot was taken (shown circled here in red).

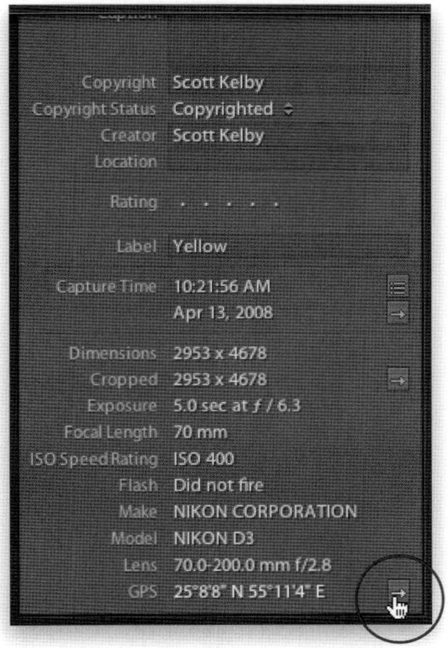

Step Three:
Just seeing that GPS info is amazing enough, but it's what comes next that always drops jaws whenever I show this feature live in front of a class. Click on the little arrow that appears to the far right of the GPS field (it's shown circled here in red).

Step Four:
When you click on that little arrow, if you're connected to the Internet, Lightroom will automatically launch your default Web browser, connect to Google Maps, and it will display a full-color photographic satellite image with your exact location pinpointed on the map (as shown here). Seriously, how cool is that!? Now, in all honesty, I've never had even a semi-legitimate use for this feature, but I've found that despite that fact, I still think it's just so darn cool. All guys do. We just can't explain why.

Finding Photos Fast!

Okay, so we've gone through the process of keywording all our important photos (the keepers), and now we finally get the pay-off: we have created a database of all our photos where we can put our hands on exactly the photo (or photos) we need, in just seconds. This has been our goal from the very start—to set things up the right way from the beginning, so we have a fast, organized, streamlined library of our entire photo collection, and we're about to take 'er out for a spin.

Step One:
Back in the original version of Lightroom, there was a Find panel, which you used to search for a photo, but you could also use the star and color label filters to search, or you could search by date, or you could search by metadata, or, well...your choices were scattered all over. In Lightroom 2, all the search options have been neatly combined into a Library Filter bar across the top of the Library module's Grid view (it's shown circled here in red). To hide this filter anytime, just press the Backslash key (\) on your keyboard.

Step Two:
To start your search, you must tell the Library Filter where you want it to search. Should it search through all of your photos, a particular folder or collection, or just the last batch of imported photos? The quickest way to do this is to go down to the filmstrip, and on the left side you'll see the path to the current location of photos you're viewing. Click-and-hold on that path and a pop-up menu appears where you can choose to see (and search) through: all your photos, the photos in your Quick Collection, your previous import of photos, or any of your recent folders or collections. If you want to search through a collection and it isn't in this list, then go to the Collections panel, click on it there, and you're ready to search just that one collection.

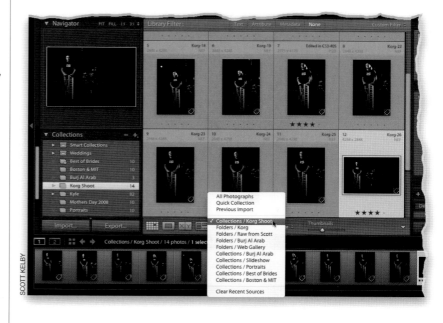

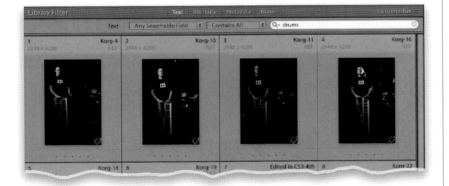

Step Three:

Now that you've told the Library Filter where to search, you can use any of the search categories: search by Text, by Attribute, or by the photo's embedded Metadata. If you click on any one in the Library Filter, a bar pops down with options for that type of search. For example, if you click on Text (as shown here), a text field appears so you can type in the word you want to search for. You can narrow your search using the two pop-up menus to the left of it. The default setting for the first pop-up menu, Any Searchable Field, will search everything: the filename, keywords, captions, embedded EXIF data—you name it—or you can choose to search any one of those individually. If you click on that pop-up menu, you can limit your search to just captions, or just filenames, or just keywords (as shown here).

Step Four:

So, let's give it a try. Click on a collection (in my example, I clicked on a collection with shots of a keyboard player), then up in the Library Filter, click on Text and the Text search options appear. Type the word you want to search for in the search field, and it starts searching (in my case, I typed the word "drums") and Lightroom instantly displays all photos that match your search (in my case, it displayed all the photos tagged with the keyword drums). By the way, did you notice there's no Go or Search button? That's because as soon as you start typing, it starts searching. To stop your search, press the Esc key on your keyboard. To clear the search field, click on the little X on the far-right side of the field.

Continued

Step Five:
Another way to search is by attribute, so click on the word Attribute in the Library Filter and its options appear. Earlier in this chapter, we used the Attribute filter to narrow things down to where just our Picks were showing (you clicked on the white flag), so you're already kind of familiar with this, but I do want to mention a few things: As for the star ratings, if you click on the fourth star, it filters things so you just see any photos that are rated four stars or higher (so you'd see both your 4-star and 5-star images, as shown here on the top). If you want to see your 4-star rated images only, then click-and-hold on the greater than or equal to (≥) sign that appears to the immediate right of the word Rating, and from the pop-up menu that appears, choose Rating is Equal to, as shown here on the bottom.

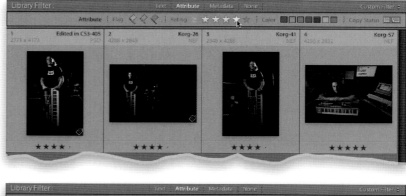

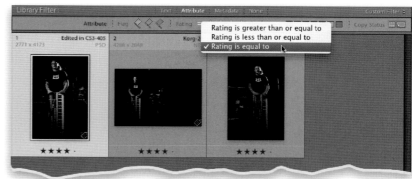

Step Six:
Two more things about the Attribute filter, then we're movin' on: First, at the far right end of the Library Filter is a pop-up menu with some additional filtering. For example, if you choose Unrated, it shows just the photos in your current collection that don't have any rating. Choose Rated, and you get every photo you've rated, no matter what its rating. Choose Flagged, and you get every photo that's flagged either as a Pick or a Reject. But, perhaps more importantly, is that it lets you save your own custom presets to this menu. So, if you realize that you often filter down to see just your photos that are 4-star rated, have a Red label, and are also flagged as Picks, you can have that whole combination appear as a preset. Just apply all those attributes, then choose Save Current Settings as New Preset and give it a name, and it'll be there from now on. Pretty cool—I know.

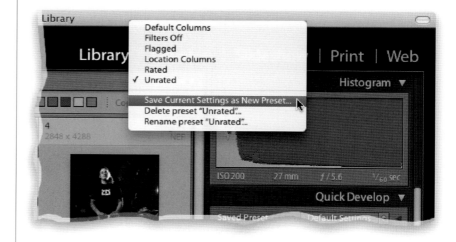

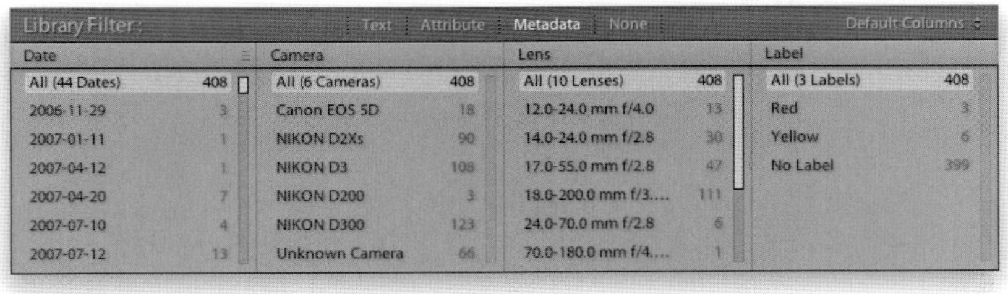

SCOTT KELBY

Step Seven:

There is one more option in the Attribute filter, and that is to show only master photos or show only virtual copies using the buttons on the right side of the Library Filter bar, next to Copy Status (to learn about virtual copies, see Chapter 4 on the Develop module). Now, I've been saving the most amazing search capability until last—Metadata. Go ahead and click on it, and you'll see a series of columns will pop down. This Metadata filter is where you search for photos using the information either: (a) embedded into your photo by your digital camera, including things like the exact time it was taken, the model camera you shot it with (including the serial number), which kind of lens you used, what your ISO was set to, what your exposure was, whether your flash fired, and dozens of other settings, or (b) information you added yourself (keywords you added on import or later, or text you added as captions, or copyright info, etc.).

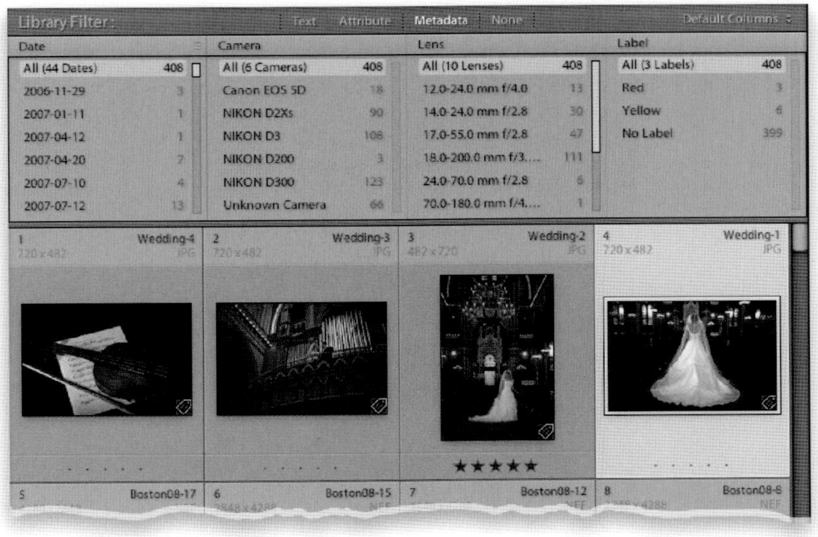

Step Eight:

Go down to the filmstrip, click-and-hold on the name of your current collection in the path, choose All Photographs from the pop-up menu, and the metadata is instantly calculated for all your photos, and displayed in these columns. If you look under the Date column (the first column) at the top, it shows that I have shots taken on 44 different dates. As you look farther down that column, it lists all 44 dates, and how many photos were taken on each date. To see just the photos taken on a particular date, click on that date (for example, if I wanted to see just the 13 photos taken on July 12, 2007, I'd simply click on that date, and then just those photos would appear in the grid).

Continued

Step Nine:

Here, we want to see just the photos taken on November 20, 2007, so I clicked on that date. See what happened when I clicked that date? Not only did the photos appear for just that date, but it updated the metadata in the columns to the right of it (as seen here), which lets you narrow things even further. For example, take a look at the second column (the Camera column), and you'll see the photos taken on that date were taken with two different cameras: a Nikon D2Xs and a Nikon D200 (hey, this was a long time ago). You can also see that five of these photos were taken with the D2Xs, and one with the D200. To see only the D2Xs shots, just click on Nikon D2Xs, and then just those five photos are displayed.

Step 10:

Now, if you want to dig a little deeper, and narrow things down even more, look over in the third column (the Lens column), and you'll see that those five photos were taken using two different lenses. If you want to see the three shots that were taken using a 70–200mm f/2.8 lens, then click on it, and now just those shots are displayed. There's a fourth column (the Label column) and it shows how many of the remaining photos visible onscreen have a label attached to them (in this case, it's just one). To see that photo, just click on the word "Yellow," in the Label column. One thing I want you to really take away from this, is that as you click on something in a column, the other columns update immediately. For example, at first it showed you the data on all the photos in your library. When you clicked on a date, then it updated the other columns with info on just the photos from that date.

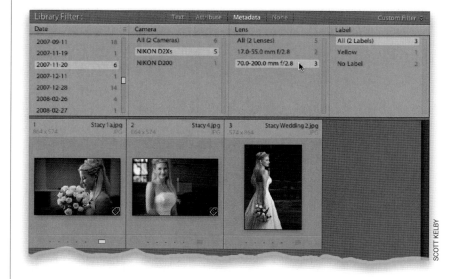

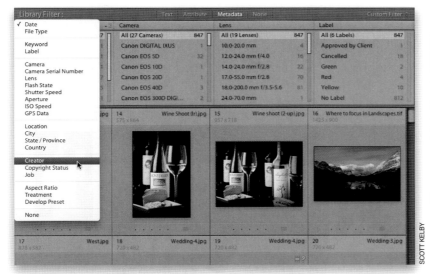

SCOTT KELBY

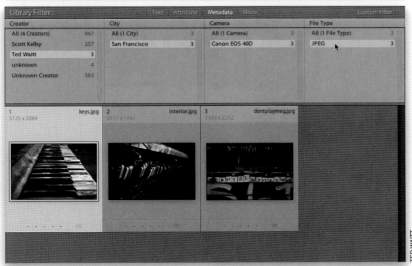

TED WAITT

Step 11:

You're not stuck with just searching with Date, Camera, Lens, and Label—you can customize this so each column displays the piece of metadata you want by clicking on the column header and choosing a new one from the pop-up menu. So, for example, let's say I wanted to find some photos that were taken by my editor, Ted Waitt, and I remember he took them in San Francisco with his Canon EOS 40D, and he emailed them to me, so they were JPEGs. From the first column, I'd choose Creator, so it lists the name of the person who shot each photo (provided, of course, metadata was added as we covered earlier in this chapter). Then, I'd click on Ted, and in the second column I'd choose City, and there I'd click on San Francisco, and it'd narrow things down again. In the third column, I'd choose Camera, and it would list all the cameras Ted used, so I'd choose the 40D. Then in the fourth column, I'd choose File Type, and it would list all the file types Ted saved his files with. Click on JPEG, and now just his JPEGs from San Francisco shot with his 40D are displayed. That is power, baby!

Step 12:

Want to take things up one last notch? (Sure ya do!) If you **Command-click (PC: Ctrl-click)** on more than one search, they're additive (go ahead, Command-click on Text, then Attribute, then Metadata, and they just pop down one after another). Now you can search for a photo with a specific keyword, that's four stars, with a yellow label, and was taken with a Nikon D300, in May of 2008, at a slower shutter speed, and is portrait (vertical). Ya know what's cool? You can even save these criteria as a preset. I am so digging this!

Renaming Photos Already in Lightroom

In Chapter 1, you learned how to rename photos as they're imported from your camera's memory card, or if you're importing photos that are already on your computer. However, once they're in Lightroom, you can also rename them very easily and quickly.

Step One:
Go to a folder or collection of photos in the Library module. In our example here, these photos are in a collection, and if you look at their names you'll see that I didn't rename them during import, so you'll see the generic names assigned by the digital camera, which are really no help at all (they're named _DSC0038.jpg, _DSC0039.jpg, and so on). Besides the fact they're not terribly descriptive names, before long you're going to have lots of photos with these same exact names, because digital cameras only have a limited number of naming options. So, press **Command-A (PC: Ctrl-A)** to select all of the photos in this collection.

SCOTT KELBY

Step Two:
To rename these photos, go under the Library menu and choose Rename Photos, as shown here, or press **F2** on your keyboard.

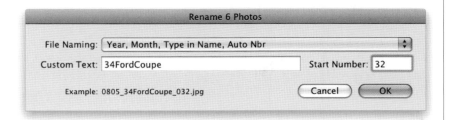

Step Three:

When the Rename Photos dialog appears (shown here), you can choose one of the built-in naming presets from the File Naming pop-up menu. For example, there's one called Custom Name – Sequence which lets you type in any name you want, then it automatically adds a sequential number after that name. If you created your own custom File Naming preset (you can find out how to do that in Chapter 1), you can choose that preset from the pop-up menu instead. In our example, I chose the preset I created back in Chapter 1, which starts with the last two digits of the year the photo was taken, then the month, then the name you type in the Custom Text field (in this case, "34FordCoupe") and a sequential number (in this case, I want it to start numbering at 32).

Step Four:

Now just click OK, and almost instantly all your photos are renamed with your new names that make sense. For example, now instead of the first photo shown here being named "_DSC0035.jpg," it's named "0805_34FordCoupe_032." The new name tells me at a glance the photo was taken in 2008 (08), in the month of May (05), the photos are of a '34 Ford Coupe, and this photo is the 32nd photo of that shoot. This whole process takes just seconds, but makes a big difference when you're searching for photos—not only here in Lightroom, but especially outside of Lightroom in folders, in emails, etc., plus it's easier for clients to find photos you've sent them for approval.

Moving Photos and How to Use Folders

If you quit Lightroom and look inside your My Lightroom Photos folder (that you created on your computer or external hard drive in Chapter 1), you'll see all the folders containing your photos, and you can move photos from folder to folder, add photos, or delete photos, right? Well, you don't have to leave Lightroom to do stuff like that—you can do it in the Folders panel, which shows the hierarchical structure inside your My Lightroom Photos folder.

Step One:

Go to the Library module, and go to the Folders panel found in the left side Panels area (shown here). What you're seeing here are all the folders of photos that Lightroom is managing (in other words, the folders you imported from memory cards or photos that were already on your computer). Anytime you see one of those "flippy triangles" you can click directly on it to reveal the subfolders inside. (*Note:* These are officially called "disclosure triangles," but the only people who actually use that term are...well...let's just say they probably didn't have a date for the prom.)

Step Two:

One of the things this Folders panel is very handy for is moving photos from one folder to another. When you move a photo in this panel, you're physically taking the photo from one folder on your computer or hard drive, and moving it to another folder (just as if you were moving files between two folders on your computer outside of Lightroom). Here's how it's done: First, click on a folder to display the photos in that folder. Then, click-and-drag any photo and drop it on the folder where you now want it to appear (as shown here, where I'm dragging a photo from my Disney Hall folder into my Slide Show folder).

Step Three:
Because you're actually moving the real file here, you get a "Hey, you're about to move the real file" warning from Lightroom. The warning sounds scarier than it is—especially the "neither this move nor any change you've made prior to this can be undone" part. What that means is, if you move this file from the Disney Hall folder to the Slide Show folder, you can't just press **Command-Z (PC: Ctrl-Z)** to instantly undo it if you change your mind. That's true, but saying it can't be undone isn't. You can undo the move by simply clicking on the Slide Show folder, finding the photo you just moved, and dragging it right back to the Disney Hall folder. So, I guess what I'm saying is it's okay to click the Move button (as shown here).

Step Four:
Once the big move has been made, if you click on the Slide Show folder to see what's inside, you'll see the photo you just moved over there in the Grid view (as shown here). So, it's pretty much just moving a file from one folder on your computer to another. In fact, it's exactly like moving a file from one folder to another—but at least here in the Folders panel, it displays how many photos are in a folder over to the right of the folder's name. For example, it originally showed three photos in my Slide Show folder, but once I dragged this other photo in there, it immediately updated to show that it now had four photos, so at least I know I dragged it into the right folder.

Continued

Step Five:

If you Control-click (PC: Right-click) on a folder, a contextual menu appears which lets you create a new subfolder inside that folder (just like you could outside of Lightroom), and lets you rename the folder. This menu also contains a Remove command, but this is where the Folders panel differs from your computer's operating system. On your computer, if you delete a folder, it goes straight into the Trash (PC: Recycle Bin). But in Lightroom, choosing Remove means this folder (and the photos inside it) will no longer be managed by Lightroom, and the folder will be removed from the Folders panel. However, this folder (and the photos inside it) will still be there in your My Lightroom Photos folder (when you choose Remove, you'll get a warning dialog telling you just that).

Step Six:

Here's a close-up of my Folders panel. Starting at the top: I've imported 92 photos that are on my desktop and 672 photos from my Pictures folder, but many of the photos that are managed by Lightroom are in the My Lightroom Photos folder, and since the flippy triangle is expanded, you can see all the subfolders of photos inside the My Lightroom Photos folder. However, you'll notice in this panel that my LaCie hard drive folders and my folder called Family appear grayed out with a question mark. That's Lightroom's way of letting me know that it can't find the original photos in these folders. You can choose Find Missing Folders from the contextual menu that appears when you Control-click (PC: Right-click) on a grayed-out folder, which opens a Finder (PC: Browse for Files or Folders) window, and if you click on the missing folder, it relinks the photos for you.

Note: The file structure you see here stinks. The right way is to have everything inside one main folder (the My Lightroom Photos folder we created), and ideally inside of that you'd have subfolders for the shoots from each year. There should be no photos referenced directly to the Desktop or Pictures folders (like you see here). So, how did mine get this way? I'm lame. Actually, it's more involved than that (meaning: I'm really lame). What you're seeing here is Lightroom running on my laptop computer—the one I use when I'm writing books, which has never been, nor sadly will ever be, very organized. For my photography work, I have a separate dedicated desktop system (no email, no writing stuff—it's just strictly for photography). On that machine, I started from scratch with Lightroom and set up the file structure properly from the start, and managing thousands of photos there is infinitely easier than managing just a few hundred here on my laptop, where chaos clearly reigns!

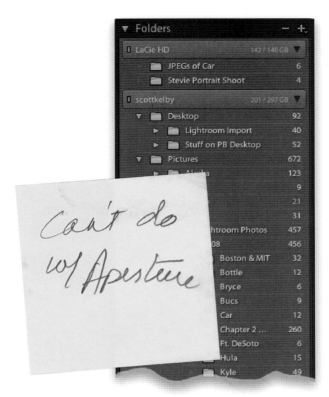

Step Seven:
The reason the LaCie hard drive folders appear grayed out is because they are on that external hard drive. When it isn't connected to my laptop, Lightroom can't find the original photos, but if I connect it to my laptop, then click on the hard drive's folders, it instantly reconnects the photos, and once they're found, they no longer appear grayed out (as shown here). Now, the Family folder is a different situation. I actually did delete that folder from my laptop's Pictures folder (not from within Lightroom), so although those photos are actually no longer on my computer, Lightroom doesn't know that (so I would need to manually delete this folder by clicking on it and then clicking the – [minus sign] button on the right side of the Folders panel's header).

Step Eight:
One more thing: Remember those Boston photos I imported in Chapter 1? Well, there were six of them. If I go onto my computer and drag five new photos into that same folder (not in Lightroom—right on my computer straight into that folder), Lightroom doesn't automatically detect that I added new photos to that folder. If you want Lightroom to manage these new photos, you'll need to click Import and re-import the whole folder of photos. It won't overwrite or alter the photos in that folder that are already being managed by Lightroom, it will just add the new ones in. Now, if you move files within the Folders panel, those get updated immediately—it's just when you add photos to a folder outside of Lightroom that you need to re-import like this. Also, once your photos are in Lightroom, you're better off only moving them within Lightroom's Folders panel, not outside.

Working in Folders? Use Stacking to Keep Things Organized

In my own workflow, I pretty much stay out of the Folders panel and just work with collections, but there's a feature called Stacking (sadly, it's only available within the Folders panel), which reduces clutter by letting you stack similar photos under one thumbnail. So, if you have 12 shots of a particular pose and stack them together, then you'll just see one thumbnail of that pose (the other 11 will be stacked behind it). You can view or hide the stacked photos with one click, and Lightroom can even do your stacking automatically, based on time intervals.

Step One:
If you're working with images in the Folders panel, you can cut some of the visual clutter by grouping similar images into stacks. Here, we've imported images from a wedding shoot, and there are numerous shots that include the same pose. This is the perfect time to group similar poses into a stack, with just one thumbnail showing and the rest of the photos with that same pose collapsed behind it. Start by clicking on the first photo of a similar pose (as seen highlighted here), then press-and-hold the Shift key and click on the last photo that has the same pose (as shown here) to select them all (you can also select photos in the filmstrip if you prefer).

Step Two:
Now go under the Photo menu, under Stacking, and choose Group into Stack, as shown here. (You can also use the keyboard shortcut **Command-G [PC: Ctrl-G]**.) If you look in the grid now, you can see there's just one thumbnail visible with that pose. It didn't delete or remove those other photos—they're stacked behind that one thumbnail. Look how much more manageable things are now that those seven photos are collapsed down to one.

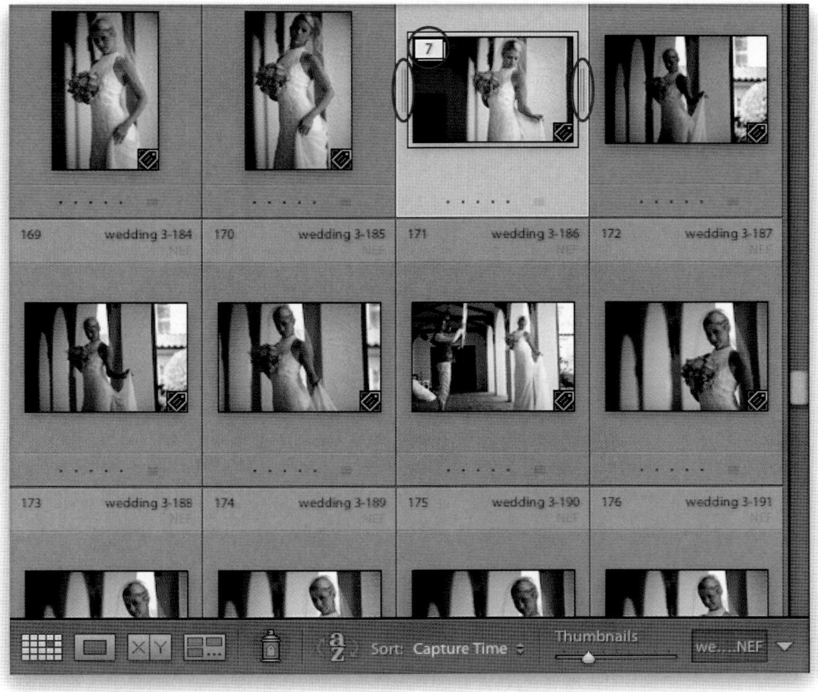

SCOTT KELBY

Step Three:

Here's the stack you just created, and the number 7 in the top-left corner of the thumbnail lets you know how many photos are grouped into that stack. To expand your selected stack back out (to see all the photos in it), just click directly on that little number 7, press the **S key** on your keyboard, or click on the two little lines on either side of the thumbnail. To restack the stack, click on the 7 twice (the first time to select all the stacked images, and the second to close the stack), press S again, or click on those two little lines again that are now on the left of the first thumbnail and on the right of the last thumbnail in the stack. To add a photo to an existing stack, just drag-and-drop it right onto the stack.

Step Four:

The first photo you selected when creating a stack will be the top photo of your stack (the photo you still see) when the stack is collapsed. If that's not the photo you want to represent your stack, you can make any photo in your stack the top photo. First, expand the stack, then Control-click (PC: Right-click) on the number (in the top-left corner of the thumbnail) of the photo you want at the top of the stack, and choose Move to Top of Stack from the contextual menu (as shown here). This contextual menu is also where you can remove a photo from the stack, or split the stack into two stacks, or choose to collapse or expand all your stacks at once.

Continued

Step Five:

If you don't feel like going through your whole folder and manually stacking photos into groups, Lightroom can do it for you, based on how much time has passed between shots. This works on the premise that while you're shooting, you're shooting fairly continuously. However, when you change poses, or lighting, or location, etc., there's a short (or long) pause while you set up the next shot. You tell Lightroom how long you think your average pause is, and everything with a shorter pause gets stacked (this works better than it sounds). To turn on this auto-stack feature, go under the Photo menu, under Stacking, and choose Auto-Stack by Capture Time to bring up the dialog you see here. As you drag the slider left or right, you'll see photos start jumping into stacks in real time. This is one of those you just have to try to see that it usually works pretty darn well.

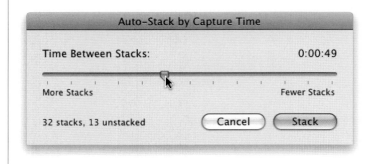

Step Six:

Here's how things look once the auto-stacking feature has been applied. By the way, if you use the auto-stack feature, it's possible that it might stack some photos together that don't actually belong together. Okay, I said it's possible, but in reality it's highly likely. Not every time, mind you, but it will happen. If that happens, it's easy to split a stack and have those other photos separated into their own stack—Control-click (PC: Right-click) on the first photo of the ones you want to split out into their own stack, and in the contextual menu that appears, go under Stacking and choose Split Stack to create two separate stacks. One last thing about stacks: once photos are in a stack, any edits you apply to your stack while it's collapsed are actually only applied to the top photo in your stack.

When you launch Lightroom for the very first time, it creates a main photo catalog for you (that's the database that keeps track of all the photos, stores all your thumbnails, etc.). But you're not stuck with that one catalog, you can create as many as you'd like (maybe one for all your client work, another for family photos, one for fine art, etc.), and load them when you need them. The advantage is it keeps your database "lean and mean" and running at top speed, rather than having one huge database for every photo you've ever taken.

Creating and Using Multiple Catalogs

Step One:
So far, we've been working with your main Lightroom catalog of photos (which was created when you launched Lightroom for the first time). However, if you wanted to, for example, create a separate catalog for managing all your family photos, then you'd go under Lightroom's File menu and choose New Catalog (as shown here).

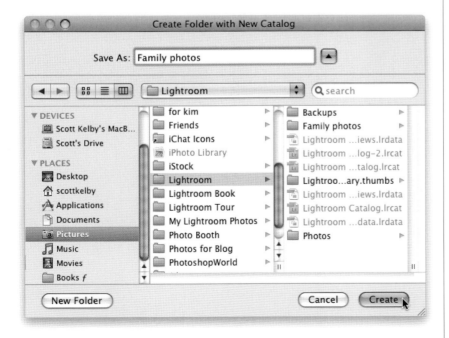

Step Two:
This brings up a Create Folder with New Catalog dialog, asking where you want to store this new catalog (it automatically creates a folder at this new location, because a new catalog consists of more than just a single database file—there are some other support folders and documents that must be created as well, so this folder keeps them all together. By the way, just so I keep things straight, I save all of my catalogs in my Lightroom folder, so I always know where they are). When you choose the location for this second catalog, give it a name (I named mine "Family photos"), then click the Create (PC: Save) button (as shown here).

Continued

Step Three:

Once you click that button, Lightroom actually closes your database, then Lightroom itself quits and automatically relaunches with your brand new, totally empty catalog, with no photos in it whatsoever (as seen here). So, click on the Import button (near the bottom-left corner of Lightroom), and let's bring in some family photos to get the ball rolling.

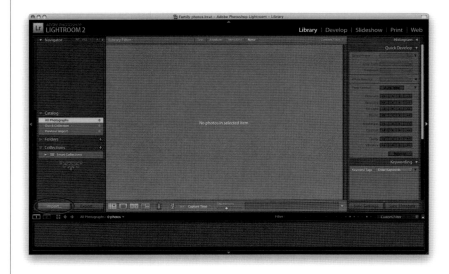

Step Four:

So you know what to do from here, as far as building a catalog of images (import more photos, add keywords, make your collections, etc., just like always). When you're done working with this new Family Photos catalog, and you want to return to your original main catalog, just go under the File menu, under Open Recent, and choose Lightroom 2 Catalog (your main catalog, as shown here). Lightroom will once again save your Family Photos catalog, quit, and relaunch with your main catalog. I know it's kinda weird that it has to quit and relaunch, but luckily it's pretty darn quick about it.

SCOTT KELBY

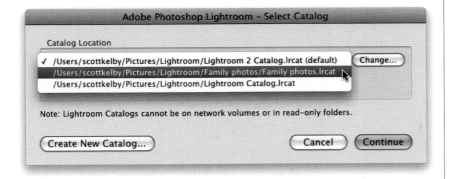

Besides switching catalogs once Lightroom is open, you can actually choose which catalog you want to work with when you launch Lightroom. Just press-and-hold the **Option (PC: Alt) key** before you launch Lightroom, and then when you launch it, it will bring up the Select Catalog dialog you see here, where you can choose (from the pop-up menu) which catalog you want it to open. *Note:* If you want to open a Lightroom catalog you created, but it doesn't appear in this Catalog Location pop-up menu (if you didn't save it in your Lightroom folder when you created it), then you can click the Change button that appears to the right of that pop-up menu and locate the catalog using a standard Open (PC: Browse) dialog.

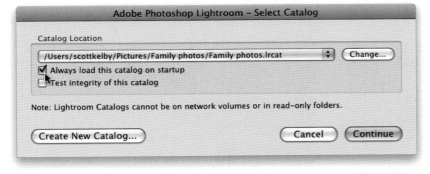

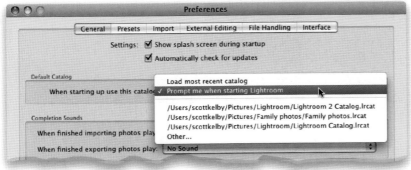

Step Six:

If you want to set it up so Lightroom always starts up with one of the new catalogs you've created (rather than the default main catalog), you can do that in this same dialog. First, choose the catalog you want to be your default start-up catalog from the pop-up menu, then turn on the Always Load This Catalog on Start-up checkbox (as shown here, at the top). Also, if you want to choose which catalog to work with every time you launch Lightroom, go to Lightroom's Preferences (found under the Lightroom menu on a Mac, or the Edit menu on a PC), click on the General tab up top, and in the Default Catalog section, from the pop-up menu, choose Prompt Me When Starting Lightroom (as shown here, at the bottom).

From Laptop to Desktop: Syncing Catalogs on Two Computers

If you're running Lightroom on a laptop during your location shoots, you might want to take all the edits, keywords, metadata, and of course the photos themselves, and add them to the Lightroom catalog on your studio computer. It's easier than it sounds: basically you choose which catalog to export from your laptop, then you take the folder it creates over to your studio computer and import it—Lightroom does all the hard work for you, you just have to make a few choices about how Lightroom handles the process.

Step One:
Using the scenario described above, we'll start on the laptop. The first step is to decide whether you want to export a folder (all the imported photos from your shoot), or a collection (just your Picks from the shoot). In this case, we'll go with a folder, so go to the Folders panel and click on the folder you want to merge with your main catalog back in your studio. (If you had chosen a collection, the only difference would be you'd go to the Collections panel and click on the collection from that shoot instead. Either way, all the metadata you added, and any edits you made in Lightroom, will still be transferred over to the other machine.)

Step Two:
Now go under Lighroom's File menu and choose Export as Catalog (as shown here).

Step Three:
When you choose Export as Catalog, it brings up the Export as Catalog dialog (shown here), where you type in the name you want for your exported catalog at the top, but there are some very important choices you need to make at the bottom. By default, it assumes that you want to include the previews that Lightroom created when you imported the photos into Lightroom, and I always leave this option turned on (I don't want to wait for them to render all over again when I import them into my studio computer). If you turn on the top Export Selected Photos Only checkbox, then it will only export photos in that folder that you had selected before you chose Export as Catalog. But perhaps the most important choice is the center checkbox—Export Negative Files. With this off, it only exports previews and metadata, it doesn't really export the actual photos themselves, so if you do indeed want to export the actual photos (I always do), then turn the center checkbox on.

Step Four:
When you click the Export Catalog button, it exports your catalog (it usually doesn't take very long, but of course the more photos in your collection or folder, the longer it will take), and when it's done exporting, you'll see the folder on your computer that you exported (as seen here). I usually save this file to my desktop, because the next step is to copy it onto an external hard drive, so you can move this folder full of images over to your studio computer. So, go ahead and copy this folder onto an external hard drive now.

Continued

Step Five:

When you get to your studio, connect your hard drive to your studio computer, and copy that folder to the location where you store all your photos (which should be that My Lightroom Photos folder we created in Chapter 1). Now, on your studio computer, go under Lightroom's File menu and choose Import from Catalog to bring up the dialog you see here. Navigate to that folder you copied onto your studio computer, and then inside that folder, click on the file that ends with the file extension LRCAT (as shown here), and click the Choose button. By the way, if you look at the capture shown here, you can see that Lightroom created three items inside this folder: (1) a file that includes the previews, (2) the catalog file itself, and (3) a Pictures folder with the actual photos.

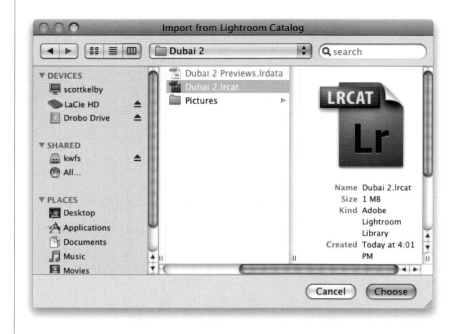

Step Six:

When you click the Choose button, it brings up a modified version of Lightroom's Import Photos dialog (seen here). Any photos in the Preview section on the right that have a checkbox turned on beside them will be imported (I always leave all of these turned on). In the New Photos section in the lower-left corner is a File Handling pop-up menu. Since we already copied the photos into the proper folder on our studio computer, I'm using the default setting which is Add New Photos to Catalog Without Moving (as shown here), but if you want to copy them directly from your hard drive into a folder on your computer, you could choose the Copy option instead. There's a third option, but I have no idea why at this point you'd choose to not import the photos. Just click Import, and these photos will appear as a folder, with all the edits, keywords, etc., you applied on your laptop.

All the changes, edits, keywords, etc., you add to your photos in Lightroom are stored in your Lightroom catalog file, so as you might imagine, this is one incredibly important file. Which is also why you absolutely need to back up this catalog on a regular basis, because if for some reason or another your catalog database gets corrupted—you're completely hosed. (Of course, unless you backed up your catalog, in which case you're not hosed at all.) The good news is Lightroom will back up this catalog database for you, but you have to tell it to. Here's how:

Backing Up Your Catalog (This Is VERY Important)

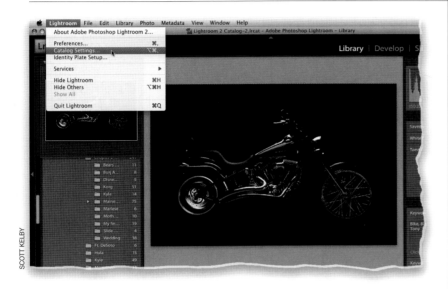

SCOTT KELBY

Step One:
Start by going under the Lightroom menu (PC: Edit menu) and choosing Catalog Settings (as shown here).

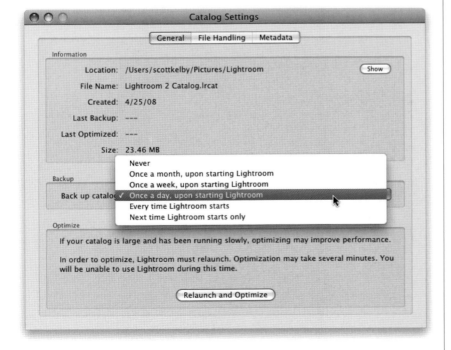

Step Two:
When the Catalog Settings dialog appears, click on the General tab up top (shown highlighted here), and in the center of this dialog is a Backup section, and a Back Up Catalog pop-up menu. Click-and-hold on that pop-up menu and a list of options for having Lightroom automatically back up your current catalog will appear. Here you choose how often you want that to be, but I recommend that you choose Once a Day, Upon Starting Lightroom. That way, it backs up each time you use Lightroom, so if for some reason the catalog database becomes corrupt, you'd only lose a maximum of one day's editing.

Continued

Step Three:

The next time you launch Lightroom, a reminder dialog will appear reminding you to back up your catalog database. Click the Backup button (as shown here), and it does its thing (it doesn't take long at all, so don't be tempted to click Backup Tomorrow or Skip Now. Those are sucker bets). Once it's done, it launches Lightroom and doesn't bother you again until the next day (at the earliest). By default, these catalog backups are stored in separate subfolders inside the folder, which lives inside your Lightroom folder, which, by default, resides in your Pictures folder. However, I recommend clicking the Choose button and putting your backups on a totally separate hard drive, because having both your working catalog and the backup copies on the same hard drive is just way too risky. This way, if your computer's hard drive crashes, you have a safe backup copy on that separate hard drive to get you back up and running (if you don't save them to a separate hard drive and your hard drive crashes, you lose both your catalog and your backups at the same time).

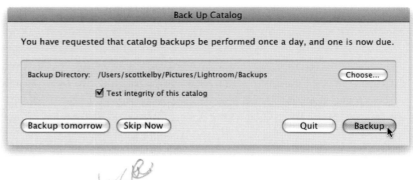

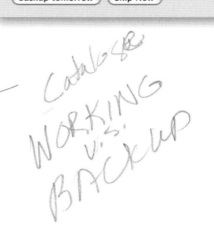

Step Four:

So now that you've got a backup of your catalog, what happens if your catalog gets corrupted or your computer crashes? How do you restore your catalog? First you launch Lightroom, then you go under the File menu and choose Open Catalog. In the Open dialog, navigate to your Backups folder (wherever you chose to save it in Step Three), and you'll see all your backups listed in folders by date and 24-hour time. Click on the folder for the date you want, then inside, click on the LRCAT file (that's your backup), click the Open button, and you're back in business.

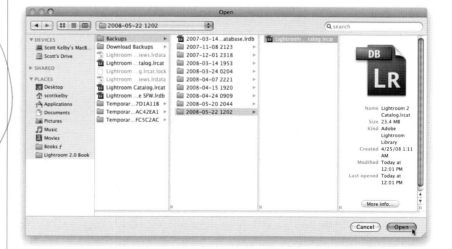

If you work for any amount of time in Lightroom, at some point you're going to see a little question mark icon appear to the right of a thumbnail, and it either means: (1) it's nothing to worry about and everything's perfectly normal, or (2) something's wrong—your photo is missing. Here's how to tell which it is, when you need to fix the problem, and how to do it if it does need fixing:

Relinking Missing Photos

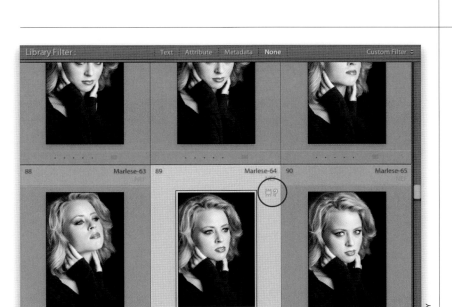

SCOTT KELBY

Step One:
If you see a little question mark appear beside a photo's thumbnail (like the one shown circled here in red), it means that Lightroom can't find the original photo that's linked to that thumbnail preview. You'll still be able to see the photo's thumbnail and even zoom in closer to see it in Loupe view, but you won't be able to do any serious editing (like color correction, changing the white balance, cropping, printing, etc.), because Lightroom needs that real original photo file before it can do those types of things. Of course, the question is, "Where is the original file, and why is it missing?"

Step Two:
There are two main reasons why photos are missing: one is that the photos are simply offline, which just means your original photos are stored on an external hard drive and that hard drive isn't connected to your computer right now, so Lightroom can't find them (as seen on the left here). So, just connect the hard drive, and Lightroom will see that drive is connected, instantly relink everything, and all goes back to normal (as seen on the right). But if you didn't store your photos on an external hard drive, then there's a different problem—you moved or deleted the original photos.

TIP: Finding Your Hard Drive Info
The Volume Browser in the Folders panel shows each storage device you have connected, how much space is free on it, and its total capacity. Also, you can click-and-hold on the + (plus sign) button and choose three different ways to display your folder info.

Continued

Step Three:
In this case, to find out where the photo was last seen, go ahead and click on that little question mark icon and a dialog will pop up telling you it can't find the original file (which you already knew), but more importantly, under the scary warning it shows you its previous location (so you'll instantly be able to see if it was indeed on a removable hard drive, flash drive, etc.). So, if you just moved the file (or the whole folder), you have to tell Lightroom where you moved it to (which you'll do in the next step).

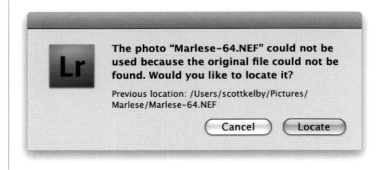

Step Four:
Click on the Locate button, and when the Locate dialog appears (shown here), navigate your way to where that photo referenced in the warning dialog is now located. Once you find it, click on it, and click the Select button, it relinks the photo. If you moved an entire folder, then make sure you leave the Find Nearby Missing Photos checkbox turned on, so that way when you find any one of your missing photos, it will automatically relink all the missing photos in that entire folder at once.

TIP: Missing Folders
If you see a question mark on a folder in the Folders panel, it means that at one point you had imported that folder of photos into Lightroom, but since then you moved the folder (or disconnected the external hard drive where it's located). If you click on the folder, it shows you the thumbnails of the photos that were in that folder. To relink them, Control-click (PC: Right-click) on the folder and choose Find Missing Folder (as shown here), then navigate to the folder's new location, click the Select button, and they're relinked.

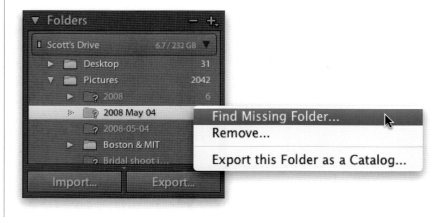

Lightroom Quick Tips > >

▼ Deleting a Collection

If you want to delete a collection, just click on it in the Collections panel and then click the – (minus sign) button on the right side of the panel header. This deletes just the collection, not the real photos themselves.

▼ Renaming a Collection

To rename a collection, Control-click (PC: Right-click) on the collection and choose Rename from the contextual menu.

▼ Adding Photos to an Existing Collection

You can add photos to any existing collection by just dragging a photo from the grid (or filmstrip) and dropping it onto your collection.

▼ Quickly Apply Keywords to Your Selected Photo

When you hover your mouse over a keyword in the Keyword List panel, a checkbox appears that lets you assign it to your selected photo.

▼ Quickly Create Subkeywords

If you Control-click (PC: Right-click) on a keyword in the Keyword List panel, there's a new menu item called Put New Keywords Inside This Keyword and until you turn it off (by choosing it again in the contextual menu), all keywords you create are created as subkeywords of this keyword.

▼ Removing Unused Keywords

Any grayed-out keywords in the Keyword List panel are not being used by any photos in Lightroom, so you can delete these orphaned keywords (which makes your keyword list cleaner and shorter) by going under the Metadata menu and choosing Purge Unused Keywords.

▼ How to Share Smart Collections Settings

If you Control-click (PC: Right-click) on a Smart Collection, you can choose Export Smart Collection Settings from the contextual menu to save the Smart Collection's criteria, so you can share it with a friend. After you send it to them, they can import it using the Import Smart Collection Settings command from the same contextual menu.

▼ Sharing Keywords

If you want to use your keywords in a copy of Lightroom on a different computer, or share them with friends or co-workers, go under the Metadata menu and choose Export Keywords to create a text file with all your keywords. To import these into another user's copy of Lightroom, go under the Metadata menu and choose Import Keywords, then locate that keyword file you exported earlier. Also, you can copy-and-paste keywords from text files directly into the Keywording panel.

▼ Turning Your Filters On/Off

Just press **Command-L (PC: Ctrl-L)** to turn your filters (flags, ratings, metadata, etc., in the Library Filter bar) on/off.

▼ Switching to the Painter Tool

You can temporarily switch to the Painter tool by simply **Command-Option-clicking (PC: Ctrl-Alt-clicking)** on the photo you want to paint on. If you're going to be doing some serious painting, then press **Command-Option-K (PC: Ctrl-Alt-K)** to permanently switch to the tool. When you're done, either click it back on its gray circular home in the toolbar or just press the same keyboard shortcut again.

▼ Making Your Panels Larger

If you want your panels to be wider (or thinner for that matter), just move your cursor right over the edge closest to the center Preview area and your cursor will change into a two-headed cursor. Now you can just click-and-drag your panels out wider (or drag them in to make them thinner). This also works for the filmstrip at the bottom.

▼ Auto Hide the Top Navigation Bar

As I mentioned, the first thing I do is turn the Auto Hide feature off (so the panels stop popping in/out all day long), and instead I show/hide them manually as needed. But you might consider turning on Auto Hide just for the top taskbar. It's the most rarely used panel, but people do seem to like clicking to jump from module to module, rather than using the keyboard shortcuts. With Auto Hide turned on, it stays tucked out of sight until you click on the gray center triangle to reveal it. Then you can click on the module you want to jump to, and as soon as you move away from the top panel, it tucks away. Try it once, and I bet you'll totally dig it.

▼ More Options for the Toolbar

By default, Lightroom displays a number of different tools and options on the toolbar below the center Preview area, but you can choose which ones you want (including some you may not have realized were available) by clicking on the little triangle at the toolbar's far right side. A menu will pop up with a list of toolbar items. The ones with checks beside them will be visible, so to add one, just choose it.

Continued

Lightroom Quick Tips > >

▼ Zooming In/Out

You can use the same keyboard short-cuts used by Photoshop to zoom in and out of your image when it's in Loupe view. Just press **Command-+ (PC: Ctrl-+)** to zoom in, and **Command--(PC: Ctrl--)** to zoom back out.

▼ The "Flag and Move" Trick

If you want to speed up the flagging-of-Picks process, try this: instead of just pressing **P** to flag a photo, and then using the Arrow key to move to the next photo, press **Shift-P**. This flags the photo as a Pick, but then automatically moves to the next photo for you.

▼ Filter Your Picks from the Filmstrip

Back in the original version of Light-room, there wasn't a Library Filter bar at the top; instead, you showed your Picks and Rejects by clicking on little flag icons on the right side of the filmstrip. Well, if you miss that way of doing things, Adobe left those filters there. So, you have your choice: do it from the top (which offers more features than just filtering by flags, stars, or colors), or the filmstrip version. However, here's a tip within a tip: you're better off Control-clicking (PC: Right-clicking) directly on the filmstrip flags and making your choice from the contextual menu, than you are trying to click on them, because they toggle back and forth, and it can get real confusing as to what you're actually seeing, real fast.

▼ Finding Out Which Collection a Particular Photo Is In

If you're scrolling through your entire Lightroom catalog (you've clicked on All Photographs in the Catalog panel), and you see a photo and want to know which collection it lives in, just Control-click (PC: Right-click) on the photo, and from the contextual menu that appears, choose Show in Collection. If it's not in any collection, it will tell you so.

▼ How Much Space Is Left on Your Hard Drive for More Photos

If you're using one or more external hard drives to store your Lightroom photos, you can quickly find out exactly how much storage space you have left on those drives without leaving Lightroom. Just go to the Folders panel (in the left side Panels area), and in the Volume Browser, you'll see a volume for each drive that you have Lightroom managing photos on (including your internal hard drive), and beside each name, it displays how much space is still available, followed by how much total space there is. If you hover your cursor over a volume, a message will pop up telling you exactly how many photos are stored on that drive that are managed by Lightroom.

▼ Removing Photos from Survey View

There's a little known shortcut for removing a selected photo from contention when you're looking at them in Survey View: just press the **/ (Forward Slash) key** on your keyboard.

▼ Where Collection Sets Live

When you create collection sets, by default they appear at the top of the Collections panel in alphabetical order. Then, after your collection sets come your Smart Collections, then your collections.

▼ The Hidden Extra Options for Smart Collections

In the Smart Collection dialog, if you Option-click (PC: Alt-click) the + (plus sign) button (which you normally use to add another line of smart criteria), instead, another section of additional options pops down which let you further tweak your first criteria, and give you refined sorting power. Very cool stuff.

Customizing
how to set up things your way

If the target audience for this book was 17-year-olds, I would have had to (by international law) name this chapter "Pimp My Lightroom," because there isn't a 17-year-old alive today that wouldn't instantly know that this chapter is about customizing how Lightroom looks and works (thanks to the MTV series *Pimp My Ride,* which brought the word "pimp" into the teen vernacular, much to the chagrin of clergymen everywhere). By the way, you may have just witnessed the first time the words "pimp" and "chagrin" were used in the same sentence (though, if you put them together, it would make a great name for a band that parents would really hate). Anyway, while I could rest on my laurels and go with a slam dunk chapter name like "Pimp My Lightroom," unfortunately the audience that actually buys my books (primarily Amish furniture salesmen and airport gift shop employees) wouldn't necessarily "get" the *Pimp My Ride* reference (they probably watch *From G's to Gents,* instead), and then they'd think I was just looking for some cheap way to work a borderline naughty word into my chapter header (I'll bet you didn't realize that this much careful thought and consideration went into each chapter name, did you?). So, I decided to play it safe. To toe the line. To not "rock the boat," and just go with the same chapter name that every author writing a book on Lightroom used for their chapter on customizing. But just between us, no matter what I called it up top, you know, and I know, "you're pimpin'!"

ng What You
See in Loupe View

When you're in Loupe view (the zoomed-in view of your photo), besides just displaying your photo really big, you can display as little (or as much) information about your photo as you'd like as text overlays, which appear in the top-left corner of the Preview area. You'll be spending a lot of time working in Loupe view, so let's set up a custom Loupe view that works for you.

Step One:
In the Library module's Grid view, click on a thumbnail and press **E** on your keyboard to jump to the Loupe view (in the example shown here, I hid the left side Panels area and the filmstrip, so the photo would show up larger in Loupe view).

Step Two:
Press **Command-J (PC: Ctrl-J)** to bring up the Library View Options dialog and then click on the Loupe View tab. At the top of the dialog, turn on the Show Info Overlay checkbox. The pop-up menu to the right lets you choose from two different info overlays—Info 1 overlays the filename of your photo (in larger letters) in the upper-left corner of the Preview area (as seen here). Below the filename, in smaller type, is the photo's capture date and time, and its cropped dimensions. Info 2 also displays the filename, but underneath, it displays the exposure, ISO, and lens settings.

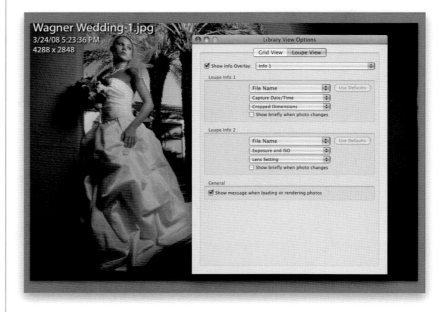

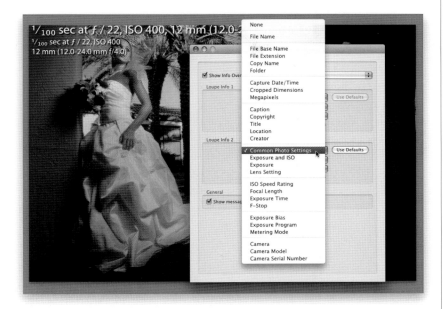

Step Three:

Luckily, you can choose which info is displayed for both info overlays using the pop-up menus in this dialog. So, for example, instead of having the filename show up in huge letters, here for Loupe Info 2, you could choose something like Common Photo Settings from the pop-up menu (as shown here). By choosing this, instead of getting the filename in huge letters, you'd get the same info that's displayed under the Histogram (like the shutter speed, f-stop, ISO, and lens set-ting found in the top panel in the right side Panels area), even though you're in the Library module. You can customize both info overlays separately by simply making choices from these pop-up menus. (*Remember:* The top pop-up menu in each section is the one that will appear in really large letters.)

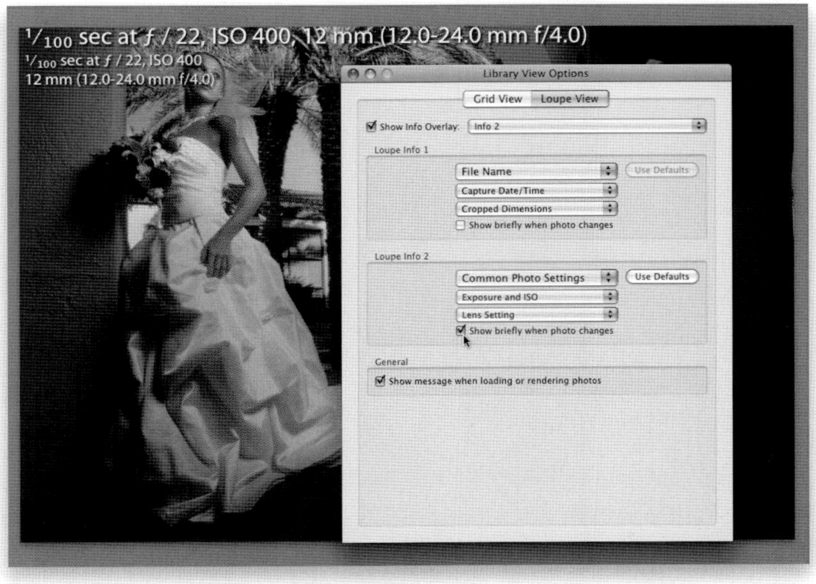

Step Four:

Any time you want to start over, just click the Use Defaults button to the right and the default Loupe Info settings will appear. Personally, I find this text appearing over my photos really, really distracting most of the time. The key part of that is "most of the time." The other times, it's handy. So, if you think this might be handy, too, here's what I recommend: (a) Turn off the Show Info Overlay checkbox and turn on the Show Briefly When Photo Changes checkbox below the Loupe Info pop-up menus, which makes the overlay tem-porary—when you first open a photo, it appears for around four seconds and then hides itself. Or, you can do what I do: (b) leave those off, and when you want to see that overlay info, press the letter **I** to toggle through Info 1, Info 2, and Show Info Overlay off. At the bottom of the dialog, there's also a checkbox that lets you turn off those little messages that appear onscreen, like "Working" or "Assigned Keyword," etc.

Choosing What You See in Grid View

Those little cells that surround your thumbnails in Grid view can either be a wealth of information or really distracting (depending on how you feel about text and symbols surrounding your photos), but luckily you get to totally customize not only how much info is visible, but in some cases, exactly which type of info is displayed (of course, you learned in the previous chapter that you can toggle the cell info on/off by pressing the letter **J** on your keyboard). At least now when that info is visible, it'll be just the info you care about.

Step One:
Press **G** to jump to the Library module's Grid view, then press **Command-J (PC: Ctrl-J)** to bring up the Library View Options dialog (shown here), and click on the Grid View tab at the top (seen highlighted here). At the top of the dialog, there's a pop-up menu where you can choose the options for what's visible in either the Expanded Cells view or the Compact Cells view. The difference between the two is that you can view more info in the Expanded Cells view.

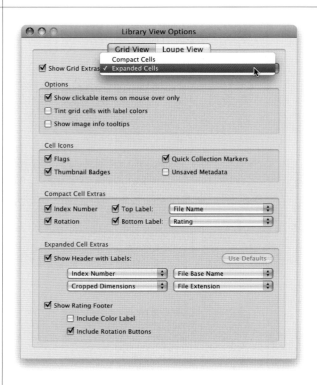

Step Two:
We'll start at the top, in the Options section. You can add a Pick flag and left/right rotation arrows to your cell, and if you turn on the Show Clickable Items on Mouse Over Only checkbox, it means they'll stay hidden until you move your mouse over a cell, then they appear so you can click on them. If you leave it unchecked, you'll see them all the time. The Tint Grid Cells with Label Colors checkbox only kicks in if you've applied a color label to a photo. If you have, turning this on tints the gray area around the photo's thumbnail the same color as the label.

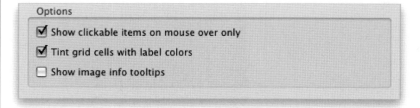

The thumbnail badges show you (from L to R) that a keyword has been applied, the photo has been cropped, and it has been edited

The gray circle in the upper-right corner is actually a button—click on it to add this photo to your Quick Collection

Step Three:
The next section down, Cell Icons, has two options for things that actually appear right over your photo's thumbnail image, and two that appear just in the cell. Thumbnail badges appear in the bottom-right corner of a thumbnail itself to let you see if: (a) the photo has had keywords added, (b) the photo has been cropped, or (c) the photo has been edited in Photoshop Lightroom (color correction, sharpening, etc.). These tiny badges are actually clickable shortcuts, so for example, if you wanted to add a keyword, you could click the Keyword badge (whose icon looks like a tag), and it opens the Keywording panel and highlights the keyword field, so you can just type in a new keyword. The other option on the thumbnail, Quick Collection Markers, adds a gray circle-shaped button to the top-right corner of your photo when you mouse over the cell. Click on this dot to add the photo to (or remove it from) your Quick Collection.

Click the flag icon to mark it as a Pick

Click the Unsaved Metadata icon to save the changes

Step Four:
The other two options don't put anything over the thumbnails—they add icons in the cell area itself. When you turn on the Flags checkbox, it adds a Pick flag to the top-left side of the cell (shown at left), and you can then click on this flag to mark this photo as a Pick. The last check-box in this section, Unsaved Metadata, adds a little icon in the top-right corner of the cell (shown at right), but only if the photo's metadata has been updated in Lightroom (since the last time the photo was saved), and these changes haven't been saved to the file itself yet (this sometimes happens if you import a photo, like a JPEG, which already has keywords, ratings, etc., applied to it, and then in Lightroom you added keywords, or changed the rating). If you see this icon, you can click on it to bring up a dialog that asks if you want to save the changes to the file (as shown here).

The metadata for this photo has been changed in Lightroom. Save the changes to disk?

☐ Don't show again   Cancel   Save

Continued

Step Five:

We're going to jump down to the bottom of the dialog to the Expanded Cell Extras section, where you choose which info gets displayed in the area at the top of each cell in Expanded Cells view. By default, it displays four different bits of info (as shown here): It's going to show the index number (which is the number of the cell, so if you imported 63 photos, the first photo's index number is 1, followed by 2, 3, 4, and so on, until you reach 63) in the top left, then below that will be the pixel dimensions of your photo (if the photo's cropped, it shows the final cropped size). Then in the top right, it shows the file's name, and below that, it shows the file's type (JPEG, RAW, TIFF, etc.). To change any one of these info labels, just click on the label pop-up menu you want to change and a long list of info to choose from appears (as seen in the next step). By the way, you don't have to display all four labels of info, just choose None from the pop-up menu for any of the four you don't want visible.

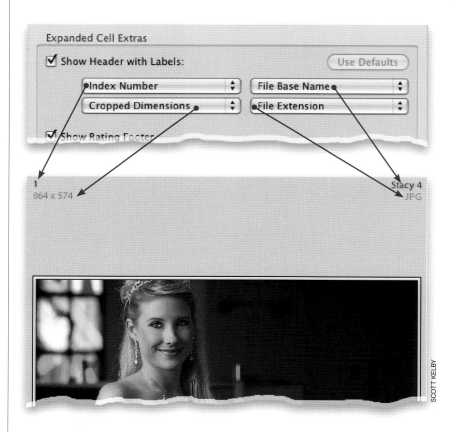

Step Six:

Although you can use the pop-up menus here in the Library View Options dialog to choose which type of information gets displayed, check this out: you can actually do the same thing from right within the cell itself. Just click on any one of those existing info labels, right in the cell itself, and the same exact pop-up menu that appears in the dialog appears here. Just choose the label you want from the list (I chose ISO Speed Rating, as seen here), and from then on it will be displayed in that spot (as shown here on the right, where you can see this shot was taken at an ISO of 200).

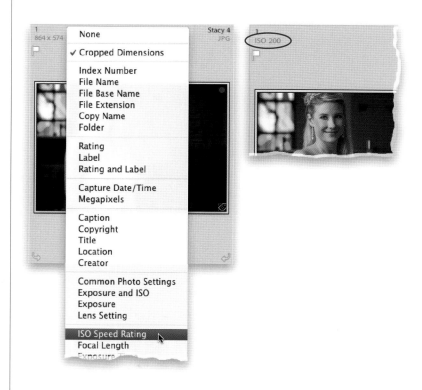

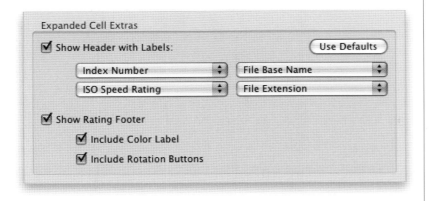

Step Seven:
At the bottom of the Expanded Cell Extras section is a checkbox, which is on by default. This option adds an area to the bottom of the cell called the Rating Footer, which shows the photo's star rating, and if you keep both checkboxes beneath Show Rating Footer turned on, it will also display the color label and the rotation buttons (which are clickable).

Step Eight:
The middle section we skipped over is the Compact Cell Extras section. The reason I skipped over these options is that they work pretty much like the Expanded Cell Extras, but with the Compact Cell Extras, you have only two fields you can customize (rather than four, like in the Expanded Cell Extras): the filename (which appears on the top left of the thumbnail), and the rating (which appears beneath the bottom left of the thumbnail). To change the info displayed there, click on the label pop-up menus and make your choices. The other two checkboxes on the left hide/show the index number (in this case, it's that huge gray number that appears along the top-left side of the cell) and the rotation arrows at the bottom of the cell (which you'll see when you move your cursor over the cell). One last thing, you can turn all these extras off permanently by turning off the Show Grid Extras checkbox at the top of the dialog.

Choosing Lightroom's Background Color

By default, Lightroom displays a medium gray background surrounding your photos, which is an ideal color because it's so neutral it doesn't affect the way your eye perceives color (after all, the last thing you want are colors surrounding your photo influencing how the actual colors in your photo look while you're trying to do color correction, right?). However, some photographers prefer a darker gray, or a lighter gray, and some like a pattern to interrupt the solid gray. So, Lightroom lets you make a few tweaks so "the background grays" are just like you like 'em.

Step One:

To change the color of the area surrounding your images, go to the Grid view (press **G**), then double-click on a vertical photo to enter Loupe view (it's easier to get access to the gray background with a vertical photo, because a horizontal photo pretty much takes up all the background area). Once your photo appears in Loupe view, Control-click (PC: Right-click) just outside the photo on the gray area surrounding your photo, and a contextual menu with different background color and texture choices will appear (as shown here).

Step Two:

Here's how the background would look if you were to choose Dark Gray from the contextual menu, and you added the Pinstripes background texture (the pinstripes are pretty subtle). To reset your background to its default, just bring up that menu again, choose Medium Gray, and turn off the Pinstripes. By the way, if you work in an office with multiple Lightroom users, it doesn't hurt to slip into their office every once in a while and change their Lightroom background to White. Most folks don't know that you can change the background color, and if they did, they'd probably look in Lightroom's preferences (and they won't find them there). Hey, it's just a thought.

Lightroom has an awful lot of panels, and you can waste a lot of time scrolling up and down in these panels just searching for what you want (especially if you have to scroll past panels you never use). This is why, in my live Lightroom seminars, I recommend: (a) hiding panels you find you don't use, and (b) turning on Solo mode, so when you click on a panel, it displays only that one panel and tucks the rest out of the way. Here's how to use these somewhat hidden features:

Make Working with Panels Faster & Easier

Step One:
Start by going to any side panel, then Control-click (PC: Right-click) on the panel header and a contextual menu will appear with a list of all the panels on that side. Each panel with a checkmark beside it is visible, so if you want to hide a panel from view, just choose it from this list and it unchecks. For example, here in the Develop module's right side Panels area, I've hidden the Camera Calibration panel. Next, as I mentioned in the intro above, I always recommend turning on Solo mode (you choose it from this same menu, as seen here).

Step Two:
Take a look at the two sets of side panels shown here. The one on the left shows how the Develop module's panels look normally. I'm trying to make an adjustment in the Split Toning panel, but I have all those other panels open around it (which is distracting), and I have to scroll down past them just to get to the panel I want. However, look at the same set of panels on the right when Solo mode is turned on—all the other panels are collapsed out of the way, so I can just focus on the Split Toning panel. To work in a different panel, I just click on its name, and the Split Toning panel tucks itself away automatically.

The Develop module's right side Panels area with Solo mode turned off

The Develop module's right side Panels area with Solo mode turned on

Using Two Monitors with Lightroom

Lightroom 2 is the first version of Lightroom to support two monitors, so you can work on your photo on one screen and also see a huge, full-screen version of your photo on another. But Adobe went beyond that in this Dual Display feature and there are some very cool things you can do with it, once it's set up (and here's how to set it up).

Step One:

The Dual Display controls are found in the top-left corner of the filmstrip (shown circled in red here), where you can see two buttons: one marked "1" for your main display, and one marked "2" for the second display. If you don't have a second monitor connected and you click the Second Window button, it just brings up what would be seen in the second display as a separate floating window (as seen here).

SCOTT KELBY

Step Two:

If you do have a second monitor connected to your computer, when you click on the Second Window button, the separate floating window appears in Full Screen mode, set to Loupe view, on the second display (as seen here). This is the default setup, which lets you see Lightroom's interface and controls on one display, and then the larger zoomed-in view on the second display.

SCOTT KELBY AND ©ISTOCKPHOTO/NGHE TRAN

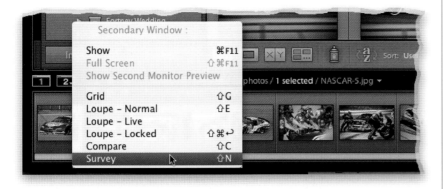

SCOTT KELBY

Step Three:

You have complete control over what goes on the second display using the Secondary Window pop-up menu, shown here (just click-and-hold on the Second Window button and it appears). For example, you could have Survey view showing on the second display, and then you could be zoomed in tight, looking at one of those survey images in Loupe view on your main display (as shown at bottom). By the way, just add the **Shift key** and the Survey view, Compare view, Grid view, and Loupe view shortcuts are all the same (so, **Shift-N** puts your second display into Survey view, etc.).

TIP: Swapping Screens

If you want to swap displays (where your main screen, panels, etc., appear on the second display and the Loupe view screen appears on your main display), if you're in Full Screen mode on your main display, press **F** to leave Full Screen mode, which lets you see the main display's title bar at the top. Now just drag-and-drop that title bar over to the right, right off the main display and onto the second display, and the two automatically swap positions.

Continued

Step Four:

Besides just seeing things larger with the Loupe view, there are some other pretty cool Second Window options. For example, click on the Second Window button and choose Loupe – Live from the Secondary Window pop-up menu, then just hover your cursor over the thumbnails in the Grid view (or filmstrip) on your main display, and watch how the second display shows an instant Loupe view of any photo you pass over (here, you can see on my main display a photo of two cars is selected in the Grid view, but my cursor is over a photo of my buddy Joe Glyda and me, which is shown in Loupe view on my second display).

Step Five:

Another Secondary Window Loupe view option is called Loupe – Locked and when you turn this on (again, choose this from the Secondary Window pop-up menu), it locks whatever image is currently shown in Loupe view on the second display, so you can look at other images on the main display (you can look at them, edit them, and then when you want to return to where you left off, you can just turn Loupe – Locked off). Also, by default, the navigation bars at the top and bottom of your image area will be visible on the second display. If you want those hidden, click on the little gray arrows at the top and bottom of the screen to tuck them out of sight, and give you just the image onscreen.

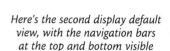

Here's the second display default view, with the navigation bars at the top and bottom visible

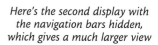

Here's the second display with the navigation bars hidden, which gives a much larger view

Step Six:
There's one other Dual Display feature you'll want to know about called Show Second Monitor Preview (you choose this from the Secondary Window pop-up menu, too), and when you choose it, a small floating Second Monitor window appears on your main display showing you what's being seen on the second display. This is pretty handy for presentations, where the second display is actually a projector, and your work is being projected on a screen behind you (so you can face the audience), or in instances where you're showing a client some work on a second screen, and the screen is facing away from you (that way, they don't see all the controls, and panels, and other things that might distract them).

Adding Your Studio's Name or Logo for a Custom Look

The first time I saw Lightroom, one of the features that really struck me as different was the ability to replace the Adobe Photoshop Lightroom logo (that appears in the upper-left corner of Lightroom) with either the name of your studio or your studio's logo. I have to say, when you're doing client presentations, it does add a nice custom look to the program (as if Adobe designed Lightroom just for you), but beyond that, the ability to create an Identity Plate goes farther than just giving Lightroom a custom look (but we'll start here, with the custom look).

Step One:

First, just so we have a frame of reference, here's a zoomed-in view of the top-left corner of Lightroom's interface, so you can clearly see the logo we're going to replace starting in Step Two. Now, you can either replace Lightroom's logo using text (and you can even have the text of the modules in the taskbar on the top right match), or you can replace the logo with a graphic of your logo (we'll look at how to do both).

Step Two:

Go under the Lightroom menu (the Edit menu on a PC) and choose Identity Plate Setup to bring up the Identity Plate Editor (shown here). By default, the name you registered your software in shows up highlighted in the large black text field in the middle of the dialog, in a font you'd never actually use. To have your name replace the Adobe Photoshop Lightroom 2 logo seen above, turn on the Enable Identity Plate checkbox at the top left of the dialog. If you don't want your name as your Identity Plate, just type in whatever you'd like (the name of your company, studio, etc.), then while the type is still highlighted, choose a font, font style (bold, italic, condensed, etc.), and font size from the pop-up menus (directly below the text field).

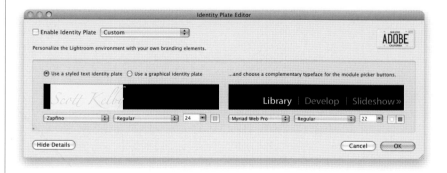

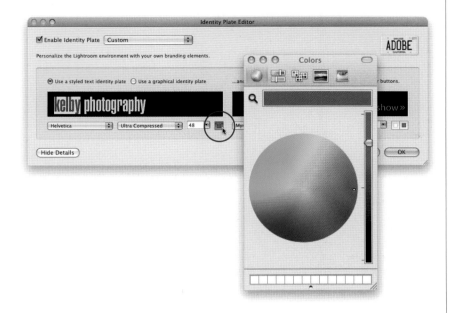

Step Three:

If you want to change only part of your text (for example, if you wanted to change the font of one of the words, or the font size or color of a word), just highlight the word you want to adjust before making the change. To change the color, click on the little square color swatch to the right of the Font Size pop-up menu (it's shown circled here). This brings up the Colors panel (you're seeing the Macintosh Colors panel here; the Windows Color panel will look somewhat different, but don't let that freak you out. Aw, what the heck—go ahead and freak out!). Just choose the color you want your selected text to be, then close the Colors panel.

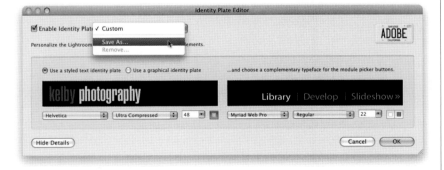

Step Four:

If you like the way your custom Identity Plate looks, you definitely should save it, because creating an Identity Plate does more than just replace the current Adobe Photoshop Lightroom 2 logo—you can add your new custom Identity Plate text (or logo) to any slide show, Web gallery, or final print by choosing it from the Identity Plate pop-up menu in all three modules (see, you were dismissing it when you just thought it was a taskbar, feel good feature). To save your custom Identity Plate, click-and-hold on the Enable Identity Plate pop-up menu, and choose Save As (as shown here). Give your Identity Plate a descriptive name, click OK, and now it's saved. From here on out, it will appear in the handy Identity Plate pop-up menu, where you can get that same custom text, font, and color in just one click.

Continued

Step Five:

Once you click the OK button, your new Identity Plate text replaces the Adobe Photoshop Lightroom 2 logo that was in the upper-left corner (as shown here).

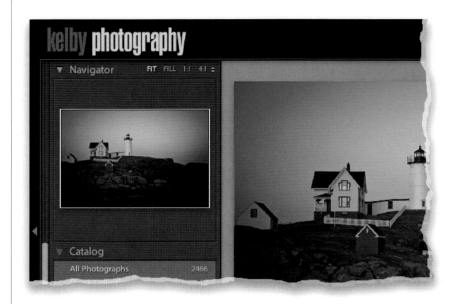

TIP: Formatting the Module Text

On the right side of the Identity Plate Editor, you can choose a font, style, and size for the module text that appears in the right side of the taskbar, as well (ya know, the words "Library, Develop, Slideshow, etc., that appear across the top-right side of Lightroom). Just choose how you want them to appear from the pop-up menus below them. If you don't see this part, click on the Show Details button at the bottom left.

Step Six:

If you want to use a graphic (like your company's logo) instead, you go to the same place (under the Lightroom menu on a Mac, or the Edit menu on a PC), and choose Identity Plate Setup, but when the dialog appears, click on the radio button for Use a Graphical Identity Plate (as shown here), instead of Use a Styled Text Identity Plate. Next, click on the Locate File button (found above the Hide/Show Details button near the lower-left corner) and find your logo file (I put my logo on a black background with white text in Adobe Photoshop), and click the Choose button to make that graphic your Identity Plate. *Note:* When you click on the Use a Graphical Identity Plate radio button, a message appears in the text field below that tells you not to make your graphic taller than 57 pixels deep (this message currently does not appear in the PC version of Lightroom 2).

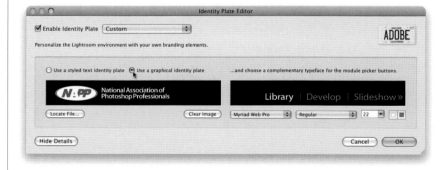

Step Seven:

When you click OK, the Adobe Photoshop Lightroom 2 logo (or your custom text—whichever was up there last) is replaced by the new graphic file of your logo (as shown here). *Note:* If you want your logo file to have a transparent background, create your logo and text on separate layers in Photoshop, then delete the Background layer, which makes the background transparent. After you delete the white Background layer, highlight your text and change the color to white (in Photoshop), then save the file in Photoshop (PSD) format to retain the transparency. If you like your new graphical logo file in Lightroom, don't forget to save this custom Identity Plate by choosing Save As from the Enable Identity Plate pop-up menu at the top of the dialog.

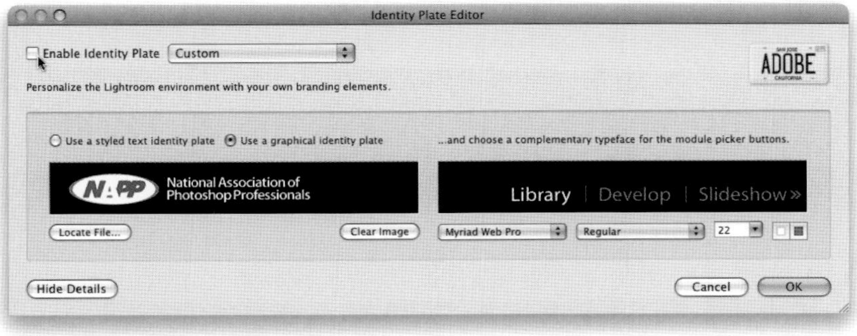

Step Eight:

If you decide, at some point, that you'd like the original Adobe Photoshop Lightroom 2 logo back instead, just go back to the Identity Plate Editor and turn off the Enable Identity Plate checkbox (as shown here). Remember, we'll do more with one of your new Identity Plates later in the book when we cover the three later modules.

Choosing What the Filmstrip Displays

Just like you can choose what photo information is displayed in the Grid and Loupe views, you can also choose what info gets displayed in the filmstrip, as well. Because the filmstrip is pretty short in height, I think it's even more important to control what goes on here, or it really starts to look like a cluttered mess. Although I'm going to show you how to turn on/off each line of info, my recommendation is to keep all the filmstrip info turned off to help avoid "info overload" and visual clutter in an already busy interface. But, just in case, here's how to choose what's displayed down there:

Step One:

Control-click (PC: Right-click) on any thumbnail down in the filmstrip and a contextual menu will appear (seen here). At the bottom of this menu are the View Options for the filmstrip. There are three options: Show Ratings and Picks will add tiny flags and star ratings to your filmstrip cells. If you choose Show Badges, it adds mini-versions of the same thumbnail badges you can see in the Grid view (which show whether keywords have been applied, whether the photo has been cropped, or if the image has been adjusted in Lightroom). The last choice, Show Image Info Tooltips, kicks in when you hover your cursor over an image in the filmstrip—a little window pops up telling you the file's name, the time and date it was taken, and its size (in pixels).

Step Two:

Here's what the filmstrip looks like when these options are turned off (top) and with all of them turned on (bottom). You can see Pick flags, star ratings, and thumbnail badges (with unsaved metadata warnings), and I hovered my cursor over one of the thumbnails, so you can see the little pop-up window appear giving me info about the photo. So, the choice is yours—clean or cluttered.

As you read in Chapter 2, besides star ratings and Pick flags, you can also use color labels to rate your photos (for example, you might use Picks to get to your keepers, then use Picks again to get to your Selects set, and then use a color label for the single best photo from the entire shoot), but which color means what? That's for you to decide because Lightroom doesn't give them descriptions. For example, you might want to name your Green label "Approved," anything flagged with a Yellow label would be "Awaiting Client Approval," and so on.

Naming Your Color Labels

Step One:
The default set of label names is simply their colors (Red, Yellow, Green, Blue, Purple), so to create your own custom label sets, go under the Metadata menu, under Color Label Set, and choose Edit (as shown here).

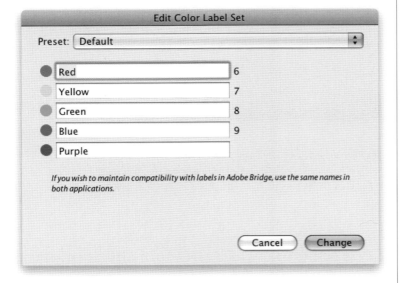

Step Two:
This brings up the Edit Color Label Set dialog (shown here) with the default set of names, which aren't too descriptive (even I knew that the red dot meant Red). There's a little note at the bottom of the dialog that tells you if you're going to be moving photos back and forth between Lightroom and Adobe Bridge, make sure the color label names in both applications are consistent (if you name the Red label "Cancelled by Client" here in Lightroom, give the Red label the same custom name in Bridge).

Continued

Step Three:

Now, just highlight each field and type in the name you want to assign to each color label (as shown here). The numbers to the right of the first four color labels are the shortcuts you'd use to apply those labels. Purple doesn't have a shortcut (my guess is that's because the star ratings already used the number **0**—it's the shortcut for a 0-star rating). Once you're happy with your new color label names, go up to the Preset pop-up menu at the top of the dialog, choose Save Current Settings as New Preset, and give your preset a name (as shown here). By the way, if you created a custom label set and later need to make a change to that set, come back to this dialog, choose your preset from the Preset pop-up menu, change the text for the label(s) you want to change, then go back under the Preset pop-up menu and choose Update Preset.

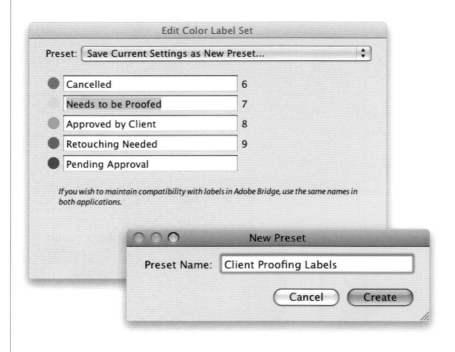

Step Four:

Since you now have multiple color label sets (well, at least two), you'll need to first tell Lightroom which set you want to use. You do that by going under the Metadata menu, under Color Label Set, and choosing the set you want (in our case, it would be the Client Proofing Labels set). Once you've made your choice, you can start labeling (it's possible that you'll create this one set, and that's the only set you'll need from here on out. In that case, you won't have to go to the Color Label Set menu again). You can assign these labels by pressing **6**, **7**, **8**, or **9**, but if you need to assign the last one, you'll have to either go under the Photo menu, under Set Color Label, and choose it from the submenu (notice how the submenu has been updated with your color label set names?), or you can choose the color label swatches from right within the grid cells themselves (if you have this view option turned on, you'll see a gray label at the bottom of the cell. Just click on it and choose your color label from the pop-up menu).

At the very bottom of the last panel in the left and right side Panels areas is a little ornamental graphic called an end mark, which is there to let you know you reached the last panel on that side. To me, the default end mark looks totally out of place in Lightroom's high-tech black interface, and the first time I saw that ornament, I said, "Please tell me there's some way to change that!" Luckily, there is—you can use another panel end mark (hey, there are some that are actually better), create your own, or download some from the Web. Here's how:

Changing Those Ornaments Below the Last Panel

Step One:
Here's the panel end mark I was talking about above (see what I was saying about the look of that default end mark?).

Step Two:
To change the panel end mark, you scroll down until you actually see the Flourish (that's the default graphic's official name—Flourish). Then you Control-click (PC: Right-click) directly on the Flourish and from the contextual menu that appears, go under Panel End Mark and you'll see a list of built-in end mark choices (as seen here).

Continued

Step Three:

If you don't want an end mark at all, choose None from that contextual menu, but if you do like the idea of having an end mark (but you just don't like the default Flourish), try one of the other built-in choices, like Tattoo (which is shown here). Besides the built-in choices, you can also create your own custom end marks (maybe you'd like your studio's logo to appear as an end mark, or your signature, or just a totally different graphic). The first step is to actually create the graphic itself in Photoshop, make its background transparent, and then put it in Lightroom's Panel End Marks folder, where it will then become one of your end mark choices (it's easier than it sounds—as you'll see).

Step Four:

Our first step in making a custom end mark is to decide how large you can make your graphic (it can be no wider than your side panels, right?). The maximum width will be different depending on which size monitor you're using, but for example, on my laptop, the side panels are 240 pixels wide, so if I wanted a graphic that spanned the whole width, I would make sure it's no wider than 240 pixels. Your best bet is to probably make a screen capture of the area where the current end mark is, and then use that same size for your new Photoshop document (also, make the resolution 72 ppi). I wanted something a little more subtle (sizewise), so I created a new document in Photoshop that was 120 pixels wide by 120 pixels deep at 72 ppi (as shown here).

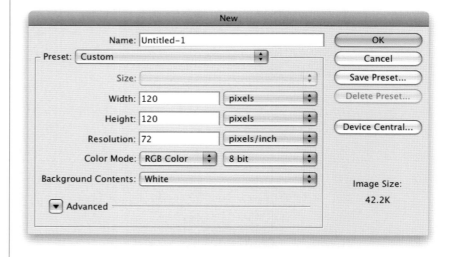

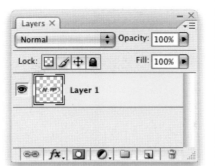

Step Five:

Next, add a new layer and either create your graphic (or import your logo), so it's on a layer above the Background layer. Once your graphic is complete, to make the background behind it transparent, click-and-drag the Background layer to the Trash to delete it (so you just have that one layer, as shown here, with no Background layer). Now, don't flatten your layer—just save your file in PNG format (that way, the background stays transparent).

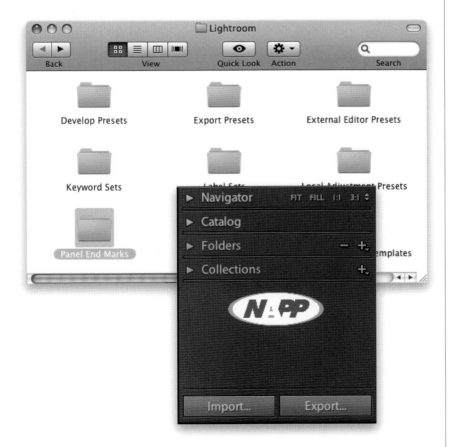

Step Six:

Now go back to Lightroom, Control-click (PC: Right-click) on the current end mark, then from the contextual menu, choose Panel End Mark, and then choose Go to Panel End Marks Folder. This brings up the folder on your computer where you store your custom end marks, so now all you have to do is drop your PNG graphic into that folder and the next time you Control-click on the current end mark, your graphic will be in the list of choices. In the image shown at the bottom, you can see where I've replaced the end mark with the NAPP logo (the logo for the National Association of Photoshop Professionals).

TIP: Downloading End Marks

Besides creating your own custom end marks, you can download some pretty cool free custom Lightroom end marks from the folks at *Lightroom Extra* at http://web .mac.com/sidjervis/iWeb/Lightroom%20 Extra/Download.html. Once downloaded, it's as easy as putting them in that same Panel End Marks folder.

Lightroom Quick Tips > >

▼ Spacebar Loupe Tricks

If you want to see your currently selected photo zoomed in to Loupe view, just press the Spacebar. Once it's zoomed in like that, press the Spacebar again, and it zooms in to whatever magnification (zoom factor) you chose last in the Navigator panel's header (by default, it zooms to 1:1, but if you click on a different zoom factor, it will toggle back and forth between the view you were in first and the zoom factor you clicked on). Once zoomed in, you can move around your image by just clicking-and-dragging on it.

▼ Hiding the Render Messages

If you chose Minimal or Embedded & Sidecar in the Initial Previews pop-up menu in the Import Photos dialog, Lightroom is only going to render higher-resolution previews when you look at a larger view, and while it's rendering these higher-res previews, it displays a little "I'm rendering" message. You'll see these messages a lot, and if they get on your nerves, you can turn them off by pressing **Command-J (PC: Ctrl-J)** and, in the View Options dialog that appears, click on the Loupe View tab (up top), then in that section, turn off the checkbox for Show Message When Loading or Rendering Photos.

▼ Quick White Balance
   Adjustment

If you see an image in the Library Grid view that needs a quick white balance adjustment, try this: press **W**, which not only switches you over to the Develop module, it gives you the White Balance Selector tool, so just click on a light gray area, then press **G** to quickly go right

back where you started (the whole thing takes just a few seconds). Try this once, and you'll be using it all the time.

▼ Jump to a 100% View

Any time you want to quickly see your image at a 100% full-size view, just press the letter **Z** on your keyboard.

▼ Opening All Your
   Panels at Once

If you want every panel expanded in a particular side panel, just Control-click (PC: Right-click) on any panel's header, then choose Expand All from the contextual menu.

▼ Changing Where
   Lightroom Zooms

When you click to zoom in on a photo, Lightroom magnifies the photo, but if you want the area that you clicked on to appear centered on the screen, press **Command-, (PC: Ctrl-,)** to bring up Lightroom's Preferences dialog, then click on the Interface tab, and at the bottom, turn on the checkbox for Zoom Clicked Point to Center.

▼ How to Link Your Panels,
   So When You Close One,
   It Closes the Other

If you set your side panels to Manual (you show and hide them by clicking on the little gray triangles), you can set them up to where if you close one side, the other side closes, too (or if you close the top, the bottom closes, too). To do this, Control-click (PC: Right-click) on one of those little gray triangles, and from the contextual menu that appears, choose Sync With Opposite Panel.

▼ The Secret Identity Plate Text
   Formatting Trick

It's surprisingly hard to format text inside the Identity Plate Editor window, especially if you want multiple lines of text (of course, the fact that you can have multiple lines of text is a tip unto itself). But, there's a better way: Create your text somewhere else that has nice typographic controls (like Photoshop), then select and copy your text into memory. Then come back to the Identity Plate Editor and paste that already formatted text right into it, and it will maintain your font and layout attributes.

▼ Shortcut for Changing
   Your Thumbnail Size

Press **Control-+ (plus sign; PC: +)** to make the thumbnails larger; press **Control-- (minus sign; PC: -)** to make them smaller.

▼ Delete Old Backups to
   Save Big Space

I usually back up my Lightroom catalog once a day (usually, the first time I start Lightroom for the day; see page 95 for more on this). The problem is that after a while, you've got a lot of backup copies—and before long you've got months of old, outdated copies taking up space on your hard drive (I really only need one or two backup copies. After all, I'm not going to choose a backup from three months ago). So, go to your Lightroom folder from time to time and delete those outdated backups.

Editing Essentials
how to develop your photos

Everything we have done up to this point—every click of a button, every slide of a slider, every drag of a dragster—has all been leading up to this one single moment. The moment when you leave the relative safety and comfort of the Library module and venture into a wild, untamed territory that many seek but only few survive. This, my friends, is the Develop module—a scary and intimidating place with more complicated-looking buttons, checkboxes, and sliders than the Space Shuttle and a 747 combined. Now, if you're thinking that all this looks too technical and advanced for you, you're right. Nobody understands this module. I don't know what it does. Adobe doesn't know. I think a lot of the sliders are just put there for looks, and moving them doesn't actually affect anything in the photo whatsoever. For example, try moving the Deflatulator slider all the way to the right. I'm not sure it really does anything, but it sure took the wind out of me. Okay, that was pretty lame, but wait—I have more. Open an image shot in RAW format, set your exposure and shadows, then try dragging the Cutlery Sharpening Amount to 75%. I'll bet your image still looks dull, and it just doesn't cut it. Are you getting any of these puns? I hope you are, because I swear, they're cracking me up.

Setting the White Balance

Getting your white balance right is one of the most important edits you can make in Photoshop Lightroom. Luckily, it's also one of the easiest. I always start by setting the white balance first, because if you get the white balance right, the color is right, and your color correction problems pretty much go away. You adjust the white balance in the Basic panel, which is the most misnamed panel in Lightroom. It should be called the "Essentials" panel, because it contains the most important, and the most used, controls in the entire Develop module.

Step One:

In the Library module, click on the photo you want to edit, and then press the letter **D** on your keyboard to jump over to the Develop module. By the way, you're probably figuring that since you press D for the Develop module, it must be S for Slideshow, P for Print, and W for the Web module, right? Sadly, no—that would make things too easy. Nope, it's just Develop that uses the first letter. (Arrrrgggh!) Anyway, once you're in the Develop module, all the editing controls are in the right side Panels area, and the photo is displayed using whatever you had the white balance set on in your digital camera (called "As Shot").

Step Two:

The white balance controls are near the top of the Basic panel, and there you'll see a White Balance (WB) pop-up menu where you can choose the same white balance presets you could have chosen in your camera, as seen here. (*Note:* The one big difference between processing JPEG and TIFF images, and those shot in RAW, is that you only get this full list of presets if you shoot in RAW. If you shoot in JPEG, you only get one preset choice—Auto—and that's it.)

Step Three:

In our photo shown in Step One, her white wedding dress looks a bit bluish, and the whole tone of the photo looks a bit cool, so it definitely needs a white balance adjustment. (*Note:* If you want to follow along here using this same image, you're welcome to download it from www.kelbytraining.com/books/lightroom2.) So, go ahead and choose Auto from the White Balance pop-up menu and you'll see how that would look (it looks even bluer). The next three White Balance presets down will all be warmer (more yellow), with Daylight being a bit warmer, Cloudy being warmer still, and Shade being a lot warmer. Go ahead and choose Cloudy (as shown here), and you can see the whole photo is much warmer—too warm, actually, because now instead of her white wedding dress being bluish, it's kind of yellowish (our goal, of course, is to get that dress to look white).

Step Four:

If you choose either of the next two down—Tungsten or Fluorescent—they're going to be way crazy blue, so you don't want either of those, and Flash is kind of like Daylight (take a moment and try each of those, just so you see how they affect the photo). The last preset isn't really a preset at all—Custom just means you're going to create the white balance manually using the two sliders beneath the pop-up menu. Now that you know what these presets look like, here's what I recommend when you're working with your own images: First, quickly run through all the presets and see if one of them happens to be "right on the money" (it happens more than you might think). If there isn't one that's right on the money, choose the preset that looks the closest to being right (in this case, I felt it was the Flash preset, which isn't nearly as warm, as seen here).

Continued

Step Five:

So now that you've chosen a preset that's kind of "in the ballpark," you can use the Temp and Tint sliders to dial in a better looking final White Balance setting. I zoomed in here on the Basic panel so you can get a nice close-up of the Temp and Tint sliders, because Adobe did something really great to help you out here—they colorized the slider bars, so you can see what will happen if you drag in a particular direction. See how the left side of the Temp slider is blue, and the right side graduates over to yellow? That tells you exactly what the slider does. So, without any further explanation, which way would you drag the Temp slider to make the photo more blue? To the left, of course. Which way would you drag the Tint slider to make the image more magenta? See, it's a little thing, but it's a big help.

Step Six:

If you think, after choosing the Flash preset, that the image is too yellow (I sure do), then click-and-drag the Temp slider slowly to the left (toward blue), until the yellow is removed from her dress and it looks white (of course, don't drag too far to the left, or it will turn blue again, like it was when you first opened the image). In the example you see here, I dragged to the left until it looked right (when I was done, the Temp reading was 4292). That's all there is to it—use a White Balance preset as a starting place, then use the Temp slider to tweak it until it looks right. Now, if you feel the image is too magenta, then try dragging the Tint slider away from magenta, toward green (again, drag slowly and don't go too far, or she'll start to look like the shrimp at the reception went bad).

Step Seven:

Now that you've learned those two ways (the preset alone, and then the preset with Temp and Tint slider tweaks), I want to show you my personal favorite way, and the way I think you'll usually get the best, most accurate results, and that is to use the White Balance Selector tool (it's that huge eyedropper on the top-left side of the White Balance section). Just click on the tool to get it, then click it on something in your photo that's supposed to be light gray (that's right—don't click on something white—look for something light gray. Video cameras white balance on solid white, but digital still cameras need to white balance on a light gray instead). In the example shown here, I clicked on a shadow area of her dress that appeared to be a light gray (where a highlight area would have been white), and just clicking once with this tool set the right white balance for me (you can see the Temp is now set to 4150, and the Tint to −15, which added a tiny bit of green to balance things out).

Step Eight:

Before we go any further, that big pixelated grid that appears while you're using the White Balance Selector tool is supposed to magnify the area your cursor is over to help you find a neutral gray area. To me, it just gets in the way, and if it drives you crazy (like it does me), you can get rid of it by turning off the Show Loupe checkbox down in the toolbar (I've circled it here in red, because my guess is you'll be searching for that checkbox pretty quickly). Now you get just the eyedropper (as shown here), without the huge annoying pixel Loupe (which I'm sure is fine for some people, so if that's you, replace "annoying" with the term "helpful").

Continued

Step Nine:

Although I'm not a fan of the "helpful" pixel Loupe, there is a feature that's a really big help when you use the White Balance Selector tool, and that's the Navigator panel on the top of the left side Panels area. What's cool about this is, as you hover the White Balance Selector tool over different parts of your photo, it gives you a live preview of what the white balance would look like if you clicked there. This is *huge*, and saves you lots of clicks, and lots of time, when finding a white balance that looks good to you. For example, move the White Balance Selector tool over the wall behind her left shoulder, and then look at the Navigator panel to see how the white balance would look if you clicked there. Pretty bad, eh? You could just click the tool as many times as you'd like to try out different white balance looks, but honestly, just looking over in the Navigator panel is quicker and easier.

Step 10:

A couple of last things you'll want to know about white balance: (1) When you're finished using the tool, either click it back where you got it from (that round, dark gray circle in the Basic panel), or click the Done button down in the toolbar. (2) In the toolbar, there's an Auto Dismiss checkbox. If you turn this on, it means that after you click the tool once, it automatically returns to its home in the Basic panel. I leave this turned off, so I can easily just click in a different area without having to retrieve the tool each time. (3) To return to the original As Shot white balance, just choose As Shot from the White Balance (WB) presets pop-up menu. (4) If you're in the Library module, and you know you need to get the White Balance Selector tool, you can press **W**, which will switch you over to the Develop module and give you the tool.

The original As Shot white balance setting, which looks cold and bluish

Here's the image after just one click with the White Balance Selector tool

Now that your white balance is set, the next thing we adjust is our overall exposure. Although there is an Exposure slider, it takes three sliders (and sometimes four) to set the overall exposure. Luckily, not only is this much easier than it sounds, Lightroom has all kinds of tools to help make your job easier.

How to Set Your Overall Exposure

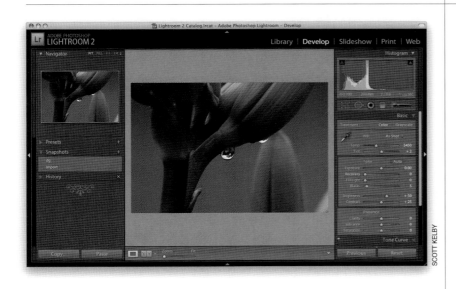

SCOTT KELBY

Step One:
To set your overall exposure, you use the Tone section of the Basic panel (that section is shown within a red rectangle here). The photo shown here (taken outdoors with a close-up macro lens) looks underexposed, and if you look up in the Histogram panel at the top of the right side Panels area, you can see there's virtually no data on the right side of the histogram (that's where all the highlights should be). So if you were wondering, "Is it underexposed?" well, there's your answer.

Step Two:
To make the overall photo brighter, just click-and-drag the Exposure slider to the right, as shown here (just like with the White Balance sliders, you get a visual cue of which way to drag by looking at the slider itself—white is on the right side of the slider, so dragging right [toward white] would make this adjustment lighter, and dragging left [toward black] would make things darker). Easy enough. However, there's one critically important thing to watch out for: if you drag too far to the right, you run the risk of losing detail in your highlights (in other words, your highlights get so bright that they literally "blow out" and you lose all detail in those areas). This is called "clipping" your highlights, and luckily Lightroom not only warns you if this happens, but in most cases, you can also fix it.

Continued

Step Three:

If you look again at the Histogram panel at the top of the right side Panels area, you'll see a triangle in the top-right corner. That is the highlight clipping warning triangle, and ideally, this triangle should always stay solid black. If it turns blue, it means you're losing highlight detail, but just in the Blue channel (which isn't great, but it's not the worst thing in the world). If it's red or green, you're losing detail in that channel. However, the worst-case scenario is that it appears solid white (as shown here), which means all three channels have lost detail, and your highlights are totally clipped. But here's the critical question: Are you clipping off highlights in an area of important detail? If not, you can ignore the warning (for example, if you have a shot where you can see the sun, that sun is going to clip, but there's no detail there anyway, so we ignore it). To find out where you're clipping, click on that white triangle, and the areas that are clipping will appear in solid red (as seen here, where we're clipping highlights inside the two water droplets).

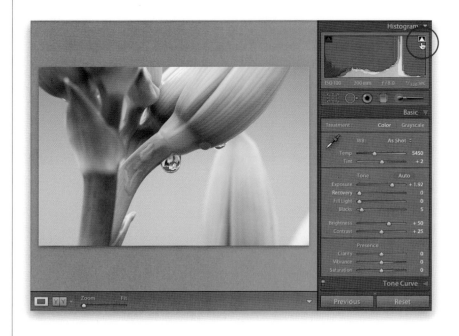

Step Four:

So, in our example here, the red areas are inside those two water droplets, and I think those areas should have detail. Now, if you lower the Exposure slider, the clipping will go away, but your exposure will be too dark again. If this happens to you (and believe me, it will. Daily), then grab the Recovery slider—one of the most brilliant features in all of Lightroom. As you click-and-drag the Recovery slider to the right, it pulls back only the very brightest highlights (those areas that were clipping), so it doesn't trash your overall exposure—you just drag to the right until the red warnings on your photo go away, and your triangle is black (as shown here).

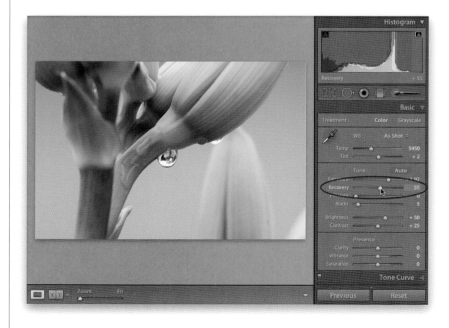

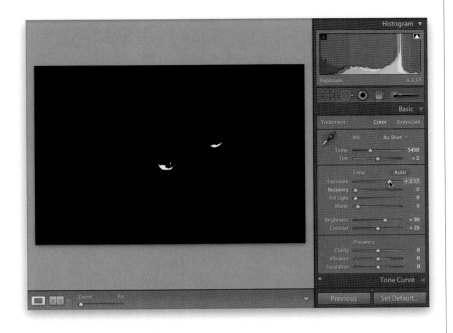

Step Five:

So when processing your photos, always start by adjusting the Exposure slider first, and then if you see a clipping warning, go to the Recovery slider and drag it to the right until your highlights come back into line. By the way, if you don't like seeing the clipped areas appear in red (or if you're working on a photo with a lot of red in it already, so you can't easily see the red clipping warnings), you can use a second method instead: press-and-hold the Option (PC: Alt) key as you click-and-drag the Exposure slider and any areas that are clipping will show up in white (as seen here). You can also hold these same keys as you click-and-drag the Recovery slider, and you just keep dragging until all the areas turn solid black again.

TIP: Toggling the Warnings On/Off

You don't have to go up there and click on that triangle every time. If you press the letter **J** on your keyboard, it toggles that red clipping warning that appears over the clipped highlights in your photo on/off.

Step Six:

We're going to jump over to a different photo for a just a moment, to tell you about another hidden benefit of using the Recovery slider: it works wonders in adding detail and drama to skies in landscape shots (especially ones with lots of clouds). Just click-and-drag the Recovery slider all the way over to the right (to 100), and watch what it does for your skies. Give it a try and see what you think.

SCOTT KELBY

Continued

Step Seven:

Okay, back to the macro shot. In adjusting our overall exposure, the next thing we use is the Blacks slider (we're intentionally skipping over the Fill Light slider until Chapter 6, because this slider is for when you're in trouble with a backlighting situation). The Blacks slider adjusts the darkest shadow areas in your photo, and dragging to the right increases the amount of black in the shadows—dragging to the left lightens up those shadow areas. I drag this slider to the right (as shown here) any time my photo looks washed out, because it can bring back color and depth to your shadow areas big time. Although, personally, I'm not nearly as concerned with losing shadow detail as I am highlight detail, if you're a "shadow detail freak" (and you know who you are), you can use the histogram's top-left corner triangle as your shadow clipping warning, or press **J**, and any shadow areas that are clipping will appear in blue on your photo. Just keep this in mind: which is more important, that you either keep detail in your shadow area, or that the overall photo looks good? 'Nuf said.

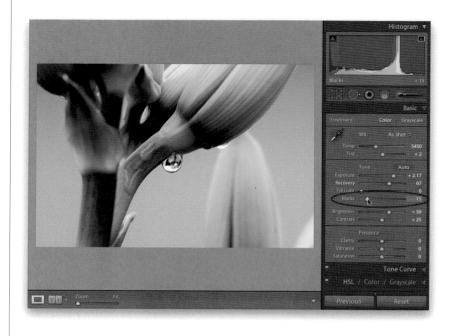

Step Eight:

The Brightness slider (shown circled here in red) acts as a midtones slider (so if you're familiar with Photoshop's Levels control, think of this as the center midtones slider). To brighten up the midtones a bit, click-and-drag this slider to the right (to darken the midtones, of course, you'd drag to the left). This slider has a broad, coarse range, so be careful not to push it so far to the right that you start clipping highlights (keep an eye on your highlight clipping triangle). We're going to ignore the pretty awful Contrast slider, because we add contrast with a much more powerful tool (the Tone Curve), which you'll learn about shortly.

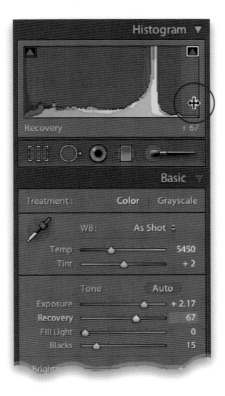

Step Nine:

The Histogram panel at the top of the right side Panels area is helpful because, by just looking at it, you can tell if your highlights are blown out. For example, if your histogram shows a bunch of pixels stacked up against the far right-side wall, it tells you right there that plenty of your highlights are clipped (ideally, you'd have a little gap at the right end of your graph, with nothing touching the right-side wall). But beyond just giving you a readout, it can help you figure out which slider adjusts which part of the histogram. Try this: move your cursor over part of the histogram and then look directly below the histogram itself, and you'll see not only the name of the slider which affects that part of the histogram, it even highlights the number field of that slider down in the Tone section for you to make it easier to find (as seen here). Here, my cursor is over the far-right side, and you can see that the Recovery slider is what would affect that far-right side of the histogram. Pretty helpful—but there's more.

Step 10:

You can actually click-and-drag anywhere right on the histogram itself, and as you drag left or right, it literally moves that part of the histogram (and the accompanying slider) as you drag. That's right, you can do your corrections by just dragging the histogram itself. You gotta try this—just move your cursor up over the histogram, click, and start dragging. By the way, in all honesty, I don't personally know anyone that actually corrects their photos by dragging the histogram like this, but it sure is fun just to give it a try.

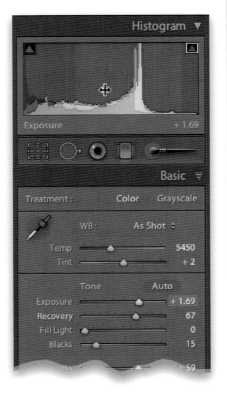

Continued

Step 11:

One thing we haven't talked about thus far is the Auto Tone button, which appears above the Exposure slider. Back in Lightroom 1, I wouldn't touch it on a bet (I called it the "overexpose my photo" button), but in Lightroom 2, Adobe came up with a new algorithm that now does a pretty decent job with it. Take a look at the before/after photo shown here, and you can see that while it doesn't do a totally kick-butt job, it doesn't do a rotten job either (at least now it might move you in the right direction, so you might use it as a starting point). Sometimes it works great, other times…not so much, but at least now it's usable.

TIP: Resetting Your Sliders

You can reset any slider to its original setting by double-clicking on the little slider "nub" (that thing that you drag), but I find it's easier just to double-click on the name of the slider—that resets it, too.

Step 12:

If you want to see a before and after during your editing process (I find this really helpful), then you'll want to know these shortcuts: To see the Before photo at any time, press the **Backslash key** on your keyboard, then press it again to see your After photo already in progress. Or, you might actually prefer seeing your before and after side by side (as shown here), in which case, you'd press the letter **Y** (or **Shift-Y** for a split-screen view). Also, if you click your cursor on the photo to zoom in, it zooms in both photos to the same magnification, which is very helpful. So, to recap this whole process: Start by adjusting the Exposure slider to get the overall brightness correct, and then use the Recovery slider, only if you have clipped highlights. Next, adjust your blacks, especially if the photo looks washed out, and lastly you'll adjust your midtones using the Brightness slider.

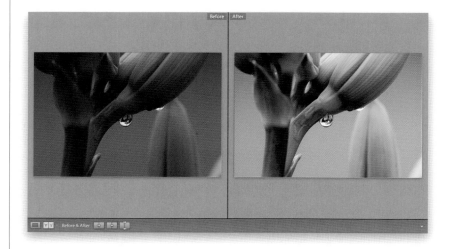

When Adobe was developing the Clarity control, they had actually considered calling the slider "Punch," because it adds midtone contrast to your photo, which makes it look, well…more punchy. So, when you see an image that needs more snap or punch (I use it on almost every photo), then get some clarity.

Adding "Punch" to Your Images Using Clarity

Step One:

Here's the original photo, without any clarity being applied. Now, because (as I said above) clarity adds midtone contrast to your photo, it makes the photo appear to have had the midtones sharpened, and that's what gives it its punch. But before you apply any clarity, to really see the effects of the slider, you should zoom in to a 1:1 view, so head over to the Navigator panel and click on 1:1 first to get you to a 100% view of your image.

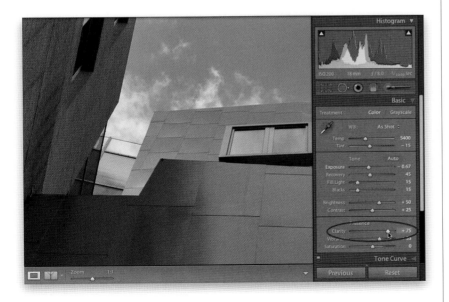

Step Two:

Now, just click-and-drag the Clarity slider to the right to add more punch and midtone contrast (dragging to the left actually decreases midtone contrast, so you might want to try a Clarity setting of −100 to soften and diffuse a portrait). I apply between +25 and +50 clarity to nearly every photo I process, with the only exception being photos that I intentionally want to be softer and less contrasty (so, for a portrait of a mother and baby, or a close-up portrait of a woman, I leave the Clarity slider set to 0 or use a negative number). For images that can really "eat up" the clarity, like architectural shots or sweeping landscapes, I'll sometimes go as high as +75 (as shown here), but as always, you just have to look at the photo, apply some clarity, and see which amount looks best to you.

Making Your Colors More Vibrant

Photos that have rich, vibrant colors definitely have their appeal (that's why professional landscape photographers got so hooked on Velvia film and its trademark saturated color), and although Lightroom has a Saturation slider for increasing your photo's color saturation, the problem is it increases all the colors in your photo equally—while the dull colors do get more saturated, the colors that are already saturated get even more so, and well...things get pretty horsey, pretty fast. That's why Lightroom's Vibrance control may become your Velvia.

Step One:

In the Presence section (at the bottom of the Basic panel) are two controls that affect the color saturation. I avoid the Saturation slider for the reasons mentioned above—everything gets saturated at the same intensity (it's a very coarse adjustment). If you click-and-drag the Saturation slider to the right, your photo does get more colorful, but in a clownish, unrealistic kind of way (as seen here—though some of the over-saturation will have been lost in the book's CMYK color conversion for printing). Once you've tried using Saturation, go ahead and return the Saturation amount back to 0.

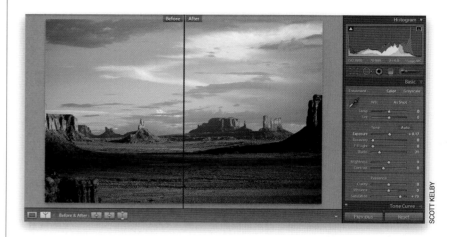

Step Two:

Now try the Vibrance slider—it affects dull colors the most, and it affects already saturated colors the least, and lastly, it does try to avoid affecting fleshtones as much as possible. This gives a much more realistic-looking color saturation across the board, without trashing your skin tones, which makes this a much more usable tool. Here's the same photo using the Vibrance slider instead, and the mountains don't look orange (I pressed **Shift-Y** to get this split-screen before/after). So, unless I'm desaturating an overly colorful photo, I pretty much avoid the Saturation slider altogether.

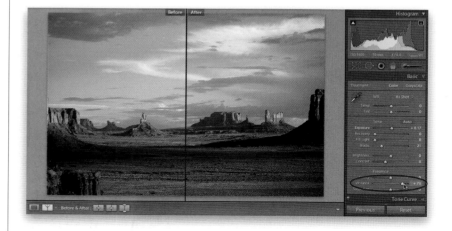

Once we've made our edits in the Basic panel, next we head down to the Tone Curve panel to adjust the overall contrast in our photos (I recommend doing your basic edits in the Basic panel, then using the tone curve to finish things off). We use this tone curve rather than the Contrast slider (in the Basic panel, which we intentionally skipped over earlier), because this gives us much more control, plus the tone curve (1) helps keep you from blowing out your highlights, (2) actually helps you see which areas to adjust, and (3) lets you adjust the contrast interactively.

Using the Tone Curve to Add Contrast

Step One:
If you scroll down past the Basic panel, you'll find the Tone Curve panel (shown here), which is where we apply contrast to our photo (rather than using the Contrast slider in the Basic panel, which seems too broad in most cases). If the photo you're viewing was shot in RAW, by default, it already has a medium amount of contrast applied to it, but if it's a JPEG, it doesn't have any contrast applied yet. Just for the purposes of teaching you how to use the tone curve, go to the bottom of the panel, and from the Point Curve pop-up menu, choose Linear, which gives you a straight-line curve and applies no contrast at all (as seen here).

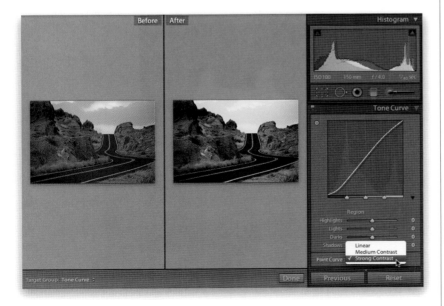

Step Two:
The fastest and easiest way to apply contrast is just to choose one of the presets from the Point Curve pop-up menu. For example, choose Strong Contrast and then look at the difference in your photo (I pressed **Shift-Y** to show you a before/after here). Look how much more contrasty the photo now looks—the shadow areas are stronger, and the highlights are brighter, and all you had to do was choose this from a pop-up menu. You can see the contrast curve that was applied in the graph at the top of the panel.

Continued

Step Three:

If you think that the Strong Contrast preset isn't quite strong enough, you can edit this curve yourself, but it's helpful to know this rule: the steeper the curve, the stronger the contrast. So to make this curve steeper, you'd move the top of the curve (the highlights) upward, and the bottom of the curve (the darks and shadows) downward. To do this, just move your cursor right over the graph (as shown here), and you'll see a little round "point" appear on the curve. As you move your cursor in the graph, you'll see the point slide up and down the curve line. So, when it's at the top, you can click-and-drag it upward, but I think it's actually easier to just use the **Up Arrow key** on your keyboard to nudge it upward a bit (it's easier than trying to click right on that moving point).

Step Four:

Here, I've nudged it up by pressing the **Up Arrow key** on my keyboard. The curve is now steeper, and I have more contrast in the highlights. I can do the same thing in the bottom left of the curve—I would just nudge the curve downward instead, which would give me a much steeper curve (as seen here), and a much more contrasty image, as you can see. Also, as you're moving your cursor over the graph, you'll notice that at the bottom of the graph itself, it tells you which part of the curve you'd be adjusting if you moved the point now.

TIP: Moving in Different Increments
Using the **Up/Down Arrow keys** moves the point in small 5-point increments. To move in 20-point increments, press-and-hold the **Shift key** while using the Arrow keys. For really precise adjustments (1-point increments), press-and-hold the **Option (PC: Alt) key** while you use the Arrow keys.

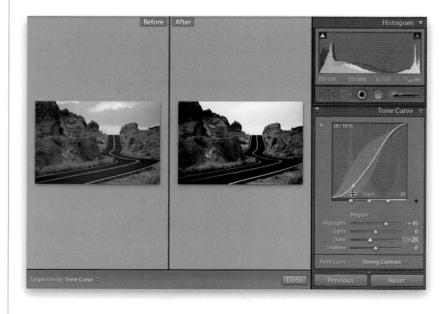

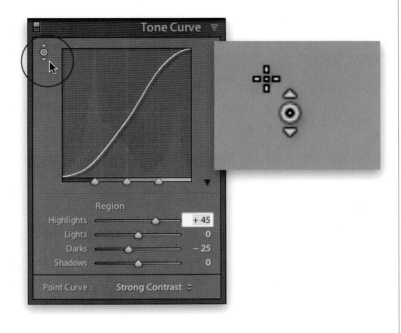

Step Five:
Another way to adjust the contrast using the tone curve is to use the Targeted Adjustment tool (or TAT, for short). The TAT is that little round target-looking icon in the top-left corner of the Tone Curve panel (when you move your cursor over it, two triangles pointing up and down will show. It's shown circled here in red). When you click on that little target icon, your cursor changes to the cursor seen here on the right—a precise crosshair cursor to the top left of a little target icon with triangles on the top and bottom. This tool lets you interactively adjust the tone curve by clicking-and-dragging it right within your photo. The crosshair part is actually where the tool is located—the target with the triangles is there just to remind you which way to drag the tool, which (as you can see from the triangles) is up and down.

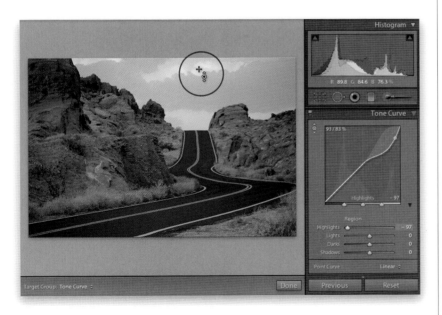

Step Six:
Now, let's put it to use. Take the TAT and move it out over your photo (over a white cloud in the sky, in this case). Look over at the tone curve and you'll see two things: (1) there's a point on the curve where the tones you're hovering over are located, and (2) the name of the area you'll be adjusting appears at the bottom of the graph (in this case, it says Highlights). To darken the clouds, just click on the clouds (as shown here) and drag straight downward (if you had dragged straight upward, it would have brightened those clouds instead). You can move around your image and click-and-drag straight upward to adjust the curve to brighten those areas, and drag straight downward to have the curve darken those areas. When you're done, click the TAT back where you found it. By the way, the keyboard shortcut to get the TAT is **Command-Option-Shift-T (PC: Ctrl-Alt-Shift-T)**.

Continued

Step Seven:

The final method of adjusting the tone curve is to simply click-and-drag the four Region sliders (Highlights, Lights, Darks, and Shadows) near the bottom of the panel, and as you do, it adjusts the shape of the curve. Here, I dragged the Highlights slider to the far left to darken the highlights in the sky. I dragged the Darks and Shadows sliders pretty far to the left to make the road and rocks much darker, and I moved the Lights slider just a little to the left to make the upper mid-tones a little darker. The only thing I knew up front was that the original photo's sky looked too light, and the road and rocks didn't look dark enough. Also, if you look at the sliders themselves, they have the same little gradients behind them like in the Basic panel, so you know which way to drag (toward white to make that adjustment lighter, or toward black to make it darker). By the way, when you adjust a curve point (no matter which method you choose), a gray shaded area appears in the graph showing you the curve's boundary (how far you can drag the curve in either direction).

Step Eight:

So, that's the scoop. To adjust your photo's contrast, you're going to either: (a) use a preset contrast curve from the Point Curve pop-up menu, (b) use the TAT and click-and-drag up/down in your photo to adjust the curve, (c) use either one of those two, then move the point up/down using the **Arrow keys** on your keyboard, or (d) manually adjust the curve using the Region sliders. *Note:* If you find that you're not using the sliders, you can save space by hiding them from view: click on the black triangle just outside the bottom-right corner of the tone curve graph (shown circled here in red). If you decide you want them back one day, click that same triangle again.

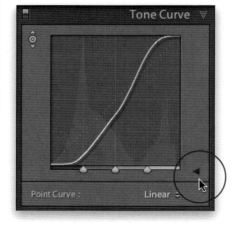

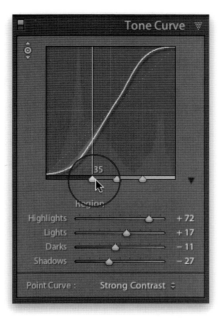

Step Nine:
There are three more things you'll need to know about the Tone Curve panel, and then we're set. The first is how to use the three slider knobs that appear at the bottom of the graph. Those are called Range sliders, and essentially they let you choose where the black, white, and midpoint ranges are that the tone curve will adjust (you determine what's a shadow, what's a midtone, and what's a highlight by where you place them). For example, the Range slider on the left (shown circled here in red) represents the shadow areas, and the area that appears to the left of that knob will be affected by the Shadows slider. If you want to expand the range of what the Shadows slider controls, click-and-drag the left Range slider to the right (as shown here). Now your Shadows slider adjustments affect a larger range of your photo. The middle Range slider covers the midtones. Clicking-and-dragging that midtones Range slider to the right decreases the space between the midtone and highlight areas, so your Lights slider now controls less of a range, and your Darks slider controls more of a range. To reset any of these sliders to their default position, just double-click directly on the one you want to reset.

Step 10:
The second thing you'll want to know is how to reset your tone curve and start over. Just double-click directly on the word Region and it resets all four sliders to 0. Lastly, the third thing is how to see a before/after of just the contrast you've added with the Tone Curve panel. You can toggle the Tone Curve adjustments off/on by using the little switch on the left side of the panel header. Just click it on or off.

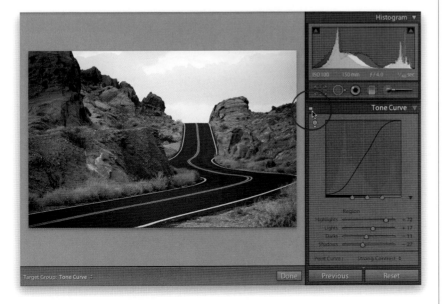

Adjusting
Individual Colors
Using HSL

If you want to make a global change to a particular color in your image (for example, let's say you want all the reds to be redder, or the blue in the sky to be bluer), one place to do that would be the in the HSL panel (HSL stands for Hue, Saturation, and Luminance), and/or the Color panel (these are grouped with the Grayscale panel, but since we're just focusing on boosting [or reducing] individual colors, we'll cover the grayscale part later in the book). Here's how this works:

Step One:

When you want to adjust an area of color, scroll down to the HSL panel in the right side Panels area (by the way, those words in the panel header, HSL/Color/Grayscale, are not just names, they're buttons, and if you click on any one of them, the controls for that panel will appear). In this example, go ahead and click on HSL (since this is where we'll be working for now), and four buttons appear in the panel: Hue, Saturation, Luminance, and All. The Hue panel lets you change an existing color to a different color by clicking-and-dragging the sliders. Just so you can see what it does, click-and-drag the Orange slider all the way to the left, and you'll see it turns the mast red. Now press the Reset button (at the bottom of the Panels area) to undo your change.

Step Two:

In this photo taken from the desk of a sailboat looking upward, if you look at the original photo in Step One, you'll see the sail kind of has a yellow color cast to it (it's supposed to be a white sail). So, to remove that yellow, you'd click on the Saturation button at the top of the HSL panel. The same eight sliders stay in place, but now those sliders control the saturation of colors in your image. Just click-and-drag the Yellow slider to the left until the yellow is removed from the sail (as shown here, where I dragged it all the way to the left).

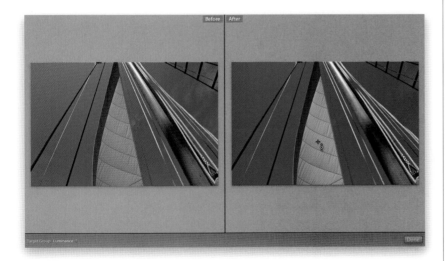

Step Three:

If you know exactly which color you want to affect, you can just grab the slider and click-and-drag it. But if you're not sure which colors make up the area you want to adjust, then you can use the TAT (the same Targeted Adjustment tool you used back in the Tone Curve panel, but now you're using it to adjust color, instead of contrast). Click on the TAT (shown circled in red here), then move your cursor over the blue sky and click-and-drag upward to increase the color saturation of the sky (you'll notice that it doesn't just move the Blue slider, but it also increases the Purple Saturation slider a little bit, as well. You probably wouldn't have realized that there was any purple in the sky, and this is why this tool is so handy here. (In fact, I rarely use HSL without using the TAT!)

Step Four:

Now click on Luminance, at the top of the panel (this panel's sliders control the overall lightness or darkness of the colors). To brighten up those sails, take the TAT, move it over the sail, then click-and-drag straight upward, and the sail will start to brighten (I dragged it to +79 to get the sail bright enough, as seen here). If you're a Photoshop user, by now you've probably realized that this is pretty much a version of Photoshop's Hue/Saturation feature, with the only real differences being that it uses two extra color sliders (Orange and Purple), Lightroom calls "L" Luminance, whereas Hue/Saturation in Photoshop calls it Lightness, and Lightroom has an Aqua slider rather than Cyan. Plus, of course, Lightroom has the TAT (which is nice). Two last things: Clicking the All button (at the top of the panel) puts all three sections in one scrolling list, and the Color panel breaks them all into sets of three for each color—a layout more like Photoshop's Hue/Saturation. But, regardless of which layout you choose, they all work the same way.

Vignetting Effects and Post-Cropping Vignettes

One of the most-requested features by users of the original version of Lightroom was post-crop vignetting. The reason is simple: Lightroom always added vignetting (edge darkening) to the original, full-sized image. So, if you cropped the photo, then added vignetting, it was still added to the uncropped image (even though you saw the cropped image onscreen—it didn't adjust the vignette to the crop). Luckily, in Lightroom 2, we have a separate control for post-crop vignetting, so you can add your vignettes without having them cropped off.

Step One:

To add an edge vignette effect, go to the right side Panels area and scroll down to the Vignettes panel. There are two different controls here: (1) The one called Lens Correction adds (or takes away) a vignette from your entire photo (before any cropping). Then (2) the Post-Crop sliders are used for any photo that you've cropped, because as you'll see in a moment, without this new Post-Crop control, when you cropped the photo, you cropped away the vignetting effect, as well.

Step Two:

We'll start with regular full-image vignetting, so drag the Lens Correction Amount slider almost all the way to the left. This slider controls how dark the edges of your photo are going to get (the further to the left you drag, the darker they get). The Midpoint slider controls how far in the dark edges get to the center of your photo. So, try dragging it over quite a bit too (as I have here), and it kind of creates a nice, soft spotlight effect, where the edges are dark, your subject (in this case, my buddy Jeff) looks nicely lit, and your eye is drawn right where you want to look.

Step Three:
Now, here comes the problem (and why Adobe added post-crop vignetting in Lightroom 2): when you go to crop the photo (as I have here, where I'm cropping in tight, so you don't see the camera he's holding), most (or often, all) of that edge darkening you added goes away. In this case, if you look at the crop, we're losing the darkening on the right side and the bottom. That's why one of the most re-quested features from Lightroom 1 users was a vignette effect that would work after cropping.

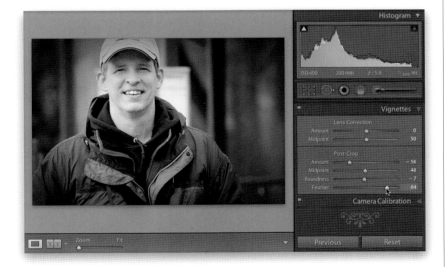

Step Four:
I went ahead and cropped the photo tight, so we could apply some post-crop vignett-ing. The Post-Crop Amount and Midpoint sliders do the same thing as always, but now you actually see the darkening on all sides, even though we cropped in (so drag the Amount slider over to the left quite a bit, and the Midpoint slider just a little bit to the right, since we're so close to his face already). The next two sliders are there to make your vignettes look more realistic than the one you applied the old way. For example, the Roundness setting controls how round the vignette is (try dragging it all the way to the left and you'll instantly see what I mean). Feather is the amount of softness of the edge, and dragging this to the right helps make the vignette softer and more natural looking. I've over-exaggerated the effect a bit here, just so you can see it at this small size, but you can see how much smoother the post-crop vignette looks compared to the original. These vignettes have become so popular (and they've become so much a part of my "look"), that I created a preset, so I can apply them with just one click.

Getting That Trendy, Gritty Portrait Look

There's a Photoshop effect for portraits that started making the rounds last year, and now it's one of the hottest and most requested looks out there, and you see it everywhere from big magazine covers to websites to celebrity portraits to album covers. Anyway, you can get pretty darn close to that look right within Lightroom itself. Now, before I show you the effect, I have to tell you, this is one of those effects that you'll either absolutely love (and you'll wind up over-using it), or you'll hate it with a passion that knows no bounds. There's no in-between.

Step One:
Before we apply this effect, I have a disclaimer: this effect doesn't look good on every photo. It looks best on photos that are dark and moody, but have multiple light sources (in particular, one or more bright lights lighting your subject's side from behind). Think gritty, because that's the look you're going for (not soft and glamorous). For the image shown here (of *Photoshop User* magazine Managing Editor Issac Stolzenbach), I used a large studio softbox (an Elinchrom 53" Midi Octa) off to the right side of the subject, and an Elinchrom RX600 Studio Strobe with no softbox—instead, just a reflector with a grid spot attachment (so the beam of the light would be hard and narrow)—behind him, opposite the main light. I started by increasing the Exposure to +0.41.

Step Two:
Now you're going to really crank just about everything up. Start in the Develop module's Basic panel, and drag the Recovery slider, the Fill Light slider, the Contrast slider, the Clarity slider, and the Vibrance slider all the way to the right (until they all read +100, as shown here). I know, it looks terrible, but we're not done yet.

Step Three:

The key to this look is to have a super-sharpened image, with vivid colors, but an overall desaturated feel (if that makes any sense). So, you do that by going to the Saturation slider and dragging it almost all the way to the left (as shown here), until there's just a little color left in the photo (so, in Step Two, we made the colors super-saturated, and then here, we're almost taking them all away. Almost). You can see how doing these two steps brings out incredible details in everything from his shirt to the floor behind him, to his hair. In some cases, it will make your subject's skin too sharp and detailed, and in that case, I'd use a little bit of the Skin Softening technique I'll show you in the next chapter, and just paint over the areas of your subject's skin that look too harsh.

Step Four:

The final step is to add an edge vignette to darken the edges of your photo, and put the focus on your subject, so go to the Vignettes panel (in the right side Panels area), and drag the Lens Correction Amount slider nearly all the way to the left (making the edges really dark). Then drag the Midpoint slider pretty far to the left, as well, but not quite as far as the Amount slider (the Midpoint slider controls how far the darkened edges extend in toward the middle of your photo. The farther you drag this slider to the left, the farther in they go). At this point, you could save this as a preset, but just understand that because each photo is different, the preset is just a starting place—you'll always have to dial in the right amount of desaturation yourself using the Saturation slider.

Virtual Copies—
The "No Risk" Way
to Experiment

Remember the wedding shot we edited earlier? Well, what if you wanted to see a version in black and white, and maybe a version with a color tint, and then a real contrasty version, and then maybe a version that was cropped differently? Well, what might keep you from doing that is having to duplicate a high-resolution file each time you wanted to try a different look, because it would eat up hard drive space and RAM like nobody's business. But luckily, you can create virtual copies, which don't really take up space and allow you to try different looks without the overhead.

Step One:

You create a virtual copy by just Control-clicking (PC: Right-clicking) on the original photo and then choosing Create Virtual Copy from the contextual menu (as shown here), or use the keyboard shortcut **Command-' (apostrophe; PC: Ctrl-')**. These virtual copies look and act the same as your original photo, and you can edit them just as you would your original, but here's the difference: it's not a real file, it's just a set of instructions, so it doesn't add any real file size. That way, you can have as many of these virtual copies as you want, and experiment to your heart's content without filling up your hard disk.

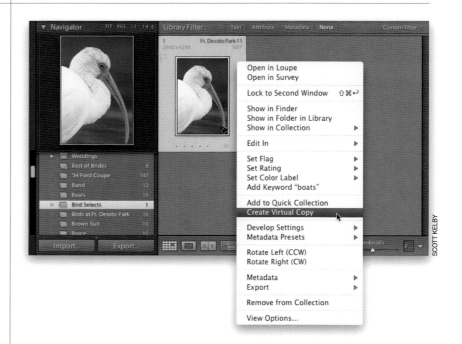

Step Two:

When you create a virtual copy, you'll know which version is the copy because the virtual copies have a curled page icon in the lower-left corner of the image thumbnail (circled in red here) in both the Grid view and in the filmstrip. So now, go ahead and process this virtual copy in the Develop module (adjust the white balance, exposure, shadows, etc.) and when you return to the Grid view, you'll see the original and the edited virtual copy (as seen here).

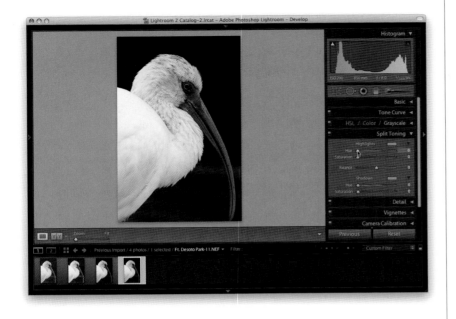

Step Three:

Now you can experiment away with multiple virtual copies of your original photo, at no risk to your original photo or your hard drive space. So, click on your first virtual copy, then press **Command-' (PC: Ctrl-')** to make another virtual copy (that's right—you can make virtual copies of your virtual copy), and then head over to the Develop module, and at the top of the Basic panel, click on the word Grayscale to create a black-and-white version. Now, make another copy and maybe try a duotone effect using the Split Toning panel (you'll learn that in Chapter 9). Make one more copy and then hit the Reset button at the bottom of the right side Panels area to return the virtual copy to its original unedited look. Now process it, but change the white balance to something cooler and more blue. By the way, you don't have to jump back to the Grid view each time to make a virtual copy—that keyboard shortcut works in the Develop module, too.

Step Four:

Now, if you want to compare all your experimental versions side by side, go back to the Grid view, select your original photo and all the virtual copies, then press the letter **N** on your keyboard to enter Survey view (as shown here). If there's a version you really like, of course you can just leave it alone, and then delete the other virtual copies you didn't like. (*Note:* To delete a virtual copy, click on it and press the Delete [PC: Backspace] key, and it's gone—no warning dialog, no nuthin'.) If you choose to take this virtual copy over to Photoshop or export it as a JPEG or TIFF, at that point, Lightroom creates a real copy using the settings you applied to the virtual copy.

Applying Changes Made to One Photo to Other Photos

This is where your workflow starts to get some legs, because once you've edited one photo, you can apply those exact same edits to other photos. For example, let's say you did a bridal shoot, where you shot 260 photos and most of those were taken in a similar lighting situation (which is fairly common). Well, now you can make your adjustments (edits) to one of those photos, then apply those same adjustments to as many of the other photos as you'd like. Once you've selected which photos need those adjustments, the rest is pretty much automated.

Step One:

Here, we'll use some photos from another bridal shoot; let's go ahead and fix the white balance. Click on one of the photos and press **W**, which is the shortcut to take that photo over to the Develop module. It automatically gives you the White Balance Selector tool, so all you have to do now is click on something light gray in the photo—I clicked on a gray part of her veil right above her head, as shown circled here in red (I pressed **Shift-Y**, so you could see a before/after split view here). So, that's the first step; fix the white balance (just a re-minder, you can download this photo and follow along at www.kelbytraining.com/books/lightroom2).

Step Two:

Now click the Copy button at the bottom of the left side Panels area. This brings up the Copy Settings dialog (shown here), which lets you choose which settings you want to copy from the photo you just edited. By default, it wants to copy everything (every checkbox is turned on), but since we only want to copy the white balance adjustment, click on the Check None button at the bottom of the dialog, then turn on the checkbox for White Balance, and click the Copy button.

Step Three:

Now press **G** to return to the Grid view, and select all the photos you want to apply this white balance change to (as shown here). If you look in the top row of the grid here, you can see that the third photo is the one I corrected the white balance on, so it's the only photo not selected.

TIP: Choosing Other Adjustments

Although here we're just copying-and-pasting a White Balance setting, you can use this function to copy-and-paste as many attributes as you want. If I've made a few edits in an area, I would just turn on the checkbox for that entire area in the Copy Settings dialog (in other words, I'd turn on the Basic Tone checkbox for my Basic panel edits, which automatically turns on all the tonal edit checkboxes. It just saves time).

Step Four:

Now go under the Photo menu, under Develop Settings, and choose Paste Settings (as shown here), or use the keyboard shortcut **Command-Shift-V (PC: Ctrl-Shift-V)**, and the White Balance setting you copied earlier will now be instantly applied to all your selected photos (as seen here, where the white balance has been corrected on all those selected photos).

TIP: Fixing Just One or Two Photos

I don't go through all of this if I'm fixing just one or two photos. Instead, I fix the first photo, then in the filmstrip (or the Grid view), I move to the other photo I want to have the same edits and I click the Previous button, which appears at the bottom of the right side Panels area in the Develop module, and all the changes I made to the previously selected photo are now applied to that photo.

Fixing a Bunch of Photos Live, While Editing Just One (Using Auto Sync)

So you just learned how to edit one photo, copy those edits, and then paste those edits onto other photos, but there's a "live-batch editing" feature called Auto Sync that you might like better (well, I like it better, anyway). Here's what it is: you select a bunch of similar photos, and then any edit you make to one photo is automatically applied to the other selected photos, live, while you're editing (no copying-and-pasting necessary). Each time you move a slider, or make an adjustment, all the other selected photos update right along with it.

Step One:

Start in the Library module by clicking on the photo you want to edit, then go to the Develop module and down in the filmstrip, Command-click (PC: Ctrl-click) on all the other photos you want to have the same adjustments as the first one (as shown here, where I've selected nine photos that all need a Fill Light adjustment). You see the first photo you clicked on in the center Preview area (Adobe calls this first-selected photo the "most selected" photo). Now, press-and-hold the Command (PC: Ctrl) key and click once on the Sync button at the bottom of the right side Panels area (as shown here).

Step Two:

When you do that, it turns Auto Sync on (you can see the button now says "Auto Sync"). Now, increase the Fill Light amount to around 60 (which makes the bottle brighter), then bring up the Blacks just a little (to keep the bottle from looking washed out), and then increase the Clarity amount to around 75 to really make it have some snap. As you make these changes, look at the selected photos in the filmstrip—they all get the exact same adjustments, but without any copying-and-pasting, or dealing with a dialog, or anything. By the way, Auto Sync stays on until you Command-click (PC: Ctrl-click) on the Auto Sync button again.

Lightroom comes with a number of built-in tonal correction presets that you can apply to any photo with just one click. These are found in the Presets panel over in the left side Panels area, where you'll find two different collections of presets: Lightroom Presets (the built-in ones put there by Adobe) and User Presets (ones you create to apply your favorite combinations of settings with just one click). Some of the built-in ones are pretty decent, and some are, well…well…let's just say that I haven't had an instance to use them yet. Here's how to put presets to work for you:

Save Your Favorite Settings as One-Click Presets

Step One:

We'll start by looking at how to use the built-in presets, then we'll create one of our own, and apply it in two different places. First, let's look at the built-in presets by going to the Presets panel (found in the left side Panels area), and clicking on Lightroom Presets (as shown here) to expand the set, and see the built-in presets within it. Adobe named these built-in presets by starting each name with the type of preset it was, so those that start with "Creative" are special effect presets, those starting with "General" are just standard tone control presets, and those that start with "Sharpen" are…do I even have to explain this one?

Step Two:

You can see a preview of how any of these presets will look, even before you apply them, by simply hovering your cursor over the presets in the Presets panel. A preview will appear above the Presets panel in the Navigator panel (as shown here, where I'm hovering over a Creative preset called B&W High Contrast, and you can see a preview of how that black-and-white effect would look applied to my photo, up in the Navigator panel, at the top of the left side Panels area).

Continued

Step Three:

To actually apply one of these presets, all you have to do is click on it. In the example shown here, I clicked on the Creative preset, Aged Photo, which gives the effect you see here.

TIP: Navigating Panels Using Keyboard Shortcuts

Want to jump right to a panel without scrolling? Press **Command-1** to jump to the Basic panel, **Command-2** for the Tone Curve panel, **Command-3** for the HSL/Color/Grayscale panel, and so on (on a PC, you'd use **Ctrl-1**, **Ctrl-2**, etc., and these shortcuts will work in each of the module's right side Panels areas).

Step Four:

Once you've applied a preset, you can apply more presets and those changes are added right on top of your current settings (in other words, they're cumulative). For example, after I applied the Aged Photo preset, I felt it looked kind of flat and lacked contrast. So, I scrolled down near the bottom of the built-in presets and clicked on the Tone Curve - Strong Contrast preset (as shown here). Then, to make the photo appear punchier, I scrolled up a bit and clicked on the Preset named, "General - Punch" to give us the image you see here. Just three clicks and I was able to add a special effect tinting, lots more contrast, and an overall sharper, punchier look. Now, let's look at using the built-in presets as a starting place to create our own custom presets.

Step Five:

Start by clicking on the Reset button at the bottom of the right side Panels area, so we're starting over from scratch (but we'll be starting with the same built-in presets we just used). Then, in the Presets panel over in the left side Panels area, first click on the Creative - Aged Photo preset, then click on Tone Curve - Strong Contrast to add more contrast. Then click on General - Punch to add more snap and Clarity to the image. Now let's increase the Blacks to 30 to really darken the shadow areas, but that makes the colors in these areas a bit too saturated. So, go to the Vibrance slider and click-and-drag it to the left until it reads –40, which desaturates the colors quite a bit, and completes our tweaking of the photo.

Step Six:

Now that we've got our look, let's save it as a preset. Go to the Presets panel, and click on the + (plus sign) button that appears on the right side of the Presets panel header. This brings up the New Develop Preset dialog (shown here). Give your new preset a name (I named mine "Desaturate With Contrast Snap"), then click the Create button to save all the edits you just made (from applying the three presets, to pumping up the shadows, to decreasing the vibrance), as your own custom preset. (*Note:* To delete a User Preset, just click on the preset, then click on the – [minus sign] button, which will appear to the left of the + button on the right side of the Presets panel header.)

TIP: Renaming Presets

To rename any preset you created (a User Preset), just Control-click (PC: Right-click) on the User Preset and choose Rename from the contextual menu, and a little dialog will appear where you can rename it.

Continued

Step Seven:

Now click on a different photo in the filmstrip, then hover your cursor over your new preset (I'm hovering over my Desaturate With Contrast Snap preset), and if you look up at the Navigator panel, you'll see a preview of the preset (as seen here, where you're seeing what your current color photo would look like if you applied the custom preset we just made). Seeing these instant live previews is a huge time saver, because you'll know in a split second whether your photo will look good with the preset applied or not, before you actually apply it.

TIP: Importing Presets

There are lots of places online where you can download free Develop module presets (like LightroomKillerTips.com). Once you've downloaded one, to get it into Lightroom, scroll down to the User Presets section in the Presets panel, then Control-click (PC: Right-click) on the User Presets header, and choose Import from the contextual menu. Locate the preset you downloaded and click the Import button, and that preset will now appear under your User Presets list.

Step Eight:

You can even put these presets to use from right within the Import Photos dialog. For example, if you knew you wanted to apply this preset to a group of photos you were about to import, you'd just choose that preset from the Develop Settings pop-up menu (as shown here), and that preset will automatically be applied to each photo as it's imported. There's one more place you can apply these Develop presets, and that's in the Saved Preset pop-up menu at the top of the Quick Develop panel in the Library module (more about the Quick Develop panel on the next page).

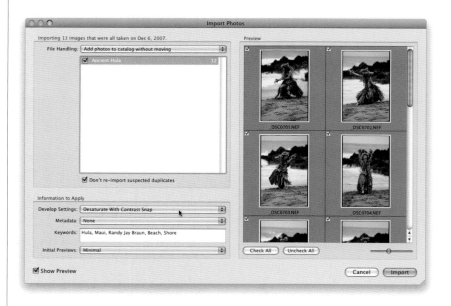

There's a version of the Develop module's Basic panel right within the Library module, called the Quick Develop panel, and the idea here is that you'd be able to make some quick, simple edits right there in the Library module, without having to jump over to the Develop module. The problem is, the Quick Develop panel stinks. Okay, it doesn't necessarily stink, it's just hard to use, because there are no sliders—there are buttons you click instead (which makes it frustrating to get just the right amount)—but for just a quick edit, it's okay (you can see I'm biting my tongue here, right?)

Using the Library Module's Quick Develop Panel

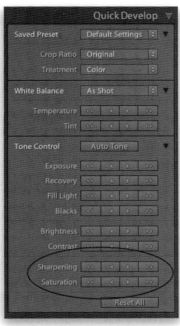

Step One:
The Quick Develop panel (shown here) is found in the Library module, under the Histogram panel at the top of the right side Panels area. Although it doesn't have the White Balance Selector tool, outside of that, it has pretty much the same controls as the Develop module's Basic panel (including the Recovery, Fill Light, Clarity, and Vibrance controls). Also, if you press-and-hold the Option (PC: Alt) key, the Clarity and Vibrance controls change into the Sharpening and Saturation controls (as seen on the right). Instead of sliders (which give us precise control over our adjustments), the Quick Develop panel uses one-click buttons (just to make us crazy). If you click a single-arrow button, it moves that control a little. If you click a double-arrow button, it moves it a lot.

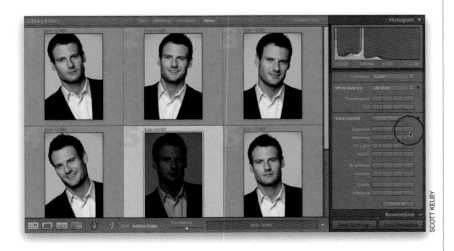

Step Two:
There are only two situations where I'll use the Quick Develop panel: One is where I see a messed-up thumbnail, and I want to see if it can easily be fixed, before I invest any time into it in the Develop module. For example, in the Grid view, click on an underexposed photo, then go over to the Quick Develop panel and click the Exposure right double-arrow button two times to get it closer to being properly exposed. Now you can make a better decision about its fate, without having to pause your sorting process by leaving the Library module and jumping over to the Develop module.

Continued

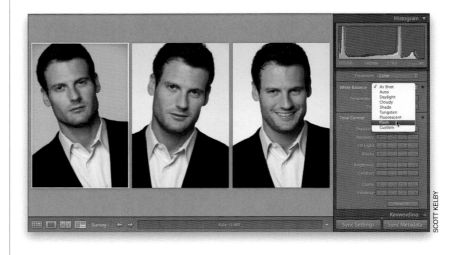

Step Three:

The other time I use the Quick Develop panel is when I'm in Compare or Survey view, because you can apply Quick Develop edits while in these side-by-side views (as shown here—just be sure to click on the photo you want to edit first). For example, the first photo shown here has a color problem—I hadn't set a custom white balance in my camera yet, so the white background looked bluish. So, click on the first photo, then choose Flash from the White Balance pop-up menu in the Quick Develop panel, and see if that fixes the problem (of course, you know it will). Also, when you make "batch corrections" using Quick Develop, every image gets the exact same amount of correction (so if you increased the exposure by 2/3 of a stop, all the selected photos go up by 2/3 of a stop). But, it's not that way when you do the same thing in the Develop module. There, if you set the exposure of one photo to +.50, every selected photo's exposure is not automatically set to +.50. There you need to use Auto Sync.

Step Four:

If you've selected a bunch of photos, but only want certain edits you made applied to them (rather than all your Quick Develop edits), then click the Sync Settings button at the bottom of the right side Panels area. This brings up a dialog (shown here) where you can choose which Quick Develop settings get applied to the rest of the selected photos. Just turn on the checkboxes beside those settings you want applied, and then click the Synchronize button.

TIP: Undo Quick Develop Changes

You can undo any individual change in the Quick Develop panel by double-clicking on that control's name.

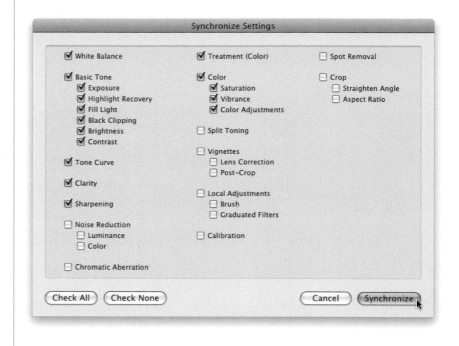

Lightroom Quick Tips > >

▼ Speed Editing

This may be my favorite new shortcut in all of Lightroom 2: to jump to the next slider in the Basic panel, just press the **. (period) key** on your keyboard (you'll see the adjustment name highlight); press the **, (comma) key** to move you back. I love it!

▼ Resetting the White Balance

To reset both the Temperature and Tint White Balance sliders to their original As Shot settings, just double-click directly on the letters WB in the Basic panel.

▼ One-Button Grayscale Preview

To quickly see how your current photo would look as a B&W photo, press the letter **V** (which converts it to grayscale), then press it again to return to color.

▼ Panel Trick for Impatient People

Have you noticed that when you expand or collapse a panel, it gently (and arguably slowly) animates this sequence (in other words, they don't snap open—they "glide" open). If you'd like to skip the fancy gliding and have those panels snap open/closed the moment you click on them, just **Command-click (PC: Ctrl-click)** on them instead.

▼ Picking Zooms in the Detail Panel

If you Control-click (PC: Right-click) inside the little preview window in the Detail panel, a little contextual menu will appear where you can choose between two zoom ratios for the preview—1:1 or 2:1—which kick in when you click your cursor inside the Preview area.

▼ Choosing What Will Be Your Before and After

By default, if you press the **\ (Backslash) key** in the Develop module, it toggles you back and forth between the original untouched image (the Before view) and the photo as it looks now with your edits. However, what if you don't want your Before photo to be the original? For example, let's say you did some Basic panel edits on a portrait, and then you used the Adjustment Brush to do some portrait retouching. Maybe you'd like to see the Before photo showing the Basic panel edits after they were applied, but before you started retouching. To do that, go to the History panel (in the left side Panels area), and scroll down until you find the step right before you started using the Adjustment Brush. Control-click (PC: Right-click) on that history state and choose Copy History Step Settings to Before. That now becomes your new Before photo when you press the \ key. I know—that's totally cool.

▼ Hiding the Clipping Warning Triangles

If you don't use the two little clipping warning triangles in the top corners of the histogram (or you want them turned off when you're not using them), then just Control-click (PC: Right-click) anywhere on the histogram itself and choose Show Clipping Indicators from the contextual menu to turn it off, and they'll be tucked out of sight. If you want them back, go back to that same contextual menu, and choose Show Clipping Indicators again.

▼ Copy What You Last Copied

When you click the Copy button in the Develop module (at the bottom of the left side Panels area), it brings up a Copy Settings dialog asking which edits you want to copy. However, if you know you want to copy the same edits as you had previously (maybe you always copy everything), then you can skip having that Copy Settings dialog pop-up up completely by pressing-and-holding the Option (PC: Alt) key, then clicking the Copy button.

▼ Making Your Current Settings the New Defaults for That Camera

When you open a photo, Lightroom applies a default set of corrections based on the photo's file format and the make and model of the camera used to take the shot (it reads this from the built-in EXIF data). If you want to use your own custom settings (maybe you think it makes the shadows too black, or the highlights too bright), go ahead and get the settings the way you want them in Lightroom, then press-and-hold the Option (PC: Alt) key and the Reset button at the bottom of the right side Panels area changes into a Set Default button. Click on it and it brings up a dialog showing you the file format or the camera make and model of the current image. When you click Update to Current Settings, from now on, your current settings will be your new starting place for all images taken with that camera, or that file format. To return to Adobe's default settings for that camera, go back to that same dialog, but this time click on the Restore Adobe Default Settings button.

Continued

Lightroom Quick Tips > >

▼ **Updating Your Presets**

If you start your editing by using a Develop module User Preset, and you like the new changes, you can update your preset by Control-clicking (PC: Right-clicking) on the old preset and choosing Update with Current Settings from the contextual menu.

▼ **Get Different Versions of Your Photo Without Making Virtual Copies**

I briefly mentioned snapshots earlier in this chapter, but I want to give you another way to think of them. Think of them as another way to have one-click access to multiple versions of your photo. When you're working in the Develop module and see a version of your photo you like, just press **Command-N (PC: Ctrl-N)** and how your photo looks at that moment is saved to your Snapshots panel (you just have to give it a name). So, that way, you could have a B&W version as a snapshot, one version as a duotone, one version in color, one with an effect, and see any of those in one click, without having to scroll through the History panel to try to figure out where each look is.

▼ **Fix Underexposed Photos Fast with Match Exposure**

If you see a series of photos of the same subject, and some of these photos are underexposed, try this quick trick to fix those fast: Click on a properly exposed photo from that series, then while it's selected, also select the underexposed photos, then go under the Settings menu and choose Match Total Exposures. It will evaluate the overall exposure from your "most-selected" photo (your properly exposed photo) and use that to fix the underexposed photos.

▼ **One of My Most-Used Presets**

The intentional vignette look is really hot right now, and it's an ideal effect to save as a one-click preset. Just go to the Vignettes panel, click-and-drag the Amount slider all the way to the left (to –100), then click-and-drag the Midpoint slider to the left to 10, and then go to the Presets panel and save that as a vignette preset. Now you can just move your cursor over this preset and you'll get an instant preview of how your image would look with a vignette applied up in the Navigator panel at the top of the left side Panels area.

Local Adjustments
how to edit just part of your images

In the original version of Lightroom, every slider you moved made what Adobe called a "global change" (the whole photo was affected equally), so if you wanted someone's shirt to be redder, and you increased the amount of red, it didn't just increase the amount of red in their shirt, it increased the amount of red in the entire photo. It was a global change. By the way, you may not know this, but Adobe has an entire department whose sole job is to come up with names for things that you would never use in everyday conversation to describe anything, like "global change." Anyway, in Lightroom 2 they added the ability to actually edit just parts of your image, instead of the whole thing. Adobe's Department of Technical Naming and Confusion (known as DOTNAC), calls these edits "local adjustments." It makes sense if you buy into that whole "global change" thing, because a global adjustment would mean it changes everything, whereas a local adjustment would mean that a city commission has to convene and decide if the change you want to propose really has merit, and if it's absolutely necessary for you to have a liquor license in the first place. I bet you didn't see that last line coming, because for a while there it sounded like I was being serious, but that would go against the very foundation of what my chapter intros are for in the first place (by the way, I'm not exactly sure what that is, but I'll know it when I see it).

Dodging, Burning, and Adjusting Individual Areas of Your Photo

My single favorite feature in all of Photoshop Lightroom 2 is the ability to make adjustments to individual areas of your photo (Adobe calls this "local adjustments"), and keep them totally non-destructive (so you can always undo them at any time!). The way they've added this feature is pretty darn clever (it makes you want something similar in Photoshop), and while it's different than using a brush in Photoshop, there are some aspects to it that I bet you'll like better. We'll start with dodging and burning, but we'll add more cool options in as we go.

Step One:

Do all your regular edits to your photo first (Exposure, Recovery, Blacks, etc.). Then, in the Develop module, in the toolbox near the top of the right side Panels area (right under the Histogram panel), click on the Adjustment Brush icon (as shown circled here), or just press the letter **K** on your keyboard. When you do this, an options panel pops down below the toolbox with all the controls for using the Adjustment Brush (as seen here).

Step Two:

With the Adjustment Brush, you have to decide first what you want to paint with the brush from the Effect pop-up menu (shown here). If you choose Exposure from the menu, then you're pretty much going to be dodging or burning (lightening or darkening certain parts of your photo), and the same holds true for Brightness (you'll be lightening or darkening the midtones where you paint). But what I think is cool is that you can paint with clarity, or sharpness, or use it so it only adds contrast where you paint, or only removes saturation where you paint. The Color effect lets you apply a tint of any color, and you can imagine what Soften Skin does.

Step Three:

In this case, I want to lighten the interior of this classic Ford Mustang, so I chose Exposure from the pop-up menu. Now, this is going to sound weird at first, but you start by choosing how much brighter you think you might want the area you're going to paint to be by dragging the Amount slider to the right (so, here I've increased the Amount to 2.02). At this point, I have no way of knowing whether that's going to be exactly the right amount or not (in fact, I have no way of knowing if it's even close), but luckily you have full control over the amount after the fact, so I intentionally drag the Amount slider to the right quite a bit. That way, I can easily see my brush strokes as I paint, and I'm not worried about messing things up, because I can always lower the Exposure there later.

Step Four:

So, go ahead and choose Exposure from the Effect pop-up menu, set your Amount to around 2.00, and paint over the dashboard area (as shown here) to brighten that area. You can see it's too bright, but again, you can always change it later (and don't worry—we will).

Continued

Step Five:

[...]hat we've painted in the dashboard, go ahead and paint over the rest of the interior (as shown here), and as you paint, you'll see a brush-size cursor that shows where you're painting and the size of your brush (you can see it on the wood grain at the top of the console here).

TIP: Changing Brush Sizes

To change your brush size, you can use the **Left and Right Bracket keys** (they're to the right of the letter P on your keyboard). Pressing the Left Bracket key makes your brush smaller; the Right Bracket key makes it bigger.

Step Six:

So, how do you know if you've really painted over the entire interior area? How do you know whether you've missed a spot? Well, when you paint with the Adjustment Brush, it puts a little "pin" (it looks like a little white ring when it's active, or a gray dot when it's not) right where you started painting (it doesn't show up until you release the mouse button after painting a brush stroke). If you move your cursor directly over this pin, it shows you (in the red mask overlay you see here) exactly where you painted, so you can see if you missed any areas (I missed the top-right corner, the bottom-right corner, and I accidentally painted a bit onto the car door). Now that you know where you painted, you can go back and paint over any areas you missed. If you painted over an area you didn't want to (like I did here on the door), press-and-hold the **Option (PC: Alt) key** and paint over that area to erase your adjustment in just that area (so here I would hold the Option key, then paint over the right edge of the door). If you want to start over from scratch, click the Reset button in the bottom of the Brush section at the bottom of the panel.

Step Seven:

Remember when I told you we could change our exposure after the fact? It's simple—first move your cursor away from that pin (so you don't see the red mask any longer). Now, you can dial in exactly how bright you want the area you painted over (the interior of the Mustang) by dragging the Exposure Amount slider. If you drag it to the left (as shown here, where I've lowered the Amount of exposure to just 0.95), the entire area you painted over is now less bright (as seen here—compare it to the image shown in Step Five). If you want it darker, keep dragging to the left. You have full control after the fact (I know—that's way cool!).

Step Eight:

If you want to affect a different area of your photo, click the New button (shown circled here in red) and then you do three things: (1) choose which effect you want to paint with from the Effect pop-up menu, (2) choose the Amount for that effect, and (3) start painting. In this case, I want to darken the car door (it's too bright, and it's drawing the eye away from our subject, which is the car's interior). So, choose Exposure from the pop-up menu, for Amount, lower it to –1.44 (as shown here), and then start painting over the car door to darken it (also shown here). It's pretty subtle at this point, but remember, we can always change it later.

TIP: Deleting Adjustments

If you want to delete any adjustment you've made, click on the pin to select that adjustment (the center of the pin turns black), then press the Delete (PC: Backspace) key on your keyboard.

Continued

Step Nine:

Okay, let's put our after-the-fact editing to work. Paint over the entire door, then go to the Amount slider and drag it way over to the left (here I dragged down to –2.52), and look how it darkened that whole area. Although the color red still tends to draw the eye somewhat, it really did a nice job of balancing out the tones in the photo, helping lead the viewer's eye to the brighter interior first.

TIP: Choosing What to Edit

If you have multiple pins, and you drag a slider, Lightroom will adjust whichever pin is currently selected (the pin filled with black), so if you want to choose which pin you want to edit, click directly on the pin first to select it, then make your changes.

Step 10:

Another nice feature of the Adjustment Brush is that you can make onscreen interactive adjustments, kind of like you do with the Targeted Adjustment tool (which you learned about in Chapter 4). So, to adjust the exposure amount for the area you painted on the door, just move your cursor directly over the pin, and your cursor changes to a bar with two arrows—one pointing left and one pointing right. Those are letting you know that you can now click-and-drag left or right to make changes (try it—click-and-drag to the right to increase the exposure in that area, or the left to decrease it).

TIP: Erasing

If you click the Erase button (in the Brush section), it doesn't erase anything—it just changes your brush so if you paint with it now, it erases your mask instead of painting one.

Step 11:

So far, we've been just lightening and darkening certain areas (dodging and burning), but the real power of the Adjustment Brush is that we can paint with other things, like sharpness, or clarity, or contrast, or color. For example, if you want to paint with sharpness (maybe you'd like the interior to look really crisp), after you click on the New button, you can either choose Sharpness from the Effect pop-up menu, or just click on the word Sharpness in the list of adjustments that appears in two columns below the Amount slider. By the way, when you make an adjustment, the little + and – icons beside each control remember your last positive or negative setting, so they're just one click away.

Step 12:

So now we can paint different effects to different areas of our image, but what if you want to paint a number of effects to the same area. For example, here we want to add clarity and sharpness to that same interior area. To do that, click the little switch to the far right of the word Effect (shown circled here in red), and a group of sliders pops down (as shown here). To add clarity and sharpness to the interior, just move those sliders. Not too shabby, eh? (*Important:* If you toggle this pop-down slider list back up, the Amount slider now controls the amount for all the adjustments you added at once—so it raises or lowers the amounts of Exposure, Clarity, and Sharpness together.) This feature is particularly handy if you did one thing, like brightened the exposure of an area, but brightening it made the colors too vibrant. You could just go and lower the Saturation amount for that area you just brightened, without having to paint over that area again. Sweet!

Continued

Step 13:

You learned the **Bracket key** shortcuts for changing brush sizes back in the tip on page 172, but in the Brush section, you can also change the brush size manually by using the Size slider. The Feather slider controls how soft the brush edges are—the higher the number, the softer the brush (I paint with a soft brush about 90% of the time). For a hard-edged brush, set the Feather to 0. The Flow slider controls the amount of paint that comes out of the brush (unless I'm using the Soften Skin effect, I leave the Flow set at 100. For skin softening, I start at around 20, and then let it build up by painting over the same spot a few times if I need to. More on skin softening later). Also, you get to create two custom brush settings (that's what the A and the B are for, shown circled here), so for example, you could set up A to be a large, soft-edged brush, and B to be a small, hard-edged brush, like the B brush settings shown here (or you can make them both soft-edged—it's totally up to you—just click on the letter, choose your settings, and it remembers them so next time you can just click on the letter).

Step 14:

To help make painting selections easier, there's an Auto Mask feature that senses where the edges of what you're painting are (based on color), and it helps keep you from spilling paint outside the area you're trying to affect. Depending on the image, and what type of object you're trying to paint within, it either does an amazing job or just so-so. Luckily, it works pretty well more often than not, so I leave this on all the time, and only turn it off if it's just not working (and paint is spilling everywhere).

Step 15:

Below Auto Mask is the Density slider, which kind of simulates the way Photoshop's airbrush feature works, but honestly, the effect is so subtle when painting on a mask like this, that I don't ever change it from its default setting of 100. At the bottom of the panel is an on/off switch (shown circled here in red), where you can turn off the effects of just the changes you made with the Adjustment Brush, so you can see how it looked before your changes. Also, to the right of it is the Reset button (to set everything back to its default settings) and a Close button, to close this panel and tuck it back up under the toolbox. A before and after of our photo is shown below, with our brightening, added clarity, and sharpening of the interior, along with darkening of the outside of the car. On the following pages, we'll look at some of the Adjustment Brush's other effects, including color tints, saturation, and retouching.

Getting Creative with the Adjustment Brush

Now that we know how the Adjustment Brush works, we can use it for more than just dodging and burning—we can use it for creative effects. We'll start with a technique that is very popular in wedding photo albums, and that is the classic "bride's in black and white, but her bouquet stays in color" effect (which, as lame as it may sound, clients absolutely love). If we were using the previous version of Lightroom, this would definitely mean a trip over to Photoshop, but thanks to Lightroom 2's Adjustment Brush, we can create the same look here just as easily.

Step One:

In the Develop module, start by clicking on the Adjustment Brush in the toolbox near the top of the right side Panels area, then from the Effect pop-up menu, choose Saturation, set the Amount slider to −100 (as shown here), and begin painting over the areas you want to be black and white (here, we're painting over everything but the bouquet). This is one instance (painting over a large background area with different colors) where I recommend turning the Auto Mask checkbox off (at the bottom of the Brush section). Otherwise, it will try to keep you from painting outside the original area you clicked in—it will let you paint over other areas, but it will fight you along the way.

Step Two:

When you get close to the bouquet, that's when I'd do two things: (1) lower the size of your brush (you can use the Size slider in the Brush section or the **Bracket keys** on your keyboard), and (2) turn the Auto Mask checkbox back on. That way, it will try to keep your brush from painting on the flowers, because their color will be much different than the white dress color and fleshtone colors you'll be painting over. The final effect is shown here, and you'll be surprised at how quickly you get this effect now in Lightroom.

Step Three:

Now let's take that idea up a notch, and apply a version of it to a different kind of image. A very popular effect for sports posters, editorial feature spreads, cover shots, and even some baseball cards is to make a player "pop out" from the background. This generally is done by removing the color from the background, applying a tint to the now grayscale background, then lightening (backscreening) it, so all the focus is on the player. Since we're applying multiple effects, click the little switch to the far right of the word Effect to bring down the slider pop-down section. Now, we'll start by painting our tint over the background, so choose Color from the Effect pop-up menu, click on the Color swatch at the bottom of the effects area and choose a blue color (as shown here), then paint over the entire background. Again, turn the Auto Mask checkbox off when painting large backgrounds with lots of color.

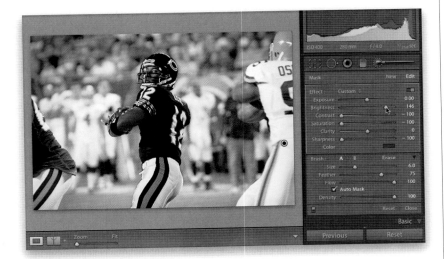

Step Four:

Once you've painted over the bulk of the background, do the same thing you did with the bride—use a smaller brush and turn the Auto Mask checkbox back on, so you can paint in the areas around the edges of the player without accidentally tinting him. Once you've got your background painted over, you can now apply multiple effects to your selected area, so go to the Saturation slider and drag it all the way to the left, to –100, to remove all the color from the background (which makes your tint really stand out). Then, to make the background less contrasty, lower the Contrast and Sharpness sliders to –100, as well. Lastly, to lighten the background, just drag the Brightness slider (the midtones) up to around 140 (as seen here) to give the backscreened look, which gives you the final multiple-effect you see here. This gives you an idea of the power of being able to make adjustments to just part of your image. Pretty cool, isn't it?

Retouching Portraits

Back in the original version of Lightroom, when it came to retouching, you basically had one thing you could do: remove blemishes. Hey, I'm thankful we could do that, because in many cases that was all I needed to do and it saved me a trip to Photoshop. But now, in Lightroom 2, you can use the Adjustment Brush to do a number of different common retouching tasks (just remember to do these after you've already toned the image in the Basic panel and then removed any blemishes—always do those first, before you use the Adjustment Brush for retouching).

Step One:

Here we've zoomed in to a 1:1 view of our cover model, Stevie. I want to make her eyes really pop (that's retouching speak) by increasing the saturation, sharpening, and clarity of her iris. Then we'll darken the brightness (to make the color richer), and then brighten the overall exposure (to make the highlights brighter). Start by getting the Adjustment Brush (in the Develop module, near the top of the right side Panels area) and clicking on the little switch to the far right of the word Effect to get the pop-down sliders. Now, increase the Saturation to 75, then paint over her iris (as shown here) with the Auto Mask checkbox turned on (which helps keep you from painting outside the iris). Now you can simply drag the Clarity and Sharpness sliders to the right, lower the Brightness a little, and increase the Exposure a little (as shown here).

SCOTT KELBY

Step Two:

Let's now brighten the white of her eye. Click the New button (near the top right of the panel), since we're going to be working on a different area, then increase the Exposure amount to 0.95 (as shown here). Paint directly over the white of her eye. Remember, if it looks too bright, we can always decrease the Exposure amount after the fact, or decrease the Brightness, as I did here (also, I'd still leave the Auto Mask checkbox turned on, to help keep your paint on just the white of her eye).

Step Three:
Click the New button again, and from the
Effect pop-up menu, choose Soften Skin.
Increase the size of your brush (use either
the Size slider in the Brush section, or the
Bracket keys on your keyboard), and
paint over her skin, avoiding any detail
areas like the eyebrows, eyelids, lips,
nostrils, hair, etc. (as shown here). This
softens the skin by giving you a negative
Clarity setting (if you look, you'll see it's at
−100) to complete the retouch (a before/
after is shown below). If you'd like to try
another enhancement, you could click
on the pin on her iris, then use the Color
swatch to choose a new color for her eye
(give that a try and see what you think).

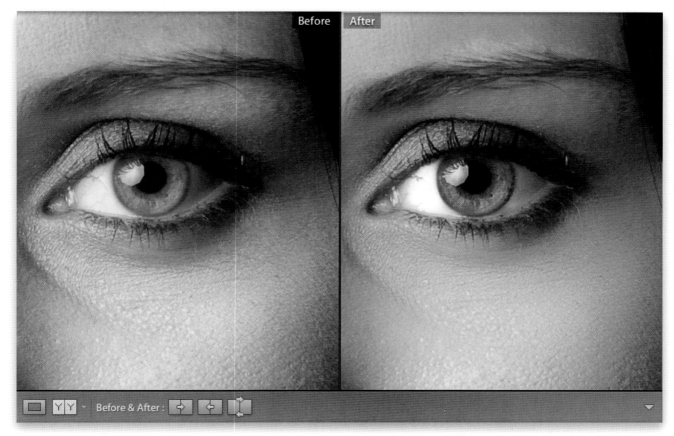

The After photo has increased color saturation, a sharper eye, the white of the eye is brighter, and her skin has been softened

Fixing Skies (and Other Stuff) with the Gradient Filter

The new Gradient Filter (which acts more like a tool) lets you recreate the look of a traditional neutral density gradient filter (these are glass or plastic filters that are dark on the top and then graduate down to fully transparent). They're popular with landscape photographers because you're either going to get a perfectly exposed foreground or a perfectly exposed sky, but not both. However, the way Adobe implemented this feature, you can use it for much more than just neutral density gradient filter effects (though that probably will still be its number one use).

Step One:
Start by clicking on the Gradient Filter tool in the toolbox (it's just to the left of the Adjustment Brush, or press **M**), near the top of the right side Panels area (it's right under the Histogram panel). When you click on it, a set of options pops down that are similar to the effects options of the Adjustment Brush (as shown here). Here we're going to replicate the look of a traditional neutral density gradient filter and darken the sky. Start by dragging the Exposure slider to the left (as shown here; if you don't see these sliders, but have + and – buttons instead, click on the little switch to the far right of the word Effect).

Step Two:
Press-and-hold the Shift key, click on the top center of your image, and drag straight down until you nearly reach the bottom of the photo (the reason I'm dragging so low is because our horizon line is near the bottom of the photo, as shown here. You can see the darkening effect it has on the sky, and the photo already looks more balanced). Generally, you'll want to stop dragging the gradient before it reaches the horizon line, or it will start to darken your properly exposed foreground. By the way, the reason we held the Shift key down was to keep our gradient straight as we dragged. Not holding the Shift key down will let you drag the gradient in any direction.

SCOTT KELBY

Step Three:
The pin shows where the center of your gradient is, and in this case, I think the darkening of the sky stopped a little short. Luckily, you can reposition your gradient after the fact—just click-and-drag that pin downward to move the whole gradient down (as shown here). What's nice about this tool is that, like the Adjustment Brush, once we've dragged out the Gradient Filter, we can add other effects to that same area. For example, go ahead and increase the Contrast to 22 (to make it more punchy), then increase the Saturation to 58 to make the sky more colorful, then lower the Sharpness so the added contrast doesn't make the sky look too sharp (a before and after is shown below). You can have more than one gradient (click the New button near the top right of the panel), and to delete a gradient, click on its pin and press the Delete (PC: Backspace) key.

Lightroom Quick Tips > >

▼ Hiding Your Pins

You can hide the Adjustment Brush pins anytime by pressing the letter **H** on your keyboard. To bring them back, press H again.

▼ Shrinking the Brush Options

Once you've set up your A/B brushes, you can hide the rest of the brush options by clicking on the little downward-facing triangle to the right of the Erase button.

▼ Scroll Wheel Trick

If you have a mouse with a scroll wheel, you can use the scroll wheel to change the Size amount of your brush.

▼ Auto Mask Shortcut

Pressing the letter **A** toggles the Auto Mask feature on/off.

▼ Controlling Flow

The numbers **1** through **0** on your keyboard control the amount of brush Flow (**3** for 30%, **4** for 40%, and so on).

▼ Seeing/Hiding the Adjustment Mask

By default, if you put your cursor over a pin, it shows the mask, but if you'd prefer to have it stay on while you're painting (especially handy when you're filling in spots you've missed), you can toggle the mask visibility on/off by pressing the letter **O** on your keyboard.

▼ Changing the Color of Your Mask

When your mask is visible (you've got your cursor over a pin), you can change the color of your mask by pressing **Shift-O** on your keyboard (this toggles you through the four choices: red, green, white, and black).

▼ Scaling the Gradient Filter from the Center

By default, your gradient starts where you click (so it starts from the top or the bottom, etc.). However, if you press-and-hold the **Option (PC: Alt) key** as you drag the gradient, it draws from the center outward instead.

▼ Shortcut for Adding New Edits

When you're using the Adjustment Brush, if you want to quickly add a new pin (without going back to the panel to click on the New button), just press the **Return (PC: Enter) key** on your keyboard, then start painting.

▼ Switching Between the A and B Brushes

The A/B buttons are actually brush presets (so you can have a hard brush and a soft brush already set up, if you like, or any other combination of two brushes, like small and large). To switch between these two brush presets, press the **/ (Forward Slash) key** on your keyboard.

▼ Inverting Your Gradient

Once you've added a Gradient Filter to your image, you can invert that gradient by pressing the **' (Apostrophe) key** on your keyboard.

▼ Auto Mask Tip

When you have the Auto Mask checkbox turned on, and you're painting along an edge to mask it (for example, you're painting over a sky in a mountain landscape to darken it), when you're done, you'll probably see a small glow right along the edges of the mountain. To get rid of that, just use a small brush and paint right over those areas.

The Auto Mask feature will keep what you're painting from spilling over onto the mountains.

▼ Changing the Intensity of the Effects

Once you've applied either a Gradient Filter or an effect with the Adjustment Brush, you can control the amount of the last-adjusted effect by using the **Left and Right Arrow keys** on your keyboard.

▼ Increasing/Decreasing Softness

To change the softness (Feather) of your brush, don't head over to the panel—just press **Shift-]** (**Right Bracket key**) to make the brush softer, or **Shift-[(Left Bracket key)** to make it harder.

▼ Painting in a Straight Line

Just like in Photoshop, if you click once with the Adjustment Brush, then press-and-hold the **Shift key** and paint somewhere else, it will paint in a straight line between those two points.

▼ Choosing Tint Colors

If you want to paint with a color that appears in your current photo, first choose Color as your Effect, then click on the Color swatch, and when the color picker appears, click-and-hold the eyedropper cursor and move out over your photo. As you do, any color you move over in your photo is targeted in your color picker. When you find a color you like, just release the mouse button. To save this color as a color swatch, just Control-click (PC: Right-click) on one of the existing swatches and choose Set this Swatch to Current Color.

Problem Photos
correcting digital camera dilemmas

It's hard to believe that with the technology packed into today's digital cameras, that you could even take a messed-up photo. Seriously, you can buy point-and-shoot cameras that use high-tech satellites circling miles above the earth in a geosynchronous orbit to pinpoint the exact longitude and latitude of your camera's position at the moment a photograph is taken, but they still haven't come up with a solid solution for red eye. I can't believe we still have to deal with red eye, but we always have—probably always will. In the future, long after we're all gone, and people travel around with jet backpacks and flying cars, and they've cured everything from spontaneous baldness to bacterial meningitis, you'll find these photographers of the future hovering on some sort of floating platform, looking at an intricate life-like 3D holographic photo, and you'll hear one of them say, "Oh no—it's got red eye. Didn't you turn on the pre-flash?" What's sad is that many digital camera manufacturers already have the technology to forever rid us of red eye, but the Red Eye Coalition and its high-powered Washington-based lobbying group have such a powerful grip over the Senate's Pop-Up Flash Committee that I doubt we'll ever see the day when we take a photo using a built-in flash and it doesn't look like our subjects are totally possessed. I'm just sorry I had to be the one to tell you this.

Undoing Changes Made in Lightroom

Photoshop Lightroom keeps track of every edit you make to your photo and it displays them as a running list, in the order they were applied, in the Develop module's History panel. So if you want to go back and undo any step, and return your photo to how it looked at any stage during your editing session, you can do that with just one click. Now, unfortunately, you can't just pull out one single step and leave the rest, but you can jump back in time to undo any mistake, and then pick up from that point with new changes. Here's how it's done:

Step One:

Before we look at the History panel, I just wanted to mention that you can undo anything by pressing **Command-Z (PC: Ctrl-Z)**. Each time you press it, it undoes another step, so you can keep pressing it and pressing it until you get back to the very first edit you ever made to the photo in Lightroom, so it's possible you won't need the History panel at all (just so you know). If you want to see a list of all your edits to a particular photo, click on the photo, then go to the History panel in the left side Panels area (shown here). The most recent changes appear at the top. (*Note:* A separate history list is kept for each individual photo.)

Step Two:

If you hover your cursor over one of the history states, the small Navigator panel preview (which appears at the top of the left side Panels area) shows what your photo looked like at that point in history. Here, I'm hovering my cursor over the point a few steps back where I had converted this photo to grayscale, but since then I changed my mind and switched back to color.

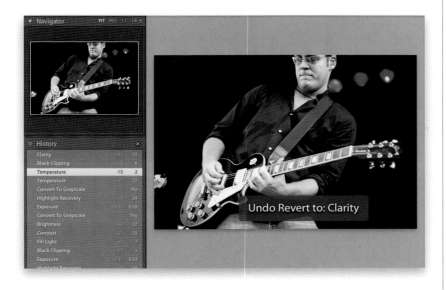

Step Three:

If you actually want to jump back to what your photo looked like at a particular stage, then instead of hovering over the state, you'd click once on it and your photo reverts to that state. By the way, if you use the keyboard shortcut for your undos (instead of using the History panel), the edit you're undoing is displayed in very large letters near the bottom of your photo (as seen here). This is handy because you can see what you're undoing, without having to keep the History panel open all the time.

Step Four:

During your editing process, if you come to a point where you really like what you see and you want the option of quickly jumping back to that point, go to the Snapshots panel (it's right above the History panel), and click on the + (plus sign) button on the right side of the Snapshots panel header (as shown here). That moment in time is saved to the Snapshots panel, and it appears with its name field highlighted, so you can give it a name that makes sense to you (I named mine "Grayscale with Exposure Increased," so I'd know that if I clicked on that snapshot, that's what I'd get—a black-and-white photo with the exposure tweaked. You can see my snapshot highlighted in the Snapshots panel shown here). By the way, you don't have to actually click on a previous step to save it as a snapshot. Instead, in the History panel you can just Control-click (PC: Right-click) on any step and choose Create Snapshot from the contextual menu. Pretty handy.

Reducing Noise

Lightroom has a built-in control for removing noise from your photos that usually appears when shooting at a high ISO or in very low light, where your camera has to do a long exposure. Although the noise reduction in the original version of Lightroom was kind of weak (I would sometimes joke that I thought Adobe forgot to connect the Noise Reduction sliders to anything), since then they've improved the noise reduction quite a bit—so much so, in fact, that it's actually fairly useful in most cases.

Step One:

There are two types of noise you're likely to run into: one adds a visible graininess throughout the photo, particularly in shadow areas; the other is color noise, where you see those annoying red, green, and blue spots. Sadly, sometimes you have both. If you see either (or both), go to the Develop module's Detail panel, where you'll find a Noise Reduction section with two sliders. Start by zooming in to a 1:1 view, so you can see how much noise is there and if you think it really needs addressing (the reason you have to make this decision is that reducing noise slightly blurs your photo, so you have to choose which annoys you more—a slightly blurry photo, or a really noisy one).

Step Two:

If the noise looks grainy, drag the Luminance slider to the right until the noise is reduced, or ideally is no longer visible. If you've got the red, green, and blue spots instead (or in addition), then try dragging the Color slider to the right. In this case, I had to really drag the Luminance slider over quite a bit (as shown here), to reduce the noise to an acceptable level. If you have to reduce color noise, keep in mind that this slider can also desaturate the colors somewhat, so just remember that.

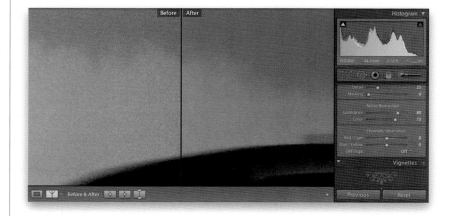

Vignetting is a lens problem that causes the corners of your photo to appear darker than the rest of the photo. This problem is usually more pronounced when you're using a wide-angle lens, but can also be caused by a whole host of other lens issues. Now, a little darkness in the edges is considered a problem, but many photographers (myself included) like to exaggerate this edge darkening and employ it as a lighting effect in portraits, which we covered in Chapter 4. Here's how to fix it if it happens to you:

Fixing Edge Vignetting

Step One:
In the photo shown here, you can see how the corner areas look darkened and shadowed. Scroll down to the Vignettes panel in the Develop module's right side Panels area, and you'll see a section for Lens Correction at the top. There are two vignetting sliders here: the first controls the amount of brightening in the edge areas, and the second slider lets you adjust how far in toward the center of your photo the corners will be brightened.

Step Two:
In this photo, the edge vignetting is pretty much contained in the corners, and doesn't spread too far into the center of the photo. So, start to slowly click-and-drag the Amount slider to the right and as you do, keep an eye on the corners of your image. As you drag, the corners get brighter, and your job is to stop when the brightness of the corners matches the rest of the photo (as shown here). If the vignetting had extended further into the center of the photo, then you'd drag the Midpoint slider to the left to make your brightening cover a larger area. That's how easy removing this problem is.

Cropping Photos

When I first used the cropping feature in Lightroom, I thought it was weird and awkward—probably because I was so used to the Crop tool in Photoshop—but once I got used to it, I realized that it's probably the best cropping feature I've ever seen in any program. This might throw you for a loop at first, but if you try it with an open mind, I think you'll wind up falling in love with it. If you try it and don't like it, make sure you read on to Step Six for how to crop more like you do in Photoshop (but don't forget that whole "open mind" thing).

Step One:

Here's the original photo. I knew when I took it, not only would it have to be cropped tighter (to hide the Octabank over his head and the light stand on the bottom right), but it would need some Photoshop work to clone in more black seamless paper in the foreground. To crop the image, go to the Develop module and click on the Crop Overlay button (circled here in red) in the toolbox above the Basic panel, and the Crop & Straighten options will pop down below it. This puts a "rule of thirds" grid overlay on your image (to help with cropping composition), and you'll see four cropping corner handles. To lock your aspect ratio (so your crop is constrained to your photo's original proportion as you crop), or unlock it if you want a non-constrained freeform crop, click on the lock icon near the top right of the panel (as shown here).

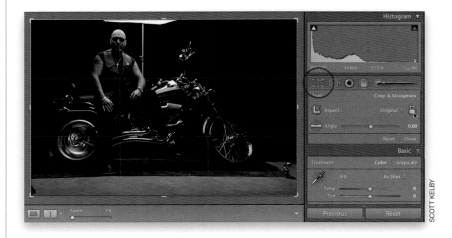

Step Two:

To crop the photo, grab a corner handle and drag inward to resize your Crop Overlay border. Here, I grabbed the top-right corner handle and dragged diagonally inward until the Octabank up top appeared outside the Crop Overlay border.

Step Three:

So, grab all four corners (you did download this photo, right? The URL for the downloads is in the book's introduction), and adjust each corner inward to eliminate as much of the lighting stand and foreground floor as possible for a nice, tight crop (as seen here). If you need to reposition the photo inside the cropping border, just click-and-hold inside the Crop Overlay border and your cursor will change into the "grabber hand" (as seen here).

TIP: Hiding the Grid

If you want to hide the rule-of-thirds grid that appears over your Crop Overlay border, press **Command-Shift-H (PC: Ctrl-Shift-H)**. Also, there's not just a rule of thirds grid, there are other grids—just press the letter **O** to toggle through the different ones.

Step Four:

When the crop looks good to you, press the letter **R** on your keyboard to lock in your crop, remove the Crop Overlay border, and show the final cropped version of the photo (as seen here). But there are two other choices for cropping we haven't looked at yet.

TIP: Canceling Your Crop

If, at any time, you want to cancel your cropping, just click on the Reset button at the bottom-right side of the Crop & Straighten section.

Continued

Step Five:

If you know you want a particular size ratio for your image, you can do that from the Ratio pop-up menu in the Crop & Straighten section. Go ahead and click the Reset button, below the right side Panels area, so we return to our original image, then click on the Aspect pop-up menu at the top-right side of the Crop & Straighten section, and a list of preset sizes appears (seen here). Choose 8x10 from the pop-up menu, and you'll see the left and right sides of the Crop Overlay border move in to show the ratio of what an 8x10" crop would be. Now you can resize the cropping rectangle and be sure that it will maintain that 8x10 aspect ratio.

Step Six:

The other, more Photoshop, way to crop is to click on the Crop Overlay button, then click on the Crop Frame tool (shown circled here in red) to release it from its home near the top left of the Crop & Straighten section. Now you can just click-and-drag out a cropping border in the size and position you'd like it. Don't let it freak you out that the original cropping border stays in place while you're dragging out your new crop, as seen here—that's just the way it works. Once you've dragged out your cropping border, it works just like before (grab the corner handles to resize, and reposition it by clicking inside the cropping border and dragging. When you're done, press **R** to lock in your changes). So, which way is the right way to crop? The one you're most comfortable with. *Note:* You'll see a finished version of another photo from this shoot, with extra black canvas area added above it in Photoshop, in Chapter 8.

When you crop a photo using the Crop Overlay tool in the Develop module, the area that will get cropped away is automatically dimmed to give you a better idea of how your photo is going to look when you apply the final crop. That's not bad, but if you want the ultimate cropping experience, where you really see what your cropped photo is going to look like, then do your cropping in Lights Out mode. You'll never want to crop any other way.

The Ultimate Cropping View

Step One:
To really appreciate this technique, first take a look at what things look like when we normally crop an image—lots of panels and distractions, and the area we're actually cropping away appears dimmed (but it still appears). Now let's try Lights Out cropping: First, click on the Crop Overlay button to enter cropping mode. Now press **Shift-Tab** to hide all your panels, and then I usually hide the Crop Overlay grid by pressing **Command-Shift-H (PC: Ctrl-Shift-H)**.

Step Two:
Press the letter **L** twice to enter Lights Out mode, where every distraction is hidden, and your photo is centered on a black background, but your cropping border is still in place. Now, try grabbing a corner handle and dragging inward, and watch the difference—you see what your cropped image looks like live as you're dragging the cropping border. It's the ultimate way to crop (it's hard to tell from the static graphic here, so you'll have to try this one for yourself—you'll never go "dim" again!).

Straightening Crooked Photos

If you've got a crooked photo, Lightroom's got three great ways to straighten it. One of them is pretty precise, and with the other two you're pretty much just "eyeing it," but with some photos that's the best you can do.

Step One:
The photo shown here has a crooked horizon line, which is pretty much instant death for a landscape shot. To straighten the photo, start by clicking on the Crop Overlay button, found in the toolbox, right under the histogram in the Develop module's right side Panels area (as shown here). This brings up the Crop Overlay grid around your photo, and while this grid might be helpful when you're cropping to recompose your image, it's really distracting when you're trying to straighten one, so I press **Command-Shift-H (PC: Ctrl-Shift-H)** to hide that grid.

Step Two:
As I mentioned above, there are three different ways to straighten your photo and we'll start with my favorite, which uses the Straighten tool. I think it's the fastest and most accurate way to straighten photos. Click on the Straighten tool, found in the Crop & Straighten section (it looks like a level), then click-and-drag it left to right along the horizon line, as shown here. See why I like straightening like this? However, there is one catch: you have to have something in the photo that's supposed to be straight—like a horizon, or a wall, or a window frame, etc.

Step Three:
When you drag that tool, it shrinks and rotates the cropping border to the exact angle you'd need to straighten the photo (without leaving any white gaps in the corners). The exact angle of your correction is displayed in the Crop & Straighten section (you can see the Angle slider in the previous step). Now all you have to do is double-click anywhere inside that cropping border to lock in your straightening. If you decide you don't like your first attempt at straightening, just click the Reset button at the bottom of the Crop & Straighten section, and it resets the photo to its unstraightened and uncropped state. So, to try again, grab the Straighten tool and start dragging. Here's the photo after being straightened.

Step Four:
To try the two other methods, we need to undo what we just did, so click the Reset button at the bottom of the right side Panels area, then click on the Crop Overlay button again (if you locked in your crop after the last step). The first of the two methods is to just drag the Angle slider (shown circled here in red)—dragging it to the right rotates the image clockwise; dragging left, counterclockwise. As soon as you start to drag, a rotation grid appears to help you line things up seen here). Unfortunately, the slider moves in pretty large increments, making it hard to get just the right amount of rotation, but you can make smaller, more precise rotations by clicking-and-dragging left or right directly over the Angle amount field (on the far right of the slider). The second method is to just move your cursor outside the Crop Overlay border (onto the gray background), and your cursor changes into a two-sided arrow. Now, just click-and-drag up/down to rotate your image until it looks straight.

Great Trick for "Dust Spotting" Your Photos

When you're searching for any dust spots or specks on your images, it's important to make sure you don't miss any areas while you're searching around an image that can easily be 50" wide or more. That's why I fell in love with this trick, which I learned while reading an interview with Mark Hamburg (known as the "Father of Photoshop Lightroom"). He mentioned an undocumented feature that helps ensure that when you're checking an image to remove specks and dust, you don't miss any areas.

Step One:
Start in the Develop module (that way, if you do find dust or specks, you can fix it right there). Now, go to the Navigator panel (at the top of the left side Panels area) and click on the 1:1 (100% size) view (shown circled here in red). If you look in the panel's small preview window, you'll see a little square (or rectangle) in the top-left corner of your photo (as shown here), which shows the area you've zoomed into, and that's what will be displayed in your Preview area, as well.

Step Two:
If you see any spots or dust in this upper-left corner of your photo, use the Remove Spots tool to remove them (more on this tool on the next page). Once you've cleaned up ("spotted") that area, press the Page Down key on your keyboard to move straight down by the exact size of that small white navigator square. When you've gone all the way down the far-left side (cleaning as you go) and you hit the bottom of your image, it automatically wraps you back up to the top of the photo, but exactly one column over, so you can begin "spotting" this area. If you keep doing this until you reach the bottom-right corner, you're guaranteed not to miss any areas.

If you've got spots, dust, specks, and other nasty junk on your lens or on your camera's sensor, it's going to show up on your photos, in the same exact place on every single photo. Luckily, a lot of simple dust and spot removal chores can be done right within Lightroom (if they're tricky, then you'll have to head over to Photoshop). However, the advantage of doing it here is once you remove the spots from one photo, you can automatically fix all the other photos based on that one photo you fixed.

Removing Spots and Other Nasty Junk

Step One:
If you find a photo that has visible dust, spots, or any other artifacts (stuff we call "nasty junk"), then head to the Develop module, because there's a tool there that can help. In the photo shown here, there are a number of different spots visible in the sky, and they're caused by dust on my digital camera's sensor (I'm really bad about keeping my sensor clean). Of course, as I pointed out above, if they're on this photo, those spots are in the same place on every photo from this shoot. I've circled some of the most obvious spots in this photo in red, just so you can see what we have to deal with.

Step Two:
The first step in getting rid of these artifacts is to zoom in tight, so you can really see what you're working on (and so you don't create a new problem—really obvious retouching). To zoom in, just double-click on the image, or you could click the 1:1 button at the top of the Navigator panel, or press **Command-+ (PC: Ctrl-+)** a couple of times until you're zoomed in nice and tight (as seen here, where I zoomed in to a 1:1 [100%] view). It doesn't matter how you get zoomed in—just get there. Now you can really see those spots. Yeech!

Continued

Step Three:

Click on the Spot Removal tool in the toolbox right below the histogram at the top of the right side Panels area, and the options for this tool will pop down below it. There are two choices for how this tool fixes your spots: Clone or Heal. Personally, I leave mine set on Heal (so it samples the lighting, texture, and tone of a nearby area), because I think it does a much better, more realistic job than Clone does. In fact, I only use the Clone option (where it copies a nearby part of the photo over the spot) in one instance, and that's where the spot I'm cloning is either on, or very near, the edge of something (like the edge of a building, or a car, etc.), or it's near the outside edge of the image itself. The reason is the Heal function doesn't like edges and it will often smudge, rather than hide, the spot, so if that happens, I switch to Clone and try again. Other than that, I'm a healer (so to speak).

Step Four:

Now, take the Spot Removal tool and move it directly over the spot you want to remove. Use the Size slider to make the round brush cursor just a little larger than the spot itself. You can also use the Left and Right Bracket keys, found to the immediate right of the letter P on your keyboard, to change the size. Each time you press the **Right Bracket (]) key**, it makes the circle larger; the **Left Bracket ([ ) key** makes it smaller. Now don't paint with this tool, just click it once and it will quickly search for a clean nearby area, then it samples that area to make your fix (and it's pretty darn clever about choosing the right area—it's not perfect, but it does a surprisingly good job).

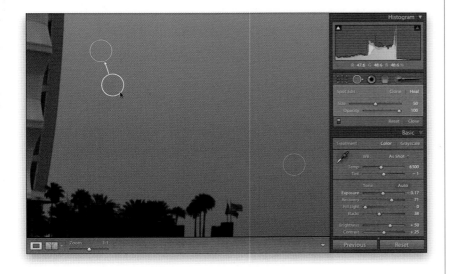

Step Five:

When you click with this tool, you'll see two circles appear: (1) a thinner one that shows the area being fixed, and (2) a thicker one that shows the clean area that the tool is sampling from to make the repair. If your background is pretty simple, like the one shown here, this one-click-and-you're-done method works pretty well, because Lightroom can find lots of open areas nearby. But, if you don't like the place it sampled from (you see an obvious change in tone or texture), you can click-and-drag that thicker sampling circle to a new spot, and as you drag, you'll see the area inside the first circle update live, so you can find a clean spot that will work pretty quickly. Also, if you think Lightroom will have a hard time finding a clean area nearby, you can lead it there—instead of just clicking once, click over the spot, hold, and drag your cursor to the area you'd like to have it sample from. When you first start dragging, a line connects both circles, and as you move further away, an arrow appears that points back to the area you're repairing.

Step Six:

To remove more spots, either click directly over them, or if they're in trickier locations, move the Spot Removal tool over the spot, click, hold, and drag out your sampler, and when you release the mouse button, the fix is in! I used that trick from the previous tutorial to make sure I didn't miss any spots in my image, and look how many little repair circles you see here (I've really got to get that sensor cleaned!).

TIP: Hiding the Circles

To hide all those circles, press **N**, which disengages the tool.

Continued

Step Seven:

Back in the first step, I mentioned that the dust on my camera's sensor created these annoying spots in the exact same position in every shot from that shoot. If that's the case (and with spots like this, it often is), then once you've removed all the spots, click the Copy button at the bottom of the left side Panels area. This brings up the Copy Settings dialog, shown here. First, click the Check None button, so everything it would copy from your photo is unchecked. Then, turn on just the checkbox for Spot Removal (as shown here) and click the Copy button.

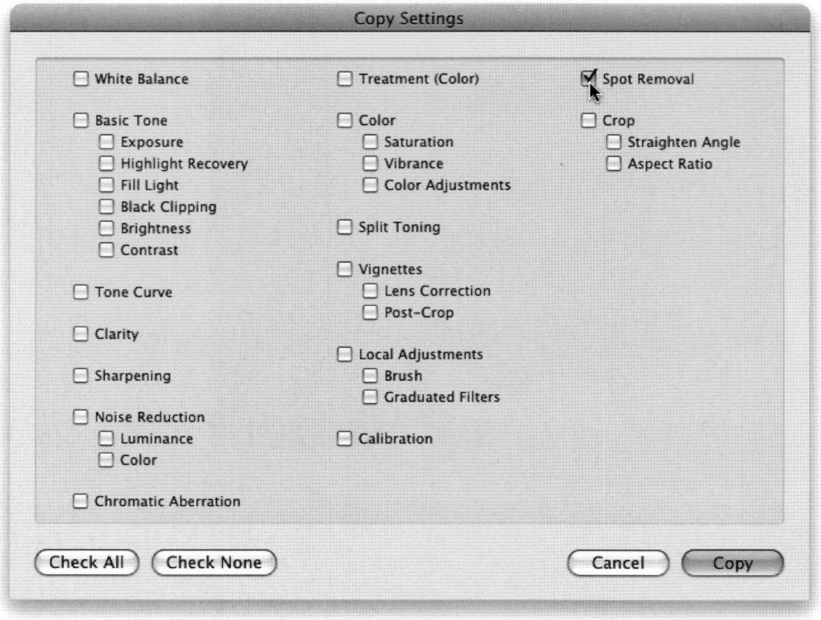

Step Eight:

Now, go to the filmstrip (or the Library module's Grid view) and select all the vertical photos (photos in the same orientation) from that shoot, then click the Paste button at the bottom of the left side Panels area, and it applies that same spot removal you did to the first photo, to all these selected photos—all at once (as shown here). To see these fixes applied, click on the Spot Removal tool again. I also recommend you take a quick look at the fixed photos, because depending on the subject of your other shots, the fixes could look more obvious than on the photo you just fixed. If you see a photo with a spot repair problem, just click on that particular circle, hit the Delete (PC: Backspace) key on your keyboard to remove it, then use the Spot Removal tool to redo that one spot repair manually.

If you wind up with red eye in your photos (point-and-shoots are notorious red-eye generators thanks to the flash being mounted so close to the lens), Lightroom can easily get rid of it. This is really handy because it saves you from having to jump over to Photoshop just to remove red eye from a photo of your neighbor's six-year-old crawling through a giant hamster tube at Chuck E. Cheese. Here's how it works:

Removing Red Eye

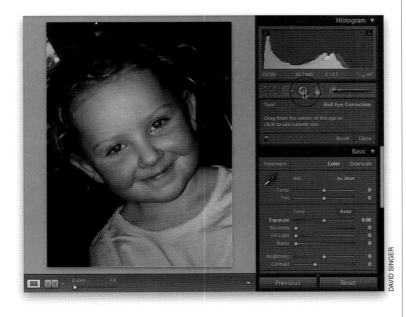

Step One:
Go to the Develop module and click on the Red Eye Correction tool, found in the toolbox right under the Histogram panel at the top of the right side Panels area (its icon looks like an eye, and it's circled here in red).

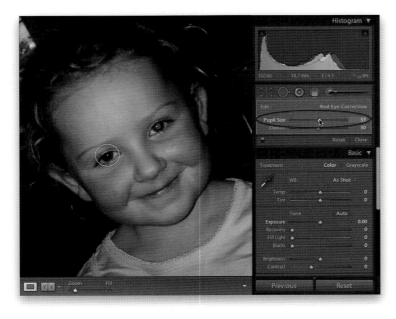

Step Two:
Take the tool and click in the center of one of the red eyes and drag down and to the side to make a selection around the eye (I used the term "selection," but it's not really a selection in the Photoshop sense—it's more a box with crosshairs in it). As soon as you release the mouse button, it removes the red eye. If it doesn't fully remove all the red, you can expand how far out it removes the red by going to the Red Eye Correction tool's options (which appear right below it, once you've released the mouse button), and clicking-and-dragging the Pupil Size slider to the right (shown circled in red here).

Continued

Step Three:

Once that eye looks good, go ahead and put a selection around the other eye (the corrected eye still stays selected, but it's "less selected" than your new eye selection—if that makes any sense at all, and I'm not sure it does). As soon as you click-and-drag out the selection, this eye is fixed too. If the repair makes the eye look too gray, you can make the eye look darker by click-and-dragging the Darken slider to the right (as shown here). The nice thing is that these sliders (Pupil Size and Darken) are live, so as you drag, you see the results right there onscreen—you don't have to drag a slider and then reapply the tool to see how it looks. If you make a mistake and want to start over, just click the Reset button at the bottom right of the tool's options.

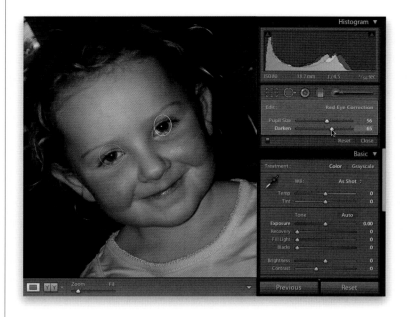

Step Four:

When you've completed your red eye repair, click your cursor back on the Red Eye Correction tool in the toolbox (as shown here) or click the Close button at the bottom right of the options, and Lightroom removes your selections so you can see the final results (seen here). That's pretty much all there is to it.

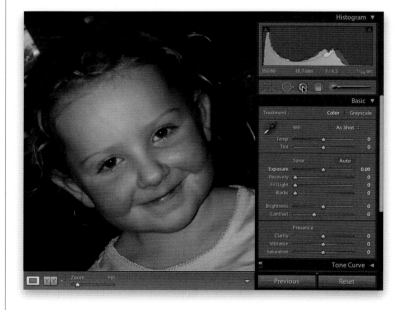

One of the most common digital photography problems is photos where the subject is backlit, so it appears almost as a black silhouette. I think the reason it's so common is because the human eye adjusts for backlit situations so well, that to our naked eye, everything looks great, but the camera exposes much differently and that shot that looked very balanced when you took it, really looks like what you see below. The Fill Light slider, found in the Basic panel, does the best job of fixing this problem of anything I've ever seen, but there is one little thing you need to add.

Fixing Backlit Photos (Using Fill Light)

Step One:
Here's an image, taken out in Nevada's Valley of Fire about 20 minutes before sunset, and while the rocks in the foreground looked pretty well exposed while I was standing there looking at the scene, of course, the camera didn't agree. To prep the photo, I increased the Recovery amount to 100% to tame some of the overly bright sky, and it did a pretty decent job. I also increased the Clarity amount (like I do to almost every photo), and since this is a landscape photo with lots of well-defined edges, I cranked it up a little higher than my usual. Now, on to fixing the problem we came here for.

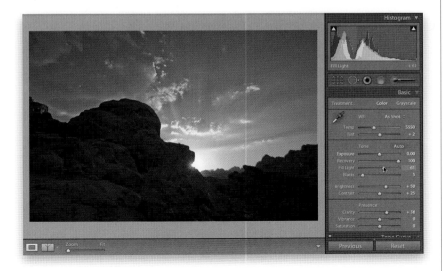

Step Two:
To open up the foreground area, just click-and-drag the Fill Light slider to the right. Unfortunately, in most cases you just can't crank it up to 100, because not only would the photo not looked balanced, but any noise in the image (which is usually the most prevalent in the shadow areas) will get amplified big time, and any noise that was hiding out in the dark shadows won't be hiding anymore. So, just keep an eye out for noise as you drag (here I was able to drag over to 61 before the noise got too bad).

Continued

Step Three:

If you do wind up adjusting the Fill Light slider to something as high as 61 (I like to stay below 40, if possible), then the photo will probably look kind of washed out. The way to fix this is simply to push a little bit of deep shadows into the image by clicking-and-dragging the Blacks slider to the right just a little bit. In most cases, you'll be able to move it just one or two ticks (so, you'll generally move it from its RAW image default setting of 5 to around 6 or 7), but in this case, with such a broad move of the Fill Light slider, I had to drag it all the way to 10 to bring back the saturation and keep the photo from looking washed out.

Step Four:

Here, I used Lightroom's Before/After view (press **Y**) to show what a big difference this technique (using Fill Light, then bringing back the deep shadows by increasing the Blacks slider) can do for our backlit photos.

Sharpening in Lightroom has come a long, long way since Lightroom 1, and now we have professional-level capture sharpening, and specialized output sharpening for print (which is actually covered in the print chapter). Here we're going to look at applying capture sharpening in the Develop module.

Sharpening Your Photos in Lightroom

Step One:
Sharpening is done in the Detail panel of the Develop module, and when you sharpen photos in Lightroom, you really need to be at a 1:1 (100%) view to really see the effects of your sharpening. The problem is when you're zoomed in to one small part of your image, it's hard to see how it's affecting the entire image. That's why, at the top of the Detail panel, there's a separate preview (seen here; if you don't see it, click on the left-facing triangle to the right of Sharpening at the top of the panel), which is there so you can zoom in tight to check the sharpening, but have your image appear at a normal size in the main Preview area.

Step Two:
To have the Detail panel zoom in on an area, just click your cursor on the spot you want to zoom in on. Once you've zoomed in, you can navigate around by clicking-and-dragging inside the preview. Although I use just the default 1:1 zoom, if you want to zoom in even tighter, you can Control-click (PC: Right-click) inside the preview, and choose a 2:1 view from the contextual menu (as shown here). Also, if you click the little icon in the upper-left corner of the panel (shown circled here in red), you can move your cursor over your main image in the center Preview area, and that area will appear zoomed in the Detail panel preview (to keep the preview on that area, just click on the area in the main image). To turn this off, click that icon again.

Continued

Step Three:
The Amount slider does just what you think it would—it controls the amount of sharpening applied to your photo. Here I increased the Amount to 91, and while the photo in the main Preview area doesn't look that much different, the Detail panel's preview looks much sharper (which is why it's so important to use this zoomed in preview). The Radius slider determines how many pixels out from the edge the sharpening will affect, and personally I leave this set at 1.0 (as seen here).

TIP: Toggling Off the Sharpening
If you want to temporarily toggle off the changes you've made in the Detail panel, just click on the little switch on the far left of the Detail panel's header.

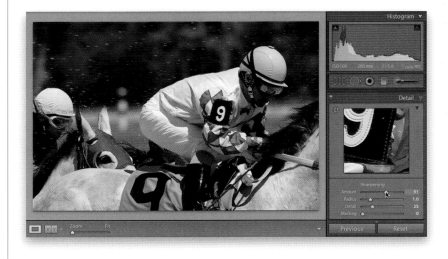

Step Four:
The Detail slider is kind of like a halo prevention control, which helps avoid one of the most negative things about sharpening, which is that if you apply a lot of sharpening, you get little halos around the edges in your image (it looks like somebody traced around the edges of your image with a small marker). So, at its default setting of 25, it's doing quite a bit of halo prevention, which works well for most photos (and is why it's the default setting), but for images that can take a lot of sharpening (like sweeping landscape shots, and architectural images, and images with lots of sharply defined edges), you would raise the Detail slider up to around 75, as shown here (which kind of takes the protection off quite a bit and gives you a more punchy sharpening). If you raise the Detail slider to 100, it makes your sharpening appear very much like the Unsharp Mask filter in Photoshop.

Step Five:

The last sharpening slider, Masking, is to me the most amazing one of all, because what it lets you do is control exactly where the sharpening is applied. For example, some of the toughest things to sharpen are things that are supposed to be soft, like a child's skin, or a woman's skin in a portrait, because sharpening accentuates texture, which is exactly what you don't want. But, at the same time, you need detail areas to be sharp—like their eyes, hair, eyebrows, lips, clothes, etc. Well, this Masking slider lets you do just that—it kind of masks away the skin areas, so it's mostly the detail areas that get sharpened. To show how this works, we're going to open a portrait I took of my in-house super-mega editor Kim Doty, and her adorable little boy Sean.

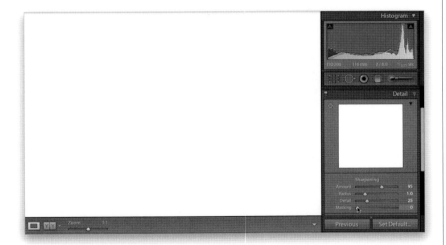

Step Six:

The best way to understand the Masking feature is to see it in action, so first zoom your main image to a 1:1 view (what I'm going to show you won't work unless you're at a 1:1 view in the center Preview area). Then press-and-hold the Option (PC: Alt) key and click-and-hold on the Masking slider, and your image area will turn solid white (as shown here). If it doesn't, it means you're not at a 1:1 view in your main Preview area, so go to the Navigator panel, click on 1:1, then try again. What this solid white screen is telling you is that the sharpening is being applied evenly to every part of the image, so basically, everything's getting sharpened.

Continued

Step Seven:

As you click-and-drag the Masking slider to the right, parts of your photo will start to turn black, and the black areas are not getting sharpened, which is our goal. Now, at first, you'll see little speckles of black area, but the farther you drag that slider, the more non-edge areas will become black—as seen here, where I've dragged the Masking slider over to 79, which pretty much has the skin in black (so it's not being sharpened), but the detail edge areas, like their eyes, lips, hair, nostrils, and outline, are being fully sharpened (which are the areas still appearing in white). So, in reality, those soft skin areas are being automatically masked away for you, which is really pretty darn slick if you ask me.

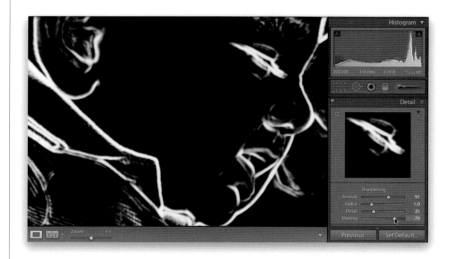

Step Eight:

When you release the Option (PC: Alt) key, you see the effects of the sharpening, and here you can see little Sean's detail areas are nice and crisp, but it's as if his skin was never sharpened. Now, just a reminder: I only use this Masking slider when the subject is supposed to be of a softer nature, where we don't want to exaggerate texture. Okay, on the next page, we're going to switch back to the horse racing photo and finish up our sharpening there.

Step Nine:

Here, I reopened the horse racing photo and, at this point, you know what all four sliders do, so now it's down to you coming up with the settings you like. But if you're not comfortable with that quite yet, then take advantage of the excellent sharpening presets that are found in the Presets panel in the left side Panels area. If you look under the Lightroom Presets (the built-in ones), you'll find two sharpening presets: one called Sharpen - Landscapes and one called Sharpen - Portraits. Clicking the Landscapes preset sets your Amount at 40, Radius at 0.8, Detail at 50, and Masking at 0 (see how it raised the detail level because the subject matter can take punchier sharpening?). The Portraits one is much more subtle—it sets your Amount at 35, Radius at 1.2, Detail at 20, and Masking at 70.

Step 10:

Here's the final before/after image. I started by clicking on the Sharpen - Landscapes preset, then I increased the Amount to 125 (which is more than I usually use, but I pumped it up so you could see the results more easily here in the book). I set the Radius at 1.0 (which is pretty standard for me), the Detail at 75 (because a detailed photo like this can really take that punchy sharpening), and I left the Masking at 0 (because I want all the areas of the photo sharpened evenly—there are no areas that I want to remain soft and unsharpened). Now, at this point I'd save this setting as my own personal "Sharpen - High" preset, so it's always just one click away.

Fixing Chromatic Aberrations (a.k.a. That Annoying Color Fringe)

Sooner or later, you're going to run into a situation where some of the more contrasty edges around your subject have either a red, green, or more likely, a purple color halo or fringe around them (these are known as "chromatic aberrations"). You'll find these sooner (probably later today, in fact), if you have a really cheap digital camera (or a nice camera with a really cheap wide-angle lens), but even good cameras (and good lenses) can fall prey to this problem now and again. Luckily, it's easy enough to fix in Lightroom.

Step One:

Here's a photo taken with an inexpensive, older, 4-megapixel, point-and-shoot camera. If you look closely, it appears as if someone has traced around the edges with a very thin red magic marker (it looks like a thin reddish fringe around the rocks). If you suspect this is happening to one of your images, first go to the Details panel and use the preview at the top of the panel to zoom in on an edge area that has that color fringe (here I zoomed in to 2:1, because it's such a low-resolution photo), so you can clearly see how your adjustments affect the edge.

Step Two:

Once you've identified which color the fringe is (it's red, in this case), go to the Chromatic Aberration section of the Detail panel and you'll see two sliders—one named Red/Cyan and one named Blue/Yellow. In our case, since our problem is red, click-and-drag the Red/Cyan slider to the right, away from red, until the fringe is gone (of course, if the fringe was blue or yellow, you'd use the next slider down and click-and-drag away from the problem color). That being said, the few times I've had to adjust for this problem, I now just use the Defringe pop-up menu, where I choose All Edges, which usually removes that edge fringe without having to move any sliders. You can see in the zoomed-in preview, it greatly reduced the red fringing on the edges.

One of the most-asked questions I get is, "Is there any way to make my RAW images in Lightroom look like the nice, rich, colorful preview I saw on the LCD on the back of my digital camera?" The reason they looked so different is that the image on your LCD is a "processed" JPEG preview image that has been color enhanced with your camera's built-in software. However, the RAW file doesn't have any of that processing—it's totally untouched, so it's up to you to do the processing. Here's how to get closer to that JPEG-processed look for your RAW images:

Using Camera Profiles to Match the Look of the Image on Your LCD

Step One:
At the time I'm writing this, these camera profiles are so new that Adobe hasn't "officially" released them yet, but is allowing you to test them out (in other words, they're Beta versions), so you have to go to the Adobe Labs site (the link is in the next step), download these free camera profiles, and then install them in Lightroom (the installer window is shown here). However, once Adobe has gotten enough feedback from photographers on how they like the individual profiles, and they've tweaked them based on that feedback, these profiles will wind up already pre-installed in Lightroom, so you'll be able to skip Step One.

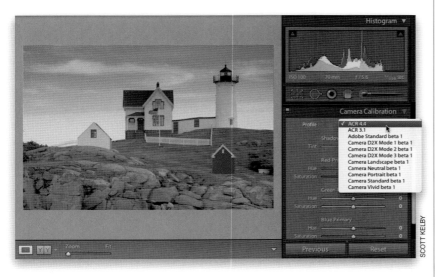

Step Two:
The way to know if these profiles are installed is to first click on a RAW photo, and then go to the Develop module. In the right side Panels area, go down to the Camera Calibration panel and, from the profile pop-up menu at the top, click on ACR 4.4, and if a menu pops up with a list of profiles for the camera you took the shot with (something like the one shown here), then they're already installed. If not, then you'll have to go to http://labs.adobe.com/wiki/index.php/DNG_Profiles to download the free Beta profiles.

Continued

Step Three:

Adobe recommends that you start by choosing the Adobe Standard Beta 1 profile (of course, once it's out of beta testing, it will just be called Adobe Standard), but if you have a Nikon or Canon dSLR camera, Adobe also included "camera matching" profiles, which are designed to replicate the different color shooting modes that are available in your camera (Lightroom knows which camera you took the shot with by reading the EXIF metadata). There are five camera-matching profiles for Canon dSLRs and eight for Nikon dSLRs, as you can see here, starting with Nikon D2X Mode 1 Beta 1. (By the way, if you don't shoot Canon or Nikon, then you'll only have Adobe Standard to choose from, but you can create your own custom profiles using Adobe's free DNG Profile Editor, also available from that download page at Adobe Labs.)

Note: At this point, for all the Nikon cameras, it shows the profile name as D2X, even if it wasn't taken with a D2X, so don't let that freak you out.

Step Four:

Here's a Before/After with only one thing done to this photo: I chose Camera Landscape Beta 1 (as shown in the pop-up menu in Step Three). It's almost like poppin' a roll of Velvia in the camera, isn't it? (Sorry, old film-days joke.) So, that's the scoop: if you bought this book as soon as it rolled off the press, you'll have to download the free profiles from Adobe Labs, but I think you can see, it's worth the two minutes of extra work. Now, if you bought this book a while after Lightroom 2 shipped, then make sure you check that pop-up menu first, because chances are they're already there.

Some cameras seem to put their own color signature on your photos, and if yours is one of those, you might notice that all your photos seem a little red, or have a slight green tint in the shadows, etc. Even if your camera produces accurate color, you still might want to tweak how Lightroom interprets the color of your RAW images. The process for doing a full, accurate camera calibration is kinda complex and well beyond the scope of this book, but I did want to show you what the Camera Calibration panel is used for, and give you a resource to take things to the next level.

Basic Camera Calibration in Lightroom

Step One:
Before we start, I don't want you to think that camera calibration is something everybody must do. In fact, I imagine most people will never even try a basic calibration, because they don't notice a big enough consistent color problem to worry about it (and that's a good thing. However, in every crowd there's always one, right?). So, here's a quick tutorial on the very basics of how the Camera Calibration panel works: Open a photo, then go to the Develop module's Camera Calibration panel, found at the very bottom of the right side Panels area, as shown here (see, if Adobe thought you'd use this a lot, it would be near the top, right?).

Step Two:
The topmost slider is for adjusting any tint that your camera might be adding to the shadow areas of your photos. If it did add a tint, it's normally green or magenta—look at the color bar that appears inside the Tint slider itself. By looking at the color bar, you'll know which way to drag (for example, here I'm dragging the Tint slider away from green, toward magenta, to reduce any greenish color cast in the shadow areas).

Continued

Step Three:

If your color problems don't seem to be in the shadows, then you'll use the Red, Green, and Blue Primary sliders to adjust the Hue and Saturation (the sliders that appear below each color). Let's say your camera produces photos that have a bit of a red cast to them. You'd drag the Red Primary Hue slider away from red, and if you needed to reduce the overall saturation of red in your photo, you'd drag the Red Primary Saturation slider to the left until the color looked neutral (by neutral, I mean the grays should look really gray, not reddish gray).

Step Four:

When you're happy with your changes, press **Command-Shift-N (PC: Ctrl-Shift-N)** to bring up the New Develop Preset dialog. Name your preset, click the Check None button, then turn on only the Calibration checkbox, and click Create. Now, not only can you apply this preset in the Develop module and Quick Develop panel, you can have it applied to all the photos you import from that camera by choosing it from the Develop Settings pop-up menu in the Import Photos dialog (also shown here).

Note: If you want to tackle the full camera calibration process, I recommend this online article by Eric Chan (http://people .csail.mit.edu/ericchan/dp/acr/). Although this article is for calibration with Adobe Camera Raw (ACR), not only are the Lightroom controls the same, but many users are recommending that you do your camera calibration in ACR (because you can download a free script that will do it for you), then copying those settings into Lightroom's Camera Calibration panel.

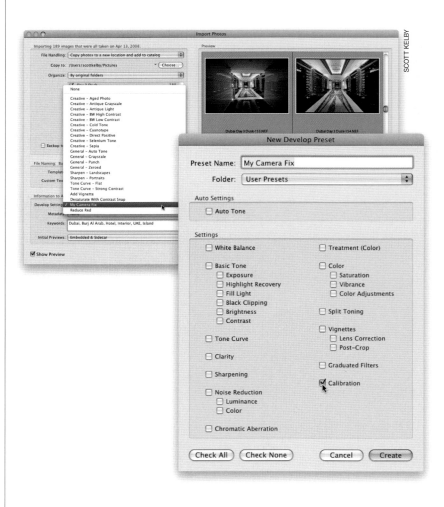

Lightroom Quick Tips > >

▼ Using the Detail Panel's Preview for Cleaning Up Spots

The Detail panel's preview was designed to give you a 100% (1:1) view of your image, so you can really see the effects of your sharpening and Clarity adjustments. But it's also great to keep it open when you're removing spots, because you leave the main image at Fit in Window size, and still see the area you're fixing up close in the Detail panel's preview.

▼ Better Noise Reduction Strategy

The Noise Reduction section, in the Detail panel, in Lightroom does an okay job, but honestly, for any serious noise issues, I jump over to Photoshop and use a plug-in I bought called Noiseware Professional, which does just an amazing job. Although, at this point, there's not a plug-in version available to use right inside Lightroom 2, I bet it won't be long before it, or something like it, will be. So, in the meantime, you can download a trial copy from their website at www.noiseware.com and install it in Photoshop (so, jump from Lightroom to Photoshop, run the Noiseware plug-in using their excellent built-in presets, and then save the file to come back into Lightroom).

▼ Undos That Last Forever

If you use Photoshop, you probably already know that the History panel there just keeps track of your last 20 steps (so, you basically have 20 undos), and if you close the document, those undos go away. However, in Lightroom, every single change you make to your photo inside Lightroom is tracked and

when you change images, or close Lightroom, your unlimited undos are saved. So even if you come back to that photo a year later, you'll always be able to undo what you did.

▼ What to Do If You Can't See Your Adjustment Brush

If you start painting and can't see the brush or the pins it creates, go under the View menu, under Tool Overlay, and choose Auto Show. That way, the pins disappear when you move the cursor outside your photo, but then if you move your cursor back over it again to start painting, they reappear.

▼ You Can Always Start Over— Even with Virtual Copies

Since none of your edits in Lightroom are applied to the real photo, until you actually leave Lightroom 2 (by jumping over to Photoshop, or exporting as a JPEG or TIFF), you can always start over by pressing the Reset button at the bottom of the right side Panels area. Better yet, if you've been working on a photo and make a virtual copy, you can even reset the virtual copy to how the image looked when you first brought it into Lightroom.

▼ Choosing Brush Size

You can press-and-hold the Command (PC: Ctrl) key and click-and-drag out a selection around your spot (start by clicking just to the upper left of the spot, and drag across the spot at a 45° angle). As you do, it lays down a starting point and then your circle drags right over the spot.

Exporting Images
saving JPEGs, TIFFs, and more

When Lightroom first came out, I did a one-day Lightroom Live! seminar tour that went to major cities across the U.S., and on that tour I heard the same question again and again, "How do I save an image as a JPEG? There's no Save or Save As under the File menu." Do you know why? It's simple. That's too easy. You see, every program has Save under its File menu, and if Adobe used a common name like that, one understood by everyone that uses a computer, and then put it in such an obvious place as the File menu, then everyone would know what to do, and then where would that leave me? That's right—out of a job. That's why I don't complain when Adobe calls something we're all used to, like "saving" files, something else (like "exporting"). Now, is exporting what you're doing? Absolutely.

But does anyone you know, who has ever had a date in their life, used the term "export" when you asked them how to save a file? Of course not. Try it out for yourself. Go up to a reasonably attractive friend or co-worker that uses any other program on earth besides Lightroom, and ask them, "What would I choose if I wanted to save a file?" They'll look at you like you just fell off the pumpkin truck and say, "Save. Duh!" (Although, maybe it's just my son that adds "Duh!" to the end of every answer to any question I pose.) So, why doesn't Adobe use the word "Save" in Lightroom (like they do in Photoshop)? It's because of a binding deal we made years ago, and under the terms of that agreement, they can't use easily understood terms until I've paid for both my kids' college educations.

Saving Your Photos as JPEGs

Since there is no Save command for Photoshop Lightroom (like there is in Photoshop), one of the questions I get asked most is, "How do you save a photo as a JPEG?" Well, in Lightroom, you don't save it as a JPEG, you export it as a JPEG (or a TIFF, or a DNG, or a Photoshop PSD). It's a simple process, and Lightroom has added some automation features that can kick in once your photo is exported.

Step One:
You start by selecting which photo(s) you want to export as a JPEG (or a TIFF, PSD, or DNG). You can do this in either the Library module's Grid view or down in the filmstrip in any other module by Command-clicking (PC: Ctrl-clicking) on all the photos you want to export (as shown here).

Step Two:
If you're in the Library module, click on the Export button at the bottom of the left side Panels area (circled here in red). If you're in a different module and using the filmstrip to select your photos for export, then use the keyboard shortcut **Command-Shift-E (PC: Ctrl-Shift-E)**. Whichever method you choose, it brings up the Export dialog (shown in the next step).

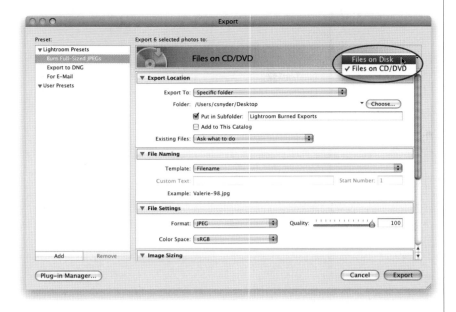

Step Three:

Along the left side of the Export dialog is the Preset section. The Lightroom Presets are the ones put there by Adobe, and then any presets you create will appear under User Presets. Click on Burn Full-Sized JPEGs as a starting point, and it fills in some typical settings someone might use to export their photos as JPEGs and burn them to a disc. However, we're using this as just a starting place, and we'll customize these settings so our files are exported where and how we want them (then we'll save our custom settings as a preset, so we don't have to go through all this every time). If, instead of burning these images to disc, you just want to save these JPEGs in a folder on your computer, then click-and-hold on the up/down triangles on the far right of where it says Files on CD/DVD at the top, and from the pop-up menu that appears (it's circled here in red), choose Files on Disk.

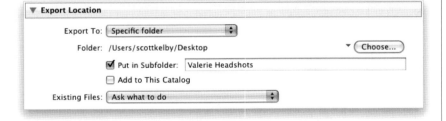

Step Four:

The next section down is Export Location, which is where you tell Lightroom where to save these files. Start by choosing to either put them in a separate folder (as I have here) or add them to the same folder as the originals. I always save mine in a separate folder, so I chose Specific Folder from the Export To pop-up menu (as shown here). If you want to save them in a separate folder, then you have to click the Choose button and locate that folder (just so I have quick access to these exported photos, I usually save them to my desktop, turn on the checkbox for Put in Subfolder, and name that folder, so they stay organized in one place, rather than scattered all over my desktop). If you want these exported JPEGs added to your Lightroom catalog, turn on that checkbox.

Continued

Step Five:

The next section down, File Naming, is pretty much like the file naming feature you already learned about back in the Importing chapter. If you don't want to rename the files you're exporting, and just want to keep their current names, then choose Filename from the Template pop-up menu and move on. If you do want to rename the files, choose one of the built-in templates, or if you created a custom file naming template (which we learned how to do back in Chapter 1), it will appear in this list to choose, too. In our example, I chose Custom Name – Sequence (which automatically adds a sequential number, starting at 1, to the end of my custom name). Then, I simply named these shots "Valerie Proofs," so the photos will wind up being named Valerie Proofs-1, Valerie Proofs-2, and so on.

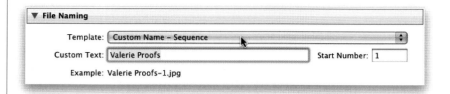

Step Six:

Under File Settings, you choose which file format to save your photos in from the Format pop-up menu (since we chose the Burn Full-Sized JPEGs preset, JPEG is already chosen here, but you could choose TIFF, PSD, DNG, or if you have RAW files, you could choose Original to export RAW). Since we're saving as a JPEG, there's a Quality slider (the higher the quality, the larger the file size), and I generally choose a Quality setting of 80, which I think gives a good balance between quality and file size. If I'm sending these files to someone without Photoshop, I choose sRGB as my color space. If you chose a PSD, TIFF, or DNG format, their options will appear (you get to choose things like the color space, bit depth, and compression settings). As for Image Sizing, by default, it exports at its current size and resolution, but if you wanted it smaller, you'd turn on the Resize to Fit checkbox, then enter the dimensions you want the exported files to be.

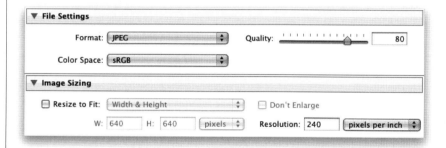

Step Seven:

If these are final images (to be printed or posted in a Web gallery, etc.), you can add sharpening by turning on the Sharpen For checkbox in the Output Sharpening section. This applies the proper sharpening based on whether the exported photos will be displayed onscreen (in which case, choose Screen) or printed (in which case, you'll choose the type of paper they'll be printed on—glossy or matte), and the amount of sharpening you want applied (as shown here). For inkjet printing, I usually choose High, which onscreen looks like it's too much sharpening, but on paper it looks just right (for the Web, I choose Standard). In the Metadata section, turn on the Minimize Embedded Metadata checkbox to remove all your personal EXIF camera data from the files, while keeping your copyright info. If you choose this, the option to write any keywords embedded in these photos to Lightroom's hierarchy is grayed out, and if you turn on the Add Copyright Watermark checkbox, it puts a visible watermark over your photo using the copyright info you added when you imported these photos into Lightroom in the first place.

Step Eight:

The final section, Post-Processing, is where you decide what happens after the files are exported. If you choose Do Nothing, they just get saved into that folder. If you choose Open in Adobe Photoshop CS3, they'll automatically be opened in Photoshop after they're exported. You can also choose to open them in another application (gasp). The Go to Export Actions Folder Now is covered later in this chapter (under emailing from Lightroom).

Continued

Step Nine:

Before you hit that Export button, this would be the perfect time to save these settings as your own custom preset, so you don't have to go through these steps each time you want to save a JPEG or two to your computer. Now, there are some changes I would suggest that would make your preset more effective. For example, if you saved this right now as a preset, when you apply it, all future JPEG exports will go into a folder named Valerie Headshots. Instead, turn off the Put in Subfolder checkbox and go and create a folder on your desktop. Name it something like JPEGs from Lightroom, then click the Choose button, find that JPEGs from Light-room folder, and choose it as your specific export folder. Also, since you'll be saving all your JPEGs into this folder, choose to have Lightroom ask you what you want to do if it encounters other files, still sitting in this folder from a previous export, with the same name as one or more of the files that you're exporting now (from the Existing Files pop-up menu, shown here).

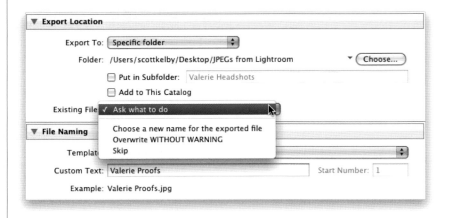

Step 10:

You also might want to consider not nam-ing all these files Valerie Proofs (hey, it's just a suggestion), because before long, you'll have thousands of Valerie Proofs, yet a surprisingly small number of these files will actually be shots of Valerie. So, I leave the Template pop-up menu set to Filename, so it uses the file's existing name (as seen here). Now, to save these updated settings as a preset, click the Add button at the bottom of the Preset section (as shown here), and a New Preset naming dialog appears, where you can name your preset, and then click the Create button.

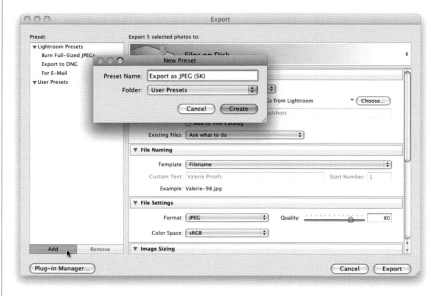

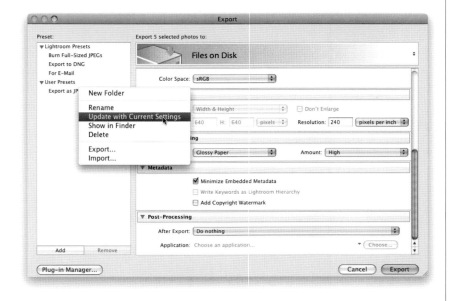

Step 11:

Once you click the Create button, your preset is added to the Preset section under User Presets, and from now on you're just one click away from exporting JPEGs your way. If you decide you want to make a change to your preset (as I did in this case, where I turned off the Add Copyright Watermark checkbox), you can update it with your current settings by Control-clicking (PC: Right-clicking) on your preset, and from the contextual menu that appears, choosing Update with Current Settings (as shown here). Now, while you're here, you might want to create a second custom preset that's a modified version of this preset—one for exporting JPEGs for use in online Web galleries. To do that, you might lower the Image Sizing Resolution setting to 72 ppi, change your sharpening to Screen, set Amount to Standard, and you might want to turn the Add Copyright Watermark checkbox back on to help prevent misuse of your images. Then you'd click the Add button to create a new preset named something like "Export JPEG for Web."

Step 12:

Once you've created your own presets, you can save time and skip the whole Export dialog thing altogether by just selecting the photos you want to export, then going under Lightroom's File menu, under Export with Preset, and choosing the export preset you want (in this example, I'm choosing the Export JPEG for Web preset we just created). When you choose it this way, it just goes and exports the photos with no further input from you. Sweet!

Emailing Photos from Lightroom

Lightroom does have an export to email feature, but it only processes your photos as small-sized JPEGs so they're easier for emailing, and sticks them in a folder. However, if you take just a minute to tweak this feature, it can do so much more. In fact, it can process the photos as JPEGs for emailing, then launch your email application, and attach your photos to the email—all automatically. Then you're really emailing from Lightroom, not just getting a folder full of small JPEGs. Here's how to set it up (luckily, it's surprisingly easy):

Step One:

The key to getting the full automation I just mentioned in the introduction to this tutorial is to create what's called an Export action, which is basically telling Lightroom what to do after it exports the photos as small JPEGs. In our case, we're going to ask Lightroom to launch our default email application and attach our photos. You set this up in two places: (1) in the Export dialog, and (2) on your computer itself (don't worry—it's easy). Start by going to the File menu and choosing Export (as shown here), or press **Command-Shift-E (PC: Ctrl-Shift-E)**.

Step Two:

When the Export dialog appears, first click on the For E-Mail preset (under the Lightroom Presets in the Preset section on the left) to see some of the basic email settings. Then scroll to the bottom of the dialog to the Post-Processing section, and from the After Export pop-up menu, choose Go to Export Actions Folder Now (as shown here).

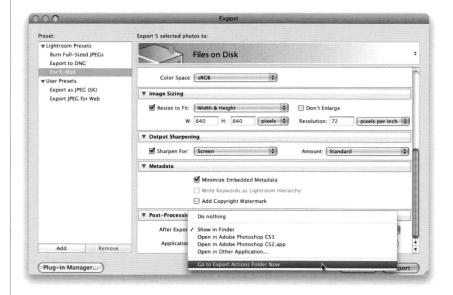

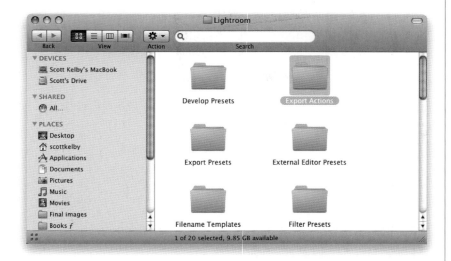

Step Three:
This brings up the folder on your computer where Lightroom's Export actions are stored (as shown here).

Step Four:
Leave that window with your Export Actions folder open, and in another window, go to the folder on your computer where your applications are stored (on a Mac, it's your Applications folder; on a PC, it's your Program Files folder). Find your email application, and what you're going to do next is create an alias (on a Mac) or a shortcut (on a PC) to that application (basically, these are pointer icons that point to the real application). To create an alias on a Mac, you'd Control-click on your email application icon, and from the contextual menu that appears, choose Make Alias (as shown here). Your alias icon will appear right beside your real email application's icon and it will have the word "alias" added to the name. On a PC, to create a shortcut, you'd Right-click on your email application icon and choose Create Shortcut from the contextual menu. Your shortcut will appear in the same folder and will have "Shortcut" added to the name.

Continued

Step Five:

Now, click-and-drag that alias (or shortcut) into Lightroom's Export Actions folder, then open that folder, and you should see your alias (as shown here). The name of this alias is what you're going to see in the After Export pop-up menu in the Export dialog, so I usually rename my alias (in this case, I renamed it "Email Photo"). Next, you're going to create a custom export preset that processes your photos as small JPEGs, then launches your email program, and attaches these smaller JPEG photos automatically (it's easier than it sounds, especially since you've done all the hard parts of this process already).

Step Six:

Now, go back to the Export dialog. When you clicked on For E-mail, in the Preset section on the left, under Lightroom Presets, it loaded some settings that work well for emailing photos (it chose a lower-quality setting, the right color space [sRGB], the proper resolution, size, etc., for emailing photos), however you can override any of these if you like (if you want a higher quality, just click-and-drag the Quality slider to the right in the File Settings section). Next, go to the Post-Processing section at the bottom, and from the After Export pop-up menu, choose Email Photo, the Export action we just created, as shown here. Lastly, you want to save all this as a preset, so click the Add button at the bottom left of the Preset section. When the New Preset dialog appears, give your preset a name (I chose "Send in Email") and click the Create button. Now, click Cancel in the Export dialog, because we only came here to create a preset, and we did, and it's saved.

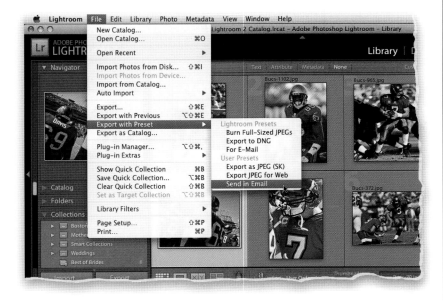

Step Seven:

Now, if you're using a PC, this will only work with Microsoft's Outlook, not with Outlook Express or Windows Mail, and there's a script you'll have to download to get this to work. So go to www.light-roomextra.com, click on the Download button at the top, then click on the Show Me button next to Other Goodies at the bottom. Download the file labeled MAPI Mailer, and install it on your PC. Make sure you read the entire Read Me file, and follow its instructions. Now let's try it out: In Lightroom, Command-click (PC: Ctrl-click) on the photos you want to send in an email to select them. Once they're selected, go under the File menu, under Export with Preset, and choose Send in Email, as shown here (that's the Export preset you created in the previous step).

Step Eight:

Lightroom takes it from there, and the next thing you'll see onscreen is a new email message window open, with all your selected photos resized and attached to the email. All you have to do now is enter the email address of the person you want to send this to, add a subject line, and hit Send. Now that you've created this Export preset, and its email Export action, the whole process will be just two steps: select the photos, and choose Send in Email. See, it was worth that little extra effort this one time to set up such an effortless Lightroom emailing system.

SCOTT KELBY

Using Export Plug-Ins (Auto-Uploading to Flickr)

Back in Lightroom version 1.3, Adobe added the ability for people to create Export plug-ins, which would enable you to process your images in Lightroom and then upload them directly to online galleries like Flickr.com (among others). In Lightroom 2, Adobe made the process of installing and managing these plug-ins much easier with the introduction of a built-in Plug-in Manager. Here's how to install one of the many free downloadable Export plug-ins written for Lightroom:

Step One:

For our project, we're going to use the excellent Flickr Export plug-in created by Jeffrey Friedl (who makes this Export plug-in available for free download at: http://regex.info/blog/photo-tech/lightroom-flickr/). So, the first step is to download Jeffrey's free Export plug-in. Next, go under Lightroom's File menu and choose Plug-in Manager to bring up the dialog you see here. To add a plug-in, click the Add button at the bottom of the section on the left (shown circled in red here). This brings up the Add Lightroom Plug-In dialog, where you navigate to the Export plug-in you downloaded. (*Note:* On a PC, you'll have to unzip the download file first.)

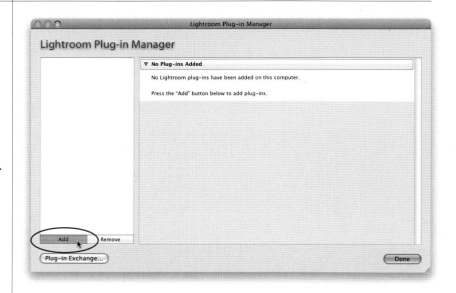

Step Two:

Once you've found that plug-in you downloaded, click the Add Plug-in button and the plug-in is installed and added to your list of plug-ins in the section on the left side of the Lightroom Plug-in Manager (as seen here, where we've only installed this one plug-in). If you click on a plug-in in this left section, the details of that plug-in appear in the main part of the dialog (as seen here), and if you want to temporarily disable this plug-in, just click the Disable button in the Status section. To delete an installed plug-in, just click on it, then click the Remove button at the bottom of the left section. When you're done working in the Plug-in Manager, click the Done button.

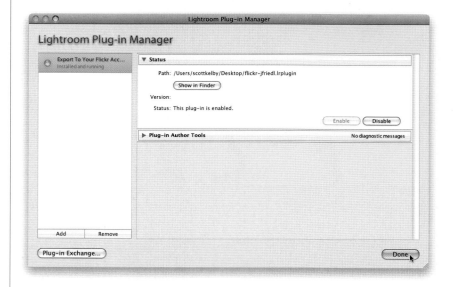

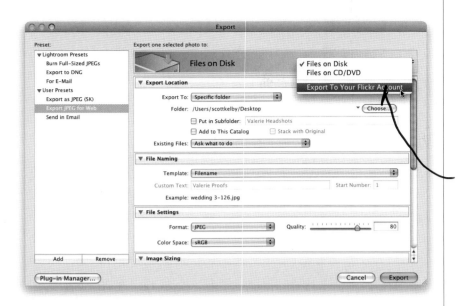

Step Three:

Now go to the Library module in Lightroom, select the photos you want to upload to your Flickr account, then press **Command-Shift-E (PC: Ctrl-Shift-E)** to bring up Lightroom's Export dialog (seen here). First, click on that custom Export preset we created earlier called Export JPEG for Web (if you didn't actually create that custom preset, you can choose Burn Full-Sized JPEGs instead). Once you click on that preset, click-and-hold on the two little triangles in the top-right corner of the Export dialog, and from the pop-up menu, choose Export To Your Flickr Account, as shown here.

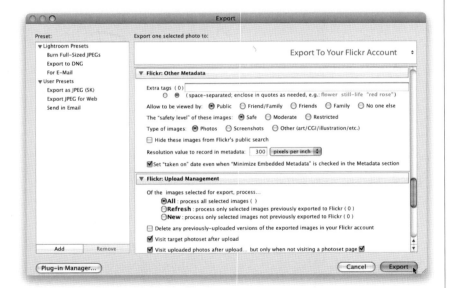

Step Four:

Choosing that from the pop-up menu, adds all the Flickr info to your Export dialog, and if you scroll down you'll see all the Flickr info fields (as shown here). When you're done, click the Export button and your images are processed as JPEGs and uploaded to your Flickr account. This probably goes without saying, but of course to do all this, you actually have to have set up a Flickr account at Flickr .com, and you have to be connected to the Internet. (Of course, if that really went without saying, I wouldn't have just said it, eh?)

Exporting Your Original RAW Photo

So far, everything we've done in this chapter is based on us tweaking our photo in Lightroom and then exporting it as a JPEG, TIFF, etc. But what if you want to export the original RAW photo? Here's how it's done, and you'll have the option of including the keywords and metadata you added in Lightroom—or not.

Step One:

First, click on the RAW photo you want to export from Lightroom. When you export an original RAW photo, the changes you applied to it in Lightroom (including keywords, metadata, and even changes you made in the Develop module, like white balance, exposure, etc.) are saved to a separate file called an XMP sidecar file, since you can't embed metadata directly into the RAW file itself (we talked about this earlier in the sorting chapter), so you need to treat the RAW file and its XMP sidecar file as a team. Now press **Command-Shift-E (PC: Ctrl-Shift-E)** to bring up the Export dialog (shown here). Click on Burn Full-Sized JPEGs just to get some basic settings in place. From the pop-up menu up in the top right, change Files on CD/DVD to Files on Disk, like we did when creating the Export as JPEG preset. Then, in the Export Location section, choose where you want this original RAW file saved to (I chose my desktop), and then in the File Settings section, under Format, choose Original (shown circled here in red). When you choose to export the original RAW file, most of the rest of your choices are pretty much grayed out.

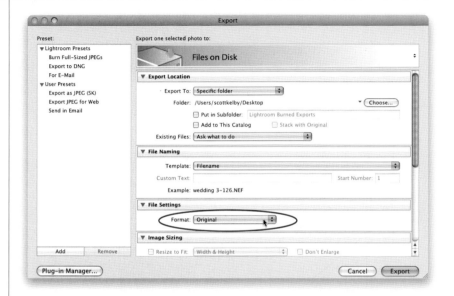

Here's the cropped, black-and-white conversion, when you include the XMP sidecar file

Step Two:

Now click Export, and since there's no processing to be done, in just a few seconds your file appears on your desktop (or wherever you chose to save it)—you'll see your file and its XMP sidecar (with the same exact name, but XMP as its file extension) right nearby (as seen here, on my desktop). As long as these two stay together, other programs that support XMP sidecar files (like Adobe Bridge and Adobe Camera Raw, for example) will use that metadata, so your photo will have all the changes you applied to it. If you send this file to someone (or burn it to disc), make sure you include both files. If you decide you want the file to *not* include your edits, just don't include the XMP file with it. (*Note:* If you converted your RAW file to DNG, there's no XMP sidecar necessary, and the metadata and edits are embedded right into the DNG file).

Step Three:

Once you've exported the original RAW file and sent it to someone, if they double-click on it, it will open in Photoshop's Camera Raw, and if you provided the XMP file, they'll see all the edits you made in Lightroom, as seen in the top image shown here, where the photo was converted to black and white, cropped, and had the tone adjusted. The bottom image shown here is what the photo looks like in Camera Raw when you don't include the XMP file—it's the untouched original file with none of the changes you made in Lightroom (so it's back to the uncropped color original.

Here's the uncropped original image in color, when you don't include the XMP sidecar file

Lightroom Quick Tips > >

▼ Exporting Your Catalog Shortcut

If, instead of just exporting a photo, you want to export an entire catalog of photos, press-and-hold the Option (PC: Alt) key, and the Export button in the Library changes into the Export Catalog button.

▼ Using Your Last Export Settings

If you want to export some photos and use the same export settings you used the last time, you can skip the whole Export dialog and, instead, just go under the File menu and choose Export with Previous, or use the keyboard shortcut **Command-Option-Shift-E (PC: Ctrl-Alt-Shift-E)**, and it will immediately export the photos with your last used settings.

▼ Using Export Presets Without Going to the Export Dialog

If you've created your own custom Export presets (or you want to use the built-in ones, as is), you can skip the Export dialog by Control-clicking (PC: Right-clicking) on the photo, and from the contextual menu, going under Export, and you'll see both the built-in and custom Export presets listed. Choose one from there, and off it goes.

▼ Sharing Your Export Presets

If you've come up with a really useful Export preset that you'd like to share with co-workers or friends (by the way, if you're sharing Export presets with friends, maybe you need some new friends), you can do that by pressing **Command-Shift-E (PC: Ctrl-Shift-E)** to bring up the Export dialog. Then, in the list of presets on the left side, Control-click (PC: Right-click) on the preset you want to save as a file, then choose Export from the contextual menu. When you give this Export preset to a co-worker, have them choose Import from this same contextual menu.

▼ Getting Your Exported Photos Back Into Lightroom Automatically

One very cool little Export feature Adobe added in Lightroom 2 is the ability to add your exported photos back into your Lightroom catalog (so, if you exported some finished images as JPEGs for a client, you can have them automatically re-imported and put with your other images). To do that, go to the Export dialog, and in the Export Location section up top, turn on the checkbox for Add to This Catalog.

▼ My "Testing Panos" Trick

If you shoot multi-photo panoramas, you know that once they get to Photoshop for stitching, it can take…well… forever (it feels like forever, anyway). And sometimes you wait all this time, see your finished pano, and think, "Ah, that's nothing special." So, if I shot a pano I'm not 100% sure is going to be a keeper, I don't use the direct Merge to Panorama in Photoshop command in Lightroom 2. Instead, I go to the Export dialog and use the For E-mail preset to export the files as small, low-resolution JPEGs, with a low Quality setting. Then, once they're exported, I open them in Photoshop, run the Photomerge feature, and because they're small, low-res files, they stitch together in just a couple of minutes. That way, I can see if it's going to be a good-looking pano (one worth waiting 20 or 30 minutes to stitch at high resolution). If it does look good, that's when I use the Merge to Panorama in Photoshop feature in the Photo menu in the Library and Develop modules, which sends over the full-size, full-resolution, full-quality images. Then I go get a cup of coffee. And maybe a sandwich.

▼ Exporting Directly to a Photo-Sharing Website

In this chapter, we talked about how you can download a free Flickr Export plug-in that allows you to upload images directly from Lightroom to Flickr .com, but these Export plug-ins are now available for most of the major photo-sharing sites (including Smugmug, Picasa Web Albums, and a dozen others).

▼ Installing Export Plug-Ins in Lightroom 2

Although Adobe introduced Export plug-ins back in Lightroom 1.3, they've made the process of installing them much easier in Lightroom 2. Just go under the File menu and choose Plug-in Manager. When the dialog appears, click the Add button below the left column to add your Export plug-in (I told you it was easier).

▼ Making Your Files Look Right on Somebody Else's Computer

I get emails from people all the time who have exported their photos as JPEGs, emailed them to somebody, and when they see them on the other person's machine, they're shocked to find out the photos don't look anything like they did on their computer (they're washed out, dull looking, etc.). It's a color space problem, and that's why I recommend that if you're emailing photos to someone, or that photo is going to be posted on a webpage, make sure you set your color space to sRGB in the File Settings section of the Export dialog.

▼ Yes, You Sharpen Twice

I get asked this question all the time, because, by default, Lightroom adds sharpening to your RAW photos. So, do you sharpen again when you export the photos? Absolutely!

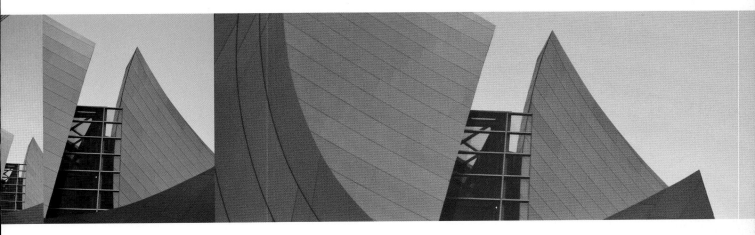

Jumping to Photoshop
how and when to do it

One big thing that Lightroom 2 brings to the table is that, because of the local adjustment tools, you have to use Photoshop much less than before. You still need it. Just not as much. Well, you still need it as much, just not as often (you know what I mean, right?). For example, if your country just launched two or three missiles, and you want to make it look like you really launched a bunch, that would be hard to do in Lightroom, but that would be no problem in Photoshop. So, your workflow would be to start by launching a few missiles—just enough to look kinda scary—then take a photo of them just as they're taking off (using a fast shutter speed). Then, import those photos into Lightroom and adjust the settings for White Balance, Exposure, Blacks, Brightness, etc., and maybe add some Clarity, and increase the Recovery amount to make the smoke from the engines look more dramatic and menacing (after all, nobody wants weenie-looking missile contrails). Then press Command-E (PC: Ctrl-E) to jump over to Photoshop. Now get the Clone Stamp tool, and start cloning as many of those missiles as you think you'll need to look really unstable. Now, be careful when you're cloning, because if the plumes of smoke look exactly the same, everybody will know you "faked it in Photoshop," and your credibility as a missile retoucher will go down the tubes. Ya know, maybe you should just stick to Lightroom.

Choosing How Your Files Are Sent to Photoshop

When you open a selected Photoshop Lightroom image in Photoshop, Lightroom makes a TIFF file, embeds it with the ProPhoto RGB color profile, chooses a bit-depth of 16 bits, and sets the resolution at 240 ppi. However, while those are the defaults, you can choose how you'd like your files sent over to Photoshop—you can choose to send them as PSDs or TIFFs, and you can choose their bit depth (8 or 16 bits) and embedded color profile (ProPhoto RGB, AdobeRGB [1998], or sRGB).

Step One:

Press **Command-, (comma; PC: Ctrl-,)** to bring up Lightroom's preferences, and then click on the External Editing tab up top (as seen here). If you have Photoshop on your computer, it chooses it as your default External Editor, so in the top section, choose the file format you want for photos that get sent over to Photoshop (I set mine to PSD, because the files are much smaller than TIFFs), then from the Color Space pop-up menu, choose your file's color space (Adobe recommends ProPhoto RGB, and if you keep it at that, I'd change your Photoshop color space to ProPhoto RGB, as well—whatever you do choose, just use the same color space in Photoshop so they're consistent). Adobe also recommends choosing a 16-bit depth for the best results (although, I personally use an 8-bit depth most of the time). You also get to choose the resolution (I leave mine set at the default of 240 ppi).

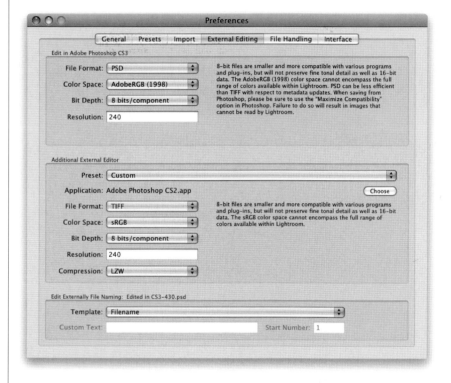

Step Two:

Lastly, in Lightroom 2, you can now choose the name applied to photos sent from Lightroom over to Photoshop. You choose this from the Edit Externally File Naming section at the bottom of the Preferences dialog, and you have pretty much the same naming choices as you do in the regular Import Photos dialog.

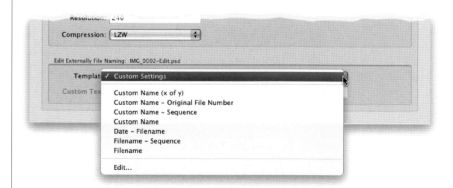

While Lightroom is great for organizing your photos, processing your images, making slide shows, and printing, it's not Photoshop. Lightroom doesn't do special effects or major photo retouching; there are no layers, no filters, or any one of the bazillion (yes, bazillion) things that Photoshop does. So, there will be times during your workflow where you'll need to jump over to Photoshop to do some "Photoshop stuff" and then jump back to Lightroom for printing or presenting. Luckily, these two applications were born to work together.

How to Jump Over to Photoshop, and How to Jump Back

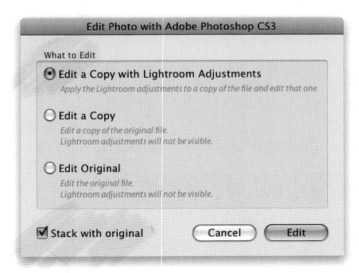

Step One:

If you need to do some things Lightroom can't do, it's time to jump over to Photoshop. For example, in this photo (from the shoot we used earlier in the book for the cropping tutorial in Chapter 4, which you can see in the Navigator panel), we need to remove the blue milk crate from the left side, remove three light stands visible in the shot, and extend the foreground so it fills the frame, plus we need to add some text, add more canvas size, and a couple of other tweaks. So, go under the Photo menu and choose Edit In, and then Edit in Adobe Photoshop (as shown here), or use the keyboard shortcut **Command-E (PC: Ctrl-E)**.

Step Two:

Now, if you're working on a JPEG or TIFF photo, this brings up the Edit Photo with Adobe Photoshop dialog, where you choose (1) to have Lightroom make a copy of your original photo, with all the changes and edits you made in Lightroom applied to the file, before it goes over to Photoshop, (2) to have Lightroom make a copy of your original untouched photo and send that over to Photoshop, or (3) to edit your original photo in Photoshop without any of the changes you've made thus far in Lightroom. If you're working on a RAW photo, you won't get this dialog—your RAW photo will just open in Photoshop.

Continued

Step Three:

Before you click the Edit button, there's a checkbox called Stack with Original, and I recommend leaving this on, because what it does is puts this copy right beside your original file, so it's easy to find later when you're done editing in Photoshop and return to Lightroom. Now, go ahead and click the Edit button, and a copy of your image, with the changes you made in Lightroom (like cropping), opens in Photoshop (as seen here). Also, to help you distinguish this copy from the original, Lightroom by default adds "Edit" to the end of the filename, so you'll know at a glance, once you bring the photo back into Lightroom later (for RAW photos, once you save the photo in Photoshop, "Edit" will appear at the end of the filename, as you see here, where I've saved the file).

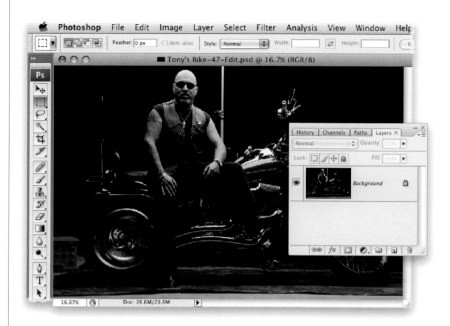

Step Four:

The first thing we're going to tackle is removing the light stand from behind our subject. To keep from accidentally cloning over Tony's arm, we're going to use the Lasso tool (L) to make a selection right down his arm, and then upward, so we enclose the area we want to remove inside a selection (as seen here). Making this selection really helps because you can only paint, or clone, inside the selected area, and since his arm appears outside the selected area, there's no way to accidentally erase or clone over it. Now, get the Clone Stamp tool from Photoshop's Toolbox (or just press S), move to a nearby area without any distractions in the background, press-and-hold the Option (PC: Alt) key, and click once to sample that area (the little crosshair above and to the right of the brush shows the area I sampled from). Now, begin painting (cloning) over the light stand (I used a hard-edged brush here, since I knew there was no danger of spilling onto his arm), and keep cloning until the light stand is gone.

Step Five:

Next, move to the back of the bike, where you'll see one of the light stands holding up the black seamless paper. Put a selection around it, as well, Option-click (PC: Alt-click) to sample a nearby area, then begin cloning the black background area over the stand (as shown here). So, that's the process you'll be doing for anything that appears in the background or foreground. Technically, some of this could have been done in Lightroom, but it would take much longer, and when you got close to the bike frame, or his arm, you'd really have a hard time making Lightroom's tools work. So, while it may be technically possible, it sure ain't easy.

Step Six:

Now, we're going to extend the seamless paper in the foreground by cloning some of the paper on the left over the missing areas at the bottom of the image, and under his foot, and basically all the way across the bottom of the photo. We don't have to worry about making a selection here, because we're cloning right to the bottom of the image, so there's nothing below it to accidentally erase, but this time you'll use a soft-edged brush. You'll do the same type of Option-click-to-sample (PC: Alt-click) routine, but this is going to take you a few minutes, so just be patient, and keep sampling slightly different areas, so you don't pick up a repeating pattern in the floor, which would be a dead giveaway that it has been retouched.

Continued

Step Seven:

Here's the finished image, after about 10 minutes of cloning. I had to sample directly under the bike and use that area to continue the background to the left side of the back tire, because that's where the blue crate was in the original photo, and I also cloned over the light stand on the right. I went for the dramatic lighting look, but I can add a lot more drama to this photo by increasing the room above his head (it's cropped awfully close to his head, but it had to be to get rid of that Octabank right above him, just like the image in the cropping tutorial in Chapter 4), so in the next step we're going to extend the black image area above his head, which as simple as that sounds, is something Lightroom can't do.

Step Eight:

Go under the Image menu and choose Canvas Size. When the Canvas Size dialog appears (shown here), turn on the Relative checkbox (so we can just type in the number of inches we want to add, rather than doing the math to add it to the current height). Then in the Height field, enter 8 inches, so it will add eight inches of height to our photo's size, but the problem is it's going to add four inches to the top, and four inches to the bottom, so go to the Anchor grid and click on the bottom-middle square. That way, the eight inches you're adding will be added above your photo. Lastly, choose Black as your Canvas Extension Color (from the pop-up menu at the bottom of the dialog, as shown here), so the eight inches you add above the photo will be in black.

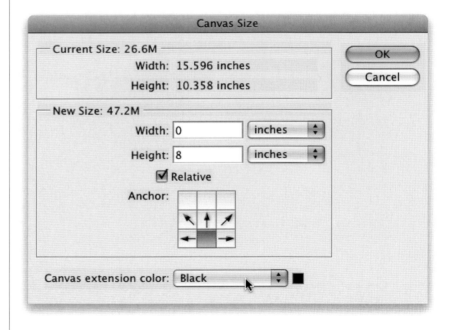

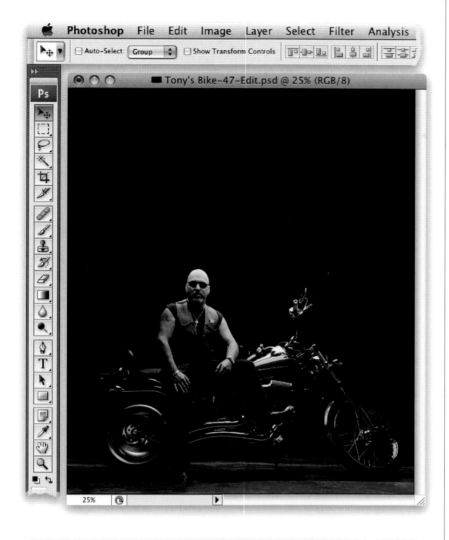

Step Nine:

When you click OK in the Canvas Size dialog, it adds the eight inches above your photo (as seen here), which creates a much more dramatic look to the image. There's only one problem: if you zoom in tight, right above his head, you can see a thin little line where the new eight inches of black you added starts (apparently, the area right over his head wasn't 100% black), so we'll have to fix this in the next step.

Step 10:

To remove this line, you're going to pretty much do what we did earlier—take the Clone Stamp tool **(S)**, Option-click (PC: Alt-click) to sample in a nearby area that doesn't have the line, and clone that area right over the little line separating the two areas. Now the addition of the canvas looks seamless.

Continued

Step 11:

Now, we're going to build a poster border around our image. Again, we could do most of this in Lightroom, but setting the different fonts and font sizes, and adding a scan of my signature, and using font spacing, and well…there's a lot of stuff that would be really tough (or impossible) to do within Lightroom, so that's why we do it here. We start back in the Canvas Size dialog, and we add three inches to the width, three inches to the height, we set our Canvas Extension Color to White, then we make sure our Anchor grid square is in the middle, so it adds the white canvas on all sides, and we click OK. Now we're going back to the Canvas Size dialog one more time, to add another three inches of white canvas space, but this time just to the bottom (as shown here).

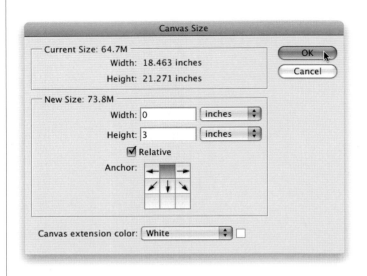

Step 12:

When you've added both of these Canvas Size adjustments, you get the white poster look you see here. Now it's time to add our text and signature. If you have a Wacom tablet and wireless pen, then you can just sign your name right on the image, below the right corner. If not, you'll need to sign a sheet of paper with a dark pen, then scan the signature, bring it into Photoshop, drag-and-drop it onto the image, and position it below the right corner. We have three lines of text we need to add with the Type tool **(T)**. I used the same font for all three lines—Trajan Pro (if you have the Adobe Creative Suite, you already have this font. If not, you can substitute Times Roman). You can add space between the letters by highlighting the text, then pressing-and-holding the **Option (PC: Alt) key**, and pressing the **Right Arrow key** on your keyboard. As you do this, the space between the letters expands, so keep holding those keys down until it looks good to you.

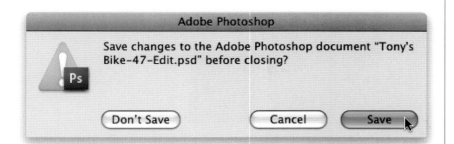

Step 13:

Now it's time to save and close the photo and return to Lightroom (and believe it or not, that's all you have to do to have it automatically return to Lightroom), so just click the Close button (at the top of the image window), then hit the Save button, as shown here. Don't choose Save As from the File menu and rename the file, or you'll "break the chain" and the photo won't go back to Lightroom. Instead, it will just be saved on your computer like any regular Photoshop file. You can actually send the layered file over to Lightroom, and Lightroom will maintain your layers (in other words, it won't flatten the layers), but since there's no layers feature in Lightroom, it treats it like a flattened image. However, if later you decide you want to take that file back to Photoshop, and have access to the layers, that's the one case where you'd click on the edited image in Lightroom, press **Command-E (PC: Ctrl-E)**, then choose Edit Original (or Edit a Copy). That way, it opens with the layers intact.

Step 14:

By the way, if you close the image in Photoshop, but click the Don't Save button, the photo closes without any of the changes you just applied in Photoshop (so when you go back to Lightroom, you'll see the original and an exact copy right beside it). In this case, we clicked the Save button, so when you switch back to Lightroom, it takes you right back to where you last were (in our case, the Develop module), and your Photoshop-edited photo, with all the edits applied, now appears within Lightroom (as seen here).

Continued

Step 15:

Remember when you first jumped over to Photoshop, and you turned on that Stack with Original checkbox in the Edit Photo with Adobe Photoshop dialog? Here's what that does: if you go to the Library module's Grid view to look at your thumbnails, you'll see that your new "Edit" copy is found right beside the original.

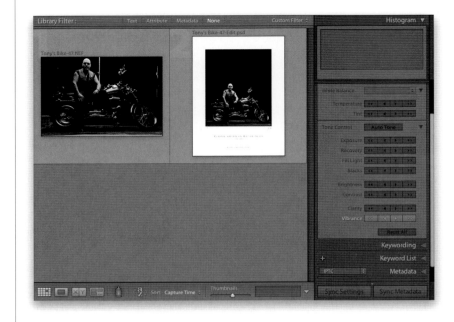

Step 16:

Now that your photo is back in Lightroom, you can treat it like any other image in Lightroom, and in this case, I want Tony and the bike a little brighter and crisper, so I increased the exposure a little bit, then I clicked-and-dragged the Recovery slider to the right quite a bit to tame some of the highlights that looked too bright when I increased the exposure. I also increased the Clarity to 70 to really make the photo look snappier. The final image is shown here. So, just to quickly recap: when you jump over to Photoshop, if it's a RAW photo, Lightroom opens the photo in Photoshop for editing, then creates a copy when you save it. If you have a JPEG or TIFF file and choose to work on the original, then you're doing just that—working on the original in Photoshop—and when you return to Lightroom, you'll see just one photo, because you've edited your original (I don't ever recommend working on the originals).

If there's a "finishing move" you like to do in Photoshop (after you're done tweaking the image in Lightroom), you can add some automation to the process, so once your photos are exported, Photoshop launches, applies your move, and then resaves the file. It's based on you creating an action in Photoshop (an action is a recording of something you've done in Photoshop, and once you've recorded it, Photoshop can repeat that process as many times as you'd like, really, really, fast).

Here's how to create an action, and then hook that directly into Lightroom:

Adding Photoshop Automation to Your Lightroom Workflow

SCOTT KELBY

Step One:
We start this process in Photoshop, so go ahead and press **Command-E (PC: Ctrl-E)** to open a portrait in Photoshop (don't forget, you can follow along with the same photo I'm using here if you like, by downloading it from the site I gave you back in the book's Introduction). What we're going to do here is create a Photoshop action that adds a popular portrait effect from my book, *The Adobe Photoshop CS3 Book for Digital Photographers*, that I called "Trendy High-Contrast Portrait Effect" (you'll recognize the look from dozens of movie posters, celebrity portraits, CD covers, etc.). Because this technique is repetitive (it uses the same steps in the same order every time), it makes it an ideal candidate for turning into an action, which you can apply to a different photo (or group of photos) much faster.

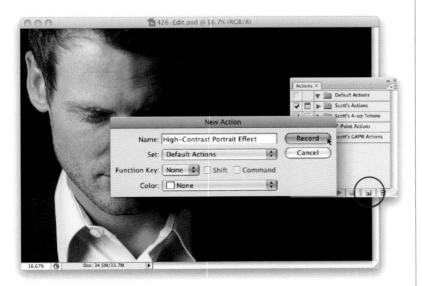

Step Two:
To create an action, go to the Window menu and choose Actions to make the Actions panel visible. Click on the Create New Action icon at the bottom of the panel (it looks just like the Create a New Layer icon in the Layers panel and is circled here). This brings up the New Action dialog (shown here). Go ahead and give your action a name (I named mine "High-Contrast Portrait Effect") and click the Record button (notice the button doesn't say OK or Save, it says Record because it's now recording your steps).

Continued

Step Three:

You're going to duplicate the Background layer twice, so press **Command-J (PC: Ctrl-J)** twice (that's the shortcut for duplicating a layer). Then go to the Layers panel and click on the center layer (as shown here).

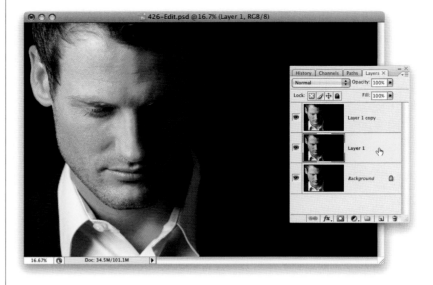

Step Four:

Now we need to remove the color from this layer (making it black and white) by going under the Image menu, under Adjustments, and choosing Desaturate (as shown here). Once the color is gone, go to the Layers panel and lower the Opacity to 80% (shown circled here in red, in the Layers panel).

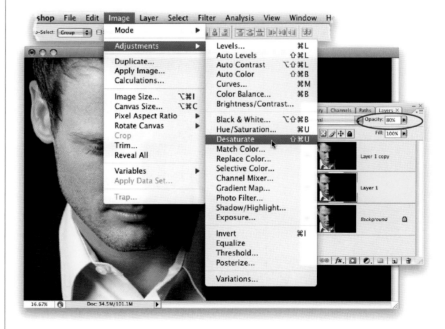

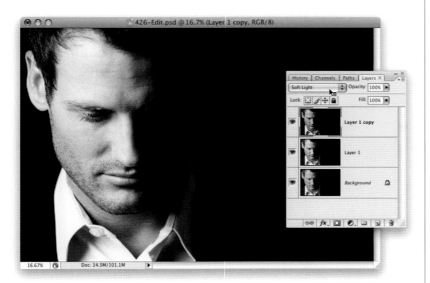

Step Five:

In the Layers panel, click on the top layer, then from the blend mode pop-up menu, near the top left of the panel, choose Soft Light (as shown here). This blends the color photo on this top layer with the grayscale photo below it and the color Background layer below that (the reason it blends a little with the original color Background layer is because we lowered the opacity of that grayscale layer to 80%), which gives us our final look (as seen here). Now, go to the Layers panel's flyout menu (near the top-right corner of the panel) and choose Flatten Image to flatten the layers down to just the Background layer. Next, save the file by pressing **Command-S (PC: Ctrl-S)** and close it by pressing **Command-W (PC: Ctrl-W)**.

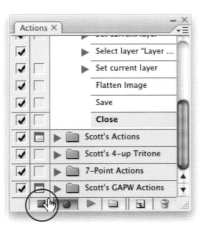

Step Six:

You may have forgotten by now, but we've been recording this process the whole time (remember that action we created a while back? Well, it's been recording our steps all along). So, go back to the Actions panel and click the Stop icon at the bottom left of the panel (as shown here). What you've recorded is an action that will apply the effect, then save the file, and then close that file. Now, I generally like to test my action at this point to make sure I wrote it correctly, so open a different photo, click on the High-Contrast Portrait Effect action in the Actions panel, then click the Play Selection icon at the bottom of the panel. It should apply the effect and close the document.

Continued

Step Seven:

Now we're going to turn that action into what's called a droplet. Here's what a droplet does: If you leave Photoshop and find a photo on your computer, and you drag-and-drop the photo right onto this droplet, the droplet automatically launches Photoshop, opens that photo, and applies that High-Contrast Portrait Effect action to the photo you dropped on there. Then it saves and closes the photo automatically, because you re-corded those two steps as part of the action. Pretty sweet. So, to make a droplet, go under Photoshop's File menu, under Automate, and choose Create Droplet (as shown here).

Step Eight:

This brings up the Create Droplet dialog (shown here). At the top of the dialog, click the Choose button and choose your desktop as the destination for sav-ing your droplet. In the Save dialog that appears, go ahead and name this droplet "Add High-Contrast Portrait Effect," and click Save. Now, under the Play section of this dialog, make sure to choose High-Contrast Portrait Effect (that's what we named our action earlier) from the Action pop-up menu (as shown here). That's it—you can ignore the rest of the dialog, and just click OK.

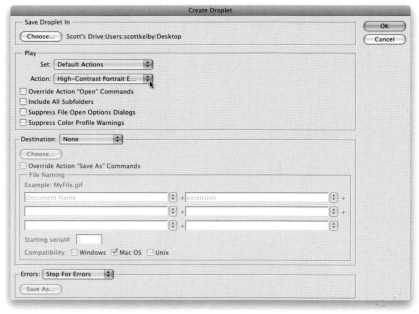

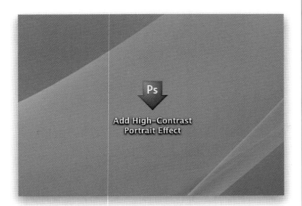

Step Nine:
If you look on your computer's desktop, you'll see an icon that is a large arrow, and the arrow is aiming at the name of the droplet (as shown here).

Step 10:
Now that we've built our Add High-Contrast Portrait Effect droplet in Photoshop, we're going to add that to our Lightroom workflow. Back in Lightroom, go under the File menu and choose Export. When the Export dialog appears, go down to the Post-Processing section, and from the After Export pop-up menu, choose Go to Export Actions Folder Now (as shown here).

Continued

Step 11:

This takes you to the folder on your computer where Lightroom stores Export Actions (and more importantly, where you can store any you create). All you have to do is click-and-drag that Add High-Contrast Portrait Effect droplet right into that Export Actions folder to add it into Lightroom. Now you can close this folder, head back to Lightroom, and click Cancel to close the Export dialog (after all, you only needed it open to get you to that Export Actions folder, so you could drag that droplet in there). Okay, now let's put it to work: In Lightroom's Grid view, select the photo (or photos) you want to have that effect applied to, then press **Command-Shift-E (PC: Ctrl-Shift-E)** to bring back the Export dialog. From the Preset section on the left, click on the right-facing triangle to the left of User Presets, and then click on the Export as JPEG preset we created in Chapter 7. In the Export Location section, click on the Choose button and select the destination folder for your saved JPEG(s) (if you want to change it). Then, in the File Naming section, you can give your photo(s) a new name, if you like. Now, in the Post-Processing section at the bottom, from the After Export pop-up menu, you'll see Add High-Contrast Portrait Effect (your droplet) has been added, so choose it (as shown here). When you click Export, your photo(s) will be saved as a JPEG, then Photoshop will automatically launch, open your photo, apply your High-Contrast Portrait Effect, then save and close the photo. Pretty slick stuff!

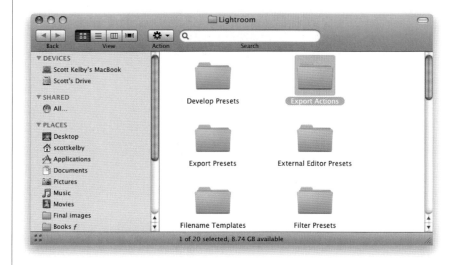

In Lightroom 2, we now have the ability to jump to Photoshop and have a RAW image open as a Smart Object (actually, it would work with JPEGs and TIFFs, too). We can take advantage of the Smart Object feature for "double-processing" a photo, which is where we create two versions of our photo—one exposed for the shadows and one exposed for the highlights—and then we combine them to get the best of both worlds. We get an image that has a range that is beyond what even the best digital cameras could capture.

Double-Processing by Opening Photos in Photoshop as a Smart Object

Step One:
Here's the original image (shown here in Lightroom), which we want to double-process in Photoshop, leveraging its Smart Object feature. The photo, besides just being kind of flat-looking, could really benefit from having the ship and water brightened, and made more saturated and vibrant, and the clouds and the sky could be darker and more dramatic. So, we'll start in Lightroom's Develop module, where we'll fix the ship and water first.

Step Two:
In the Develop module, increase the Exposure amount (click-and-drag the slider to the right), until the ship looks pretty bright and the water gets that emerald look that the water down in the Bahamas often has (as seen here). Then increase the Recovery amount a little bit, so the whites on the boat aren't too bright. Lastly, click-and-drag the Blacks slider to the right to bring back the saturation of color in the shadow areas (as shown here), which keeps the photo from looking washed out, and then increase the Fill Light just a little bit. Okay, so at this point, we have a version of the photo exposed for the boat and water.

Continued

Step Three:

To take our image over to Photoshop as a Smart Object, go under Lightroom's Photo menu, under Edit In, and choose Open as Smart Object in Photoshop (as shown here). Because this photo was taken in RAW format, it will actually open the RAW photo in Photoshop (just like when you normally export to Photoshop, and Lightroom will create a copy in TIFF or PSD format when you save it). Don't worry, your original RAW file is still in Lightroom.

Step Four:

Here's the processed photo open in Photoshop as a Smart Object (you know it's a Smart Object by its name in the title bar and by the little page icon that appears in the bottom-right corner of the layer's thumbnail in the Layers panel). Now that we're here, I want to briefly talk about the advantage of using Smart Objects: in this case, the main advantage is you can reprocess your image anytime in Adobe Photoshop's Camera Raw (which has the exact same sliders and controls as the Develop module in Lightroom, so you'll feel right at home), so you can make your adjustments there, and when you click OK, your changes are applied to the photo. This will make more sense in a moment as we put this to use. Now we need to create a second version of this image—one exposed for the sky—so Control-click (PC: Right-click) on the Smart Object layer, and from the contextual menu that appears, choose New Smart Object via Copy (as shown here).

Step Five:

By the way, the reason I had you choose New Smart Object via Copy, rather than just duplicating the layer like always, is this: when you duplicate a Smart Object layer, the duplicate is tied to the original layer, so if you edit the duplicate, the original updates with the same changes (they're essentially linked together). But when you choose New Smart Object via Copy instead, it does duplicate the layer, but it breaks that link, and now you can edit each one separately. So now, go to the Layers panel and double-click on the duplicate layer's thumbnail, which brings up the Camera Raw window. Lower the Exposure slider until the sky looks nice and dark (like you see here). By the way, did you notice that the sliders are the same ones, in the same order, as those in Lightroom's Basic panel?

Step Six:

When you click OK, it applies those changes, but just to the duplicate layer (as seen here, in the Layers panel, where the bottom layer is the Smart Object exposed for the highlights, and the top layer is the darker one exposed for the sky and the shadows). They are perfectly aligned with one another—pixel for pixel— right in the same position, so now we'll be able to blend the two together (in the next step).

Continued

Step Seven:

Press-and-hold the Option (PC: Alt) key, and click on the Add Layer Mask icon at the bottom of the Layers panel (it's the third icon from the left). This adds a black mask over your darker image (which means it has hidden the darker layer behind a black wall, so now you see the original brighter layer below it). Now, we can reveal just the parts of the darker layer that we want revealed by painting. So, press **D** to set your Foreground color to white, then get the Brush tool from the Toolbox (or just press **B**), choose a very large, soft-edged brush from the Brush Picker in the Options Bar, and begin painting over the sky (as shown here). As you do, it paints in the darker version of the sky. At this point, stay away from the ship and the horizon line—just paint over the biggest parts of the sky.

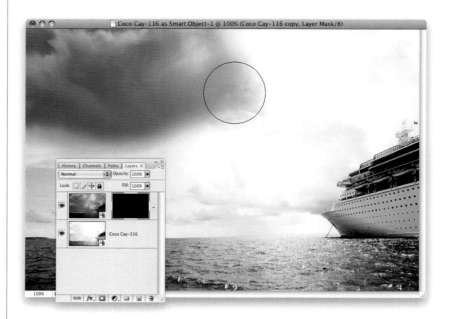

Step Eight:

Now shrink your brush size *way* down, so it's a pretty tiny brush (like the one you see here above the ship, or smaller), and carefully paint right up along the ship, and along the horizon line. Take your time, and carefully paint it in, and try not to paint the darker version onto the ship—just paint right up to the edge; same thing with the water. You can vary your brush sizes while you're painting by using the **Left** and **Right Bracket keys** on your keyboard (they're to the right of the letter P—the Left Bracket makes your brush smaller; the Right Bracket makes it bigger). This is going to take a few minutes, so don't rush through it. Remember, though, we are just practicing on my photo, so it doesn't have to be perfect this time, but kinda get in the ballpark with it.

Step Nine:
Once I had the darker sky painted in (see the image in the previous step), I thought the boat and water looked a little too bright (it looked like it had been faked), so go back to the Layers panel, and this time double-click on the layer thumbnail for the original Smart Object layer (the bottom layer of the two), so you can reprocess this layer a little bit darker. When it appears in the Camera Raw window, just click-and-drag the Exposure slider back to the left a little bit, so the boat isn't so bright (originally I had set the Exposure at +1.58, and here I've lowered it to +1.20, so it's not so bright).

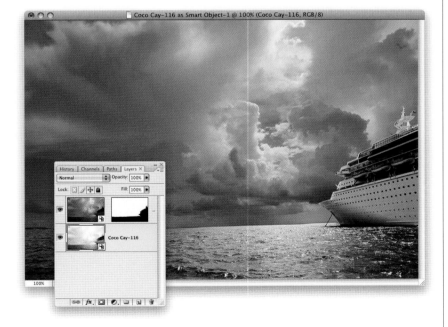

Step 10:
When you click OK, it updates your Smart Object layer with your new darker ship adjustments (as seen here, where the two layers now look much more balanced).

Continued

Step 11:

Now you can either save the file with its layers intact (if you think you might want to go back later and edit the layers individually), or if you're done and ready to print or email the photo, just go to the Layers panel's flyout menu (near the top-right corner of the panel), and choose Flatten Image (as shown here) to remove the layers and flatten it down to just a single Background layer.

Step 12:

The last thing I would do before saving the file is apply a little Unsharp Mask, so go under the Filter menu, under Sharpen, and choose Unsharp Mask. When the dialog appears: for Amount, enter 85; for Radius, enter 1.0; and for Threshold, enter 4; and then click OK (as shown here). Then go under the Edit menu, and choose Fade Unsharp Mask. Now, in that dialog, change the blend mode (in the Mode pop-up menu) to Luminosity, and then click OK. By changing the blend mode to Luminosity, you're applying the sharpening to just the detail areas of the photo—not the color areas—so you avoid some of the halos and other problems associated with sharpening color images. You can see the original flat-looking image at the bottom here, and you can see the final processed and sharpened image in the example above it. So that's how you double-process Lightroom images in Photoshop. Pretty cool, isn't it?

One of my favorite features in Lightroom 2 makes it easy to use one of my favorite features in Photoshop—the Photomerge feature, which automatically and seamlessly stitches panoramas together.

Stitching Panoramas Using Photoshop

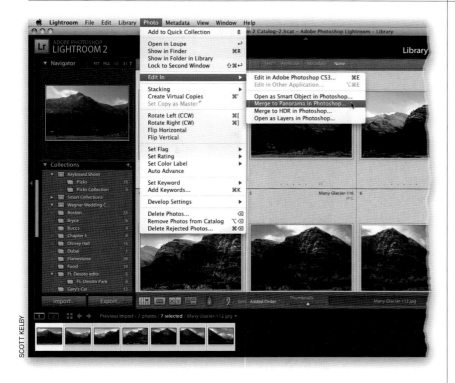

Step One:

In Lightroom's Grid view, select the photos you want to stitch together (the images shown here are of Glacier National Park in Montana). Here I've selected a series of seven photos, and when I shot these, I made sure each photo overlapped the next one by around 20%, because that's about how much overlap Photoshop needs between images to stitch these seven photos into one single panoramic image. Once the photos are selected, go under the Photo menu, under Edit In, and choose Merge to Panorama in Photoshop.

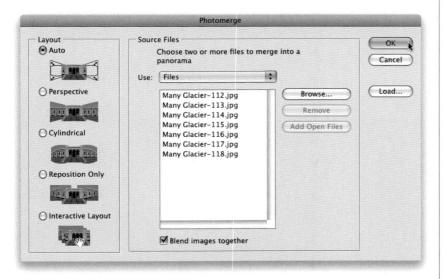

Step Two:

The dialog that will appear is Photoshop's Photomerge dialog (shown here), and in the center of the dialog, you'll see the names of the seven images you selected in Lightroom. In the Layout section on the left side, leave it set at Auto, so Photomerge will automatically try to align and blend the images together for you, then click the OK button in the upper-right corner of the dialog.

Continued

Step Three:

When Photoshop is done aligning and blending your photos, a new document will appear with your seven images combined into a single panoramic image (as seen here). Parts of each photo wind up in this document as a separate layer (as seen in the Layers panel here), so if you wanted to tweak the masks created by Photomerge, you could (but we don't). Let's go ahead and flatten the image by choosing Flatten Image from the Layers panel's flyout menu near the top-right corner of the panel.

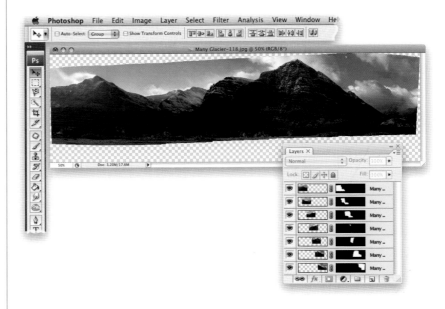

Step Four:

Now that we've flattened the image, we'll need to crop the image down to size to get rid of the areas that were adjusted to make the image stitch together properly. Sometimes this is pretty minor, other times it's more pronounced, like this, but either way, you're just a simple crop away from having your pano look right. Get the Crop tool (from the Toolbox, or just press **C**) and click-and-drag it out over the area you want to keep, as shown here (I drag it out as far as I can, without having any white areas show up on the edges after I crop. In this pano, I did have some white area in the top left of the image after I cropped, which I just filled in using the Clone Stamp tool **[S]**). Once your cropping border is in place, press the Return (PC: Enter) key to lock in your crop.

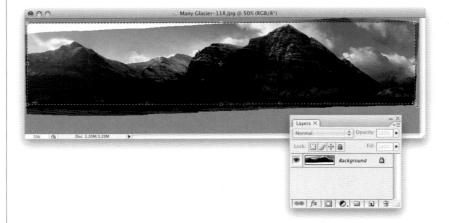

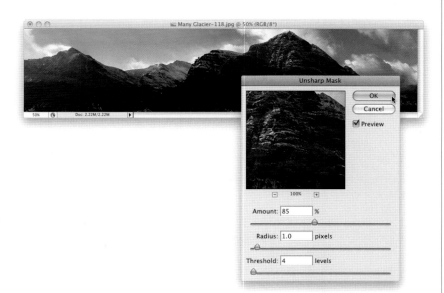

Step Five:
To finish things off, go under the Filter menu, under Sharpen, and choose Unsharp Mask. When the dialog appears: for Amount, enter 85; for Radius, enter 1.0; and for Threshold, enter 4; then click OK (as shown here). Then go under the Edit menu, and choose Fade Unsharp Mask. Now, in that dialog, change the blend mode (in the Mode pop-up menu) to Luminosity, and then click OK to apply this sharpening just to the detail areas of the image, and not the color areas.

Step Six:
Here's the final cropped image in Photoshop (I pressed the **F** key on my keyboard three times and the **Tab key** once to hide all the panels and menus, and center my pano on a black background, as shown here. To return to the regular Photoshop view, just press F, and then the Tab key, one more time).

Merging HDR Images in Photoshop

HDR (High Dynamic Range) images (a series of shots of the same subject taken at different exposures to capture the full tonal range) have become really popular, and in Lightroom 2, you can take the images you shot for HDR straight from Lightroom over to Photoshop's Merge to HDR feature. You start by shooting bracketed on your camera. Here, I set up my camera to shoot five bracketed shots with one stop between each shot—one with the standard exposure, one 2 stops darker, one 1 stop darker, one 1 stop brighter, and one 2 stops brighter (for five shots total).

Step One:

In Lightroom, select your bracketed shots. Here, I've selected the five shots I bracketed with my camera, but you can use as little as three shots, or as many as nine (personally, I like either three or five. Nine just seems like overkill and it takes forever to process). Once you've selected them, go under the Photo menu, under Edit In, and choose Merge to HDR in Photoshop.

Step Two:

This launches Photoshop, and brings up the Merge to HDR dialog. Your image will look pretty horrible, but don't let that throw you—it gets better later in the process. The thumbnails in the left column show your bracketed shots, and you can see the one in the middle shows 0.0 (that's the standard exposure for the shot), and you'll see the ones above it show 1 stop brighter and 2 stops brighter (the ones below are –1 and –2). There's really only one control in this dialog, and that's the Set White Point Preview slider, which appears under the histogram on the right. If your photo's highlights look really blown out, you could click-and-drag this slider to the right until you reach the end of the black graph, but I haven't been able to tell any significant difference when I do this, so I don't do anything here, I just click OK.

Step Three:

This opens your image in Photoshop, and it still looks pretty lame, but one reason is because you're in 32-bit mode (which is outside the range of what today's monitors can display. Well, outside the range of any monitor I could buy, anyway), so to get this puppy fixed up, you'll need to first convert it to 16-bit mode by going under the Image menu, under Mode, and choosing 16 Bits/Channel (as shown here).

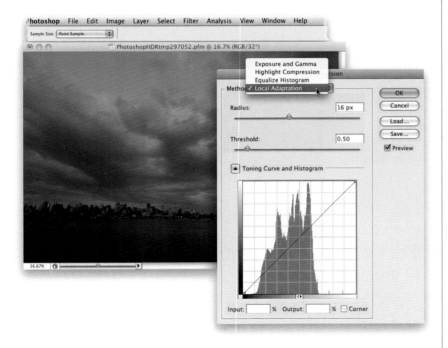

Step Four:

When you do this, your photo still won't look that good. The HDR Conversion dialog will appear, and once it does, you'll want to click on the little down-facing triangle that appears to the left of Toning Curve and Histogram, so those options appear (seen here). The default Method will be set to Exposure and Gamma, but you need to click on that pop-up menu and choose Local Adaptation (as shown here). Just choosing Local Adaptation does wonders for the look of your image, and you finally start to make some progress to getting an HDR look to your photo, but we still have some processing to do.

Continued

Step Five:

To balance out the tones in your image, and maximize the tonal range, you're going to click on the two toning curve points (one at the top of the curve and one at the bottom) and drag them in toward the black histogram graph (which looks like some steep mountains). So, click-and-drag the top corner point to the left, until it reaches the right edge of the black graph (as shown here), to increase the highlights. Next, drag the bottom corner point to the right until it reaches the left edge of the graph (also seen here) to really pump up the shadows. Now things are starting to look a lot better.

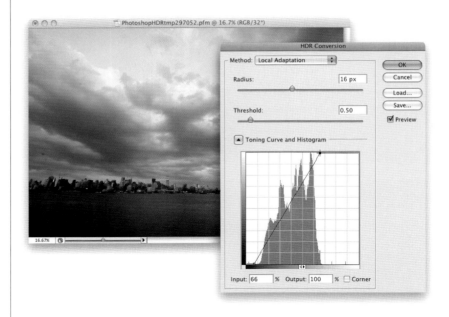

Step Six:

If you want to add more points to the graph (like a center point to control the midtones, or quarter-tone points between the top point and the center point, so you can add more contrast like we learned earlier in the Tone Curve panel of the Develop module, in Chapter 4), just click on the curve, then use the **Up/Down Arrow keys** on your keyboard to adjust the points. *Remember:* The steeper the curve, the more contrast it adds. Also, one thing to look out for is little halos that appear around the edges of things in your image, which make things look kind of blurry. Because of this, I usually wind up lowering the Radius amount quite a bit, just to retain detail and avoid those halos (as shown here). Now click OK to apply these changes.

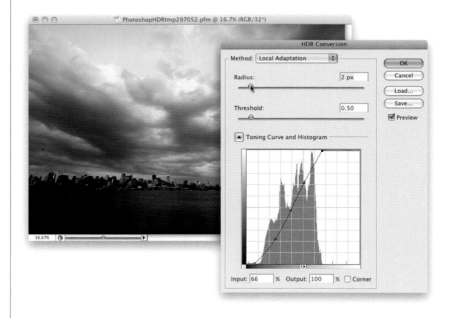

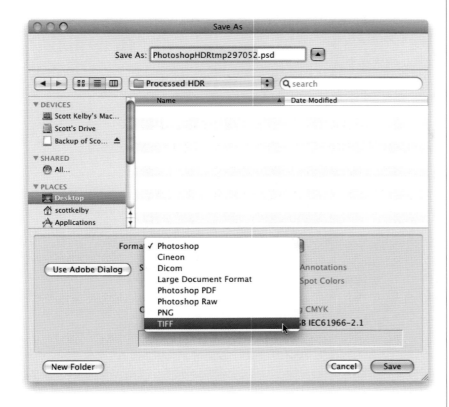

Step Seven:

Now let's save the file, so press **Command-Shift-S (PC: Ctrl-Shift-S)** to bring up the Save As dialog (seen here). For the next step to work, you have to save the file in TIFF format, because we're going to open this image next in Camera Raw for final processing (Camera Raw only opens TIFFs, JPEGs, and, of course, RAW photos. It won't open the default format for this photo, which is PSD). So, choose TIFF from the Format pop-up menu (as shown here) and choose to save it to your desktop. Click the Save button and then click OK in the TIFF Options dialog. Now, just close your image.

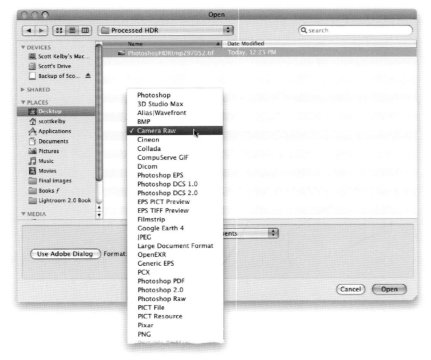

Step Eight:

Go under Photoshop's File menu and choose Open (PC: Open As). When the Open (PC: Open As) dialog appears, click on the TIFF photo you just saved, and from the Format (PC: Open As) pop-up menu at the bottom of the dialog, choose Camera Raw (as shown here) to have the TIFF image open for processing in Camera Raw.

Continued

Step Nine:

Now for some final tweaks in Camera Raw: To make the clouds more dramatic, click-and-drag the Recovery slider over to around 65 and increase the Clarity to around 60 (as shown here). If you want the blue sky to be more blue, click-and-drag the Temperature slider towards blue, until it reads −8, then increase the Vibrance amount to +19 (as shown), and click the Open Image button. Of course, the final step is (as always) to add some sharpening, so go under the Filter menu, under Sharpen, and choose Unsharp Mask. For Amount, enter 120%; for Radius, enter 1.0; and for Threshold, enter 3, and click OK.

Step 10:

The final HDR-processed image is shown here, with the original, regular-exposure image smaller below.

SCOTT KELBY

Step 11:
If you now wanted to get this image back into Lightroom, you'd go to your desktop, and click-and-drag the image file into the same folder on your computer where your original bracketed photos are stored. Then go back to Lightroom, go to the Folders panel (in the Library module) and Control-click (PC: Right-click) on the folder you just dragged your image into (the folder with all your bracketed photos from that shoot). This brings up a contextual menu, where you'll choose Synchronize Folder (as shown here).

Step 12:
The Synchronize Folder dialog will appear (shown here), and you can see that the top choice is already checked, and is indicating that you're importing one new photo (that's the finished HDR you dragged into that folder). Click Synchronize, and that photo is imported into Lightroom, and will now appear in that folder. Just remember, if, like me, you work in collections most of the time (because that's where all your good photos are), just bringing this photo into your folder won't put it in your collection. You'll have to find that photo in your folder inside Lightroom, and drag-and-drop it onto your collection. Okay, so that's the scoop on how to merge your HDR photos in Photoshop, and how to get your finished photo back into Lightroom (if that's where you want it).

Lightroom Quick Tips > >

▼ The Missing Options Dialog
for RAW Photos Going
to Photoshop

If you're a Lightroom 1 user upgrading to Lightroom 2, here's something that might catch you by surprise: when you press **Command-E (PC: Ctrl-E)** to take your RAW file over to Photoshop, it used to bring up a dialog asking if you wanted to make a copy of the RAW file with Lightroom adjustments included, or a copy with no Lightroom adjustments, or just open the original file. What was weird was that the second and third options were grayed out (the only choice was to make a copy with your Lightroom adjustments). Now, thankfully, since you have no choice anyway, the file just goes over to Photoshop. Even better, it doesn't make a copy of the file unless you actually save your file after editing in Photoshop. If you close it and don't save changes, Lightroom no longer makes that useless copy.

▼ Choosing the Name of Your
Photoshop Edited Files

Back in Lightroom 1, it automatically added "Edit in CS3" to end of any photo you edited over there, but now in Lightroom 2, you get to choose exactly what these edited files are named. Just go to Lightroom's preferences (press **Command-, [comma; PC: Ctrl-,]**), and then click on the External Editing tab, and at the bottom of the dialog, you'll see the Edit Externally File Naming section, where you can choose your own custom name or one of the preset file naming templates.

▼ Cutting Your File's
Ties to Lightroom

When you move a file over to Photoshop for editing, and you save that file, the saved file comes right back to Lightroom. So, how do you break this chain?

When you're done editing in Photoshop, just go under Photoshop's File menu and choose Save As, then give the file a new name. That's it, the chain is broken and the file won't go back to Lightroom.

▼ Get Rid of Those
Old PSD Files

If you upgraded from Lightroom 1, do you remember how each time you jumped over to Photoshop, it created a copy of your photo and saved it alongside the original (in PSD format), even if you never made a single change to it in Photoshop? If you're like me, you probably have a hundred or more PSD photos with no visible changes, just taking up space on your drive and in Lightroom. To quickly get rid of them, go to the Library module, and in the Catalog panel, click on All Photographs. Then, up in the Library Filter, click on Metadata. In the first field on the left, click on the header and choose File Type from the pop-up menu. It will list how many PSDs you have in Lightroom, and if you click on Photoshop Document (PSD), it will display just those files, so you can see which ones you never used or just flat out don't need, and you can delete them so you get that space back.

▼ Getting Consistent Color
Between Lightroom
and Photoshop

If you're going to be going back and forth between Lightroom 2 and Photoshop, I'm sure you want consistency in your color between the two programs, which is why you might want to change your color space in Photoshop to match Lightroom's default color space of ProPhoto RGB. You do this under Photoshop's Edit menu: choose Color Settings, then under Working Spaces, for RGB, choose ProPhoto RGB. If you prefer to work in the Adobe RGB (1998) color

space in Photoshop, then just make sure you send your photo over to Photoshop in that color space: go to Lightroom's Preferences dialog, click on the External Editing tab up top, then in the Edit in CS3 section, for Color Space, choose AdobeRGB (1998).

▼ How to Get Photos Back
Into Lightroom After Running
an Export Action

If you created an action in Photoshop and saved it as an export action in Lightroom (see page 247), when your photos leave Lightroom and go to Photoshop to run the action, that's the "end of the line" (the photos don't come back to Lightroom). However, if you want those processed photos to be automatically imported back into Lightroom, do this: Use Lightroom's Auto Import feature to watch a folder (see Chapter 1), and then when you write your Photoshop action, have it save your processed files to that folder. That way, as soon as the action is run, and the file is saved out of Photoshop, it will automatically be re-imported into Lightroom.

▼ How to Get Much
Better Looking High
Dynamic Range Images

Although in this chapter I showed you how to jump from Lightroom to Photoshop to create High Dynamic Range (HDR) photos, unfortunately Photoshop's built-in HDR feature isn't the greatest (and that's being kind). Every pro photographer I know who is into creating HDR images uses a program called Photomatix Pro (you can download a free trial version from their website at www.hdrsoft.com). Try it once, and I doubt you'll use Photoshop's HDR feature again.

Gorgeous B&W
converting from color to black and white

I don't know many photographers who don't just love black and white. Well, actually the color black. You see, once you become a serious photographer, you want to sell your prints. Of course, once that happens once or twice, you're no longer satisfied with what you sold your first prints for, so now you have to find a way to charge more. But here's the catch: you can't just sell the same prints and charge more, right? You'd have to shoot new stuff, better stuff, in fact better stuff than you can actually shoot, which is tough, because in reality you can only shoot as good as you can shoot. So, what's going to make up for your lack of talent and vision? Black clothing. You need a black shirt, pants, socks, coat, shoes, etc. Black clothing on a photographer is like magic because that tells the world you're not just a photographer, you're an artist and obviously mourning something deep inside your soul. Perhaps an emotional loss, but you're so tortured by it that you can't talk about it. The only way to express your inner angst is through your "art," which is now worth a whole lot more because you're no longer some schmuck with a camera trying to make a buck, you're a deep, mysterious artist they could never understand. This makes your work irresistible to people who love buying the work of tortured artists (which is just about everybody). So now you're living in a luxury apartment on the Upper East Side and you've decorated it all in just one color—white. Why white? Because you needed to make a personal statement about monochromaticity, corporate plundering, and man's inhumanity to man. That, and you're really sick of black.

Finding Out Which Photos Might Look Great in Black & White

I absolutely love B&W photos (I think most photographers are secretly B&W freaks), but unfortunately, not every color photo makes a good black and white (in fact, some photos that look great in color look just dreadful in black and white. Of course, at the same time, some photos that look boring in color look stunning as B&W images). So, before I start actually converting photos to black and white in the Develop module, I use this Library module technique to quickly see which photos from a shoot might look great in black and white.

Step One:
Start in the Library module by clicking on the collection of photos you want to test to see which ones in that collection might make nice B&W photos. Press **Command-A (PC: Ctrl-A)** to select all the photos in that collection (in the example shown here, I have a collection set from a wedding, and inside that set I had created a collection of just the Picks from that wedding. So, I clicked on that Picks collection and selected all of those photos, as shown here).

Step Two:
Now, press **Command-N (PC: Ctrl-N)** to create a new collection. When the Create Collection dialog appears, in the options at the bottom of the dialog, turn on the checkbox for Make New Virtual Copies. That way, when you click the Create button, this new collection will be made up of virtual copies, which you can use to experiment with without disturbing your color originals. (*Note:* Since this collection was inside my collection set, it assumes that you want to save this collection in the same set, as shown here.)

Step Three:
Once the images appear in their own collection, they'll all still be selected, so go to the Quick Develop panel (in the right side Panels area), and from the Treatment pop-up menu near the top, choose Grayscale (as shown here), and it converts all of these virtual copies to black and white. Now, it doesn't do a great job of the conversion; in fact, it does a pretty flat-looking conversion, but it does give you a really good idea of which photos will look good as B&W photos and which won't.

Step Four:
At this point, I press **Shift-Tab** to hide all the panels (so I can focus on the images), then I scroll through the B&W converted images, and when I see one that looks good, I press the letter **P** on my keyboard to mark it as a Pick (as shown here). Once I have all my Picks marked, I click on the Picks flag filter (up in the Library Filter at the top of the window), so only my Picks are showing, then I press **Command-A (PC: Ctrl-A)** to select them all. Next, click on the left-facing triangle on the right to make the right side Panels area visible, and at the bottom of the Quick Develop panel, click the Reset All button to return your Picks to color. Now you can jump over to the Develop module where you'll start converting these "best of the bunch" photos to black and white, using the methods you'll learn starting on the next page.

Better Black and White By Doing It Yourself

There are two auto conversion methods for converting your images from color to black and white (one in the Basic panel and another in the HSL/Color/Grayscale panel), and no matter where you choose to do it from, the results are the same. Now, to me it looks just too flat, and I honestly think you can do much better by doing it yourself. We'll start with my preferred method for most color-to-black-and-white conversions, which lets you build on what you've already learned in the Develop module chapter of this book.

Step One:

In the Library module, find the photo you want to convert to black and white, and first make a virtual copy of it by going under the Photo menu and choosing Create Virtual Copy, as shown here (the only reason to do this is so when you're done, you can compare your do-it-yourself method with Lightroom's auto-conversion method side by side. By the way, once you learn to do the conversion yourself, I doubt you'll ever want to use the Auto method again).

Step Two:

Press **Command-D (PC: Ctrl-D)** to deselect the virtual copy, and then go down to the filmstrip and click on the original photo. Now press **D** to jump to the Develop module, and in the right side Panels area, scroll down to the HSL/Color/Grayscale panel and click on Grayscale on the far right of the panel header (as shown here). This is one way to apply the auto conversion, which gives you the kind of flat-looking B&W conversion you see here (consider this your "before" photo). By the way, if you toggle the panel on/off button (shown circled here in red), you can see how bad this black and white would have looked if Lightroom didn't do an auto conversion.

Step Three:

Now, press the **Right Arrow key** on your keyboard to switch to that virtual copy you made, go to the Basic panel (at the top of the right side Panels area), and in the Treatment section at the top, click on Grayscale (the other auto conversion method). I want to create a really rich, high-contrast B&W image, so the first thing to do is click-and-drag the Blacks slider over to the right until the photo doesn't look so flat and washed out (as shown here). Now, there are those who believe that you should never let any part of your photo turn solid black, even if it's a non-essential, low-detail area like a shadow under a rock. I'm not one of those people. I want the entire photo to have "pop" to it, and in my years of creating B&W prints, I've found that your average person reacts much more positively to photos with high-contrast conversions than to the flatter conversions that retain 100% detail in the shadows. If you get a chance, try both versions, show your friends, and see which one they choose.

Step Four:

Of course, once you darken the shadows, the whole photo is going to look quite a bit darker, so I usually go back and raise the Exposure amount as much as I can without blowing out the highlights. Actually, if you blow the highlights out a little, don't worry, because next I'm going to have you click-and-drag the Recovery slider to the right to make that lighter sky a little darker, and doing that will bring back those clipped highlights. (*Remember:* I use this increase-the-Recovery move any time I have a light sky, especially if it has lots of white puffy clouds. This one doesn't have lots of those, but just dragging the Recovery slider to the right helps the whole sky look better.)

Continued

Step Five:

We're going for a high-contrast black and white, so we can add more contrast by clicking-and-dragging the Clarity slider quite a bit to the right (here I dragged to +60), which gives the midtones more contrast and makes the overall photo have more punch.

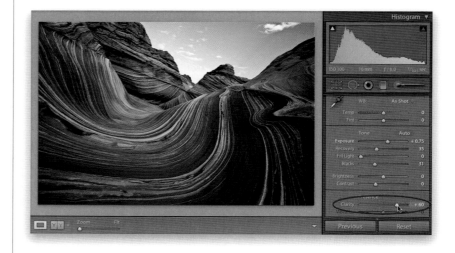

Step Six:

Now we're going to pump up the overall contrast, but we're not going to use the Contrast slider (it's just too broad, so I generally don't use it). Instead, scroll down to the Tone Curve panel and, from the Point Curve pop-up menu at the bottom, choose Medium Contrast to make your highlights brighter and your shadows deeper (as shown here). I'm only choosing Medium Contrast because this is a JPEG image, and some contrast was already applied when the JPEG was originally made from the RAW photo. If this was a RAW photo, I would have chosen Strong Contrast instead, because the default amount of contrast for RAW images is already Medium.

Step Seven:
If you think the image looks a little too dark, try clicking-and-dragging the Brightness (midtones) slider over to +25 (as shown here in the right side Panels area). The final step is to add some sharpening. Since this is a landscape photo, the easiest thing to do is to go over to the left side Panels area, in the Presets panel, and choose Sharpen – Landscapes from the built-in presets (as shown here on the left side of the window) to apply a nice amount of sharpening for landscapes. So that's it. It's not that much different from adjusting a color photo, is it? But you can see how much more dramatic the results are in the before/after images shown below. Now, what if you wanted to darken just the sky some more? You'll learn that next.

How to Tweak Individual Areas When You Convert to Black and White

The method you just learned is how I do 95% of the color-to-black-and-white conversions I do in Lightroom, but sometimes there's a particular area of the photo you want to adjust during this conversion process, and that can be done in the Develop module's HSL/Color/Grayscale panel. I usually still do the conversion the way I showed you on the previous pages, but when I see an area that needs adjusting, I head straight for the HSL/Color/Grayscale panel, because it's usually the quickest and easiest way to get the job done.

Step One:
Start off in the Library module by selecting your photo and then making a virtual copy of it, so we can see a before/after like we did in the last project. Rather than digging through the menus, you can just press **Command-' (apostrophe; PC: Ctrl-')**, which is the shortcut for making a virtual copy of your currently selected image. Now, click back on the original, press **D**, to go to the Develop module, and in the Treatment section at the top of the Basic panel, click on Grayscale. Then press the **Right Arrow key** on your keyboard to switch to your virtual copy and click the Grayscale button again (as shown here).

Step Two:
The photo looks flat and washed out, so click-and-drag the Blacks slider over to the right until the shadows look nice and rich (as shown here). Once you've done that, you can click-and-drag the Exposure slider over to the right, until the highlights just start to clip, and then you can pull those clipped highlights back (and make the sky a bit more dramatic) by increasing the Recovery amount quite a bit (here I dragged over to 64).

Step Three:
To add more overall contrast, scroll down to the Tone Curve panel and, from the Point Curve pop-up menu at the bottom, choose Medium Contrast (as shown here). Once again, I'm choosing medium because this is a JPEG image, and contrast was already applied when the JPEG was made from the original RAW photo. If this were a RAW photo, I would have chosen Strong Contrast, instead. So the foreground now looks better, but the sky still looks really weak. This is the kind of situation—where one part of the photo needs tweaking—where I know I need to go to the HSL/Color/Grayscale panel, because it lets me adjust individual colors.

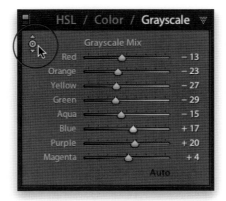

Step Four:
Go to the HSL/Color/Grayscale panel and click on the word Grayscale, on the far right of the panel header, to bring up the Grayscale Mix sliders. If you know exactly which sliders you need to adjust, have at it—start draggin'—but honestly, I think it's much easier to use the Targeted Adjustment tool (the TAT), which is found in the upper-left corner of the panel. Just click on it to select the tool (it's shown circled here in red. The triangles on the top and bottom will appear when you click on it).

Continued

Step Five:

Now move your cursor out over your image, right over the area you want to adjust (in this case, we want to darken the sky, so move the TAT out over the sky, as shown here). If you look closely at the TAT's cursor, you'll see it has a circle with one triangle pointing upward, and one pointing down. That's there to tell you that you use this tool by clicking-and-dragging it up or down.

Step Six:

Click the TAT on the clouds and drag straight downward, and the TAT automatically moves all the sliders necessary to adjust the colors in the area under your cursor. Look at what this did for the sky, which is now much darker and more dramatic and really helped to balance the overall image.

Step Seven:
Now move the TAT over the rock forma-tion on the left side (as shown here), then click-and-drag upward to lighten these areas (once again, it knows which sliders control the colors under your cursor, and it automatically moves those sliders as you drag—the higher your drag, the larger the adjustment). Just remember that when you make your adjustments with the TAT, it moves one or more sliders; if those same colors appear in other places in your image, those areas will get ad-justed, too. Just so you know. Take a look at the before/after below.

Adding a Split-Tone Effect to Your Black-and-White Photos

There is a B&W darkroom technique called "split toning," where you apply a tint of one color to the highlights and another color to the shadow areas. It wasn't a hugely popular technique (in fact, I'm not a fan of split toning myself), but since the first version of Lightroom came with an easy built-in Split Toning panel, now you see it showing up fairly often (in fact, it may have single-handedly saved the art of split toning).

Step One:

Here's our original color image, shown in Lightroom's Develop module. Although the actual split toning is done in the Split Toning panel (shown here, in the right side Panels area), you should probably convert the photo to black and white first. (I say "should," because you can apply a split-toning effect on top of your color photo, but…well…yeech!)

Step Two:

Start in the Basic panel (at the top of the right side Panels area), and in the Treatment section, click on Grayscale to convert the photo to black and white. You can do a little tweaking to the photo to make it nice and contrasty, as I did here, by increasing the Blacks amount and increasing the Recovery amount quite a bit to darken the sky and give it some drama. I also increased the Clarity to +61 to really give it some snap.

Step Three:

Now that you've got a decent-looking B&W photo, scroll down to the Split Toning panel (shown here). In the panel, you'll see there are Hue and Saturation sliders for both the highlights and the shadows, which let you add one tint to the highlight areas and a separate tint to the shadows. A nice new thing Adobe added in Lightroom 2 is the little color swatches—click on the one next to Highlights and it brings up the Highlights color picker, and along the top are some common split-tone highlight colors. Click the yellowish swatch at the top (the second swatch from the left, as shown here) to apply a yellow tint to the highlight areas in your photo (you can see the result in the Preview area). To close the color picker, click on the X button in the upper-left corner.

Step Four:

Now click the color swatch in the Shadows section to bring up the Shadows color picker. From the swatches up at the top of the picker, click on the blue swatch (as shown here) to assign a blue color to the shadow areas. You can see the completed split-tone effect right onscreen, as soon as you click this blue swatch. The shadow areas (down in the mountains) are primarily blue, but the lighter areas of the clouds and the snowcaps on the mountains (the highlights) are yellow. That's it—you've made your first split tone. There are a couple of other controls you'll want to know about, so we'll cover those next.

Continued

Step Five:

The Balance slider (found between the Highlights and Shadows sections in the Split Toning panel) does just what you'd think it would—it lets you balance the color mix between the highlights and shadows. For example, if you want the balance in your image more toward the yellow highlights, you'd just click-and-drag the Balance slider to the right, as shown here.

Step Six:

Now we're going to undo the split-tone effect we just applied, so press **Command-Z (PC: Ctrl-Z)** a few times, until you return to the untinted grayscale version of your photo (as shown here). We're doing this because I want to point out a "gotcha" you'll run into when you try to make your own custom split-tone effect by just clicking-and-dragging the sliders. Start by clicking-and-dragging the Highlights Hue slider to the right, way over to the blue area, then take a look at your image. It still looks grayscale. Where's the blue? That's the "gotcha!" The reason nothing changed is that, by default, the Saturation slider (the amount of color) is set to 0, so you can't see the color unless you then go and raise the Saturation amount (I know, this doesn't make sense. Don't get me started).

Step Seven:

There is a workaround to this: if you press-and-hold the Option (PC: Alt) key and then start clicking-and-dragging the Highlights Hue slider, it temporarily bumps up the Saturation amount to 100%, so you can easily see which color tint you're choosing (the Saturation slider doesn't actually move, but the effect is the same—you see the tint at 100% saturation until you release the Option key, then it returns to 0%). I normally don't even mess with this "press-and-hold the Option key" method—I recommend just clicking-and-dragging the Highlights Saturation slider to 25 first, then clicking-and-dragging the Hue slider. That way, you get a better idea of how the tint color is going to look, because with the Option key method, the color is so oversaturated (at 100%), it's really hard to judge what the final image, or color, is going to look like.

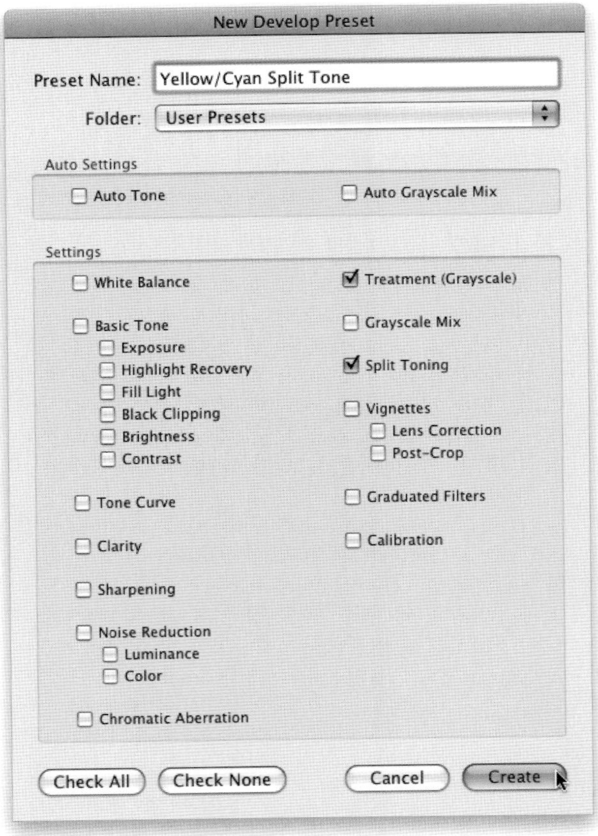

Step Eight:

If you've created a particular split tone that you like, and you think you might use it again on some different photos, save it as a preset. Head over to the left side Panels area, and in the Presets panel, click on the + (plus sign) button to add a new preset. The New Develop Preset dialog will appear (seen here). First, click the Check None button at the bottom to turn off all the checkboxes from the other Develop panel settings. Next, turn on just the Treatment (Grayscale) checkbox (so it converts your photo to black and white first) and the Split Toning checkbox, then give your preset a name, and click the Create button. Now those settings are saved as a one-click preset in your Presets panel (I named this one "Yellow/Cyan Split Tone").

Creating Duotones Using the Split Toning Panel

The thing I use the Split Toning panel the most for is for creating duotones—there's no faster way to make 'em (but if you are wondering if there is another way, there is. You could use the Adjustment Brush, set your Effect to Color, choose a color from the color picker to be your duotone color, convert your photo to black and white, and then paint over the entire photo with the brush, but doesn't that seem like an awful lot of work? Worse yet, you can't save it as a preset, so you'd have to do it manually every single time. Ouch!).

Step One:
Start by converting your photo to black and white using any method you like (the photo I'm using had already been converted to black and white, so there's not much to do here, except show you the original B&W image in the Develop module).

Step Two:
Go to the Split Toning panel (in the right side Panels area of the Develop module) and click on the color swatch in the Highlights section. This brings up the Highlights color picker (seen here). Go ahead and click on the center color swatch (as shown here), then close the color picker by clicking on the little round X button in the upper-left corner.

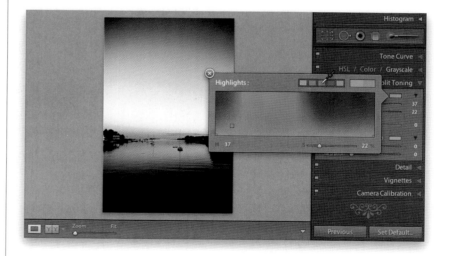

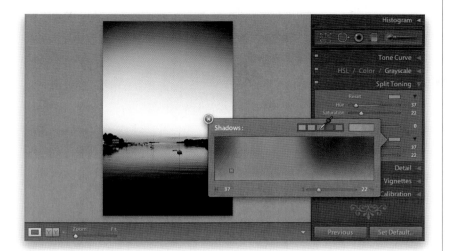

Step Three:
Now, click on the Shadows color swatch to bring up its color picker. The key to creating a duotone is simple—just choose the exact same color for your shadows as you did for your highlights (in other words, choose the same color swatch for both highlights and shadows). So, in this case, you'd click that same center color swatch, then close the color picker, and you're done—instant duotone.

Step Four:
Before you save this as a duotone preset, there is one thing you *might* want to change, and that's the saturation amount that's applied to both the highlights and shadows when you click their swatches. To me, the saturation is a bit too high, which makes it look more like a tint, and less like the usually more subtle colors of a duotone. So, just go to the Saturation sliders and pull them back a little (clicking-and-dragging to the left), until the effect is more subtle, as shown here. Now, go ahead and save this duotone as a preset over in the Presets panel in the left side Panels area. Also, now that you know the technique, you can stop using the color swatches at the top of the color picker, and instead choose your own custom colors in the picker (common duotone colors are oranges, browns, reds, and blues over a B&W image).

Lightroom Quick Tips > >

▼ One-Click B&W Preview

If you're looking at an image and wonder if it will make a good black and white, just press the letter **V** and it converts to black and white. If it doesn't look good, just press V again. This is great anytime you want a quick preview of how your image might look as a black and white.

▼ Separating Your Virtual Black & Whites from the Real Black & Whites

In this chapter, we talked about creating a collection full of virtual copies, so we could find out which ones look good as black and whites. However, you might convert a single photo to black and white, and then decide to make a virtual copy (which is fine). Then you might make another, and another, and pretty soon it's hard to remember which was the original and which one's a copy, since they're all grouped together in the filmstrip. So, to see just your virtual copies, go up to the Library Filter bar (if it's not visible, press the \ **[Backslash key])**, and then click on Attribute. When the Attribute options pop down, click on the little curled page icon at the far right of the bar to show just the virtual copies. To see the real original "master" B&W files, click the filmstrip icon just to the left of it. To see everything again (both the virtual and original masters), click the None button.

▼ Painting Duotones

Another way to create a duotone effect from your B&W photo is to click on the Adjustment Brush, and then in the options that pop down, choose Color from the Effect pop-up menu. Now, click on the Color swatch to bring up the color picker, choose the color you want for your duotone, and close the picker. Then, turn off the Auto Mask checkbox

and paint over the photo, and as you do, it will retain all the detail and just apply the duotone color.

▼ B&W Contrast: The Difference Between RAW and JPEG

If you import a RAW photo into Lightroom, by default, contrast is added to the photo as part of Lightroom's RAW conversion process. (You can see how much by going to the Tone Curve panel, and looking at the Point Curve pop-up menu at the bottom of the panel. You'll see that Medium Contrast is selected in the pop-up menu.) However, if you import JPEG photos, there is no contrast applied by Lightroom whatsoever (that pop-up menu will be set to Linear). Since, when it comes to B&W photos, contrast is king, with a JPEG image you may want to start by choosing Medium Contrast from the Point Curve pop-up menu to see if it can handle the extra contrast. If it does, try Strong Contrast.

▼ Grayscale Conversion Tip

If you click on the word "Grayscale" in the HSL/Color/Grayscale panel, it converts your photo to grayscale and it's kind of a flat-looking conversion, but the idea is that you'll use those color sliders to adjust the conversion. The problem is, how do you know which color sliders to move when the photo is now in black and white? Try this: once you've done your conversion and it's time to tweak those color sliders, press **Shift-Y** to enter the Before & After split-screen view (if it shows a side-by-side view instead, just press Shift-Y again). Now you can see the color image on the left side of the screen, and black and white (grayscale) on the right, which makes it much easier to see which color does what.

▼ Tip for Using the Targeted Adjustment Tool (TAT)

If you're using the HSL/Color/Grayscale panels' TAT to tweak your B&W image, you already know that you click-and-drag the TAT within your image and it moves the sliders that control the colors underneath it. However, you might find it easier to move the TAT over the area you want to adjust, and instead of dragging the TAT up/down, just use the **Up/Down Arrow keys** on your keyboard, and it will move the sliders for you. If you press-and-hold the Shift key while using the Up/Down Arrows, the sliders move in larger increments.

▼ Using the HSL/Color/Grayscale panel? Color Correct Your Photo First

If you're going to be using the Grayscale panel to make your B&W conversion, before you go there, start by making the color image look right first (balance the exposure, blacks, contrast, etc., first, then you'll get better results from the Grayscale panel).

▼ Getting a Before/After of Your B&W Tweaking

You can't just press the \ **(Backslash key)** to see your before image after you've done the edits to your B&W image, because you're starting with a color photo (so pressing \ just gives you the color original again). There are two ways to get around this: (1) As soon as you convert to grayscale, press **Command-N (PC: Ctrl-N)** to save the conversion as a snapshot. Now you can get back to your grayscale original anytime by clicking on that snapshot in the Snapshots panel. Or, (2) after you convert to grayscale, press **Command-' (PC: Ctrl-')** to make a virtual copy, and then do your editing to the copy. That way you can use \ to compare the original conversion with any tweaks you've been making.

Slideshow
sharing your photos onscreen

It's kind of funny that in this digital day and age, we still use the term "slide show," even though traditional slides are nearly as outdated as records. For example, my 11-year-old son has never seen a record album. For him, music has always come from either CDs or iPods. Although I have many photographic slides, my son has never seen a real slide show using real conventional color slides. But it's not just him. I speak at conferences and tradeshows, and if I walked into the room where I was scheduled to speak and asked the class moderator where the slide projector was, he'd look at me like I was from Mars. Yet, Adobe Photoshop Lightroom still uses this term. So, today, in this very book, I'm suggesting that not only should we, in the photography industry, use a different term for what was previously called a slide show, but I actually want to propose the new term. I have crafted a new word that I feel better represents the experience of viewing photographic images onscreen, and thus I'm quite certain this term will be quickly and unilaterally embraced by the worldwide photographic community. It's "flobotnor" (flow·bot·nore). So, once it's officially adopted (any day now, I'm sure), you'll see future releases of Lightroom where the Slideshow module will have been renamed the Flobotnor module. Of course, you'll have the satisfaction of knowing that not only were you there when it all happened—you helped shape modern history. These are amazing times, my friend. Amazing times, indeed.

Creating a Quick, Basic Slide Show

Here's how to create a quick slide show using the built-in slide show templates that come with Photoshop Lightroom 2. You'll probably be surprised at how easy this process is, but the real power of the Slideshow module doesn't really kick in until you start customizing and creating your own slide show templates (which we cover after this, but you have to learn this first, so start here and you'll have no problems when we get to customizing).

Step One:

Start by jumping over to the Slideshow module by pressing **Command-Option-3 (PC: Ctrl-Alt-3)**. There's a Collections panel in the left side Panels area, just like there is in the Library module, so you have direct access to the photos in any collection. First, click on the collection that has the photos you want to appear in your slide show, as shown here. (*Note:* If the photos you want in your slide show aren't in a collection, it will make your life a lot easier if they are, so head back to the Library module [press the letter **G**], and make a new collection with the photos you want in your slide show, then jump back over to the Slideshow module, and click on that collection in the Slideshow's Collections panel.)

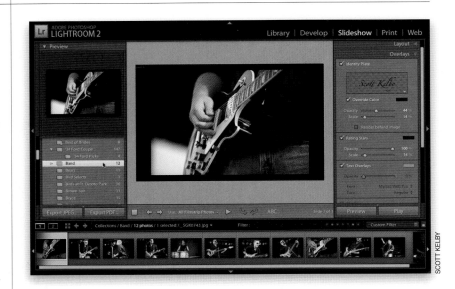

Step Two:

By default, it's going to play the slides in the order they appear down in the filmstrip (the first photo from the left appears first, the second photo appears next, and so on), with a brief dissolve transition between slides. If you only want certain photos in your collection to appear in your slide show, then go to the filmstrip, select just those photos, and choose Selected Photos from the pop-up menu in the toolbar below the center Preview area (as shown here). As you can see, you can also choose to have just flagged photos in your slide show.

Step Three:

If you want to change the order of your slides, just click-and-drag them into the order you want them. (In the example shown here, I clicked on a photo on the far right that I wanted to appear as the second slide, and dragged it over so it appeared right after the first slide in the filmstrip.) So, go ahead and do that now—click-and-drag the photos into the order you'd like them to appear in your slide show. (*Note:* You can always change your mind on the order any time by clicking-and-dragging right within the filmstrip.)

Step Four:

The center Preview area shows you a large preview of how any selected slide is going to look (here I clicked on a different slide, just because I was getting tired of seeing that close-up of a Les Paul). When you first switch to the Slideshow module, it displays your photos in the default slide show template, which has a black background and your custom Identity Plate in the upper-left corner in white letters (as seen in the previous steps). If you want to try a different look, you can apply any of the built-in slide show templates that come with Lightroom. For example, go to the Template Browser (in the left side Panels area) and, under Lightroom Templates, click on the Caption and Rating template (as shown here), which puts your photo on a light gray gradient background, and adds a white stroke around your photo and a drop shadow. If you've added a star rating to your photo, the stars will appear over the top-left corner of your image on the slide, and if you added a caption in the Library module's Metadata panel, it will appear at the bottom of the slide (both are seen here).

Continued

Step Five:

When it comes to choosing slide show templates, you can get a preview of each template by just hovering your cursor over the name of the template in the Template Browser, and a preview of that look will appear in the Preview panel at the top of the left side Panels area (as seen here). If you want to remove a photo from your slide show, just remove the photo from your collection by clicking on it and pressing the Delete (PC: Backspace) key on your keyboard (or choose Selected Photos from the toolbar and make sure you don't select that photo). By the way, this is another advantage of collections vs. folders. If you were working with a folder here, instead of a collection, and you deleted a photo, it would actually remove it from Lightroom and from your computer. Yikes!

Step Six:

If you want a quick preview of how your slide show will look, go to the toolbar below the center Preview area, and click the Preview button (it's a right-facing triangle—just like the Play button on a DVD player). This plays a preview of your slide show within that center Preview area, and although the slide show is the exact same size in that window, you're now seeing it without guides, with transitions, and with music (if you chose to add music, which we haven't covered yet, so you probably haven't, but hey, ya never know). To stop your preview, press the square Stop button on the left side of the toolbar; to pause it, press the two vertical lines where the Play button used to be (as shown here).

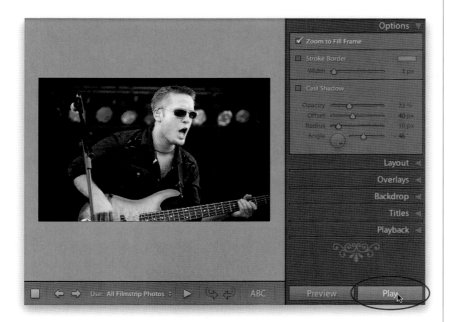

Step Seven:

Once you've seen the preview, you can do any last minute tweaking (like changing the order of the slides by clicking-and-dragging them down in the filmstrip), and then it's time to see "the big show" (the full-screen version)! To see it, you click the Play button at the bottom of the right side Panels area (shown circled here in red).

TIP: Life Is Random

By default, your slides play in the order that they appear down in the filmstrip, but if you want your slides to appear in a completely random order, go down to the Playback panel in the right side Panels area and turn on the Random Order checkbox.

Step Eight:

Once you click that Play button, your slide show starts at full-screen size (as shown here). To exit full-screen mode and return to the Slideshow module, just press the Esc key on your keyboard. Okay, that's it—you've created a basic slide show. Next, you'll learn how to customize and create your own custom slide shows.

TIP: Creating an Instant Slide Show

I mentioned this in an earlier chapter, but I think it has to be included here, too, and that is you can create an impromptu slide show anytime without coming here to the Slideshow module. Whichever module you're in, just go to the filmstrip, select the photos you'd like to see in an instant slide show, then press **Command-Return (PC: Ctrl-Enter)**, and it starts—full screen, using whatever template and settings you used last in the Slideshow module.

Adding Opening and Closing Title Slides

One way to customize your slide show is to create your own custom opening and closing title slides (I usually only create an opening slide). Besides just looking nice, having an opening slide serves an important purpose—it conceals the first slide in your presentation, so your client doesn't see the first image until the show actually begins (in earlier versions of Lightroom, your client would see the first image in the slide show onscreen before you even clicked the Play button).

Step One:
You create opening/closing slides in the Titles panel (found in the right side Panels area in the Slideshow module). To turn this feature on, turn on the Intro Screen checkbox and your title screen appears for just a few seconds (as seen here), then the first photo appears again, so you might have to toggle this checkbox on/off a few times while you're building this slide, just so you can see what you're building. The little color swatch to the right lets you choose a background color (by default, the background color is black). To add text, you add your Identity Plate text (or graphic) by turning on the Add Identity Plate checkbox (shown circled in red here), and your current Identity Plate text appears (as seen here).

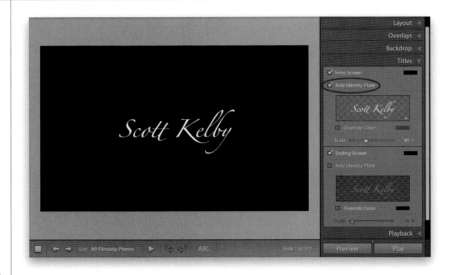

Step Two:
To customize your Identity Plate text, click on the little down-facing triangle in the bottom-right corner of the Identity Plate preview (right under the Add Identity Plate checkbox) and choose Edit from the pop-up menu that appears to bring up the Identity Plate Editor, seen here. Now you can highlight the existing text, type in any text you'd like (in this case, I added the bride's and groom's names), and choose a different font from the Font pop-up menu. Click OK to apply this text to your intro slide.

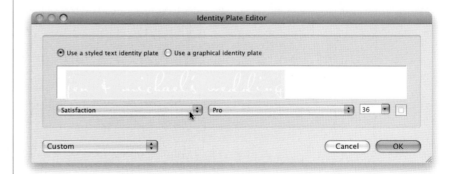

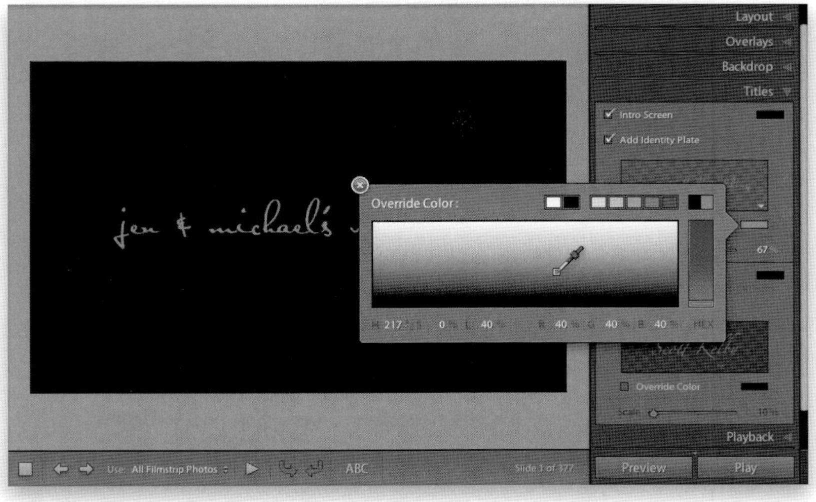

Step Three:

You can control the color of your Identity Plate text by turning on the Override Color checkbox (found under the Identity Plate preview). Once you turn that on, click once on the color swatch to its right and a large color picker (shown here) appears. At the top are some handy color swatches in white, black, and different shades of gray. You can choose one of those, or drag the bar up/down on the far right to choose a hue, and then you can choose your color's saturation from the large color picker gradient (here, I'm choosing a gray color, and you can see that color instantly reflected in the text). You can also control the size of your Identity Plate text by using the Scale slider at the bottom of the Intro Screen section.

Step Four:

Once your text is formatted the way you want it (good luck on that, by the way, because editing text in the Identity Plate Editor is…well…it's clunky as hell, and that's being kind), you can preview the slide show in the Preview area (as I did here. I also changed the background color of the title slide to a medium gray, just to mix things up a bit). If you hit the Play button, the full-screen slide show starts with your title slide displayed first, before the first photo in your filmstrip. The Ending Screen works the same way: to turn it on, you turn on the Ending Screen checkbox in the Titles panel, and you can choose that screen's background color, Identity Plate size, etc., just like you did with the intro screen.

SCOTT KELBY

Customizing the Look of Your Slides

The built-in templates are okay, but after you create a slide show or two with them, you're going to be saying stuff like, "I wish I could change the background color" or "I wish I could add some text at the bottom" or "I wish my slide show looked better." (*Note:* You're not saying you wish your photos looked better— you wish your slide show looked better.) Well, this is where you start to create your own custom look for your slides, so not only does it look just the way you want it, your custom look is just one click away from now on.

Step One:
Although you might not be wild about Lightroom's predesigned slide show templates, they make great starting points for creating your own custom look. Here, we're going to create a wedding slide show, so start by going to the Slideshow module's Collections panel (in the left side Panels area) and click on the wedding collection you want to use. Then, go up to the Template Browser and click on Exif Metadata to load that template (seen here, which puts your photos over a black background with a thin white border, info about your photo in the top right and below your photo, and your Identity Plate in the upper-left corner).

Step Two:
Now that we've got our template loaded, we don't need the left-side panels anymore, so press **F7** on your keyboard to hide them. The first thing I do is get rid of all the EXIF info (after all, your wedding clients probably won't care what your ISO or exposure settings were), so go to the right side Panels area, to the Overlays panel, and turn off the Text Overlays checkbox (as shown here). Your Identity Plate will still be visible, but the info in the upper-right corner and below the photo is now hidden.

TIP: Resizing Custom Text
Once you create custom text, you can change the size by clicking-and-dragging the corner points outward (to make it larger), and inward (to make it smaller).

Step Three:

Now let's choose how big your photos are going to appear on the slide. For this design, we're going to shrink the size of the photos a bit, and then move them up toward the top of the slide, so we can add our studio's name below them. Your photo is positioned inside four page margins (left, right, top, and bottom), and you can control how big/small these margins are in the Layout panel found in the right side Panels area. By default, all four margin guides are linked together, so if you increase the left margin to 81 pixels, all of the other margins adjust so they're 81 pixels, as well. In our case, we want to adjust the top and bottom separately, so first click on Link All to unlink the margins (the little "lights" beside each margin go out). Now, click-and-drag the Bottom margin slider to the right until it reads 180 px (as shown here), and you'll see the photo scale down in size inward, leaving a larger margin below the photo.

TIP: Moving Guides

You don't actually resize the photos on your slide—you move the margin guides and your photo resizes within the margins you create. You can do this visually (rather than in the Layout panel) by moving your cursor over a guide, and you'll see it change into a "moving bar" cursor (by the way, I have no idea if "moving bar" is its official name, but it is a double-headed arrow), and now you can click-and-drag the margins to resize the photo. If you move your cursor over a corner (where two guides intersect) you can drag diagonally to resize those two guides at the same time.

Continued

Step Four:

Now that our photo is in position, let's move our studio name Identity Plate below the photo. Click on it (up in the top-left corner of your slide) and drag it so it appears under your photo (when you drag it, it does this weird Spiderman thing of clinging to the edges. This is supposed to help you center your text by having it snap to the edges. At least, that's the theory).

TIP: Zoom to Fill Frame

If you see a gap between the edges of your photo and the margin guides, you can fill that gap instantly with a very cool feature called Zoom to Fill Frame. Turning on this checkbox (found in the Options panel at the very top of the right side Panels area) increases the size of your photos proportionally until they completely fill the area inside the margins. Give this a try—you'll probably use it more than you'd think.

Step Five:

To customize your Identity Plate text, go to the Overlays panel, click on the little triangle in the bottom-right corner of the Identity Plate preview, and choose Edit to bring up the Identity Plate Editor (seen here). Type in the name you want to appear below each photo (in my case, I typed in Kelby Photography, with two spaces between each letter to make the text look more airy, in the font Trajan Pro at 24 points), and click OK. Choosing the right point size isn't so critical, because you can change the size of your Identity Plate by either using the Scale slider (in the Overlays panel), or by clicking on your Identity Plate text on the slide and then clicking-and-dragging any corner point outward (which scales the text up).

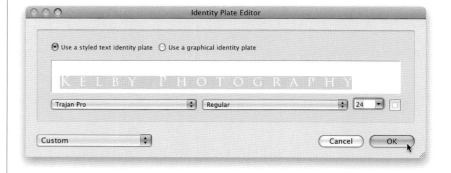

Step Six:
Let's take a look at how our custom slide layout is coming together by hiding the margin guides—press **Command-Shift-H (PC: Ctrl-Shift-H)**, or you could go to the Layout panel and turn off the checkbox for Show Guides. If you look at the text below the photo, you can see it's not bright white—it's actually a very light gray (I like that better, because it doesn't draw the eye as much if it's not solid white), and to get this more subtle light gray look, you just lower the Opacity amount up in the Identity Plate section of the Overlays panel (here you can see I've got the Identity Plate Opacity lowered to just 55%). Also, if you want to rotate your Identity Plate text, click on it first, then use the two Rotate arrows found down in the toolbar (I've circled them here in red for you).

Step Seven:
Although we're not going to use them for our project here, there are some other Overlays panel features you should know about. For example, if your slide has a lighter background color, you can add a drop shadow to your Identity Plate text. You have to click on your Identity Plate text first, then go to the bottom of the Overlays panel and turn the Shadow checkbox on. You can now control the opacity, how far offset your shadow is from your text, the radius (softness) of your shadow, and the angle (direction) of the shadow. By the way, to change the background color of your slide, go to the Backdrop panel, click on the Background Color swatch, and choose a new color from the color picker. Then, since your text color was white, go to the Overlays panel and turn on the Override Color checkbox found in the Identity Plate section.

Continued

Step Eight:

Before we leave this white background example, I wanted to point out the drop shadow behind the photo. That's controlled in the Options panel (the first panel in the right side Panels area). To turn on/off this drop shadow behind your photo, use the Cast Shadow checkbox (shown circled in red here). You have the same controls here as you did with the Identity Plate (opacity, offset amount, softness, and direction). Just so you can see it, I also changed the Stroke Border color swatch to black (our starting template had it set to white) and I increased the Width to 4 px (just so you can see it). Okay, let's finish up our custom template, and then we'll look at some of the other options (there are not that many left, but some of 'em are handy, so we'll cover them next).

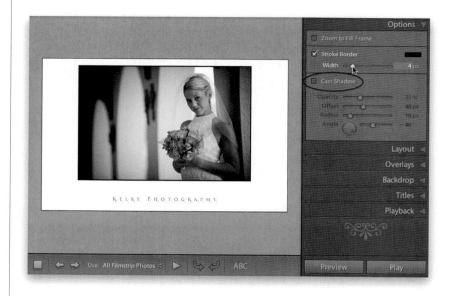

Step Nine:

I've returned to our black background (remember, I just changed to white to show you the shadow features), and I clicked on a different image (so we don't get sick of that same photo), and now we're going to save our template, so in the future we can apply it with just one click in the Template Browser (it remembers everything: the text, the background color, the opening and closing title slides—you name it). To do this, press **F7** to make the left side Panels area visible again, then go to the Template Browser and click on the + (plus sign) button on the far right of the panel header. This brings up the New Template dialog (shown here), where you can name your template and choose where you want to save it (I save mine in the User Templates folder, as shown here, but you can create your own folders and choose to save into one of them by choosing it from the Folder pop-up menu).

Step 10:
Now that you've saved your custom slide design as a template, you can apply this same exact look to your next wedding by going to the Slideshow module, and in the Collections panel, clicking on the collection from this new wedding. Then in the Template Browser, under User Templates, click on My Wedding Template, and this look will be instantly applied to your collection of photos. Now that you know how to customize a slide show, and save it as your own custom template, there are a few other customization features I need to share, and then we'll move on to other slide show stuff.

Step 11:
Besides adding text using the Identity Plate, you can add other lines of text info to your photo (either custom text that you type in, or info that Lightroom pulls from the photo's EXIF data or metadata). You can add these by clicking on the ABC button down in the toolbar, which adds a pop-up menu and a text field to the right of it. The default setting is Custom Text, and you can type the text you want in the text field. If you click-and-hold on the words Custom Text, a pop-up menu appears that lets you choose text that may be embedded into your photo's metadata. For example, if you choose Date, it displays the date the photo was taken (as shown here), and you can resize and reposition the text like it was an Identity Plate. If you choose any of the other options, it only pulls that information if it's in the file (in other words, if you didn't add caption info in the Metadata panel, choosing Caption here won't get you anything).

Continued

Step 12:

So, if you'd like to have a string of info visible during your slide show, you can do that by choosing Edit from the text overlay pop-up menu in the toolbar, which brings up the Text Template Editor (seen here). Here you can choose to create a string of info by clicking on the Insert button to the right of each field you want included. For example, here I wanted the filename, then the exposure, the ISO, the focal length of the lens I shot it with, and then my copyright info. To do that, you'd click on Custom Text under Example at the top, and press Delete (PC: Backspace), then beside Filename, click on Insert, and then I typed two dashes to add some visual separation between bits of info, then click the Insert button beside Exposure, and so on. It shows a preview of how your text will look at the top of the dialog.

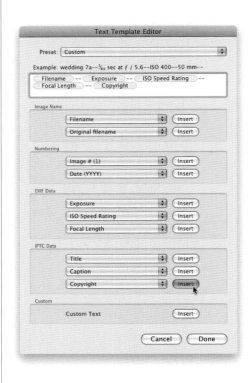

Step 13:

When you click the Done button, the string of text will appear on your slide, and you can just click-and-drag it where you want it to appear. Now, of course, you don't have to add all those different lines of info, you can have as many or as few as you'd like, and you don't have to have it go right over your photo (as I did here), I just wanted to show you what could be done. Also, instead of just one of these text blocks, you can have multiple blocks, and resize them by just clicking on a corner point and dragging it inward (to scale it down in size) or outward (to make it bigger). If you want to change the font, you can do so using the Font and Face pop-up menus under Text Overlays in the Overlays panel.

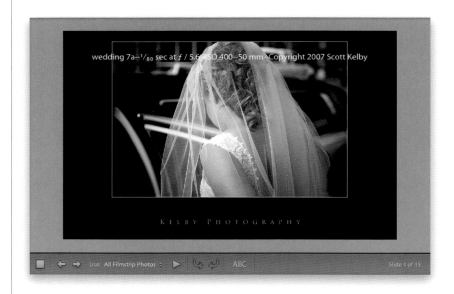

Step 14:

We're going to wrap up with some more background stuff (and then on the next page, we'll look at using a photo as your background). We're going to create a gradient as our background, so go to the Backdrop panel and turn on the Color Wash checkbox (as shown here). By default, this adds a light gray gradient to the top right of your slide, graduating down diagonally to whatever your background color is (in this case, our background color is black, so turning on Color Wash gives you a light gray to black diagonal gradient as your background, as seen here). If you want to choose a different color for your color wash (think of this color as the top-right color), you can click on the color swatch to the right of the Color Wash checkbox, and it will bring up the Color Wash color picker. By the way, the two sliders below Color Wash control the angle of your gradient and the opacity.

Step 15:

If you want to change the other color in your gradient, turn on the Background Color checkbox (at the bottom of the panel), then click on the color swatch to the right and a color picker appears (shown here). I chose a pretty dark gray as my bottom color for the gradient, so now the gradient goes from a light gray at the top right down to a dark gray at the bottom left (as seen here). Of course, you don't have to just use grays—you can choose other colors by dragging the Hue bar, which sits on the bottom of the tall gradient on the far-right side of the color picker. When you're done with all your background tweaks and text tweaks, click the Play button (at the bottom of the right side Panels area) and see your final customized slide show in full-screen mode without all the guides and panels.

Using a Photo as Your Slide Background

Besides a solid color and a gradient fill, you can choose a photo as your slide background, and you can control the opacity of this background photo, so you can create a subtle screen effect. My only complaint about this feature is that the same background appears on every slide (except the title slides, of course). So, you can't vary the background effect from slide to slide, or jump back to a solid background. Other than that, it rocks. Here's how it's done:

Step One:
First a little setup: go to the Template Browser and click on the template named Caption and Rating. Now, let's simplify the layout: In the Options panel (at the top of the right side Panels area), turn on the Zoom to Fill Frame checkbox, then click on the bottom-right corner of the guides and drag inward until your photo is smaller with a wide aspect ratio (like the one shown here). In that same panel, change the Stroke Border color to black and increase the stroke width to 2 pixels, then turn off the checkbox for Cast Shadow. Now go down to the Overlays panel and turn off both the Text Overlays checkbox and the Star Ratings checkbox (so we don't see stars over our photo).

Step Two:
Go to the filmstrip, find the photo you want to use as a background image, and drag-and-drop it right onto the Background Image well in the Backdrop panel (as shown here; you may have to turn the Background Image checkbox on first), and that image now appears as the background behind your currently selected photo. The background photo appears at 100% opacity, which usually means it's going to compete with your foreground photo, and for that reason we usually would create a "backscreened" effect for the background photo, so it appears washed out and more subtle.

Step Three:

Now we'll create that backscreened effect, but first you'll see that the Color Wash checkbox is turned on, so there's a slight gradient going over the background photo. This might look good or it might look pretty bad—it just depends on the photo you choose, but as a general rule I turn the Color Wash checkbox off, as shown. Now, to create the backscreened effect, change the background color to white (click on the Background Color swatch), then lower the Background Image Opacity to 40% (as shown here), and the photo fades. By the way, if you prefer that your photo fades to black, rather than white (again it depends on the photo you choose), leave the Background Color set to black.

TIP: Other Ideas for Slide Show Backgrounds

When it comes to using photos as backgrounds, you don't have to just use photos—you can use any image as a full-page background, including illustrations saved as either JPEGs or TIFFs and imported into Lightroom. For example, my buddy Matt Kloskowski (at LightroomKillerTips .com) put together some great holiday illustrations to use as slide backgrounds (back on December 24, 2007, just in case you want to go there and download them).

Step Four:

When you press the Preview button (as I did here), or the Play button, you'll see the slides play with the photo you chose as the background image (as I mentioned in the intro, this same background will appear behind each photo). If you want to turn this feature off, turn off the Background Image checkbox in the Backdrop panel.

SCOTT KELBY

Adding Background Music

The right background music can make all the difference in a slide show presentation, and if you get a chance to see the pros show their work, you'll find they choose music that creates emotion and supports the images beautifully. Lightroom lets you add background music to your slide shows, but there's one catch (and it's a big one), and that is that the music only plays while you're in Lightroom—if you save the file as a PDF for emailing (or putting on disc), the music isn't saved with the PDF.

Step One:
Once you've got the photos you want in a collection and you've created a slide show template you like, it's time to add some background music. (In case you were wondering, I created that little logo and text on the left side over in Photoshop, then I saved it as a JPEG and used it as my graphical Identity Plate. I didn't have to worry about getting the size just right, because there's a Scale [size] slider in the Identity Plate section of the Overlays panel. In the example shown here, I scaled the imported Identity Plate graphic down to 36%.)

Step Two:
Go to the Playback panel near the bottom of the right side Panels area (shown here). We'll start by turning on the Soundtrack checkbox (as shown here). Okay, that part was simple, but it's the next part—actually selecting which song will play behind your slide show—that takes a little doing, and the process is different depending on whether you're on a Mac or a Windows PC.

Step Three:

The Mac version of Lightroom requires that you use Apple's iTunes software (and don't worry—if you have a Mac, it's already installed). You start by either importing a song from a CD into iTunes, or you can download songs (at 99¢ each) from the iTunes Store (just for simplicity's sake, we'll assume you're either going to buy and download a song, or you've already got a song that will work in iTunes). Now, create a new playlist (click on the + [plus sign] button in the bottom-left corner of the iTunes window) and name it (I called mine "Slideshow Music"). Then drag-and-drop the song you want to use as background music into this playlist in the left column of the iTunes window. Okay, that's all you have to do in iTunes—basically you created a playlist, and dragged the song you want as background music into it.

Step Four:

Back in Lightroom, go to the Playback panel again, to the right of Soundtrack, and click-and-hold on the two little triangles to bring up a pop-up menu with a list of your iTunes music playlists (as seen here). Choose that Slideshow Music playlist from the list of playlists, and now the song (or songs) in that playlist will play as background music behind your slide show. (*Note:* If you don't see your new playlist, choose Refresh Playlist from iTunes from the top of the pop-up menu.)

TIP: Eliminating the Music Gap

iTunes has to launch before the background music can start playing, so before I show a slide show, I launch iTunes myself from the Mac OS X Dock. That way, the slide show doesn't start with silence while you're waiting for iTunes to launch and start playing the song.

Continued

Step Five

If you're running Lightroom on a Windows PC, you don't use iTunes, you just put an MP3 song into a folder (anywhere on your computer), then in Lighroom's Playback panel, below the Soundtrack checkbox, you click on the Click Here to Choose a Music Folder link (shown circled here). A Browse for Files or Folders dialog will appear, where you can choose the folder containing your one MP3 song (if you put more than one song in there, they'll play in alphabetical order).

Note: On a Windows PC, the song you put in that folder absolutely has to be in MP3 format or it won't play (so no WAVs, or WMAs, or AIFs—it has to be a real MP3 file).

Step Six:

At this point, I always preview my slide show to make sure the background music fits with the photos, so click the Preview button at the bottom of the right side Panels area (shown circled here), and your slide show will play in the center Preview area, and within a couple seconds, your background music will start playing, as well. If you need to change the background music, on a Mac you'd need to delete the current song in your slide show playlist and replace it with a different song (or choose a new playlist). On a Windows PC, you'd need to remove the current song from that folder, and drop a different MP3 song in its place (or choose a different folder).

SCOTT KELBY

Besides choosing your music, Lightroom's Playback panel in the Slideshow module is where you choose how long each slide stays onscreen, how long the transition (fade) between slides is, and even the color of the transition. You can choose to play your slides in order or randomly, and you get to choose whether you want your slide show to repeat after your last slide or end at the last slide.

Choosing Your Slide Show Preferences

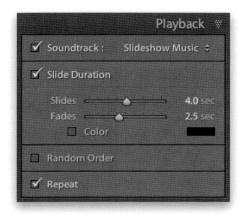

Step One:
We'll start with setting how long your slides stay onscreen, which you choose using the Slides slider in the Playback panel (click-and-drag to the right to keep them onscreen longer, or to the left for shorter). We're going to skip over the Fades slider until the next step, so there are just two more controls: your slides play in the order they appear in the filmstrip, unless you turn on the Random Order checkbox. Lastly (new in Lightroom 2), is a checkbox to turn off the Repeat function, and when this is off, your slide show will end when you reach the last slide, rather than looping and playing all over again.

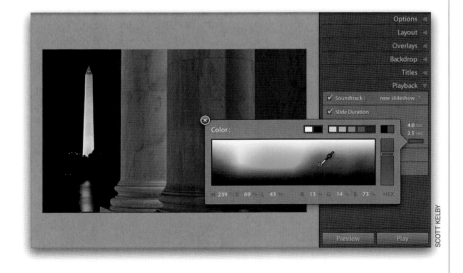

Step Two:
Now, on to Fades. The Fades slider is where you choose how long it takes once the transition between slides starts. But beyond that, another new thing Adobe added in Lightroom 2 is the ability to choose the color of your fade (your transition) between slides. By default, it's always been black (so your slide briefly fades to black before the next slide appears), but now if you turn on the Color checkbox, you can click on the color swatch to its right, and a color picker pops up where you can choose a different solid color (in this example, your slide would briefly fade to a bluish purple before the next slide appears).

Emailing Your Slide Show

If you want to show someone your slide show and they happen to be nearby, then no sweat—you can show it right within Lightroom. But if they're not standing nearby (perhaps it's a client across town or across the country), you can email them a PDF of the slide show. There are two limitations though: one is you can't control the length of the transitions (that's set by the PDF), and the second is you can't include the background music. That second one gets me, but I do have a workaround you'll learn in just a moment.

Step One:
To save your slide show as a PDF (which is ideal for emailing because it compresses the file size big time), click on the Export PDF button at the bottom of the left side Panels area (shown circled in red here).

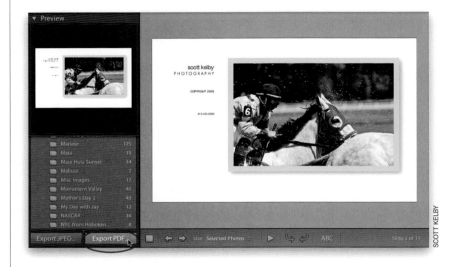

Step Two:
Go ahead and name your slide show in the Export Slideshow to PDF dialog. In the bottom part of the dialog is a Quality slider, and the higher the quality, the larger the file size (which is a consideration when emailing), so I usually use a Quality setting of between 80 and 90. I also always turn on the Automatically Show Full Screen checkbox, so they see the slide show without any other onscreen distractions. The width and height dimensions are automatically inserted in the Width and Height fields, but if you need the images to be smaller for emailing, you can enter a smaller width or height and Lightroom will automatically scale the photos down proportionally.

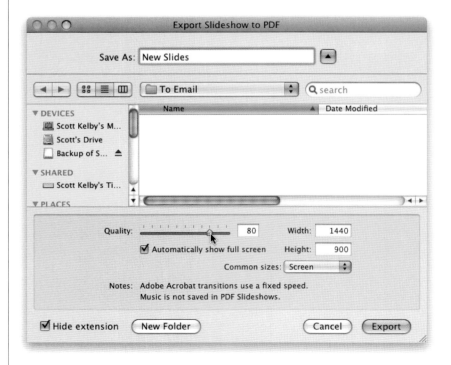

Step Three:
Here's the saved slide show as it appears on my computer, exported as a PDF file. The entire slide show, with 17 large-sized photos, is only 3.7 MB, which should email just fine (many email accounts have a 5-MB limit on attachments), so open your email software and include this PDF as an attachment.

Step Four:
When your client (friend, relative, parole officer, etc.) double-clicks on your PDF, it will launch their Adobe Reader, and when it opens, it will go into full-screen mode and start your slide show, complete with smooth transitions between slides. Now, of course there is no background music (as I mentioned in the intro on the previous page), but if you have Acrobat Professional, you can open the PDF document you created in Lightroom and add background music there that will play automatically when your client gets your PDF. Just keep an eye on the file size when you start embedding music. If it's a long song, it could really balloon your file size.

TIP: Adding Filenames to a PDF
If you're planning on sending this PDF slide show to a client for proofing purposes, be sure to go to the Slideshow module first and make the filename text overlay visible before you make the PDF. That way, your client will be able to tell you the name of the photo(s) they've approved.

Lightroom Quick Tips > >

▼ Detailed Slide Design

Although you can create your slide shows from scratch in Lightroom, there's nothing that says that you have to design your slides in Lightroom. If there are things you want to do that you can't do in Lightroom, just build the slides over in Photoshop, save them as JPEGs, then re-import the finished slides into Lightroom, and drop those into your slide show layout, add your background music, etc.

▼ Preview How Photos Will Look in Your Slide Show

On the far-right side of the toolbar that appears under the center Preview area, you'll see some text showing how many photos are in your current collection. If you move your cursor over that text, your cursor turns into a scrubby slider, and you can click-and-drag left or right to see the other photos in your slide show appear in your current slide show layout (it's one of those things you have to try, and then you'll dig it).

▼ What Those Rotate Arrows Are For

If you look down in the toolbar, you'll see two rotation arrows, but they're always grayed out. That's because they're not for rotating photos, they're for rotating any custom text you create (you add custom text by clicking on the ABC button in the toolbar).

▼ A Better Start to Your Slide Show

One of my biggest slide show complaints about Lightroom 1 was that when you started your slide show, the person viewing it always saw the first slide onscreen before the slide show even started (so, if you're showing a bride and groom the photos from their wedding, when they sit down, they see the first image onscreen, without any music, any drama, etc., which totally kills any emotional impact). You saw earlier in this chapter that you can have opening and closing title slides in Lightroom 2, right? So, go ahead and set up a title slide (or just leave it black, but turn on the title slide feature in the Titles panel). Now, here's the tip: When you make a slide show presentation for a client, before the client is in front of your monitor, start the slide show, and as soon as it appears onscreen, press the Spacebar to pause it. Now when your client sits in front of your screen, they don't see your first photo—they see a black screen (or your title screen). When you're ready to begin your presentation, press the Spacebar again and your slide show starts.

▼ Adding a Copyright Watermark to Your Slides

If you want to add a transparent copyright over your photos (so if you email somebody a PDF, they won't want to print the images themselves), go to the Overlays panel, turn on the Identity Plate, and choose Edit from the Identity Plate pop-up menu (found in the bottom-right corner of the Identity Plate preview). When the Identity

Plate Editor appears, click in the text field, erase the current Identity Plate, then press Option-G (PC: Alt-0169 on your numeric keypad) to create a copyright symbol, and click OK. Once the symbol appears, position it where you'd like it. Use the Scale slider to increase the size, and lower the Opacity slider to make it transparent. Now that copyright symbol will appear over every image in your PDF slide show.

▼ Collections Remember Which Template You Used Last

The Collections panel now also appears in the Slideshow module (which you learned about in this chapter), but these collections have memory—they automatically remember the last slide show template you used for the photos in that collection. However, they don't remember the exact photos you used—they just remember the template itself, so your layout looks the same, but if you originally selected just a few photos in that collection for your slide show (and changed the Use pop-up menu to Selected Photos in the toolbar at the bottom of the Preview area), they don't remember those. So, you'll want to Control-click (PC: Right-click) on the collection, and choose Create Slideshow from the contextual menu. This creates a new collection with just the photos you used in that particular slide show, in the right order, along with the template, so when you want that exact same slide show again (same look, same photos, same order), you're one click away.

Print
printing your photos

It could be argued that this is the single most important module of all of Photoshop Lightroom's modules, because it's all about "the print." Everything we do is, ultimately, to produce a final printed image. In fact, one of my friends, the award-winning nature photographer Vincent Versace, has a saying he's quite fond of: "We are in service of the print." He must be right, because he's a brilliant photographer, and one heck of a Photoshop instructor, too. However, Vincent himself will be the first one to tell you he's a better chef than he is a photographer. Now, if you've seen any of Vincent's photography (some of his original prints go for upwards of $5,000 a pop), you know he's got to be one hell of a cook. Vincent has invited me over to his house for dinner on numerous occasions, but I've never gone. You know why? Because

I'm afraid Vincent will slip hallucinogenic drugs into my food. Why do I think that? It's because I think Vincent slips hallucinogenic drugs into his own food. Always. So, it only stands to reason that if he's cooking dinner, I'm going to wind up singing "Purple Haze" while staring intently at a ball of yarn. Maybe that's why everybody loves Vincent's cooking so much. By the time the main course comes around, they're all hopped up on crank and everything tastes yummy. Of course, I could be wrong. But if you get a chance to hear Vincent speak at a conference, see if you don't subscribe to my "don't eat the brownies" theory afterwards. However, I think Vincent's statement that "We are in service of the print" has some merit. Not that I really understand it, but I've noticed it really starts to sound good after a few appetizers.

:tting Up Your Photos for Printing (It All Starts Here)

If you really like everything else in Photoshop Lightroom, it's the Print module where you'll fall deeply in love. It's really brilliantly designed (I've never worked with any program that had a better, easier, and more functional printing feature than this). In Lightroom 2, Adobe took it up another notch by incorporating a version of Photoshop's Contact Sheet II feature (and I like the implementation of it here better). The built-in templates make the printing process not only easy, but also fun, and they make a great starting point for customizing and saving your own templates.

Step One:

Start in the Print module by clicking on the collection that has the photo (or photos) you want to print. By default, whichever photo you have selected will appear in the Print module's center Preview area. If you want to print more than one photo, then go down to the filmstrip and Command-click (PC: Ctrl-click) on the photos you want to print. Also, a few lines of info appear over the top-left corner of your photo. This info doesn't actually print on the photo, and if you find it as distracting as I do, you can turn off this info display by going under the View menu and choosing Show Info Overlay (which turns it off). You can also just press the letter **I** on your keyboard.

Step Two:

The Print module uses layout templates just like the Slideshow and Web modules do, and the default template in the Print module is called Maximum Size (this template positions your photo so it prints as large as possible on your selected paper size with the full image showing, even if it has to rotate the photo on its side, as seen in the previous step). If you don't want the photo auto-rotated like this, go to the Image Settings panel (in the right side Panels area), and turn off the checkbox for Rotate to Fit (as shown here), and your image won't be rotated.

Step Three:

If you selected more than one photo to print (down in the filmstrip), you get to choose how these are printed (one per page or multiple photos on the same page). For example, here I've selected seven photos, and if you look at the right end of the toolbar below the Preview area, you'll see Page 1 of 7 (circled here in red). That lets you know that, although you're only seeing one photo right now onscreen, there are actually six more photos that are queued up to print with the same layout. To see the other pages queued up to print, use the Previous/Next arrow buttons on the left end of the toolbar. (*Note:* Compare this to printing in Photoshop, where to print seven photos, you'd have to open seven separate documents and then print each one of them separately, and it makes you really appreciate printing from Lightroom.)

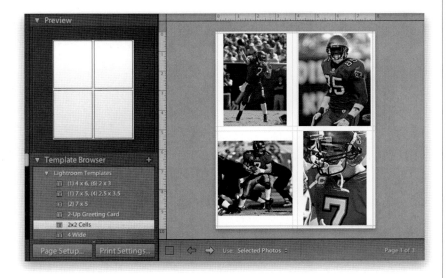

Step Four:

Your other choice is to print more than one photo on each page. To do that, just click on any multiple-photo template in the built-in templates (if you hover your cursor over any of the templates in the Template Browser, a preview of the layout will appear in the Preview panel at the top of the left side Panels area). For example, go to the Template Browser and click on the 2x2 Cells template, and it puts your photos in two columns and two rows (as shown here—you can see a preview of that template's layout up in the Preview panel). Here, I selected nine photos, and if you look at the right end of the toolbar, you'll see Lightroom will make three prints: two with four photos each, and the last print will just have that one leftover photo up in the top-left corner.

Continued

Step Five:

If you want to print the same photo, at the same exact size, multiple times on the same page, then you can go to the Image Settings panel and turn on the checkbox for Repeat One Photo Per Page, as shown here. If you want to print multiple photos on the same page, but you want them to be different sizes (like one 5x7" and four wallet-size photos), then turn to page 328 for details on how to set that up.

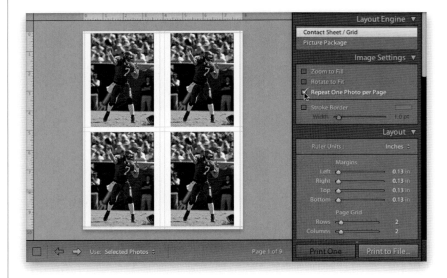

Step Six:

If one of the built-in templates works for you, then you're pretty much set, but before you go any further, you'll need to let Lightroom know what size paper and which printer you'll be printing to. You do this by clicking on the Page Setup button found at the bottom of the left side Panels area (it's shown circled here in red). This brings up the Page Setup dialog (the Mac version is shown here, but the Windows version, called the Print Setup dialog, looks and works very similarly). There are basically three things you need to do here: (1) choose your printer from the Format For (PC: Printer Name) pop-up menu (if your printer doesn't appear in the list, you need to install your printer's driver software), (2) choose the paper size you want to print on from the Paper Size pop-up menu (I chose 16x20" paper here), and (3) in the orientation section, click on an icon (PC: Portrait or Landscape radio button) to choose whether you want to print tall or wide.

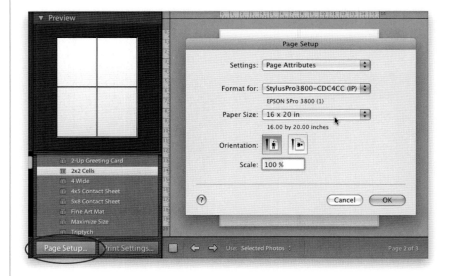

Step Seven:
Now click the OK button in the Page Setup (PC: Print Setup) dialog (you can see the new page size by taking a quick glance at the rulers, along the top and left side of the center Preview area. If the rulers aren't visible, press **Command-R [PC: Ctrl-R]**). Now that you've chosen your paper size, printer, and orientation, next let's look at how to resize and position your photo on the page.

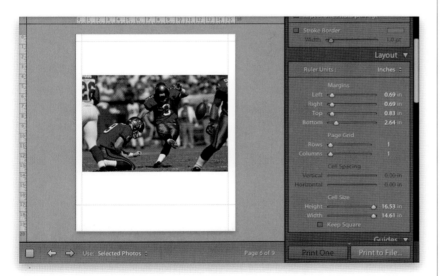

Step Eight:
As a starting point, go to the Template Browser and click on the Fine Art Mat template. Go to the Layout panel in the right side Panels area, and take a look at the Margins sliders. They're showing you that for this photo, there's a 0.69-inch margin on the left and right sides of your photo, and then at the top, there's a slightly larger 0.83-inch margin. The bottom margin is much larger at 2.64 inches, which gives the photo the fine art mat look you see here. So, if those are the margins, why is my photo so far from the top and bottom margins? It's because Lightroom puts each photo in its own a separate cell (kind of like a spreadsheet cell). This cell idea works great when you want to put multiple photos on the same page (which Lightroom really excels at), but it does make it a little funky when you just want to fit one photo on a page, because now you have to mess with the margins and the size of your cell. In the next step, we'll do something that will help make all of this make more sense.

Continued

Step Nine:

Just for the sake of understanding margins and cells, select nine photos down in the filmstrip, then go to the Layout panel. In the Page Grid section of the panel, using the sliders, increase the Rows to 3 and the Columns to 3. You can see here how it put each of those nine photos into its own separate little cell, but all nine of those photos fit within the margin settings we had in place (if you remember, we had the same 0.69-inch border on the left and right, a slightly deeper margin up top, and then a 2.64-inch margin at the bottom of the page). You can still see all those in place, and your photos can't extend out into those areas—they're protected by your margins (you can change your margins using the Margins sliders—dragging to the right makes the margins bigger; dragging all the way to the left removes that margin, so you can print to the edge of the page, if your printer allows that, of course).

Step 10:

If you look at the capture back in Step Nine, you'll also notice that the photos don't perfectly fill up each cell, because some are tall and thin, and others are wide with a gap at the top and bottom. If you want to have your images completely fill each cell, scroll up to the Image Settings panel in the right side Panels area, and turn on the Zoom to Fill checkbox (as shown here). This enlarges the photos so they completely fill each cell (as seen in the Preview area here). Now the photos fill the cell, and they're right up against each other.

Step 11:

If you want to add some space between these cells, go back to the Layout panel and, in the Cell Spacing section, click-and-drag the Vertical and Horizontal sliders to the right (I dragged mine over to 0.67 inches, which adds that white space between each column and between the rows, as well). So, the Cell Spacing sliders do just what you'd expect—they add space between the cells, but even though we added space, you'll notice that our margins are still exactly the same. How could that be? It's because the cells themselves shrunk in size—they had to, because the margins protected the area outside the photos, so the only thing they could do to allow more space is to shrink the photo cells themselves (in Step 10, each cell was 5.51 inches by 4.87 inches, but after we added cell space, each photo, and its cell, was shrunk down to 5.07 inches by 4.43 inches to fit in the same space).

Step 12:

Now, if you wanted more space around the sides and more space below the photos, you could increase the margins (and luckily, the cells are smart enough to scale themselves down in size automatically, because now they have to fit in less space). So, go to the Margins section of the Layout panel, and using the sliders there, increase the Left and Right margins to 1.25 inches, increase the Top margin to 1.77 inches, and increase the Bottom margin to 5.29 inches, and then look at how the layout looks now. The cells are smaller, but the space between them remains the same. So, to recap: (1) you control how much of the page is allowed to have an image on it using the Margins sliders, (2) you have your images fill each cell by turning on the Zoom to Fill checkbox, and (3) you choose how much space appears between each cell using the Cell Spacing sliders.

Continued

Step 13:

Before we go any farther, if you've tweaked a layout like we have here and you like it, don't forget to save it as a printing template. Go to the left side Panels area, and on the right side of the Template Browser header, click the + (plus sign) button, and when the New Template dialog appears, give your new custom template a name, choose to save it in the User Templates folder, then click Create. Now, next time you want this same setup, you're just one click away. Okay, let's look at resizing just one photo on the page. In the Template Browser, click on Fine Art Mat again.

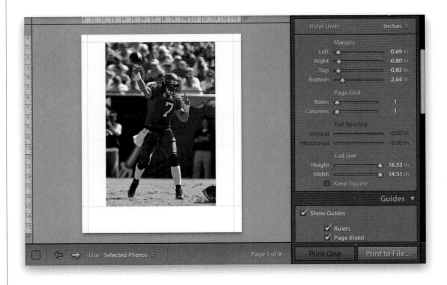

Step 14:

As far as resizing a single image on a page goes, if you want to move the photo left, right, higher up on the page, or lower down on the page, you'll use the Margins sliders in the Layout panel. If you want to resize the entire photo while it remains centered on the page, then use the Cell Size sliders in the Layout panel, instead. Once you've dragged the Cell Size sliders in a bit, so you can see the cell guides, you can actually just move the cell guides by clicking-and-dragging directly on them (as seen here, where I'm moving the right guide inward). A little readout with the dimensions of that part of the cell appears beside the guide as you drag (as seen here). Depending on whether you have a tall or wide photo, you may only have to adjust the top or side cell guide to get the image positioned the way you want it. However, if you're going to cut your photo to size once it's printed, there is an advantage to having the cell guides snug up against your photo (more in the next step).

Step 15:
At this point, go to the Guides panel (in the right side Panels area) and turn off the Show Guides checkbox, so you get a clean view of the photo on the page without all the cell and margin guides (I also turned off the rulers by pressing **Command-R [PC: Ctrl-R]**). Now, scroll down to the Overlays panel, turn on the checkbox for Page Options, and then turn on the Crop Marks checkbox (as shown here) to have Lightroom print crop marks to help you cut the photo to size, once it's printed (you can see the crop marks appear outside each corner of the image in the preview shown here). The crop marks appear where your cell guides were, so if they're snug up against your photo, they'll appear in the right position. If you only moved one side of the cell, those crop marks will appear where the cell border is, not where your photo is (just a quick heads up on that, just in case).

Step 16:
The final step is to actually print the file, which is handled down in the Print Job panel. There are some important things you'll need to know (like how to set up the color management, resolution, what the sharpening is all about, etc.), and I've covered that in a separate tutorial starting on page 339 of this chapter, but I wanted to show you in context what you'd do after you've gotten your photo laid out on the page the way you want it. The nice thing is that once you learn how to set this Print Job panel up, you won't have to fuss with it every time—most of the choices will already have been made. In many cases, you'll be able to skip this panel, and simply click either the Print One or Print button (found at the bottom of the right side Panels area), and it will use your last Print Job panel settings and simply print the photo without any further input from you. So that's the basics of laying out your photo(s) for printing.

Adding Text to Your Print Layouts

If you want to add text to your print layouts, it's pretty easy, as well, and like the Web and Slideshow modules, you can have Lightroom automatically pull metadata info from your photos and have it appear on the photo print, or you can add your own custom text (and/or Identity Plate), just as easily. Here's what you can add, and how you can add it:

Step One:
Start by selecting a photo, then choose that Fine Art Mat template in the Template Browser to get you started. Next, grab the bottom cell guide and drag upward to move your photo up higher in the frame (as seen here; if you don't see the cell guides, turn on the Show Guides checkbox in the Guides panel). Now, the easiest way to add text to your print is to go to the Overlays panel and turn on the Identity Plate checkbox, and your nameplate appears on your print (if you're not familiar with how to set up your Identity Plate, jump back to Chapter 3 for a step by step). Once it's there, you can click-and-drag it right where you want it (in this case, drag it down and position it in the center of the space below the photo, as shown here).

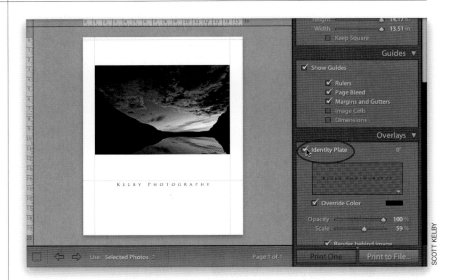

Step Two:
Besides adding your Identity Plate, Lightroom can also pull text from your metadata (things like your exposure settings, camera make and model, the filename, or caption info you added in the Metadata panel of the Library module). You do this in the Overlays panel by turning on the Photo Info checkbox (as shown here) and choosing which type of info you want displayed at the bottom of your cell from the pop-up menu on the right. You can change the size of your text right below it, but the largest size is 16 points, and on a print this size, it's still pretty tiny (as barely seen here).

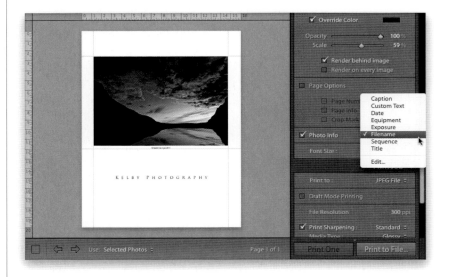

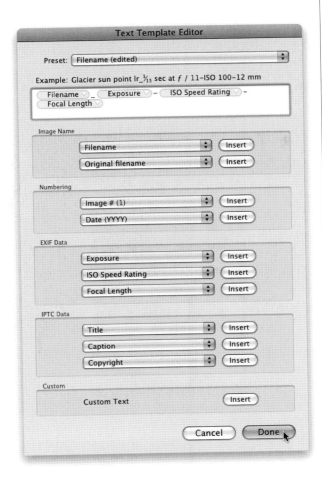

Step Three:

Now, besides just pulling the filename and metadata stuff, you can also create your own custom text (but it's going to show up at the bottom of the cell and this text is stuck there—you can't reposition it like you can the Identity Plate text, which is why I usually use that instead). If you choose Custom Text from the Photo Info pop-up menu, a field appears below it, so you can type in your custom text. You can also choose Edit from that same pop-up menu to bring up the Text Template Editor (shown here), where you can create your own custom list of data that Lightroom will pull from each photo's metadata and print under that photo. In this case, I chose to add text showing the filename, exposure, ISO, and the focal length of the lens by clicking the Insert button beside each of these fields in the Editor. I can't imagine why anyone would want that type of information printed beneath the photo. But you know, and I know, there's somebody out there right now reading this and thinking, "All right! Now I can put the EXIF camera data right on the print!" The world needs these people.

Step Four:

If you're printing pages for a photo book, you can have Lightroom automatically number those pages. In the Overlays panel, turn on the Page Options checkbox, then turn on the checkbox for Page Numbers. Lastly, if you're doing a series of test prints, you can have your print settings (including your level of sharpening, your color management profile, and your selected printer) appear on the bottom-left side of the print (as seen here) by turning on the Page Info checkbox.

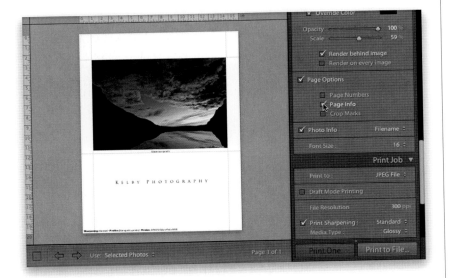

Printing Multiple Photos on One Page

You saw earlier in this chapter how to print the same photo, at the same exact size, multiple times on the same print. But what if you want to print the same photo at different sizes (like a 5x7" and four wallet sizes)? That's when you want to use Lightroom's Picture Package feature (it's new in Lightroom 2).

Step One:

Start by clicking on the photo you want to have appear multiple times, in multiple sizes, on the same page. Go to the Template Browser in the left side Panels area and click on the built-in template named (1) 4x6, (6) 2x3, which gives you the layout you see here. If you look over in the Layout Engine panel at the top of the right side Panels area, you'll see that the engine running this feature is Picture Package (as seen circled here in red).

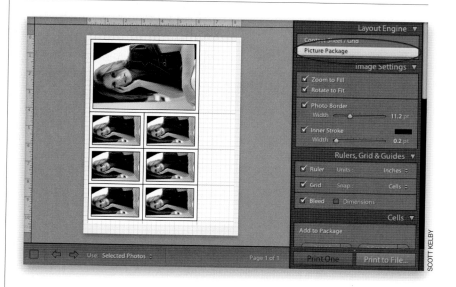

Step Two:

If you look at the Preview area in Step One, you can see that, by default, it puts a little white border around each photo. If you don't want the white border, go to the Image Settings panel and turn off the Photo Border checkbox (as shown here). Also, by default, the Zoom to Fill checkbox is turned on, so your photo is cropped in a little bit. If you don't want your photo cropped like that, turn the Zoom to Fill checkbox off.

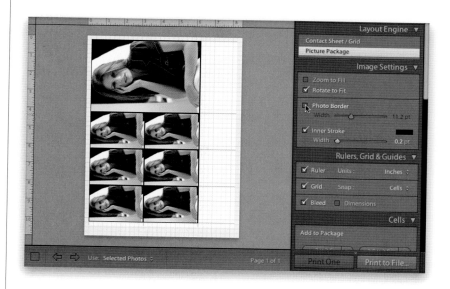

Step Three:
Another option it has on by default is that it puts a black stroke around each image (you can control the size of this stroke, using the Width slider right below the Inner Stroke checkbox). To remove this stroke, turn off the Inner Stroke checkbox (as shown here. You'll still see a thin stroke that separates the images, but does not print). Now your images are back to their original cropping, they're right up against each other (there's no extra white border), and you've removed the black stroke around the photos (by the way, if you like this layout, don't forget to save it as your own custom template by clicking on the + [plus sign] button on the right side of the Template Browser header).

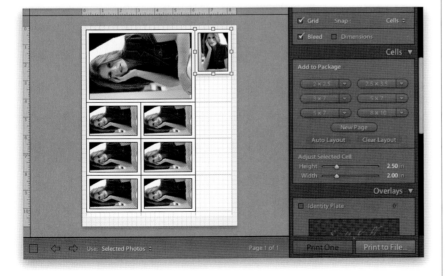

Step Four:
Adding more photos is easy—just go to the Cells panel (in the right side Panels area) and you'll see a number of pill-shaped buttons marked with different sizes. Just click on any one of those to add a photo that size to your layout (I clicked on the 2x2.5 button, and it added the new cell you see selected here). So, that's the routine: you click on those buttons to add more photos to your Picture Package layout. To delete a cell, just click on it, then press the Delete (PC: Backspace) key on your keyboard.

Continued

Step Five:

If you want to create your own custom Picture Package layout from scratch, go to the Cells panels and click on the Clear Layout button (as shown here), which removes all the cells, so you can start from scratch.

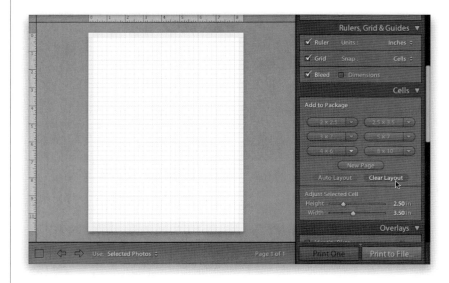

Step Six:

Now you can just start clicking on sizes, and Lightroom will place them on the page each time you click one of those Add to Package buttons (as shown here). As you can see, it doesn't always place the photos in the optimum location for the page dimensions, but Lightroom can actually fix that for you.

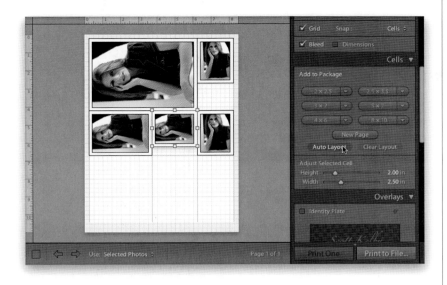

Step Seven:
If you click on the Auto Layout button, at the bottom of the Add to Package section (as shown here), it tries to automatically arrange the photos so they fit more logically, and gives you extra space to add more photos. Okay, hit the Clear Layout button and let's start from scratch again, so I can show you another handy feature.

TIP: Dragging-and-Copying
If you want to duplicate a cell, just press-and-hold the **Option (PC: Alt) key**, click-and-drag yourself a copy, and position it anywhere you'd like. If one of your photos overlaps another photo, you'll get a little yellow warning icon up in the top-right corner of your page.

Step Eight:
If you add so many cells that they can't fit on one page, Lightroom automatically adds new pages to accommodate your extra cells. For example, start by adding an 8x10, then add a 5x7 (which can't fit on the same letter-sized page), and it automatically creates a new page for you with the 5x7. Now add another 5x7 (so you have two-up), then a 2x2.5 (which won't fit on the same page), and it will add yet another page. Pretty smart, eh? (By the way, I think this "automatically do the obvious thing" is a big step forward in software development. In the past, if something like this happened, wouldn't you have expected to see a dialog pop up that said, "This cell cannot fit on the page. Would you like to add an additional page?") Also, if you decide you want to add another blank page yourself, just click on the New Page button that appears below the Add to Package buttons.

Continued

Step Nine:

If you want to delete a page added by Lightroom, just hover your cursor over the page you want to delete, and a little red X appears over the top-left corner (as seen here, on the third page). Click on that X and the page is deleted. Now, on the page with the two 5x7s, click on each of the 5x7s, press the Delete (PC: Backspace) key to remove them, and then go and turn on the Zoom to Fill checkbox up in the Image Settings panel.

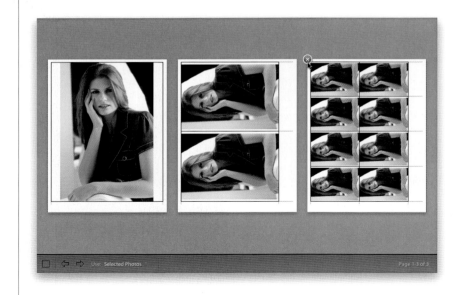

Step 10:

You can also manually adjust the size of each cell (which is a handy way to crop your photos on the fly, if you have Zoom to Fill turned on). For example, go ahead and add two 3x7 cells on this second (now empty) page, which gives you a tall, thin, cropped image. Click on the bottom image (to bring up the adjustment handles around the cell), then click-and-drag the bottom handle upward to make the cell thinner (as seen here). You can get the same effect by clicking-and-dragging the Adjust Selected Cell sliders, at the bottom of the Cells panel (there are sliders for both Height and Width). There's only one real downside, and that is you can't have different photos at these different sizes—it has to be the same photo repeated for each different size (interestingly enough, this Picture Package feature was borrowed from Photoshop, but Photoshop actually does let you use different photos in your cells, not just one repeated).

Step 11:

If you do want different images to appear in each cell (as shown here), you'll need to use the standard Contact Sheet/Grid feature in the Layout Engine panel. Start by selecting the photos you want in the filmstrip (in this case, you'd need to click on four photos, since there are four cells), then go to the Template Browser, and from the built-in templates, click on 4 Wide. Once the photos appear in their cells, you can reposition them inside the cells by clicking-and-dragging right on the photos themselves (if you look at the top photo here, you'll see my cursor has changed into a Grabber Hand, which you use to reposition the image inside the cell).

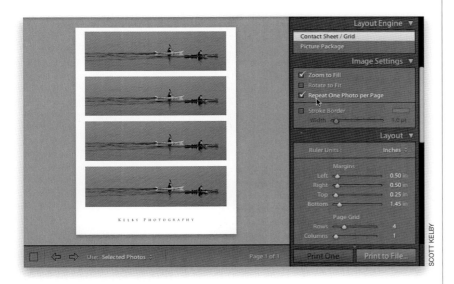

Step 12:

You can actually get the same photo repeated on a page (and in the exact same size) using the Contact Sheet/Grid layout engine. Using the same 4 Wide template, click on the photo you want repeated in all four cells, then go to the Image Settings panel in the right side Panels area and turn on the Repeat One Photo Per Page checkbox, as shown here. Now that one photo will be repeated in all the cells.

Continued

Step 13:

I use this Repeat One Photo Per Page technique for artistic looks. Here's a layout I created (with the layout settings shown in the Layout panel here). If you want to create this same layout (and save it as a custom template), first change the page setup to Landscape (by clicking on the Page Setup button at the bottom of the left side Panels area), then go to the Layout panel, and in the Page Grid section, choose 1 for Rows and 5 for Columns. Down at the bottom of the panel, in the Cell Size section, turn on the checkbox for Keep Square to get the perfectly square cells you see here. I have the space between each photo (the Horizontal Cell Spacing slider) set to 0.15 inches, but depending on the size of the paper you'll be printing on, you might have to make this larger or smaller. I also added my Identity Plate (created with some text in Photoshop using the font Trajan Pro, which I put over a scan of my signature with the layer opacity lowered to around 10%) by turning on the Identity Plate checkbox in the Overlays panel.

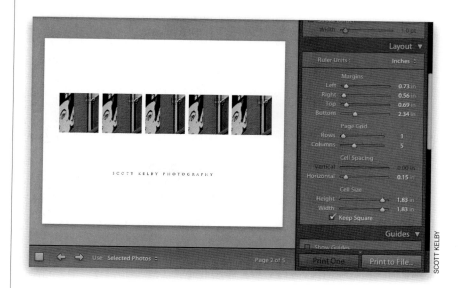

Step 14:

In this layout, I only changed three things: I lowered the number of Columns to 3 (as seen in the Layout panel here), changed the Horizontal Cell Spacing to 0.67 inches, and then up in the Image Settings panel, I turned off the Repeat One Photo Per Page checkbox, so I was able to use three different photos, instead of having that one photo repeat itself in all the cells.

SCOTT KELBY

Step 15:
Let's take that same layout and tweak it just a bit for an entirely different look. First, change the page setup to Portrait. Then, in the Layout panel's Page Grid section, change the number of Rows to 2, and the number of Columns to 2 (you may have to tweak your margins and cell spacing), and you've got this new layout (if you like it, don't forget to save it as your own custom template in the Template Browser). Also, once you save that, try creating a layout with 3 Rows and 3 Columns, for a nine-photo grid.

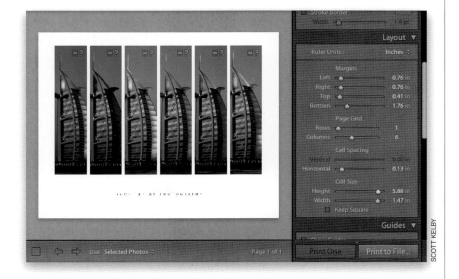

SCOTT KELBY

Step 16:
Now let's turn off the Keep Square feature, and go with a tall, thin layout using six selected photos (go to the Layout panel and turn off the Keep Square checkbox at the bottom of the panel). Change the page setup back to Landscape. In the Page Grid section, set the number of Rows to 1 and the number of Columns to 6. In the Margins section, set the Bottom slider to 1.76 inches, so it moves all six photos in the cells up closer to the top of the page, and change your Horizontal Cell Spacing to 0.13 inches. Then click-and-drag your Identity Plate down below the photos (as seen here; if it is rotated, you can click on the degrees to the right of the Identity Plate checkbox, and choose No Rotation). So, there are a few layout ideas to get your creative juices flowing, now that you know how to create your own custom multi-photo layouts.

Having Lightroom Remember Your Last Printing Layouts

In Lightroom 2, Adobe added the Collections panel right in the Print module, so now you have access to different collections without having to go back to the Library module. But what's cool is that they also added a little "under the hood" feature for the collections that makes them more powerful—Lightroom remembers the last print layout you used for each collection (even if you created it from scratch, and didn't save it as a template). However, there is one big "Gotcha!" and you're about to learn how to avoid it.

Step One:
Start by going to the Print module, then in the Collections panel (in the left side Panels area), click on a collection of images (in this case, it's a collection of B&W portraits of a child). Now, in the filmstrip, Command-click (PC: Ctrl-click) on the images that you want to print. Also, in the left side Panels area, in the Template Browser, click on the built-in Triptych template to get the layout you see here. In the Image Settings panel on the right, turn on the Stroke Border checkbox to put a thin stroke around the outside of each image. Now you can go ahead and print this layout (it's actually not necessary to print them now, but at this point you would print them for your client).

Step Two:
Okay, so you've printed those and you move on to other portraits from a different collection. The cool thing is, when you click on a different collection of photos, Lightroom automatically remembers the last layout you used for this collection (as shown here, where the last layout used for these color portraits was the Fine Art Mat, and as soon as you click on this collection, that layout loads).

Step Three:

Pretty cool so far, right? But, here's where it gets dicey. So, a few weeks after you printed the B&W portraits, the client calls and says, "Our daughter's grandparents visited us today, and they are so crazy about that print with the three photos on one page that they want four copies for themselves and some for our relatives up north." So you think, "Great—no problem—I'll just go back to that collection and it will remember the layout." So, you click on that collection, and sure enough it remembered the layout, but (and here's the gotcha) it doesn't remember which three photos you used in that layout. (Yikes!) So, what do you do? Have the client take a photo of the layout and email it to you so you can see which photos you used, and their order and position in each cell? See, it's a pretty big gotcha.

Step Four:

Here's how you avoid the gotcha: when you actually do make a print, once it prints out and looks the way you want it to, Control-click (PC: Right-click) directly on that collection (over in the Collections panel) and, from the contextual menu that appears, choose Create Print (as shown here).

Continued

Step Five:

This brings up the Create Print dialog and the key thing to do here is to make sure the Include Selected Photos checkbox is turned on (as shown here). That way, when you create this new collection, only the photos that are actually in this print are saved in this new print collection. By the way, print collections look just like any other collection, but by default it adds the word "Print" to the end of the collection name, and I recommend that you leave that in place, so you'll quickly know which collections are regular and which are just used when you're printing. Now click the Create button.

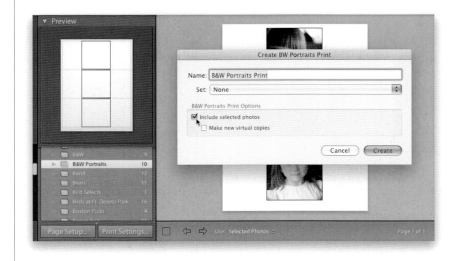

Step Six:

Now if your client calls and asks for more prints, you'll click on the print collection instead, and Lightroom will not only remember the layout, but also which photos, in which order, were used in that layout. All you have to do is click on the photos again in the filmstrip (to select them), and they pop right back into the layout, in the right order and placement within the print cells (as shown here). Plus, it remembers all the print settings, page setup settings, and the whole ball of wax, so you can just hit Print and go. The 20 seconds it takes to make a print collection like this can save you tons of time (and embarrassment) down the road.

The Final Print and Color Management Settings

Once you've got your page set up with the printing layout you want, you just need to make a few choices in the Print Job panel, so your photos look their best when printed. Here are which buttons to click, when, and why:

Step One:
Get your page layout the way you want it to look (in the capture shown here, I clicked on Page Setup at the bottom of the left side Panels area and set my page to a tall [portrait] orientation, and then I went to the Template Browser and clicked on the Fine Art Mat template. Lastly, I added my Identity Plate below the photo). Once that's done, it's time to choose our printing options in the Print Job panel, at the bottom of the right side Panels area.

Step Two:
In Lightroom 2, you have the choice of outputting your image to a printer, or just creating a high-resolution JPEG file of your photo layout (that way, you could send this finished page to a photo lab for printing, or email it to a client as a high-res proof, or use the layout on a website, or… whatever). You choose whether it's going to output the image to a printer or save it as a JPEG from the Print To pop-up menu, at the top right of the Print Job panel (as seen here). If you want to choose the Print to JPEG File route, go to the next tutorial in this chapter for details on how to use the JPEG settings and export the file.

Continued

Step Three:

Since we've already started at the top, we'll just kind of work our way down. The next setting down in the panel is a checkbox for Draft Mode Printing, and when you turn this on, you're swapping quality for speed. That's because rather than rendering the full-resolution image, it just prints the low-res JPEG preview image that's embedded in the file, so the print comes out of your printer faster than a greased pig. I would only recommend using this if you're printing multi-photo contact sheets. In fact, I always turn this on when printing contact sheets, because for printing a page of small thumbnail images, it works beautifully—the small images look crisp and clear. Notice, though, that when you turn Draft Mode Printing on, all the other options are grayed out. So, for contact sheets, turn it on. Otherwise, leave this off.

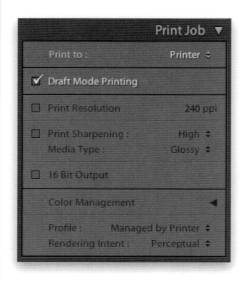

Step Four:

Make sure the Draft Mode Printing checkbox is turned off, and now it's time to choose the resolution of your image. If you want to print at your file's native resolution, then turn the Print Resolution checkbox off. Otherwise, when you turn the checkbox on, the default resolution is 240 ppi (fine for most color inkjet printing). I use Epson printers, and I've found resolutions that work well for them at various sizes. For example, I use 360 ppi for letter-sized or smaller prints, 240 ppi for 13x19" prints, or just 180 ppi for a 16x20" or larger. (The larger the print size, the lower the resolution you can get away with.) In this instance, I'm printing to an Epson Stylus Pro 3800 on a 17x22" sheet, so I would highlight the Print Resolution field and type in 180 (as shown here), then press the Return (PC: Enter) key. *Note:* If printing at 180 ppi freaks you out, just leave it set to the default of 240 ppi, but at least try 180 ppi once on a big print, and see if you can tell a difference.

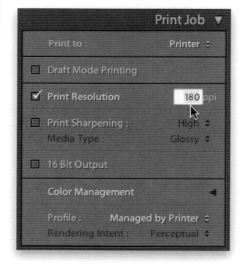

Step Five:
Next is the pop-up menu for Print Sharpening, and in Lightroom 2, Adobe really made this a powerful tool (the output sharpening in earlier versions was just too weak for most folks' tastes). Now when you tell Lightroom which type of paper you're printing on and which level of sharpening you'd like, it looks at those, along with the resolution you're printing at, and it applies the right amount of sharpening to give you the best results on that paper media at that resolution (sweet!). So, start by turning on the Print Sharpening checkbox (I always turn this on for every print, and every JPEG file), then choose either Glossy or Matte from the Media Type pop-up menu. Now choose the amount of sharpening you want from the Print Sharpening pop-up menu (I generally use High for glossy and Standard for matte paper, like Epson's Velvet Fine Art). That's all there is to it—Lightroom does all the work for you.

Step Six:
The next checkbox down reveals another new Lightroom 2 feature: 16-bit printing, which gives you an expanded dynamic range on printers that support 16-bit printing. (*Note:* At the time this book was published, 16-bit printing in Lightroom 2 was only available for Mac OS X Leopard users, but, of course, that is subject to change if Adobe releases an update for Windows.) So, if you're running Mac OS X Leopard, and you have a 16-bit-capable printer, like some of the new Canon printers (or if you've downloaded a 16-bit printer driver, like the ones Epson released in early 2008 that make your current printer 16-bit capable), then you should turn the 16 Bit Output checkbox on (as shown here).

Continued

Step Seven:

Now it's time to set the Color Management options, so what you see onscreen and what comes out of the printer both match. (By the way, if you have any hope of this happening, you've first got to use a hardware monitor calibrator to calibrate your monitor. Without a calibrated monitor, all bets are off. I use the X-Rite i1Display 2 to calibrate my monitor.) There are only two things you have to set here: (1) you have to choose your printer profile, and (2) you have to choose your rendering intent. For Profile, the default setting is Managed by Printer (as shown here), which means your printer is going to color manage your print job for you. This choice used to be out of the question, but today's printers have come so far that you'll actually now get decent results leaving it set to Managed by Printer (but if you want "better than decent," read on).

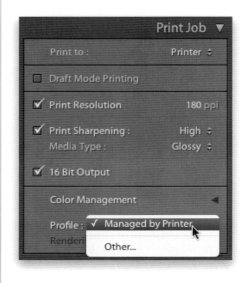

Step Eight:

You'll get better looking prints by assigning a custom printer/paper profile. To do that, first go to the website of the company that manufactures the paper you're going to be printing on. On their site, find the ICC color profiles they provide for free downloading that exactly match (a) the paper you're going to be printing on, and (b) the exact printer you're going to be printing to. In our case, I'm printing to an Epson Stylus Pro 3800 printer, and I'm printing on Epson's Exhibition Fiber Paper. Epson partnered with PixelGenius to create free downloadable color profiles for this paper for various Epson printers, so I went to http://pixelgenius.com/epson to download the free color profile for my printer, and then installed it (directions for installation are included on the website).

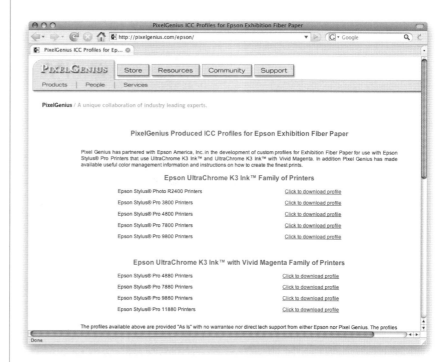

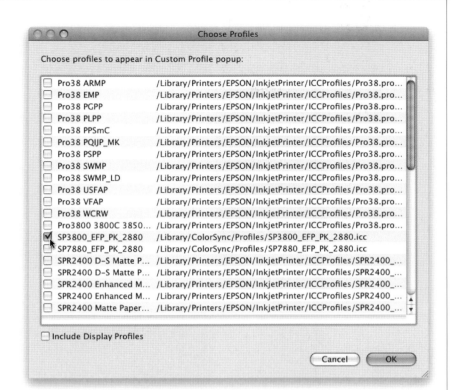

Step Nine:
Once your color profile is installed, click-and-hold on the Profile pop-up menu (right where it says Managed by Printer), and choose Other. This brings up a dialog (shown here) listing all the color profiles installed on your computer. Scroll through the list and find the paper profiles for your printer, then find the profile(s) for the paper(s) you normally print on (in my case, I'm looking for that Epson Exhibition Fiber Paper, or EFP for short), and then turn on the checkbox beside that paper (as shown here). Once you've found your profile(s), click OK to add it to your pop-up menu.

Step 10:
Return to that Profile pop-up menu in the Print Job panel, and you'll see the color profile for your printer is now available as one of the choices in this menu (as seen here). Choose your color profile from this pop-up menu (if it's not already chosen; in my case, I would choose the SP3800_EFP_PK_2880, as shown here, which is Epson's secret code for the Stylus Pro 3800, Exhibition Fiber Paper, PK, at 2880 dpi). Now you've set up Lightroom so it knows exactly how to handle the color for that printer on that particular type of paper. This step is really key to getting the quality prints we're all aiming for, because at the end of the day, it's all about the print.

Continued

Step 11:

Under Rendering Intent, you have two choices: (a) Perceptual, or (b) Relative (Colormetric). Theoretically, choosing Perceptual may give you a more pleasing print because it tries to maintain color relationships, but it's not necessarily accurate as to what you see tonally onscreen. Choosing Relative may provide a more accurate interpretation of the tone of the photo, but you may not like the final color as much. So, which one is right? The one that looks best on your own printer. Relative is probably the most popular choice, but personally, I usually use Perceptual because my style uses very rich, saturated colors, and it seems that Perceptual gives me better color on my particular printer. So, which one should you choose? The best way to know which one looks best for your printer is to print a few test prints for each photo—try one with Perceptual and one with Relative—when the prints come out, you'll know right away which one works best for your printer.

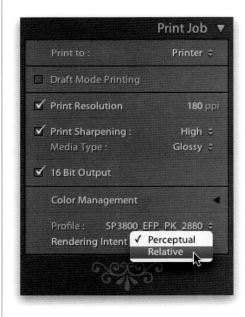

Step 12:

Now it's time to click the Print button at the bottom of the right side Panels area. This will bring up the Print dialog (shown here. If you're using a Mac, and you see a small dialog with just two pop-up menus, rather than the larger one you see here, click the little arrow button to the right of the Printer pop-up menu, shown circled here in red, to expand the dialog to its full size, more like the one shown here).

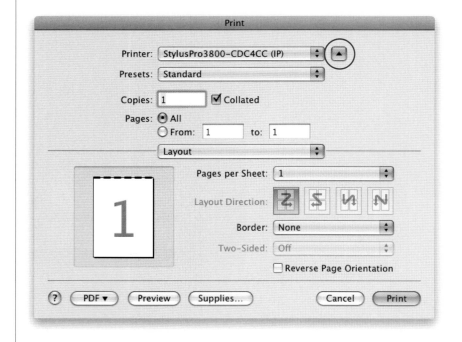

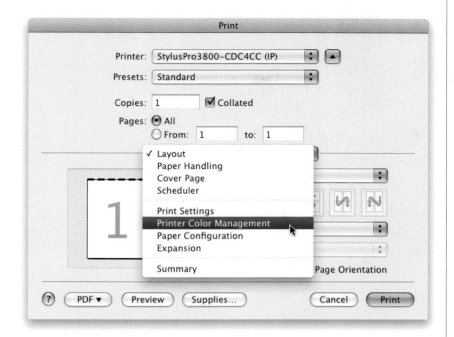

Step 13:

Click-and-hold on the dialog's main section pop-up menu, and choose Printer Color Management (as shown here). By the way, the part of this dialog that controls printer color management, and your pop-up menu choices, may be different depending on your printer, so if it doesn't look exactly like this, don't freak out. On a PC, click on the Properties button next to the Printer Name pop-up menu to locate it instead.

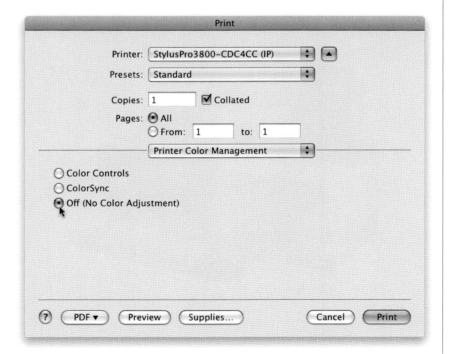

Step 14:

When the Printer Color Management options appear, by default, your printer's color management will be turned on. Since you're having Lightroom manage your color, you don't want the printer also trying to manage your color, because when the two color management systems start both trying to manage your color, nobody wins. Click the Off radio button, so there's no color adjustment (as shown here). On a PC (this may be different, depending on your printer), in the Media Settings section, under Mode, click the Custom radio button and choose No Color Adjustment from the pop-up menu.

Continued

Step 15:

Now switch to the Print Settings section (or Media Settings on a PC) of the Print dialog (again, your pop-up menus may be different, and on a PC, these will be in the Properties dialog for your printer), and for Media Type, choose the exact paper you'll be printing to from the pop-up menu (as shown here, where I chose Premium Luster Photo Paper, which is what Epson recommends for printing on their Exhibition Fiber Paper).

Step 16:

In that same Print Settings section, for Mode click on the Advanced Settings radio button, turn off the High Speed setting checkbox (if it's turned on), then choose SuperFine – 1440dpi from the Print Quality pop-up menu (as seen in the previous step. Again, this is for printing to an Epson printer using Epson paper. If you don't have an Epson printer...why not? Just kidding—if you don't have an Epson printer, you're prob- ably not using Epson paper, so for Print Quality, choose the one that most closely matches the paper you are printing to). On a PC, under Print Quality, choose Quality Options from the pop-up menu. In the resulting Quality Options dialog, you can turn off the High Speed check- box and choose your Print Quality by setting the Speed slider. Now sit back and watch your glorious print(s) roll gently out of your printer.

When I was on the road with my Lightroom Live! seminar tour, one of the most-asked questions was, "How can I save these print layouts as JPEGs?" Unfortunately, back then, the answer was, "You can't." Luckily, in Lightroom 2, you now can save these layouts as JPEG files, so you can send them to a photo lab, or have someone else output your files, or email them to your client, or one of the dozen different things you want JPEGs of your layouts for. Here's how it's done:

Saving Your Page Layout as a JPEG

Step One:
Once your layout is all set, go to the Print Job panel (in the right side Panels area), and from the Print To pop-up menu (at the top right of the panel), choose JPEG File (as shown here).

Step Two:
When you choose to print to a JPEG, a new set of features appears. First, ignore the Draft Mode Printing checkbox (it's just for when you're actually printing contact sheets full of small thumbnails). For File Resolution, the default is 300 ppi, but if you want to change it, move your cursor directly over the File Resolution field (the 300), and your cursor will change into a "scrubby slider" (it's that hand with the two arrows, as seen here). Now you can click-and-drag left to lower the resolution amount, or click-and-drag right to increase it.

Continued

Step Three:

Next is the pop-up menu for Print Sharpening (which has been dramatically improved in Lightroom 2). What you do here is tell Lightroom which type of paper you'll be printing on (Matte or Glossy), and which level of sharpening you'd like applied (Low, Standard, or High). Lightroom looks at your choices (including resolution) and comes up with the optimum amount and type of sharpening to match your choices. So, start there (I apply this print sharpening to every photo I print or save as a JPEG). If you don't want this output sharpening applied to your exported JPEG, just turn off the Print Sharpening checkbox.

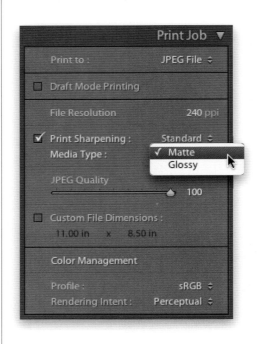

Step Four:

You've got a couple more choices to make before we're done. Next, is JPEG Quality (I usually use 80, because I think it gives a good balance between quality and compression of the file size, but you can choose anything you want, up to 100). Below that is the Custom File Dimensions section. If you leave the checkbox turned off, it will just use whatever page size you had chosen in the Page Setup dialog (in this case, it was an 11x8.5" letter-sized page). If you want to change the size of your JPEG, turn on the Custom File Dimensions checkbox, then move your cursor over the size fields and use the scrubby slider (shown here) to change sizes. Lastly, you set your Color Management Profile (many labs require that you use sRGB as your profile, so ask your lab). If you want a custom color profile, go back to the last tutorial for info on how to find those, and you can find info on the Rendering Intent setting there, too. Now just click the Print to File button at the bottom of the right side Panels area to save your file.

I wish Lightroom had the built-in ability to add custom borders, edges, and frames around your photos, but unfortunately it just doesn't. However, you can do a little workaround that lets you use your Identity Plate, and a special option in the Identity Plate section, to get the same effect right within Lightroom itself. Here's how it's done:

Adding Cool Frame Borders to Your Prints

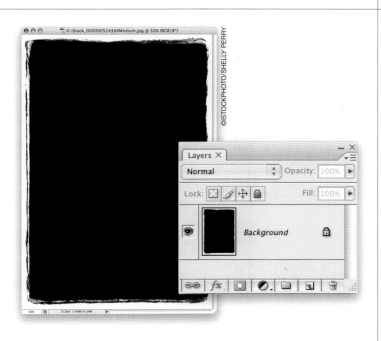

Step One:
We're going to start in Photoshop with prepping our edge file for use in Lightroom. I downloaded the edge border you see here from iStockphoto.com (it cost me $4 for the high-res 300 dpi download, but you can download it for free from this book's website—just look in the Introduction for the URL). The edge comes flattened on the background, so to start, click the Magic Wand tool (nested below the Quick Selection tool) within the black area in the center to select that area. Press-and-hold the Shift key and click on some of the outside edge areas to add those to our selection. Lastly, go under the Select menu and choose Similar to pick up any stray areas we missed. Then press **Command-Shift-J (PC: Ctrl-Shift-J)** to put this edge up on its own separate layer (as shown in the next step).

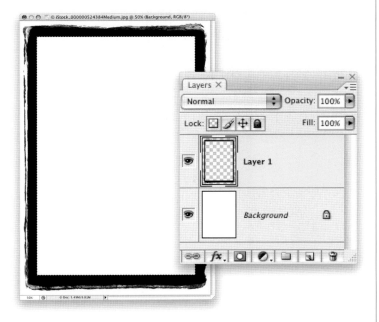

Step Two:
We need a hole cut out of this solid black edge graphic in the shape of a rectangle (so our photo can show through). So, get the Rectangular Marquee tool **(M)** and click-and-drag a rectangular selection that's almost as big as our edge graphic (as shown here), then press the Delete (PC: Backspace) key to knock a large rectangular hole out of our graphic.

Continued

Step Three:

For this to work properly, our file can't have a solid white background or it will cover our photo when we bring it into Lightroom—instead the background has to be transparent. To do that, go to the Layers panel and click-and-drag the Background layer into the Trash (at the bottom of the panel) to delete it (prior to CS3, you had to unlock the Background layer first). That leaves us with just our edge border on a transparent layer. Now we can save it, so go under the File menu and choose Save As. When the dialog appears, you'll need to choose a file format that supports transparency (JPEG doesn't), so choose PNG as your format, give the file a name, and click Save (you'll probably get a warning that because this is a layered file, you'll have to save a copy of the file instead—no problem, just click Save).

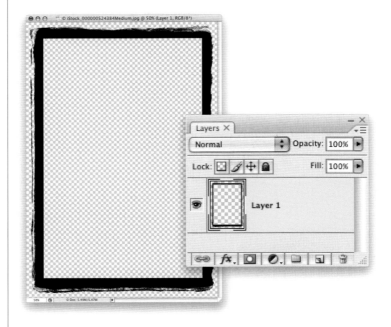

Step Four:

All right, that's all the prep work in Photoshop—now back to Lightroom. Click on the photo you want to have an edge frame, then jump over to the Print module. In the Print module, in the Overlays panel, turn on the Identity Plate checkbox. Then, in the Identity Plate pop-up menu, choose Edit to bring up the Identity Plate Editor you see here. In that dialog, click on the Use a Graphical Identity Plate radio button (because we're going to import a graphic, rather than using text), then click on the Locate File button (as shown here), locate your saved PNG edge file, and click Choose to load it into your Identity Plate Editor (you can see the top of our edge frame in the small preview window shown here).

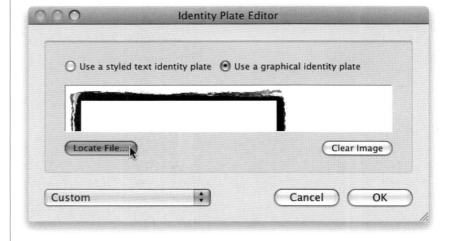

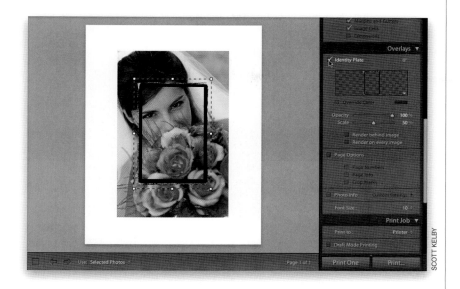

Step Five:

When you click OK, your edge frame will appear, hovering over your print (almost like it's on its own layer). The size and position won't be right, so that's the first thing you'll want to fix (which we'll do in the next step, but while we're here, notice how the center of our edge is transparent—you can see right through it to the photo below it. That's why we had to save this file without the Background layer, and as a PNG—to keep that transparency intact).

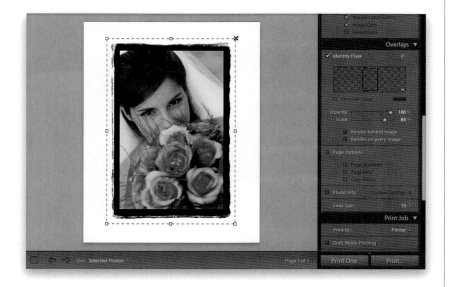

Step Six:

To resize your border, you can either click-and-drag a corner point outward (as shown here), or use the Scale slider in the Overlays panel. Once the size looks about right, you can reposition the edge by simply clicking-and-dragging inside the edge frame borders. You may need to resize your image, as well, using the Margins sliders in the Layout panel.

Continued

Step Seven:

When it's right where you want it, just click your cursor outside the border and it will deselect. The final photo with the edge frame border is shown here. Now, if you decide you want to keep this border and use it in the future, go back to the Identity Plate Editor and from the Custom pop-up menu at the bottom-left corner of the dialog, choose Save As to save this frame border as an Identity Plate you can use anytime to add a quick border effect.

Step Eight:

We created a vertical frame, but how do you add this frame edge to a horizontal photo, like the one shown here? If you change your page setup to Landscape (by clicking on the Page Setup button at the bottom of the left side Panels area), the Identity Plate will rotate automatically. If you are printing a horizontal photo in a Portrait setup, you can rotate the Identity Plate by clicking on the degree field that appears to the right of the Identity Plate checkbox in the Overlays panel and choosing the rotation angle (as shown here). You'll probably have to resize and reposition the frame (as I did here) to make it fit just right, but now your single frame edge is doing double duty.

SCOTT KELBY

Lightroom Quick Tips > >

▼ Can't See Your Rulers?

If you're pressing **Command-R (PC: Ctrl-R)** and you can't see your printing rulers (the ones that appear above the top of your photo, and along the left side), it's because you have to make your guides visible first. Press **Command-Shift-H (PC: Ctrl-Shift-H)** or just choose Show Guides from the View menu. Now when you use that shortcut, you'll be toggling the rulers on/off.

▼ Enabling 16-Bit Printing

If your inkjet printer was made in the last year or two, it probably supports 16-bit printing, but to take advantage of it, make sure you have the latest printer driver (which can be downloaded for free from your printer manufacturer's website). *Note:* 16-bit printing currently only works for Mac users, and only those using Mac OS X Leopard.

▼ Changing Your Ruler Units

To change the unit of measure for your rulers, just Control-click (PC: Right-click) on either ruler, and a contextual menu of measurements (Inches, Centimeters, Millimeters, Points, and Picas) will appear, so you can choose the one you'd like.

▼ Changing the Preview Area Background Color

Although you can't change the color behind your photo (it stays solid white), you can change the color of the gray canvas area that surrounds your printed page. Just Control-click (PC: Right-click) anywhere on that gray background area and a contextual menu will pop up where you can choose different colors.

▼ Workaround for Getting a Different Print Background Color

If you want a different color background to print behind your photos, the trick is to go to Photoshop and create a new document that is the exact same size as the page you'll be printing in Lightroom (i.e., make a 16x20" page in Photoshop). Fill this new Photoshop document with a solid color, then save it as a JPEG. Now, make that photo your Identity Plate, and in the Overlays panel, turn on the checkbox for Render Behind Image.

▼ Adding Photos to Your Printing Queue

Adding more photos to print couldn't be easier—just go to the filmstrip and Command-click (PC: Ctrl-click) on any photo you want to add to your print queue, and Lightroom instantly creates another page for it in the queue. To remove a photo from the print queue, it's just as easy: go to the filmstrip and Command-click (PC: Ctrl-click) on any already selected photo to deselect it (Lightroom removes the page from your queue automatically, so you don't print a blank sheet).

▼ When You Can Get Away with Draft Mode Printing

When you're printing contact sheets, I always recommend using Draft Mode Printing, which uses the cached previews (or built-in previews, if necessary) for printing, rather than the high-resolution versions of the photos—so it prints in a fraction of the usual time, yet the print quality still looks great because the photos are so small. However, a lot of people fall in love with the speed, and as long as you're printing large images, you should give it a try and see if you find the quality reasonable (I'm always having people bring me prints to show

off that they made using Draft Mode Printing). Just remember, if you put more than one image on a page, it's worth trying (turn it on in the Print Job panel).

▼ Precise Margins Way Quicker Than Using the Margins Sliders

If you need to reposition your image on the page, you can adjust the Margins or Cell Size sliders. But if your guides are visible, it's easier just to click-and-drag a margin guide itself, because as soon as you start dragging, the position of the guide (in inches) appears above the top of the guide, so it's easy to quickly set two side or top and bottom margins to the exact same amount.

▼ Sending Prints to a Lab?

If you use Lightroom 2's new ability to save a page layout to JPEG, so you can send your prints to a lab for final printing, then here's a great tip: make a new template that has your usual page size, layout, etc., but make sure you set your color profile to the color space your lab prefers (which is usually sRGB for color labs). That way, when you save it as a JPEG, you won't forget to embed the right color space.

▼ Choosing How the Identity Plate Prints

There are two other options for how the Identity Plate is used in multi-photo layouts. If you choose Render on Every Image, it puts your Identity Plate right smack dab in the middle of each photo, in each cell (so if you wanted to use your logo as a watermark by lowering the opacity of that Identity Plate, that would work). If you choose Render Behind Image, it prints on the background, as if it was a paper watermark (scale it up so it is slightly larger than your image).

Web
getting your photos on the web

Okay, this is a weird chapter because it was originally the only chapter in the book just for Macintosh users. The reason why was simple. I'm a Macintosh user, and I wanted my Macintosh brethren to share a special bond with me—one that only came from having a special chapter that Windows users didn't get to enjoy. You see, in every-day computing life, Macintosh users get the short end of the stick. There's less Macintosh software, less Macintosh hardware, fewer Macintosh magazines, fewer Macintosh peripherals, and about a bazillion fewer games for the Macintosh platform. So, this was my cry for help—my personal crusade to some-how even the score by including a chapter just for Mac users. It was my way of striking back at the anti-Macintosh subculture that has for far too long held sway in the overall

computing world and kept Mac users down. Well, it could be that, or it could've been the fact that the Windows version of Photoshop Lightroom 1 didn't have a Web module until Beta 4, so there was no reason to make Windows users read this chapter. Ahh, you'd like it to be that, wouldn't you? You'd like there to be some logical explanation— something that made perfect sense as to why this chapter was just for Mac users. Then it would perpetuate the Microsoft world domination scheme that has kept Macintosh users from having an Apple-branded two-button mouse for more than 20 years. You'd like that wouldn't you? Wait. Huh? Apple came out with a two-button Bluetooth mouse? Really? Oh. I didn't realize that. I'm so embarrassed. Really, this is so embarrassing. Forget this ever happened.

Building a Quick, Simple, Online Photo Gallery

Want to put up a quick online photo gallery of your vacation photos, or want to put proofs up online for a client's approval? It's easier than you'd think; you start with a built-in template and then add your little tweaks to customize it your way. The nice thing is you do most of your editing right on the page itself, so all your changes happen live, in real time. It's this live onscreen editing that makes the process so easy, and even if you have no Web design experience whatsoever, you'll be able to create a great-looking gallery in about five minutes. Here goes:

Step One:

Start by going to the Library module, and in the Collections panel in the left side Panels area, click on the collection of photos you want to put in your online gallery. Now, go to the Web module and Photoshop Light-room instantly puts them into a Web gallery (seen here in the center Preview area). The default Web Gallery template is a gray HTML webpage with thumbnails (seen here), and when you click on a thumbnail, it displays a larger version of the photo. The photos appear in your gallery in the same order they appear in the filmstrip below, so to change their order, just drag-and-drop them into the order you want in the filmstrip.

Step Two:

By default, this template displays your thumbnails in three columns and three rows (as seen in Step One), but you can change this really easily. Just go to the Appearance panel (in the right side Panels area) and in the Grid Pages section, there's a mini-preview of your thumbnail grid that's more than a preview—it's live! Just move your cursor out over the grid and click-and-drag out how many rows and columns you want (I dragged over so there would be four columns, and the Web gallery instantly adjusted, as seen here). This is such an intuitive way to choose your columns and rows, and the fact that it updates live really makes it fun.

Step Three:
At this point, we've just been working with thumbnails, but when you (or your client) click on a thumbnail, it will be displayed at a larger size (as seen here). So, how large will they appear? That's up to you. By default, they appear at 450 pixels wide, but you can choose the size you'd like in the Appearance panel, in the Image Pages section, using the Size slider. Right below that is a checkbox for toggling on/off a stroke border around this larger image, and you get to choose the width and color of the stroke border there, as well. At the top of this panel is a checkbox for turning on/off the drop shadow behind your photos. The Section Borders check-box turns on/off the little lines that appear between your site title and the text below it at the top of the page, and the line between your photo and your contact info at the bottom of the page (you can choose the color of those section border lines, as well). There's one more section in this panel (Grid Pages), but it's for the thumbnails, not the larger-size previews.

Step Four:
You edit the text on your webpage right on the page itself, which makes this process fast and easy. You just click on the placeholder text that's there, it highlights, and you type in your new text, then press the Return (PC: Enter) key to lock in your changes. Here, I've changed the site title.

TIP: Removing a Photo
By default, your Web gallery will include all the photos in your selected collection. If you want to remove a photo from your gallery, you'll either have to delete it from your collection or choose Selected Photos from the Use pop-up menu at the left side of the toolbar beneath the center Preview area, and then only your selected photos will appear in your gallery.

Continued

Step Five:

Basically, that's the plan—you click on placeholder text, right there on the page itself, and type in your own custom text. So, go ahead and enter the information you want on your webpage by clicking on the placeholder text, typing in your new text, and then hitting the Return (PC: Enter) key on your keyboard to lock in your changes. Here, I've updated my page with the information I might put on a typical online proofing page for a client. So now you've got your own text in place, you've chosen how many rows and columns you want for your thumbnails, and how large your larger images will appear on the page. You can go with this default HTML page, but Lightroom comes with some pretty decent built-in templates—and not just in HTML format, there are a number of Flash-based templates, as well.

Step Six:

To get a preview of these built-in templates, go to the Template Browser (in the left side Panels area) and just hover your cursor over a template, and a preview of that template will appear in the Preview panel at the top (as seen here). If the template is Flash-based, you'll see the a little "*f*" appear in the bottom-left corner of the preview; otherwise you'll see "HTML" there instead. To apply one of these templates, just click on it (here, I've clicked on the Paper White template, which has a white background, your thumbnails appear on the left in a scrolling list, and you have slide show controls below the larger image in the center). *Note:* One advantage of these Flash-based templates is that they have built-in slide show capabilities, with smooth transitions between each image. Also, people viewing your page can't just click-and-drag your photo onto their computer, like they can with HTML-based pages.

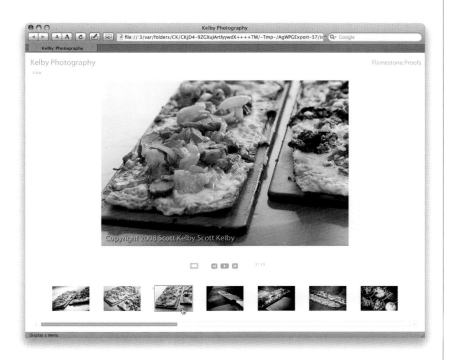

Step Seven:
While you can't control the number of rows or columns, there are different layouts you can choose from with these Flash-based templates. Go to the Appearance panel (in the right side Panels area), then at the top of the panel, in the Layout section, click-and-hold on the pop-up menu on the right side (as shown here), and choose Scrolling, which instantly reconfigures your page with the scrolling list of thumbnails at the bottom (as seen here). You can see a few other controls in this Appearance panel, including pop-up menus where you can choose your large image size and your thumbnail image size.

Step Eight:
Once you've chosen your final template, chosen the sizes you want for everything, chosen your layout, and added your custom text, make sure you test your final webpage by clicking on the Preview in Browser button at the bottom of the left side Panels area. This launches your Web browser, and displays your gallery as it will be seen on the Web (as shown here), so click on a few thumbnails to make sure it works the way you want it to. If you're ready to upload your gallery to the Web, jump over to page 370, but before you do that, there's still plenty you can do to customize the look and feel of your page (that's coming up), and there are some absolutely kick-butt built-in Flash-based templates that aren't found in the Template Browser (you access them in a totally different way), which we're going to cover later in this chapter.

Adding an Email or Website Link to Your Gallery

If you're using Lightroom's Web gallery for online client proofing, you're probably going to want your client to be able to email you right from the page, or you might want to have a link to your main homepage, or your studio's website, etc. Here you'll learn how to do both (it's easier than you'd think).

Step One:

Although we've been editing our text right on the webpage itself, adding an email link to your page is one thing you have to go to the right side Panels area to do. So, go to the Site Info panel (shown here), and you'll see that the top section of this panel shows you all the text fields for the custom text you can add directly on the page itself (so technically, you could add the text here instead, but it's just easier to do it on the page). However, there is an extra feature here: Lightroom remembers the info you last added in each of these fields, and adds them to a pop-up menu, so you can quickly choose that same info again in the future (click on one of the little triangles at the top right of each text field to access that menu).

Step Two:

Right below Web or Mail Link, by default, it reads "mailto:user@domain." To add your email link, you just have to change the "user@domain" to your email address (in my case, it would read, "mailto:skelby@ photoshopuser.com," as shown here, with no spaces in between anything), then press the Return (PC: Enter) key to lock in your change. *Note:* If, instead of an email link, you want to add a link to another webpage, just type the full URL in this field (like http://www.scottkelby.com).

Step Three:
The default text for this webpage or email link on your Web gallery reads, "Contact Name," but you can change it to whatever you'd like in the Contact Info field (which is right above the Web or Mail Link field). Just click on it and type in what you'd like your webpage or email link to say (I just use either "Contact Scott," as shown here, or "Email Scott," but choose whatever works best for you).

Step Four:
Here's how the page will look in your Web browser (I just clicked the Preview in Browser button at the bottom of the left side Panels area), and up in the top-right corner, there it is—my Contact Scott link. If your client clicks that link, it will launch their email application and open a new email message already addressed to you. All they have to do is enter a subject, jot you a quick note, and click Send.

TIP: Web Links
If you're using this gallery for client proofing, chances are this will be a page within your current website, and not your entire site itself. That's why you might want to consider having a Web link back to your main homepage. For example, let's say I posted a proofing page at www.scottkelby.com/flamestone. Then, I would have a Web link back to www .scottkelby.com, and I would change the Contact Info text to read "Home Page."

Customizing Your Gallery Layout

So far, we've done just the basics: we used a built-in template as a starting point, we changed the text, picked the size and number of our thumbnails and larger images, and added a contact link. However, you can take the customizing process a lot further using the controls in the right side Panels area.

Step One:

One thing you can do to customize your page is to have your Identity Plate replace the site title text that appears in the top-left corner. Earlier we just typed in the name of our studio, but now we're going to add a logo graphic to replace it. (Here, I have chosen the Ivory template from the Template Browser in the left side Panels area.)

Step Two:

Go to the Appearance panel in the right side Panels area and turn on the Identity Plate checkbox, then click on the down-facing triangle in the bottom-right corner of the Identity Plate preview, and choose Edit from the pop-up menu to bring up the Identity Plate Editor (shown here). Click on the Use a Graphical Identity Plate radio button at the top of the dialog, then click the Locate File button, and find the logo you want to use as your Identity Plate (I used a quick logo I put together in Photoshop). Once you've chosen your graphic, click the OK button.

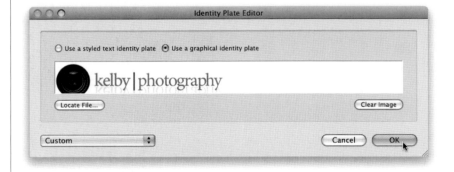

Step Three:

Here's the page with the Identity Plate graphic in place. *Note:* You can't resize the Identity Plate here in the Web module, so make sure you make your graphic the right size to fit your page before you place it into Lightroom.

Step Four:

If you look at the page, there is a problem: although we brought this Identity Plate in to replace our site title, the old site title text is still there. Because the Identity Plate graphic says the same thing that I would have typed in for the site title, we need to remove the old site title text. So, in the Site Info panel, just delete the text in the Site Title field (you can see how much better the page looks here, compared to the one in Step Three). To finish things off here, I updated the other two text fields (as seen here), by clicking on them and typing in some custom text.

Step Five:

You can also customize how the thumbnails look. In the Appearance panel, you can turn off the stroke border around your photos by turning off the Photo Borders checkbox in the Grid Pages section (shown circled here). By the way, if you like the borders, you can choose which color you'd like them to be by clicking on the color swatch to the right of the Photo Borders checkbox. At the top of this panel, there's a checkbox for toggling on/off the drop shadow that appears behind your thumbnails (here's how the page looks without the thin black stroke around the photos and with the drop shadow turned off).

Continued

Step Six:

If you've added copyright info to your images (either when you imported them into Lightroom, or later in the Metadata panel in the Library module), by default that copyright info will appear over the bottom of your thumbnail and larger-sized photo (as seen here). You can turn this feature off in the Output Settings panel by turning off the Add Copyright Watermark checkbox. While we're here, this is also where you control the quality of the larger-sized images that will be displayed on your page using the Quality slider (as shown here).

Step Seven:

If you're using this gallery for online proofing, the next two features might come in handy. You can have each photo's filename displayed above the photo (well, you can actually choose other options besides the filename), and you can add a caption (pretty much whatever you want) below the photo. You turn these text features on in the Image Info panel. The Title checkbox turns on the text above the photo, and you use the pop-up menu to the right of it to choose what info gets displayed up there (you can choose to have the filename appear up top, as I have here, or the date the photo was taken, the exposure, etc.). The Caption checkbox works the same way, but that text appears below your photo. In the example here, I chose Custom Text from the pop-up menu, which brought up a text field right beneath it (highlighted here), where I typed in my own custom text to appear beneath each photo.

Step Eight:
There are a couple more tweaks you can make here. Up in the Appearance panel, you can turn off the little horizontal divider lines that separate your Identity Plate from the text below it, and that appear across the bottom of your page, by turning off the Section Borders checkbox (as seen here). Also, the Show Cell Numbers checkbox in the Grid Pages section puts a large sequential number in each cell, as shown here (this makes it easy for the client to tell you, "I like numbers 5, 8, 14, 22, and 23"). When you've finished tweaking your Web gallery, you might want to save it as a template (I sure would), so you can reapply it any time with just one click. Go to the Template Browser and click the + (plus sign) button to add the current look as a template.

Changing the Colors of Your Gallery

If there's a color that appears on your Web gallery, you can change it. From the background color, to the color of your cells, to the text, to the borders, you can change pretty much everything, and that applies to both HTML and Flash-based templates. Here's how it's done:

Step One:
If you scroll down to the Color Palette panel in the right side Panels area, you'll see you have color control over, well…just about everything. Here's one of the default Flash-based templates (called Classic) and it features a white background, light gray accents, and light gray slide show controls and text.

Step Two:
We'll start by changing the color of the header at the top of the page. In the Color Palette panel, click on the color swatch to the right of Header. When the color picker appears, click on the black color swatch at the top of the picker to change the header at the top to solid black (as shown here).

Step Three:

Changing the background color is just as easy. Click on the color swatch to the right of Background, then when the color picker appears, choose the color you'd like for your background (here, I chose kind of a light tan/beige look). By the way, if the color picker appears and the large gradient in the center only shows black, white, and grays, that's only because the color bar (at the far-right side of the color picker) is set all the way at the bottom. To reveal full-color gradients, click on the little rectangular knob (I know, it's not a knob, but I don't know what else to call it), drag it straight upward, and the colors will be revealed. The higher you drag the slider upward, the more vivid and saturated the colors will look.

Step Four:

Our last color tweak here is for the text in the header and in the menu bar right under it. The word Proofs at the right side of the header is a bit too dark, so go to the Color Palette panel, click on the color swatch to the right of Header Text, and in the color picker, click on a lighter gray color swatch at the top of the picker. Then, do the same thing for the menu text (as shown here, where I chose a much darker gray color for my menu text, so it's easier to read over that darker gray menu bar that I also changed). You also get to choose the color for the background of the slide show controls, and the color of the little icons inside the control buttons. Here, I chose a light gray for the button background (from the Controls Background color picker) and a darker gray for the icons (from the Controls Foreground color picker). So, that's pretty much the deal—just go to the Color Palette panel, click on the color swatch beside the area you want to adjust, and when the color picker appears, choose a new color. Pretty quick and easy.

Using Cooler Flash Templates

Remember earlier when I mentioned that there were actually some really cool built-in Flash-based templates, but you didn't access them from the Template Browser? These three templates are found in the Engine panel (at the top of the right side Panels area), and they were created by a company called Airtight Interactive (www.airtightinteractive.com). These guys have developed a number of very cool, free, Flash-based templates, and back in Lightroom 1.3, Adobe included these right in Lightroom for us, and I just love 'em! Here's how to put them to work:

Step One:

To get to these other Flash-based templates, go up to the Engine panel at the top of the right side Panels area (shown here) and first click on Airtight AutoViewer. This creates a slide show gallery, with the current image highlighted, and the previous and next image partially visible, but dimmed (as shown here, in the Preview in Browser view). In the Color Palette panel you can choose the background and border colors. In the Appearance panel, you can control the width of the border around each photo, and the Padding slider lets you choose how much space is between each photo. You can use the navigation arrows that appear on the left and right of your page to move backward and forward through your photos, and to play the slide show, just click the Play button that appears at the bottom of the page when you move your mouse.

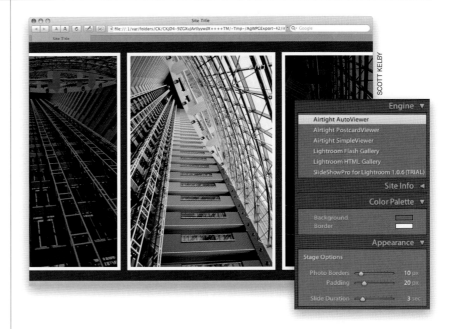

Step Two:

Now click on Airtight PostcardViewer in the Engine panel, and your images appear as small postcards on the page. In the Post Cards section of the Appearance panel, you can choose how many columns you want, how thick the borders are, and how much space there is between the photos.

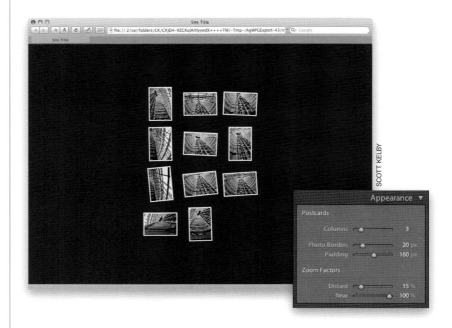

Step Three:
When you click on one of these tiny post-cards, that postcard zooms to a larger size and comes "front and center" (as seen here). In the Zoom Factors section of the Appearance panel, the Distant slider controls how big the small thumbnail postcards will be (the default setting of 15% means they'll appear at 15% of their actual size). The Near slider controls how big the photo will appear when you click on one of those small postcards. The default 100% setting means it will appear as large as it can and still fit within the webpage window. So if you set this to a smaller size, like 75%, it will only scale to 75% as large as it could in the current window. If you click on the large-view image, it returns to the smaller postcard thumbnail view. Also, once the page has been created, people viewing your gallery can navigate around using the Arrow keys on their keyboard.

Step Four:
The last one of these Airtight Flash galleries is called Airtight SimpleViewer (and it's the one I probably use the most). It creates a simple grid of thumbnails on the left side of the page, and when you click on a thumbnail, a larger version is displayed on the right. In the Color Palette and Appearance panels, you get to adjust page colors and the number of rows and columns for your grid, as well as its position. The Site Info panel (which is available for all three of these Airtight galleries) lets you type in a title of your gallery, which will appear in the tab at the top of your Web browser's window (it will replace the default phrase "Site Title," which I have circled here in red). So there you have it—three other very cool Flash-based templates hidden over in the Engine panel.

Putting Your New Gallery on the Web

The last part of this process is actually getting your new gallery up live on the Web. You can either export your gallery to a folder and then upload it yourself, or use the Web module's built-in FTP capabilities for uploading your gallery to a Web server. If you don't already have a company that hosts your website on their server, that will be your first order of business. Try Googling "free Web hosting," and in about two seconds, you'll find loads of companies that are willing (read as: dying) to host your new site absolutely free.

Step One:
Now that your Web gallery is complete, you have two choices for getting your finished gallery up on the Web: (1) Export the files to a folder and upload the contents of that folder to your website (this is the method required by many Web hosting companies and almost all of the free hosting services, who have you do your uploading directly from a regular Web browser). Or if you're a bit more Web savvy, you can (2) use Lightroom's built-in FTP uploader to send your gallery right from Lightroom straight to your Web server (if you're wondering what FTP means, then you definitely want to go with Option #1). For now, we'll assume you're going with the first option (exporting to a folder), so click the Export button at the bottom of the right side Panels area (as shown here).

Step Two:
This brings up a Save Web Gallery dialog (shown here), where you name your exported gallery folder and choose where you want it saved. So give your folder a name, then click the Save button (as shown here).

TIP: Getting More Cool Flash-Based Web Galleries
If you're looking for more Lightroom Web galleries, my favorite site for them is LightroomGalleries.com. They have a number of free downloadable Web galleries you can access from right within Lightroom's Engine Panel. Also, for $25, you can get the most sophisticated gallery out there: SlideShowPro (from http://slideshowpro.net).

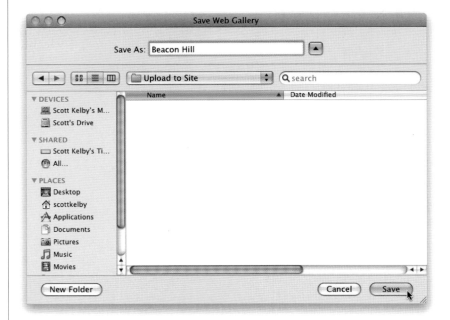

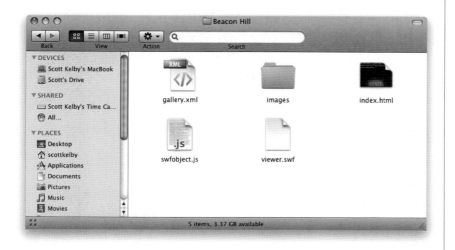

Step Three:
Once you click the Save button, Lightroom generates the webpage(s), and optimizes the photos for the Web for you (you can see the progress in the top left of Lightroom's taskbar). Once it's done, look in the folder you chose to save it in and you'll see the files and folders needed for your webpage. The file named index.html is your homepage, and the additional folder and files contain your web-optimized photos and other pages and resources your site needs. You'll need to upload everything in this folder to your website for your gallery to go live on the Web. Now, if instead you went with the second option (you're Web server savvy, and comfortable with FTP uploads and server protocols), then you'll need to configure your FTP upload first. So, scroll down to the Upload Settings panel in the right side Panels area, and from the FTP server pop-up menu, choose Edit.

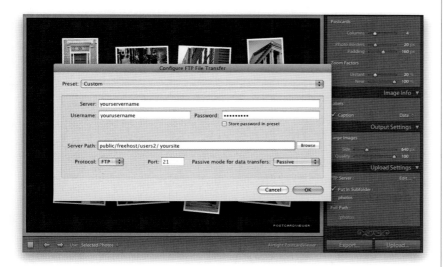

Step Four:
This brings up the Configure FTP File Transfer dialog (shown here), where you enter your server name, password, and the path to your homepage folder on the Web. Once you've entered this info, I recommend saving this as a preset (so you don't have to enter it again) by going to the Preset pop-up menu up top and choosing Save Current Settings as New Preset. By the way, if you don't choose the Store Password in Preset option, when you upload, it will ask you for your password again. Once you've entered your FTP info, click OK, and then click on the Upload button (at the bottom of the right side Panels area), and Lightroom will generate your webpage(s), optimize your photos for the Web, and upload the whole thing to your Web server, so your new gallery goes live on the Web.

Lightroom Quick Tips > >

▼ Save Time Using the Site Info Panel's Pop-Up Menus

Lightroom keeps track of any text you add in the title fields, contact field, Web or Mail Link field, and the description field, so rather than typing in the same stuff all over again, each time you create a Web gallery, you can just go to the Site Info panel (in the right side Panels area) and at the top right of each field, you'll see a little triangle. Click on it and a pop-up menu of the most recent text you entered in that field appears. Choose the one you want, and Lightroom enters it for you.

▼ Hiding the Border Around Each Cell

All of the HTML templates that come with Lightroom have borders around each cell, except for two: Ivory (which is solid white) and Midnight (which is solid black). However, if you want to customize any of the other HTML templates, there is no checkbox to turn the cell borders on/off. The trick is to go to the Color Palette panel, click on the Grid Lines color swatch, and choose the exact same color for the grid lines as the background color of the cells, and they'll disappear. Want to take it a step further? You can do the same trick with the cell color. Click on the Cells color swatch in the Color Palette panel, make the cell color the same as the background color of the page, and now your photos have no grid lines and no cells—they just appear right on the background, giving you an airy, unclut-tered look.

▼ Saving a Specific Gallery Design, and the Photos In It

Just like in the Print and Slideshow modules, the Collections panel in the Web module lets you save a Web gal-lery collection, which includes both the layout and the specific photos, in the same order, that you used to create your current gallery. That way, if you ever need to go back to that exact gal-lery, with the same layout and photos already in order, you can. To do this, just Control-click (PC: Right-click) on a collection and, from the contextual menu that appears, choose Create Web Gallery. When the naming dialog appears, make sure you turn on the Include All Filmstrip Photos checkbox, so the collection is created using only the photos that actually wound up in your gallery.

▼ You Can't Change the Size of Your Thumbnails

Although you do get the option of choosing the size of the preview (larger-size) image people see when they click on a thumbnail, there is no option for changing the size of the thumbnails themselves (just thought I'd help keep you from pulling your hair out looking for it).

▼ Save Space by Hiding the Upload Settings Panel

If you're not using Lightroom's built-in FTP feature to upload your Web gallery directly to your server, then you might as well hide the Upload Settings panel, so your right side Panels area is shorter and you spend less time scrolling. To do that, Control-click (PC: Right-click) on the panel header, and a contex-tual menu appears, where you'll see checkmarks beside each visible panel. To hide the Upload Settings panel, just choose it from the menu. To get it back, choose it again.

▼ Sampling Colors from Another Webpage

If you find a page on the Web that has a color scheme you really like, you can use the exact colors on your page really easily. Just go to the Color Palette panel and click on the color swatch of whatever you want to change. For example, let's say you want to change your background color, so click on the Background color swatch and, when the color picker appears, your cursor changes into a large eyedropper. Nor-mally, you'd click on a color in the color picker itself, but if you click-and-hold, you can actually leave Lightroom (keep holding the mouse button down) and move this cursor out over that webpage, and as you move it, it samples the color of whatever's beneath it. When you get the new background color you like, just release the mouse button. Of course, to make this work, you'll have to be able to arrange your windows to see Lightroom and your Web browser onscreen at the same time.

▼ What to Do If You See a Warning Icon Above the Image Pages Size Slider

The Image Pages slider (in the middle of the Appearance panel) lets you choose the size of the preview (larger) image people see when they click on a thumbnail. However, if you're in thumbnail view, and look at the top right of the Image Pages slider, you'll always see a little warning icon. That's letting you know that before you try to use this slider, you should click on a thumbnail first, so you can see the larger preview image (which is what that slider adjusts), because without seeing the larger size, you're kind of just dragging that slider blindly.

Portrait Workflow
my step-by-step on-location portrait shoot process

When I wrote the first edition of this book, back when Photoshop Lightroom 1 was first released, I wanted to do something different—something that no other Lightroom book would have, and that was a step-by-step workflow chapter that took the reader from beginning to end, starting with the live shoot, all the way through to the final print. I did both a wedding shoot and a landscape shoot, and showed the whole process, so you could use it as a jumping off place to create your own workflow. When you read that here, it doesn't sound all that groundbreaking, but nobody else had done it, and nobody else did it (for Lightroom 1 anyway), but it was such a good idea that I thought I'd steal it from myself and do it again in this new Lightroom 2 version of the book. But I didn't want to do the same wedding workflow again, or a landscape workflow again. Instead, I wanted to document my step-by-step Lightroom 2 workflow for a location portrait shoot of Oscar-winning movie star, George Clooney. I wanted to keep the lighting gear small and compact, because at first I wasn't sure if I'd be shooting him in a hotel or at his home, and if I limited my gear to just a couple of Nikon SB-800s on some lightweight light stands, I'd be ready for either setting. When the call came in from his publicist, there were a lot of questions like, "You're who?" and "Do you want me to call the police?" and "You're scaring me," etc. So then I called Tom Hanks' publicist, and….

Workflow Step One: It All Starts with the Shoot

This workflow is for location or environmental portrait photographers. In our example, we're going to start with a location shoot taken in a small recording studio (this shoot is one I did for keyboard manufacturer Korg, for a promotion concept for a new keyboard accessory). I had no idea how much room I'd have to work with in the recording studio or the control room, so I decided to go with a light, flexible off-camera flash setup, rather than hauling in a bunch of studio strobes and softboxes. First, I'll quickly take you through the location shoot setup.

Step One:

Today's high-tech recording studios can have really amazing interiors, but the studio we wound up shooting the promo in just wasn't one of those. Once we got on location, I realized our challenge was going to be to not over-light the studio, but instead, to try to hide as much of the background as possible. Here, I'm set up in the studio's control room, and it was so small that I was really glad I brought such a small, simple lighting setup. I mounted a Nikon SB-800 flash on a light stand, using a swivel mount to hold both the flash and a shoot-through umbrella (so the flash fires through the umbrella, which helps to spread and soften the light).

Step Two:

I used two cameras during this shoot: For the control room shots, I wanted a really wide look, so I used a full-frame Nikon D3 with a 14–24mm f/2.8 lens. The final image (which you'll see later in the chapter) was taken at 200 ISO, at f/5.6, at 1/60 of a second. I shot tethered directly from the camera into my laptop (shown here), and then into Photoshop Lightroom (see page 20 in Chapter 1 for how to set up to shoot tethered into Lightroom), and the wireless Nikon flash was triggered by a Nikon SU-800 transmitter sitting on top of my camera.

RAFAEL "RC" CONCEPCION

Step Three:
The second location in the studio was the main recording room. They had these color-changing lights going the whole time, which looked cool while you were standing there, but it made getting the lighting right a little trickier. I used the same shoot-through umbrella setup, but for these shots, I added a second SB-800 flash on a light stand, but without an umbrella to soften the light. I also added a HonlPhoto Speed Snoot, which is basically a black nylon tube you put around the end of your flash head to narrow the beam of your flash big time. It works wonders. I placed this second flash right where the photo here was taken from (the "behind-the-scenes" photos on these pages were taken by RC Concepcion), directly across from the white umbrella, so it would put a brighter kicker light on the opposite side of my subject's face.

Step Four:
Here's another view of the setup (with me sitting on the floor, shooting up at my subject). You can see the placement of the main light (with the shoot-through umbrella), and the second light is just out of the frame, on the far-right side of the photo. Again, I'm shooting tethered directly into my laptop (and Lightroom), so I can see the images full screen just seconds after I take them. That way, I can really see what the light is doing, and adjust the position and intensity of the flashes, and even try tweaking the files right in Lightroom during the shoot. For a "down-and-dirty" job like this on-location recording studio shoot, a lightweight portable lighting setup like this (which fits in a small 2-lb. shoulder bag) does a surprisingly good job.

RAFAEL "RC" CONCEPCION

Workflow Step Two: Right After the Shoot, Do This First

Once the shoot is over, before you head back to your studio to start the sorting/editing process in Lightroom and Photoshop, you've got some absolutely critical "first-things-first" stuff to do, and that is to back up your photos, right now, before anything else—I actually back up while I'm still on location (using two OWC Mercury On-The-Go High-Speed 80-GB portable hard drives). Here's the step by step on backing up:

Step One:

When you shoot tethered (directly from your camera to your laptop, like I did at this shoot), your photos are already in your computer, and they're already in Lightroom, but they're not backed up anywhere yet—the only copies of those photos are on that computer. If anything happens to your laptop, those photos are gone forever. So immediately after the shoot, I back up those photos (while I'm still there on location). Although you can see the photos in Lightroom, you need to back up the photo files themselves. A quick way to find that folder is to go to Lightroom and Control-click (PC: Right-click) on a photo from that shoot and choose Show in Finder (PC: Show in Explorer) from the contextual menu, as shown here.

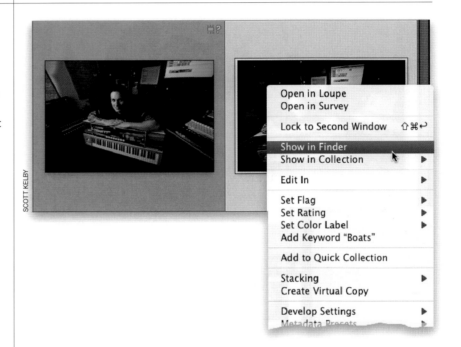

Step Two:

This opens a Finder (PC: Windows Explorer) window of the folder with your actual photo files inside, so click on that folder and drag the whole thing to your backup hard drive (this has to be a separate external hard drive—not just another partitioned disk on the same computer). If you don't have an external drive with you, then at the very least, burn that folder to a CD or DVD before you leave the location.

Okay, your photos are in Lightroom, they're backed up to a separate hard drive (or CD/DVD), so now it's time to make a collection of the "keepers" (the photos that have a chance of being seen by the client), and get rid of the shots that are out-of-focus, the flash didn't fire, or are just generally messed up (the Rejects). We're going to make our lives easy by creating a collection set right off the bat, and then we'll make a collection inside that set for our best images, and one for the final images we'll show to the client.

Workflow Step Three: Finding the "Keepers" & Making a Collection

Step One:
In the Library module, go to the Collections panel (in the left side Panels area), click on the + (plus sign) button on the right side of the panel header, and choose Create Collection Set from the pop-up menu. When the Create Collection Set dialog appears, name your new collection "Keyboard Shoot," and then click the Create button. Now we've got a set where we can save our Picks and our final images to show to the client.

Step Two:
In the Folders panel (in the left side Panels area), click on the folder of photos from the studio shoot. Once they appear in the Grid view, double-click on the first one (so it zooms into Loupe view), then start the process of flagging your Picks (your best shots from the shoot) by pressing the letter **P** on your keyboard each time you see one, and your Rejects (shots that are out-of-focus, badly composed, messed up, etc.) by pressing the letter **X** when you see one of those. Use the **Arrow keys** on your keyboard to move through all your images (remember, just Picks and Rejects—no star ratings, etc.). More on Picks and Rejects in the tutorial on page 42 in Chapter 2.

Continued

Step Three:

Once you've chosen your Picks (and deleted your Rejects by choosing Delete Rejected Photos from the Photo menu), go up to the Library Filter above the Preview area, click on Attribute, and then click on the white Picks flag (shown circled here in red) to filter your images so only the Picks are showing. Now, press **Command-A (PC: Ctrl-A)** to select all the Picks, and then press **Command-N (PC: Ctrl-N)** to create a new collection. When the dialog appears, name this collection "Picks," from the Set pop-up menu, choose that Keyboard Shoot set you created back in Step One, make sure the Include Selected Photos checkbox is turned on, and click the Create button (more on collections on page 42 in Chapter 2).

Step Four:

This saves your Picks into their own collection inside your Keyboard Shoot set (shown circled here in red).

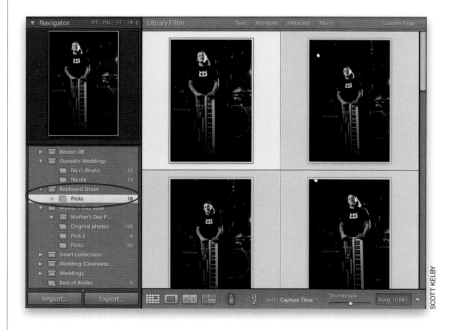

Now that you've whittled things down to the images you're going to show the client, it's decision time: are you going to let your client look at the proofs "as is," or do you want to tweak 'em a bit first in Lightroom's Develop module? If you're leaving them "as is," jump over to page 385. But, if you want to take a couple of minutes and tweak the white balance, exposure, and other simple adjustments, then stick with me here. By the way, these are just some quick tweaks—we don't want to invest a bunch of editing time now, because the client is only looking for two final images.

Workflow Step Four: Tweaking the Picks

Step One:
In our project, we shot in two different locations in the studio, so we have two different lighting setups. I'll only have to tweak one photo from each of these locations (two photos total), and then I'll apply those edits to all the other similar photos. In the Grid view, start by clicking on a photo from one of those locations, then press **D** to jump over to the Develop module. Start with a quick white balance tweak (get the White Balance Selector tool **[W]** from the top of the Basic panel and click on something that's supposed to be a light gray). Here I clicked on a gray piece of gear in the audio rack, and it made my subject's skin tone a little warmer (which is good).

Step Two:
If you look at the histogram back in Step One (at the top of the right side Panels area), you can see that the white highlight clipping warning triangle is on, and if you click on that triangle, it will highlight in red the areas being clipped. When I clicked on the warning triangle for this photo, his left cheek lit up in red (so, that second flash behind him was blowing out his cheek). To fix that, just click-and-drag the Recovery slider to the right (as shown here). Since I was already in the Basic panel, I went ahead and increased the Clarity to +57 to give the photo some extra punch.

Continued

Step Three:

Now we're going to add an edge vignette to hide some of the background junk that might distract the viewer. So, scroll down to the Vignettes panel and decrease the Lens Correction Amount to around −78 and the Midpoint to 28 (as shown here). For more on creating vignettes (and we why add them), jump back to page 150 in Chapter 4.

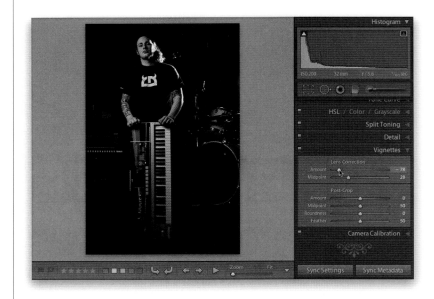

Step Four:

Once I added the vignette, it made the subject look a little too dark (which is not uncommon when you darken the edges of an entire photo as much as we just did), so I went back up to the Basic panel and increased the exposure a little by clicking-and-dragging the Exposure slider to the right to +0.41 (as shown here). So, like I said, we just make a few quick tweaks (white balance, exposure, recovered some clipped highlights, added some clarity, and added a vignette). Now, let's take the changes we made to this one photo and apply them to the other photos with similar lighting.

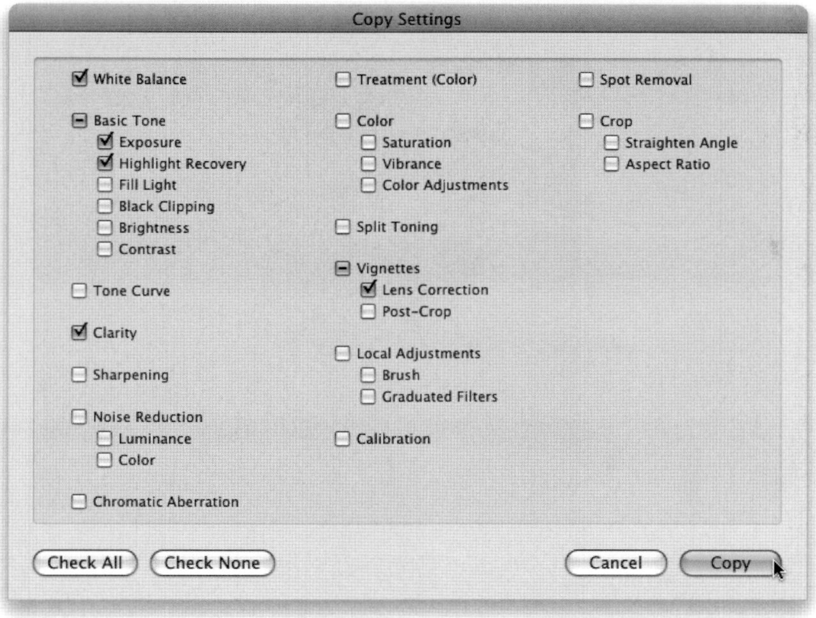

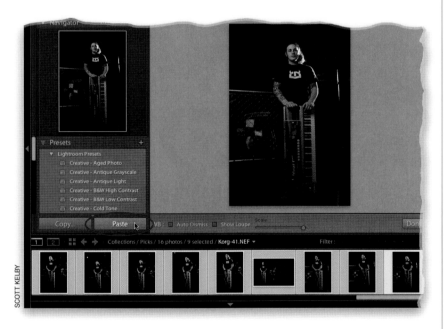

Step Five:
Click on the Copy button, found at the bottom of the left side Panels area, to bring up the Copy Settings dialog (shown here). First, click the Check None button at the bottom of the dialog (so it unchecks all the checkboxes), then turn on just the checkboxes beside the things you actually did to the photo, and click the Copy button (more on copying-and-pasting settings between photos back on page 156 of Chapter 4).

Step Six:
Go to the filmstrip and select all the other photos that have similar lighting, then click the Paste button (shown circled here) to apply the settings you copied to all those selected photos at once.

Continued

Step Seven:

Now find one of the photos from the other lighting setup (as seen here), and make any tweaks you need to it (I pretty much made the same Basic panel adjustments and added a vignette at the end, as shown here). Then, just repeat Steps Five and Six (copying the settings from your tweaks to this one photo and pasting them onto all the other photos taken in this part of the studio with similar lighting). Below is a before and after, and you can see the tweaks are nothing major, but of course I'd prefer that my client saw a proof of the photo on the right, rather than the before photo on the left, especially since these tweaks took less than two minutes total. Just remember: at this stage, do minor tweaks—save the big editing for the ones the client approves.

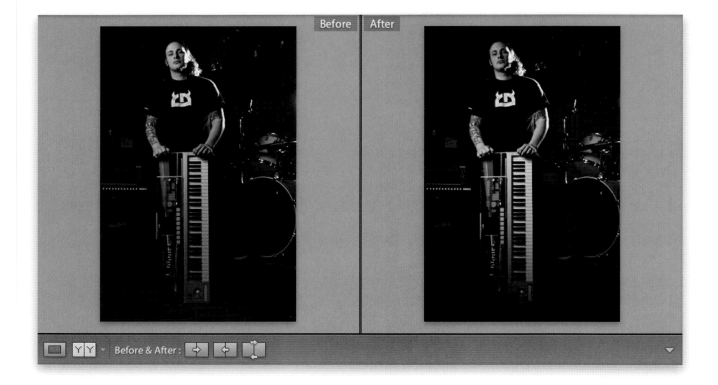

At this point, we've got the photos we want to show our client tweaked (or you're showing them pretty much "as is"), and it's time to put these proofs on the Web so the client can make a decision. We're going to use Lightroom to create a simple proofing webpage—the same one I use myself for client proofing—and it just takes a couple of minutes to get it up and running, because we're going to customize one of the built-in templates that come with Lightroom 2.

Workflow Step Five: Letting Your Clients Proof on the Web

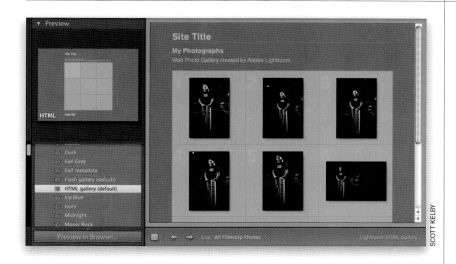

Step One:
Go to the Web module, and in the Collections panel in the left side Panels area, click on your Keyboard Shoot Picks collection. This loads your photos into whichever Web template you used the last time you were here in the Web module. Also, in the toolbar, make sure that All Filmstrip Photos is selected in the Use pop-up menu. We're going to customize one of the built-in templates, so go to the Template Browser panel in the left side Panels area and click on HTML Gallery (Default), as shown here. One of the main reasons I like using this particular template for proofing is that it puts a large number in the top-left corner of each cell, which makes it easier for clients to tell you which photos they've approved.

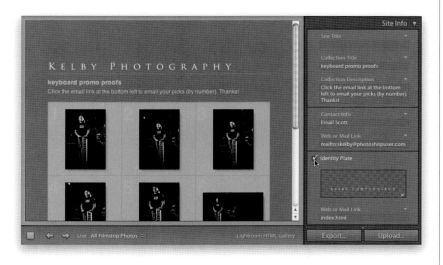

Step Two:
Let's spend two minutes customizing the look and text of this template. First, if you have an Identity Plate with your studio's name, turn that on (as shown here, in the Site Info panel in the right side Panels area). If not, just click directly on the words "Site Title" (right on the webpage itself) and type in your studio's name. Then add any other lines of text you want by clicking on the placeholder text and adding your own. Also, add your email address in the Web or Mail Link field, beneath the Contact Info field, in the Site Info panel (all this is explained in detail starting back on page 356 in Chapter 12).

Continued

Step Three:

One thing I always change in this default template is the color (darkness) of the numbers. I've had clients mention that they really didn't notice them at first, so I always make them a little darker. Scroll down to the Color Palette panel (in the right side Panels area), and you'll see a Numbers color swatch. Click on it to bring up the Numbers color picker, and click on a darker gray color swatch at the top (as shown here). You see a live preview as you choose different shades of gray, so just pick one that contrasts with the background enough that the numbers easily stand out, then close the color picker by clicking on the little X in the upper-left corner.

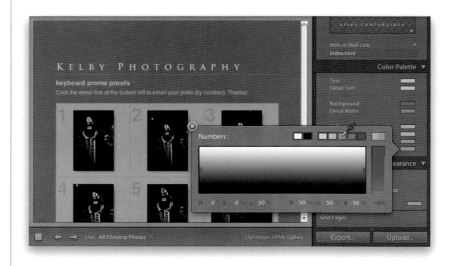

Step Four:

You're pretty much ready to go, but at this point, I always preview the webpage to see how the final will look (and to test everything to make sure it works, including my email link). So, click the Preview in Browser button at the bottom of the left side Panels area, and it will launch your Web browser and open your proofing page, so you can see a real preview of the final working webpage (as seen here). I click on the thumbnails to see if I like how the larger-sized previews look, one of which is shown here (if this larger preview seems too small, you can change the size in the Appearance panel), and I always check the email link to see if it launches my email program and puts in the right email address. If everything looks good, click the Export button at the bottom of the right side Panels area to save your HTML web-page for uploading to the Web. If you're hosting your own website on your server, you can direct Lightroom to an FTP site by clicking the Upload button instead (right next to the Export button. Again, more on all of this stuff back on page 370).

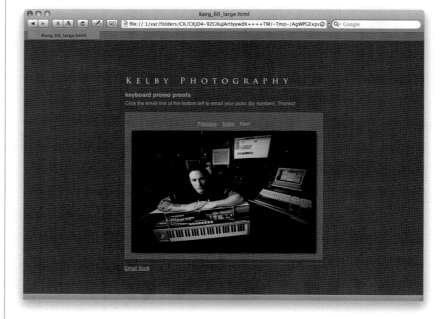

Once the client gets back to me with their picks, then I start working on the final images—first in Lightroom, and then, if necessary, I jump over to Photoshop. In this case, since we'll be adding a lot of text and a logo, we'll have to jump over to Photoshop at some point, because Photoshop has professional control over both, but in Lightroom, we can handle most of what we need to do.

Workflow Step Six: Making the Final Tweaks & Working with Photoshop

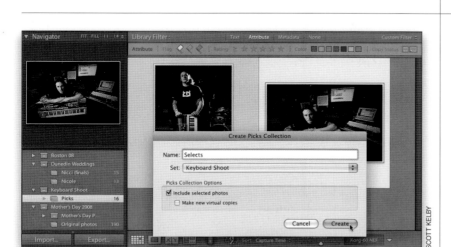

Step One:
Once the client emails me their picks, I go back to the Library module and I flag those images as Picks. In this case, the client only chose two shots, but in many cases (like in a wedding or portrait shoot), I might have 20 or 30 picks from the client, so I flag all of those. Once you've flagged them, go up to the Library Filter (above the Preview area), click on Attribute, and then click on the white Picks flag to see just the client picks. Then press **Command-A (PC: Ctrl-A)** to select them all, and put them in their own collection (within the Keyboard Shoot collection set) called "Selects" (as shown here. Again, more on collections and Picks in Chapter 2).

Step Two:
In this case, the client wanted more of a "concert lighting" look for the vertical photo, so we're going to have some color light spill onto the background and the edges of our subject using the Adjustment Brush in the Develop module (this is definitely something we would've had to do in Photoshop before Lightroom 2). So, press **D** to go to the Develop module and click on the Adjustment Brush (near the top of the right side Panels area), and in the options panel that appears, turn off the Auto Mask checkbox (near the bottom of the panel, if it's turned on), choose Color from the Effect pop-up menu at the top, then click on the Color color swatch and choose a yellowish color from the color picker (as shown here).

Continued

Step Three:

Using the Brush Size slider, choose a large size for your brush, and start painting over the background on the right side of the photo, letting a little of the color spill over onto your subject (as shown here). By the way, for more detailed info on the Adjustment Brush, there's almost a whole chapter on it (Chapter 5), and it starts on page 168.

Step Four:

Now, let's switch colors: click on the Color color swatch again, and this time choose a magenta color (you'll have to take the Eyedropper tool and click on magenta in the gradient color map). Then, take the brush and paint over the left side of the photo, and again, let a little of the color spill over onto his arms and the side of the keyboard (as shown here).

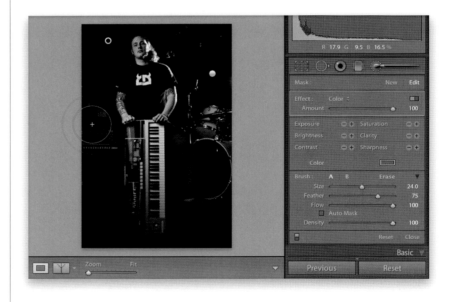

Step Five:

Even though we added a vignette earlier to take your eye off some of the distracting elements in the background, the background still looks a little too bright to me (maybe adding the colored lights drew more attention to it), so we're going to darken (burn) those areas. Click on New (at the top of the panel), choose Exposure from the Effects pop-up menu, set the Amount to around –1.00, and then paint over the background areas, avoiding the subject and the keyboard (as shown here). Now let's jump over to Photoshop to add our text and logo.

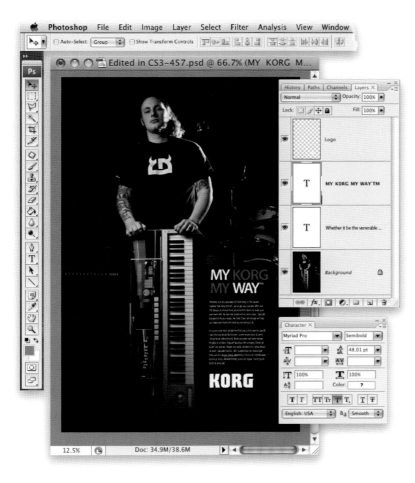

Step Six:

Press **Command-E (PC: Ctrl-E)**, and Lightroom sends a copy of your RAW file over to Photoshop (of course, if you wanted to maintain the RAW editing capabilities while in Photoshop, you could, instead, go under the Photo menu, under Edit in, and choose Open as Smart Object in Photoshop. For more info on opening your photo as a Smart Object in Photoshop, look back on page 253 in Chapter 8). Now we're going to do just about the easiest thing you can do in Photoshop— add text. Get the Type tool **(T)**, and type in your text (I used the font Myriad Pro for all the text). Then lastly, I opened the logo (it was its own separate document), and I used the Move tool **(V)** to click-and-drag it over into this document, and then positioned it below the column of text. Now you can just save and close the document, and it goes right back to Lightroom (with the layers still intact, even though you can't see the individual layers in Lightroom).

Continued

Step Seven:

When you return to Lightroom, you'll see the copy of the photo you edited in Lightroom, and the original RAW photo to the left of it in the filmstrip. Now, I mentioned in the previous step that this image still has all its layers, but you can't see them individually (it displays the photo, as if it's a flattened file). To reopen this photo in Photoshop and have the layers still intact, you'll press **Command-E (PC: Ctrl-E)**, and then a little dialog will appear asking if you want to open a copy or not. You'll want to choose Edit Original, then click the Edit button, and now your layered file will open in Photoshop (if you choose Edit a Copy with Lightroom Adjustments, it will open a flattened copy of your file; if you choose Edit a Copy, it will open your original layered file, but it will make a copy of it).

Step Eight:

Here's a before and after with the original RAW file on the left, and the file after our tweaks and adding text on the right (just in case you were wondering, I had to use Compare view to do this before/after view, because now there are actually two separate files—the original and the copy. So, I first clicked on the original file, and then clicked the Reset button at the bottom of the right side Panels area to get the original untouched RAW file. Then, I selected both versions of the file in the filmstrip and pressed the letter **C** on my keyboard to enter Compare view). Now, the second Selects collection image needs similar tweaks (and text added), but it has a problem of its own that will also need some Photoshop attention, because it's something Lightroom still can't do.

Step Nine:
Here I've taken the second Selects collection photo over to Photoshop, and I've added the text, although I had to split the text up into two sections to make it work with the layout of the ad, but that's not the problem. The problem is that I used such a wide-angle lens (a 14–24mm, but out wide at 14mm) on a full-frame sensor that the right edge of the photo is really starting to distort (look at the monitor and the laptop on the far right side—they're stretching to the right). Luckily, Photoshop can cure a lot of this with a really easy trick.

Step 10:
First, seeing all that text can be visually distracting for what you're going to do next, so go ahead and hide your text by clicking on the Eye icon to the left of each Type layer and the logo layer in the Layers panel. Next, with the Background layer selected, get the Rectangular Marquee tool **(M)** and make a tall, rectangular selection of the entire right side of the photo, from just to the right of the keyboard on over (as shown here). Now press **Command-J (PC: Ctrl-J)** to put a copy of just that selected area up on its own separate layer.

Continued

Step 11:

Now press **Command-T (PC: Ctrl-T)** to bring up Photoshop's Free Transform bounding box (it's what you use to scale, rotate, shear, add perspective, etc.). Grab the far-right side handle and click-and-drag inward to reduce the stretched look (as shown here). It does a pretty amazing job of bringing things almost back to normal (they'll still be a little stretched, but not nearly what you had before, so it will be much less obvious and distracting). When you're done "unstretching" it, press the **Return (PC: Enter)** key to lock in your transformation. Press **Command-E (PC: Ctrl-E)** to merge the Background layer and the transformed layer, and then you'll have to use the Crop tool **(C)** to crop the photo (so the old stretched stuff on the right side is cropped away).

Step 12:

Here's the final image after fixing the edge distortion, and making all the Type layers, and the logo layer, visible again. Now you can just save the file, close the image window, and that file is sent back to Lightroom with all your layers still intact. Next, we'll look at how to deliver the finished files to your client.

Once both of your images have had their text and logos added, it's time to deliver the final images to the client, and these are most often delivered in one of three ways: (1) you make final prints for the client, (2) you email high- or low-resolution copies of the final images to the client, or (3) you burn the final images to CD/DVD and deliver them the old-fashioned way. Here's a quick look at all three, with printing it yourself, of course, being the one that takes the most work, so we'll start with the two easier ones first.

Workflow Step Seven: Delivering the Finished Image

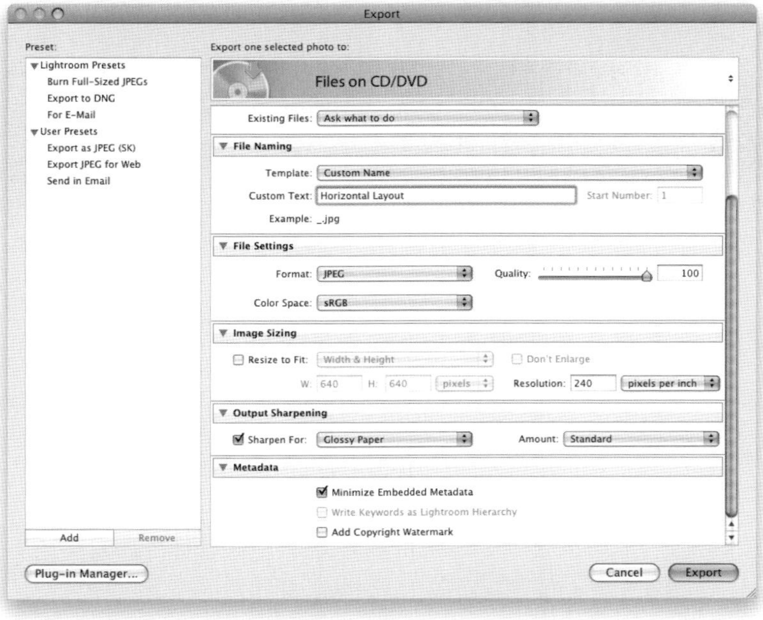

Step One:
To save your images to a CD/DVD, start by pressing **Command-Shift-E (PC: Ctrl-Shift-E)** to bring up the Export dialog (seen here). In the list of Lightroom Presets on the left, click on Burn Full-Sized JPEGs. Under File Naming, choose and enter a Custom Name, then in the File Settings section, for your JPEG quality, choose 100. Make sure the Sharpen For checkbox in Output Sharpening is turned on (I chose Glossy Paper and Standard Amount), then turn on the Minimize Embedded Metadata checkbox in the Metadata section, so your personal camera info is removed (but not your copyright info). Now click Export, and get a blank disc ready to insert into your CD/DVD drive.

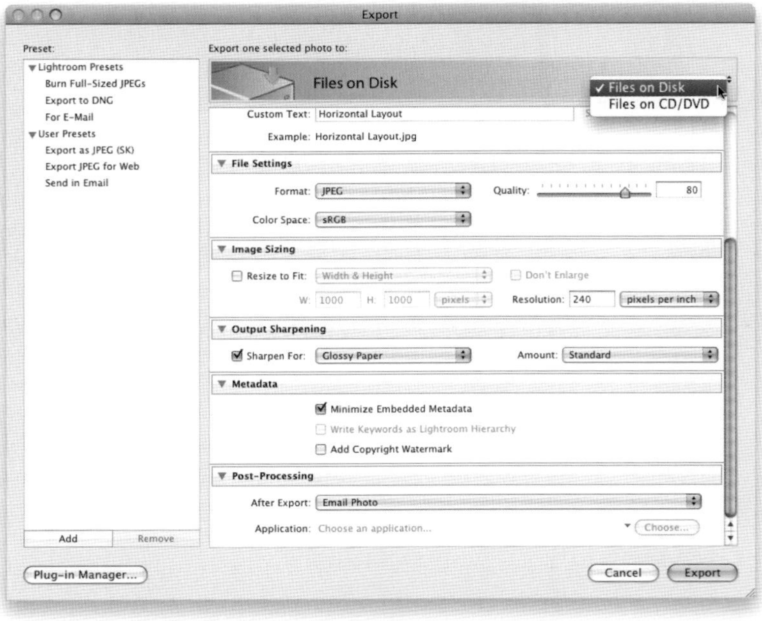

Step Two:
If you're going to email the images, then click on the For E-Mail preset (in the Lightroom Presets on the left side of the Export dialog; or just choose the Send in Email preset we made back in Chapter 7), then at the top-right corner of the dialog, choose Files on Disk from the pop-up menu (if it's not already selected), as shown here, so it just saves the files, rather than burning them to disc automatically. Lower the File Settings Quality to 80 (so the file sizes are smaller for emailing), then turn off the Resize to Fit checkbox in the Image Sizing section. Make sure the Sharpen For (in Output Sharpening) and Minimize Embedded Metadata (in Metadata) checkboxes are turned on. Then in the Post-Processing section, choose Email Photo (which we created in Chapter 7) from the After Export pop-up menu (as seen here).

Continued

TIP: Choosing Your Export Action

To email your images if you don't have the Email Photo export action available in the After Export pop-up menu, you'll choose Do Nothing, instead. Once you click the Export button, your images will be saved on your computer, and you can attach the files in your email message.

Step Three:

If, instead, you're going to output prints yourself, first jump over to the Print module and, in the Template Browser in the left side Panels area, click on the Maximum Size template to give you the page layout you see here. The default Page Setup for the Maximum Size template is US Letter (8½x11"), and Lightroom automatically rotates your photo, so it fits as large as possible on this letter-sized sheet. However, if I'm making a print for a client, I generally print something larger than letter-sized, and I like seeing my layout upright (the orientation in which I'm printing. I can't tell you how many little things I've caught at the printing stage over the years, but if my print is sideways [like it is here], the chances of me catching something are pretty slim).

Step Four:

So, to change the page setup, click the Page Setup button at the bottom of the left side Panels area. When the dialog appears, choose the printer, paper size, and orientation (I chose wide [landscape] here, so I could see my image right-side up, instead of on its side), then click OK to apply these settings. The side margins looked a little too close to the edge (making the image look unbalanced on the page), so I went to the Layout panel (in the right side Panels area) and increased the Left and Right margins to 0.64 (as seen here).

Step Five:
Now it's time to print the image (this is covered in-depth starting back on page 339 in Chapter 11). Scroll down to the Print Job panel (in the right side Panels area), and from the Print To pop-up menu at the top, choose Printer. Then for Print Resolution, since I'm printing to a color inkjet printer, I can leave it at 240 ppi. Make sure the Print Sharpening checkbox is turned on, choose the amount of sharpening from the pop-up menu on the right (I generally choose High for glossy prints), and then choose the type of paper you'll be printing on from the Media Type pop-up menu (I chose Glossy here). If your printer supports 16-bit printing (and you're running Mac OS X Leopard), then you can turn on the 16 Bit Output checkbox (at this point, only Macs running Leopard support 16-bit printing). Then, in the Color Management section, choose your Profile and set your Rendering Intent (again, covered in Chapter 11).

Step Six:
Now click the Print button (at the bottom of the right side Panels area), and the Print dialog will appear (the one shown here is from a Mac running OS X Leopard, but the Windows print dialog has the same basic features, just in a different layout). Choose Printer Color Management from the pop-up menu in the middle of the dialog, and turn this color management Off (as shown here), since you want Lightroom managing your color, instead of your printer (because the last thing you want is two color management schemes both trying to determine the right color, and then it's "Lightroom vs. Printer" and nobody wins).

Continued

Step Seven:

Now choose Print Settings from the pop-up menu in the middle, and choose the type of paper you're printing to (I'm printing to Epson's Exhibition Fiber Paper, so for Media Type, I chose Premium Luster Photo Paper). Then under Mode, click on the Advanced Settings radio button, from the Print Quality pop-up menu, choose SuperPhoto – 2880dpi (provided you're printing to an Epson Stylus Pro 3800, of course), and if you've cleaned the heads on your printer recently, you can actually leave the High Speed checkbox turned on. (*Note:* High Speed works fine, as long as you've got a reasonably new computer. If you've got an older computer, leave High Speed off, or the printer will pause and wait for the computer to catch up, which can degrade print quality.) Now, just click the Print button.

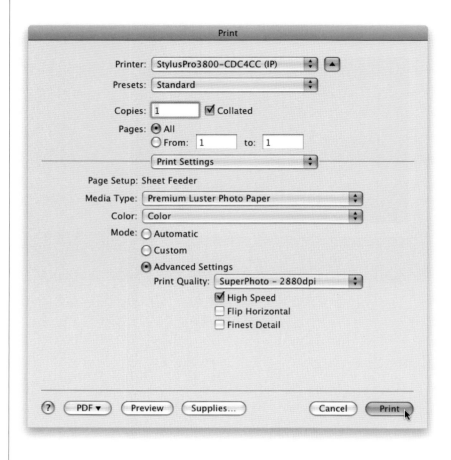

Step Eight:

When you click the Print button, sit back, and wait for that puppy to roll out of the printer. There you have it: my location portrait workflow, from beginning to end. Remember, this workflow stuff is at the very end of the book for a reason— because it only makes sense after you've read the rest of the book (everything that comes before this), so if anything didn't make sense, make sure you go back and reference the page numbers and chapters I gave you here, so you can learn in-depth about anything you might have skipped over, or didn't think you'd need, earlier in the book.

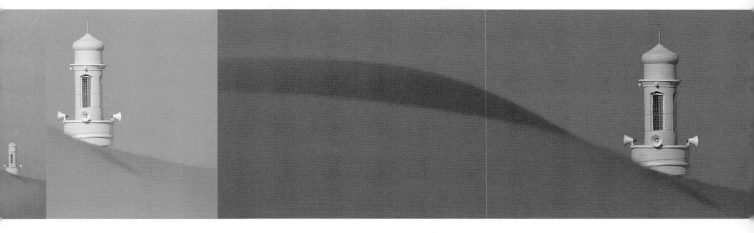

Travel Workflow
my step-by-step travel photography process

So far, in my Lightroom books, I've done three start-to-finish workflows. In the first book, I did a wedding workflow and a landscape workflow, and then in this book, I included a location portrait shoot, but those were all geared toward working professionals, and everything dealt with showing the final proofs to the client, and making prints for your client, and so on, but a lot of you (us) don't have clients. Instead, we have dependents, and when we return from an exotic locale (Houston), these dependents (and people masquerading as our friends) may want to share our experiences, and the best way to share them is either to: (a) show photographs from our trip, or (b) actually bring indigenous people from that area to give personal accounts of their lives, of their struggle to survive in a hostile world, and to tell us how much the price of gas has gone up in their region (answer: plenty). These people are known as "Texans" and will often attack if startled. The answer, of course, is (c) show photographs of Texans. Anyway, being a professional travel photographer is truly a dream job, since as best as I can tell, no one on earth really has that job as their sole means of support. Here's why: the next time you go to some cool destination, look around—everybody has a camera. Why would anyone pay us to shoot travel photos while they're surrounded by people shooting travel photos? If you find that you're not surrounded by people taking travel photos, that only means you probably live in the most uninteresting place on earth (Dallas).

Workflow Step One: Importing and Organizing

With this travel photography workflow scenario, *we* are the client, and we're creating the images for our family and friends, and our final images will be displayed in a slide show (when friends and family are nearby), and on a Web gallery for those farther away. This makes the presentation of the images much more important, and because we're shooting to a memory card (like normal), rather than shooting tethered to a laptop, it makes the workflow faster and easier. Here's what I do in these scenarios:

Step One:

I was lucky enough to get to do a speaking gig for Adobe in Dubai (located in the United Arab Emirates), and since I only had to speak one day, I spent the rest of the time shooting in the city (which was just amazing) and out in the nearby desert (the photo shown here was taken by my brother Jeff). I generally shoot on a tripod for any serious work, and I had a Gitzo Traveler tripod with me on the trip, but when I went out to the desert the first time, I learned that in the soft sand it was more trouble than it was worth (and it got sand in, well…everything), so I shot handheld the rest of the time (the sun was so bright that it really wasn't a problem). My main camera was a Nikon D3 with the Nikon 70–200mm VR f/2.8 lens you see here. (By the way, the cast on my leg was from a hairline fracture that happened a week or so before the trip, during either: [a] A taekwondo sparring match, where I threw a front round-kick at my opponent's head, and when he came up to block it, my foot caught the corner of his elbow. He went down, but then I couldn't put my foot down for a week. Or, [b] I was on my treadmill, watching a movie, and I slipped off because I wasn't paying attention. I really like the [a] story, but sadly…well, you know.)

JEFF KELBY

SCOTT KELBY

Step Two:

I'm fairly paranoid about losing my original photos, so when I'm out in the field, before I even leave the shoot, I pop out my memory card and back up right there on the spot to an Epson P-5000 (it has CompactFlash and SD card slots built in), which is a portable 80-GB hard drive with a huge, beautiful crisp LCD monitor (there's also a cheaper 40-GB model—the P-3000). However, this is only temporary "in-the-field" storage. Once I get back to my hotel room, I connect my memory card reader and my two OWC Mercury On-The-Go high-speed portable hard drives to my computer (as shown here), and import the photos into Photoshop Lightroom.

Step Three:

When you connect your memory card reader to your laptop, Lightroom's Import Photos dialog appears (if it doesn't, just go to the Library module and click the Import button at the bottom of the left side Panels area). I set this up so one set of photos from the card goes onto the first drive (and into my Lightroom catalog) by clicking on the Choose button to the right of Copy To, and choosing my first external hard drive. Then I turn on the Backup To checkbox and click its Choose button, so I have a backup copy of these photos sent to my second drive automatically (I never erase a memory card until I know I have at least two backup copies of the images from that card). For more on importing, adding your copyright info on import, and that stuff, jump back to Chapter 1.

SCOTT KELBY

Continued

Step Four:

Once the photos are imported, take a quick look through them and mark your Picks and Rejects (pressing **P** for Picks and **X** for Rejects). Once you've flagged any really bad shots (this only takes two minutes because the really bad ones jump out at you), go to the Photo menu and choose Delete Rejected Photos (as shown here).

Step Five:

When you travel for any period of time, you're going to wind up shooting in different places (for example, I shot in the city, on the water, on a beach, at the conference, in the old town area, etc.), and your best bet to keep all these different (yet still connected) shoots organized is to create a collection set first, so you can put all your different shoots sorted by topic inside that set. So, first go to the Collections panel, click on the + (plus sign) button on the right side of the panel header, choose Create Collection Set (as shown here), and give your new set a name.

Step Six:

Now go to the Library Filter bar above the center Preview area (press **\ [the Backslash key]** if it's not visible), click on Attribute, then click on the white Picks flag to show just your best shots from this shoot. Next, press **Command-A (PC: Ctrl-A)** to select all your Picks, then press **Command-N (PC: Ctrl-N)** to create a new collection. When the Create Collection dialog appears, from the Set pop-up menu, choose the collection set you just created (as shown here), give your new collection a descriptive name, then click Create. Now your Picks from that shoot will appear inside your main collection set (this is the key to staying organized—your best shots from each shoot will wind up being just one click away, right inside your collection set for that shoot).

Step Seven:

Now you're ready to pop in another card from another shoot on the same trip (so let's do that). Go ahead and import another set of photos from your memory card, and then we'll go through the same routine: (1) import your photos and make a backup copy on your second drive; (2) flag your Picks and Rejects, then get rid of your Rejects; (3) turn on the Picks flag filter (up top) to find your best photos from the shoot; and then (4) select all the Picks, make a new collection, and save it inside your trip's collection set (as shown here). You're going to repeat this each time you bring in another card of photos from this trip. Each time you add another set of keepers, they'll be right inside that collection set.

Workflow Step Two: Editing Our Images in Lightroom 2

Now that we're down to just the Picks (the best photos from each location on the trip), we can take some time to tweak the photos in the Develop module. We can do more in Lightroom 2 than we ever could before at this stage, so we'll have to see how the editing process goes on these photos to see whether we'll really need to jump over to Photoshop or not (like the way I'm building some digital imaging suspense there?).

Step One:
Click on one of the photos you want to tweak in Lightroom, then press **D** to jump over to the Develop module. The shot shown here has a number of things I'd like to fix. First, it's crooked (yikes!), and just very flat looking. Besides that, the sky is about the same color as the sand, and although we won't be able to make it a bright blue (it would just look too fake), it should at least look a little blue, right? Also, the photo is just washed out, and it needs to be punchier all around.

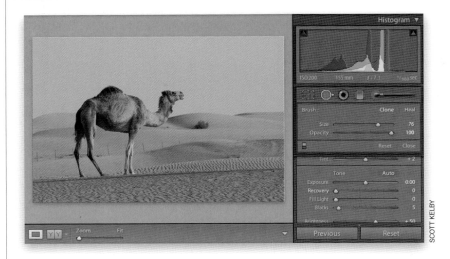

Step Two:
Let's straighten the photo first, so click on the Crop Overlay tool in the toolbox right below the Histogram panel (or press **R** on your keyboard). When the Crop Overlay border comes up, move your cursor outside the border, and click-and-drag to rotate it (as shown here) until the image looks straight.

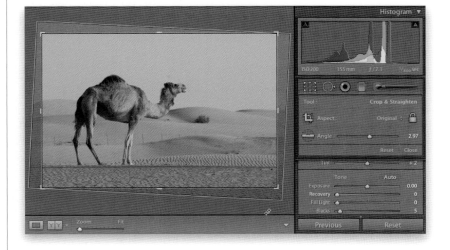

Step Three:
Press Return (PC: Enter) to lock in your straightening. Now let's tweak the settings in the Basic panel to get this photo looking better. Start by increasing the Exposure a little bit (which brightens the highlights), but be careful not to clip any highlights (keep an eye on the highlight clipping warning triangle, up in the top right of the histogram). The photo looks washed out, so click-and-drag the Blacks slider to the right until the shadow areas start to look more balanced and the colors look more saturated. Lastly, go ahead and click-and-drag the Clarity slider to the right (I dragged over to +39) to add some midtone contrast and punch to the image.

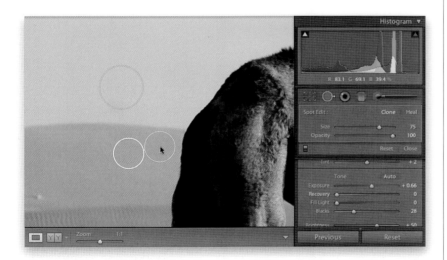

Step Four:
Once the photo is tweaked, some of the dust spots on it (which weren't apparent when the photo was washed out) really jump out, so press **N** to get the Spot Removal tool, and click it over the spots (as shown here) to remove them (see Chapter 6 for more on this tool). There are spots in a number of different places on this photo (I've really got to clean my sensor), so click on all of them to get rid of them. Okay, at this point the photo looks straight, it looks pretty balanced tone-wise, and the spots have been removed. However, there are four or five other photos, taken at the same time, in the same light (and of the same camel), that need fixing, too. Luckily, since we fixed this one photo, we can apply these same fixes (including the spot removal) to those other photos.

Continued

Step Five:

Press **G** to return to the Library module's Grid view. When you're in Grid view, there is no Copy Settings button, like there is in the Develop module, but you can still get to that same Copy Settings dialog by pressing **Command-Shift-C (PC: Ctrl-Shift-C)**. When the dialog appears, first click the Check None button (to uncheck everything), then turn on the checkboxes for the changes you made to the image so far (I turned on the checkboxes for Exposure, Black Clipping, Clarity, Spot Removal, and Crop). When you're done, click Copy to copy your settings.

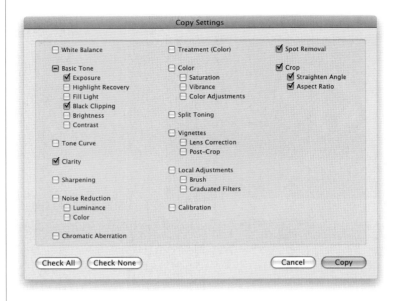

Step Six:

Now, in Grid view, select the other photos you want to apply those same edits to (as shown here), by Command-clicking (PC: Ctrl-clicking) on them. You can see these other photos look pretty flat, just like the original photo did.

SCOTT KELBY

Step Seven:

Now press **Command-Shift-V (PC: Ctrl-Shift-V)** to paste those copied settings onto all of your selected photos (as shown here). Don't forget, it also applies the straightening and the spot removal. Luckily, all the shots needed straightening pretty badly, but if they didn't, I would have just left the Crop checkbox turned off in the Copy Settings dialog. You may also want to check the spot removal on each one to make sure it didn't do anything funky (again, see Chapter 6 for more on spot removal).

Step Eight:

Now let's move on to a different photo from the same shoot, so choose it in the Grid view and press **D** to go to the Develop module. We'll address some different issues in just a minute, but if you look, this photo shares most of the same problems as the one we just fixed (it's even crooked, too. Hey, it was hot out there!).

Continued

Step Nine:

Let's go ahead and press **Command-Shift-V (PC: Ctrl-Shift-V)** to paste those same edits onto this photo (it did a pretty darn good job!). Now, if you hadn't copied the settings from the other photo, you could use a little trick that I use just about every day, and it's incredibly handy: Just go to the filmstrip, and click back on that photo you fixed earlier. Then click directly on another photo that needs a similar fix, and click the Previous button at the bottom of the right side Panels area, and Lightroom takes the settings from the last photo you clicked on and applies them to this photo. Try it—you'll use this more than you'd think.

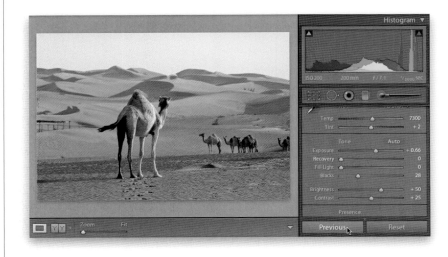

Step 10:

One of the problems that this photo has is that the sky is the same color as the sand, and like I mentioned in the first step, it doesn't have to be a bright blue sky, but it has to have at least a little blue. So, click on the Adjustment Brush in the toolbox, then from the Effect pop-up menu, choose Color, and click on the Color color swatch to bring up the color picker (shown here). Choose a blue color, then close the color picker by clicking on the little X in the top-left corner. (For more on the Adjustment Brush, see Chapter 5.)

Step 11:
Set your brush to a large size, turn on the Auto Mask checkbox (so it keeps you from painting on the sand), and start painting over the sky (as shown here) to add a slight blue tint to it (I know, it's pretty subtle, but if you do much more, it will look pretty obvious). A before and after is shown below. *Note:* At this point, the photo is fine for the Web or for a slide show, but if I was going to print a 13x19" print or larger, then I'd press **Command-E (PC: Ctrl-E)** to jump over to Photoshop, and there I'd use the Clone Stamp tool to carefully remove the fence posts and tin roof in the center of the left side. When I was done, I'd just save and close the photo, and it would come right back here to Lightroom.

Workflow Step Three: Creating a Slide Show

When I come back from a trip, I usually do a slide show for friends and family, and Lightroom is perfect for onscreen presentations like this. You can add background music, it puts a smooth dissolve between your images, and now, in Lightroom 2, you can add beginning and ending title screens, as well. But before you start making your slide show, there's a decision you'll have to make about how many images you want in your slide show, and how to manage them. We'll start with that part first.

Step One:

At this point, you've got a collection set with a number of different collections of Picks inside it. So, the question is: do you want to use all the photos in every collection you've saved, or do you want to create a separate collection of just the "best of the best"? I go this second route, otherwise, you're going to have one long slide show, and when it comes to slide shows, less is more. In the Library module, start by pressing **Command-N (PC: Ctrl-N)** to create a new collection (name it "Slideshow"), turn off the Include Selected Photos checkbox, and save this new slide show collection inside the collection set you created earlier (as shown here).

Step Two:

Now go over to the Collections panel and Control-click (PC: Right-click) directly on this new, empty Slideshow collection, and from the contextual menu that appears, choose Set as Target Collection (as shown here).

Step Three:

Now that you've made this empty Slide-show collection your target collection, you can quickly go through each collection of Picks inside your collection set, and when you see a photo you'd like in your final slide show, just press the letter **B**, and that photo will be added to your target collection (your Slideshow collection). What you've done, by making that Slideshow collection your target collection, is borrowed the keyboard short-cut from Lightroom's Quick Collection. Normally, if you pressed B, it would add your photo to Lightroom's temporary Quick Collection, but once you choose a collection as the target collection, now pressing **B** moves the current photo into that collection. In our case, this is perfect for letting us quickly go through each Picks collection, find the ones we want in our slide show, and add them to the Slideshow collection by pressing just one letter.

Step Four:

Once you've gone through all the collections in your collection set and added the "best of the best" shots to your Slideshow collection, go ahead and click on it (as shown here) to see the photos you've added to this collection. Now, we're ready to start building our slide show.

Continued

Step Five:

Jump over to the Slideshow module (you can just press **Command-Option-3 [PC: Ctrl-Alt-3]**), and by default, it applies the slide show template you used last to the photos in your collection. But in our case, we're going to change templates, and quickly modify it the way we want it. So in the Template Browser (in the left side Panels area), under the Lightroom Templates, click on Caption and Rating. This template automatically displays text for any captions you've added to the photo in the Library module's Metadata panel, plus any star ratings you've assigned. I haven't done either to this photo, so you don't see anything but some little dots under the photo.

Step Six:

Now let's do a little customizing of our own. First, go up to the Options panel (at the top of the right side Panels area), and turn off the Cast Shadow and Stroke Border checkboxes. Then scroll down to the Overlays panel, and turn off the check-boxes for Rating Stars and Text Overlays (that removes those little dots). Lastly, scroll down to the Backdrop Panel and turn off the Color Wash checkbox (as shown here), so instead of a dark gray–to–light gray gradient, our background is now just a solid gray (if you want to change the background color, just click on the color swatch at the bottom right of this panel).

Step Seven:

Let's add some background music: Go down to the Playback panel and choose some background music. If it's a travel slide show, I usually go and buy a song (from the iTunes Store) from a movie soundtrack filmed in that area. For example, if I was doing a slide show of my trip to Italy, I might use a song from the soundtrack for the movie *Under the Tuscan Sun*. However, for this slide show of Dubai City, I actually bought a belly dancing song from the iTunes Store called "Mastoom Mastoom/Asmar Asmar" by Turku, from the album *Alleys of Istanbul* (I know what you're thinking: "That's gotta rock!" But it actually does fit surprisingly well). More on adding music to your slide show back on page 308 in Chapter 10.

Step Eight:

Go to the Titles panel, and turn on the Intro Screen checkbox, then use the Identity Plate Editor to create the text that will appear on your opening title slide (see page 296 in Chapter 10 for how to create custom Identity Plate text). Now you can hit the Play button to see your slide show start, which starts with the title slide (as shown below), and then the background music plays as the slide show begins. If you turned off the Repeat checkbox in the Playback panel, the slide show will play until it reaches the last slide. Of course, you could add a "The End" slide after the last slide by going to the Titles panel and turning on the checkbox for Ending Screen (if you do that, don't forget to create the text for the ending slide using the Identity Plate Editor).

Workflow Step Four: Putting Up a Web Gallery

If the people you want to show your travel photos to are not physically nearby, so they can't sit with you while you show them your slide show, you'll probably want to create a Web photo gallery you can post, so they can see it. Because this is the final presentation, rather than just proofs, like we did in the previous workflow (from the recording studio), we can get a little more creative with our Web gallery layout choices. Here goes:

Step One:

For your Web gallery, you can use the same Slideshow collection you just made a few minutes ago, but if you didn't make one, go back to the "Creating a Slide Show" project just a few pages back, and follow steps one through three to create a separate collection of just the images from your collection set that you want to appear in your Web gallery. Once you've got that collection, click on it, then jump over to the Web module by pressing **Command-Option-5 (PC: Ctrl-Alt-5)**. Once there, go to the Engine panel (at the top of the right side Panels area), and click on Airtight Simple-Viewer (as shown here). Then, in the Site Info panel, type in the name you want for your site in the Site Title field, under HTML Information. In the Image Info panel, I also changed the Caption pop-up menu to Date.

Step Two:

We don't need to do much customizing here, but one thing I would like to change is the thickness of the border around the photos. It seems a little too thick, so go to the Output Settings panel, and where it says Photo Borders, click-and-drag the slider to the left until it reads 7, which gives us a much thinner white border around our photos, (as shown here).

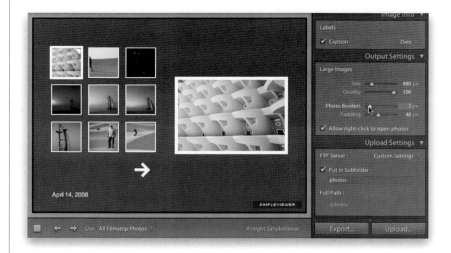

Step Three:

If you want to change the order that your photos appear in the gallery, just click-and-drag them into the order you want down in the filmstrip (in the example shown here, I moved a photo of my brother Jeff from the fifth slide to the first slide). *Note:* If you want to learn a lot more about creating Web galleries in Lightroom, jump back to Chapter 12.

Step Four:

Unless you want to tweak the colors of your webpage (the background color, stroke color, etc., which you would do in the Color Palette panel), then it's time to test our Web photo gallery. Click on the Preview in Browser button at the bottom of the left side Panels area, and it compiles your page, launches your Web browser, and displays your finished webpage, as shown here. If it looks good to you, back in Lightroom, click the Export button at the bottom of the right side Panels area, and save your webpage into its own folder, ready for uploading. Well, there you have it, my own workflow for shooting and processing images from my travel photography. I hope both of these workflows give you some ideas for customizing your own workflow to work as fast and as efficiently as possible.

Bonus Video: My Wedding Photography Workflow

When I wrote the first version of this book, I felt it was really important to include a chapter at the end that brings it all together, where I could show the process from beginning to end, starting with the shoot and ending with the final print. Once I wrote that workflow chapter (for wedding photographers), I thought I should add another one for landscape photographers. Well, this time around, I wrote one for portrait photographers and one for travel, but I just couldn't leave it alone—I had to add a special bonus video just for wedding photographers.

Do This First:

My workflow video starts on location at the church, during the formal portrait shoot of the bride. Although in the last version of the book I used a studio strobe and softbox on location, this time I went with a very small, lightweight, portable solution using an off-camera dedicated flash and… well, you'll have to watch the video to see the setup. I also shot tethered directly into Lightroom on the video, and you'll see me do the camera-to-computer setup there, as well. We don't spend too much time at the shoot, because the workflow is really about what we do in Lightroom 2, so you'll see me take the images from the shoot into Lightroom, and do our sorting in the Library module, our editing in the Develop module, etc., all the way to the final print for the bride.

SCOTT KELBY AND ©ISTOCKPHOTO/NGHE TRAN

Here's Where You'll Find It:

You can find the live on-location Lightroom wedding shoot at **www.kelbytraining .com/books/lightroom2**. When you get to that webpage, you'll need to enter a password to access the video. Your password is **Lightroom2 rocks** (with no space between Lightroom and 2). (It's lame—I know.) Well, that's it folks. I really hope you enjoy the bonus video, and that it helps you in your own Lightroom 2 workflow.

So, you've made it to the end of the book and now you can see how Lightroom 2 is going to change the digital photography workflow forever. Well, if you're hungry for more Lightroom learning, I put together a couple pages of different resources that I'm involved with, so even though you've finished the book, we don't have to stop learning about Lightroom 2 together.

Where to Go Next for More Lightroom Learning

Photoshop User Magazine (The How-to Magazine for Adobe® Photoshop® Users):
I'm Editor and Publisher of *Photoshop User* magazine, and in each issue we have a magazine within a magazine—a special section of the publication dedicated to teaching you the latest techniques in Lightroom. *Photoshop User* magazine is sent free to all U.S. members of the National Association of Photoshop Professionals (NAPP). It's also available at newsstands all over the U.S. and Canada. You can find out more about *Photoshop User* magazine and NAPP at www.photoshopuser.com.

Adobe® Photoshop® Lightroom® Killer Tips Videocast and Blog:
Each week my buddy (and my co-host of *Photoshop User TV*) Matt Kloskowski hosts *Adobe Photoshop Lightroom Killer Tips*—a free tips and tricks video podcast for Lightroom users. Check it out at www.lightroomkillertips.com, where Matt also posts lots of cool Lightroom news and tips on his accompanying blog. You can subscribe for free on Apple's iTunes Store and then watch it right from within iTunes, or you can watch it right there on the website.

Continued

My Lightroom® Live! Seminar Tour:
When the original version of Lightroom
shipped, I launched a nationwide one-day
Lightroom Live! seminar tour that went
to major cities across the U.S., and now
with the amazing things in Lightroom 2,
I'm taking the tour back out on the road.
The tour is sponsored by Adobe Systems,
Inc. and produced by NAPP, and it starts
with a live on-location shoot, right there
in the class, with full studio lighting and
all the info on how we're shooting it, the
equipment used, etc. Then we take these
shots into Lightroom, and you see the
whole step-by-step workflow unfold live
in front of your eyes. It's kind of like a live
version of this book, but it all happens in
just one day—there's never been a tour
like it, so I hope you'll join me when we
come out your way. For info, or to sign up,
visit www.kelbytraining.com.

DAVE MOSER

**The National Association of Photo-
shop Professionals (NAPP): The
Photoshop Lightroom Authority!**
This is the world's largest photography,
graphics, and digital imaging professional association in the world, with
nearly 60,000 members in the U.S. and
221 countries around the world. They
were nice enough to support this book,
because, well…I'm their President.
I started the organization nine years ago
because there was no central resource
for learning about Photoshop 365 days
a year. Now, we've expanded our training
to include Lightroom, and besides including a special Lightroom section in each
issue of *Photoshop User* magazine, we
also produce the world's largest Photoshop
event, The Photoshop World Conference
& Expo, where we've added a full conference track, and a pre-conference workshop,
just for Lightroom users. Find out more
at www.photoshopworld.com.

Index

\ (backslash) key, 74, 140, 165
[ ] (bracket) keys, 172, 176, 200, 256
, (comma) key, 165
. (period) key, 165
+ (plus sign) button, 54, 56, 57, 97
1:1 previews, 18, 19
16-bit printing, 341, 353
32-bit mode, 263
64-bit mode, 33, 238
100% view, 126

A

A/B buttons, 184
actions
    creating in Photoshop, 247–252
    Export, 226, 227–229, 252, 268
Actions panel, 247, 249
Add Layer Mask icon, 256
Adjustment Brush, 170
    Auto Mask feature, 176, 178, 179,
        180, 184
    Auto Show option, 217
    creative effects using, 178–179
    dodging and burning with, 170–174
    effects applied with, 175, 178–179
    hiding pins for, 184
    interactive adjustments, 174
    landscape retouching with, 408–409
    portrait retouching with, 180–181,
        387–388
    quick tips about, 184
    resizing, 172, 176, 184
    settings for, 176, 184
Adobe Bridge, 70
Adobe Camera Raw (ACR), 70, 216,
    265–266
    See also **Raw photos**
Adobe Photoshop. *See* **Photoshop**
Adobe Photoshop Lightroom. *See*
    Lightroom
Adobe Photoshop Lightroom Killer
    Tips videocast and blog, 417
Adobe RGB color space, 268
After Export pop-up menu, 228, 251,
    252

Airtight Interactive templates, 368
alias icons, 227–228
Amount slider
    Adjustment Brush, 171
    Detail panel, 208
Appearance panel, 357, 359, 362, 363,
    365, 368, 369
artifact removal, 199–202
Attribute filter, 76–77
attributes
    finding photos by, 76–77
    sorting photos by, 45, 49, 53, 288
Auto Dismiss checkbox, 134
Auto Hide & Show feature, 37, 99
Auto Import settings, 21
Auto Layout button, 331
Auto Mask feature, 176, 178, 179, 180,
    184
Auto Sync mode, 158
Auto Tone button, 140
automated importing, 21
Auto-Stack feature, 88

B

Backdrop panel, 305
backgrounds
    print, 353
    slide show, 305, 306–307
    Web gallery, 367
backing up
    catalog database, 95–96
    photos during import, 11–12
    workflows for, 378, 401
backlit photos, 205–206
backscreened effect, 306–307
backslash (\) key, 74, 140, 165
Balance slider, 284
Basic panel, 130–142
    Auto Tone button, 140
    Blacks slider, 138
    Brightness slider, 138
    Clarity slider, 141, 381
    Contrast slider, 138, 143
    Exposure slider, 135–140
    Fill Light slider, 205–206
    Grayscale conversions, 275, 278, 282
    Histogram panel, 139
    Recovery slider, 136, 137

Saturation slider, 142
    Temp slider, 132
    Tint slider, 132
    Vibrance slider, 142
    white balance controls, 130–134
before-and-after views, 140, 165, 288
black-and-white conversions,
    272–288
    Develop module used for, 274–277
    duotones created from, 286–287
    finding candidates for, 272–273
    quick preview for, 165, 288
    quick tips about, 288
    split-tone effect and, 282–285
    tweaking individual areas of,
        278–281
blackout modes, 40–41
Blacks slider, 138, 206, 275, 278, 405
Blue Primary slider, 216
Blue/Yellow slider, 212
borders, frame, 349–352
bracket ([ ]) keys, 172, 176, 200, 256
Brightness slider, 138, 277
browser preview option, 359, 415
brush size adjustments, 172, 176,
    200, 217, 256
Brush tool (Photoshop), 256
burning and dodging, 170–177

C

calibrating monitors, 342
Camera Calibration panel, 213,
    215–216
Camera Raw, 70, 216, 265–266
    See also **Raw photos**
cameras
    default settings for, 165
    filtering photos by, 78
    fixing problems caused by, 212,
        215–216
    importing photos from, 5–19
    profiles for, 213–214
    shooting tethered from, 20–21
Candidate image, 52
Canvas Size dialog (Photoshop),
    242, 244
Caption and Rating template, 293,
    306

captions
  slide show, 293, 303
  Web gallery, 364
Cast Shadow checkbox, 302
Catalog panel, 59
Catalog Settings dialog, 95
catalogs, 89–96
  backing up, 95–96
  creating, 89–90
  exporting, 92–94, 234
  restoring, 96
  selecting, 91
  syncing, 92–94
CDs, burning photos to, 393
Cell Size sliders, 324, 353
Cell Spacing sliders, 323
Cells panel, 329
Chan, Eric, 216
chromatic aberrations, 212
Clarity slider, 141, 276, 381, 405
clipping warnings, 165
  highlight, 135, 136, 137, 381
  shadow, 138
Clone option, 200
Clone Stamp tool (Photoshop),
  240, 243, 260, 409
collection sets, 54–55, 100
collections, 45
  adding photos to, 99
  creating, 45–46, 50
  deleting, 99
  locating photos in, 100
  portrait workflow and, 380
  print layouts for, 336–338
  Quick Collections, 58–59
  renaming, 99
  sets of, 54–55, 100, 379
  slide show, 292, 314, 410–411
  Smart Collections, 56–57, 99, 100
  subcollections of, 55
  travel workflow and, 402–403
  Web gallery, 356, 372
Collections panel
  Library module, 46, 356, 379
  Print module, 336, 337
  Slideshow module, 292, 314
  Web module, 372, 385
color fringe, 212
color labels
  finding photos by, 78

  marking photos with, 53
  naming, 121–122
Color Management options, 345
Color Palette panel, 366–367, 368,
  369, 372
color picker, 184, 366, 367, 408
color profiles, 342–343
Color Space settings, 222, 234, 238,
  268
Color Wash checkbox, 305, 307
colors
  adjusting individual, 148–149
  camera calibration, 215–216
  Lightroom background, 110
  print background, 353
  slide show background, 305
  Web gallery, 366–367, 372
Colors panel, 117
Compare view, 51–53
comparing photos
  Compare view for, 51–53
  Survey view for, 47–49
Configure FTP File Transfer dialog,
  371
contact information, 15, 31
contact sheets, 340, 353
contrast adjustments
  Contrast slider, 138, 143
  Tone Curve panel, 143–147, 276,
  279
Contrast slider, 138, 143
Convert Photo to DNG option, 8
Copy button, 156, 165
Copy Metadata dialog, 71
Copy Settings dialog, 156, 165, 202,
  383, 406
copying-and-pasting settings,
  156–157, 383, 406–407
copyright information, 15, 31, 314,
  364
correcting problem photos. See
  fixing problem photos
Create Collection dialog, 46, 50, 54,
  272, 403
Create Droplet dialog, 250
Create Folder with New Catalog
  dialog, 89
Create New Action icon, 247
Create Print dialog, 338

Create Snapshot option, 189
Create Virtual Copy option, 154,
  274
Crop Frame tool, 194
Crop Marks checkbox, 325
Crop Overlay tool, 192–194, 195,
  196, 197, 404
Crop tool (Photoshop), 260
cropping photos, 192–195
  canceling crops, 193
  Lights Out mode for, 195
  locking in crops, 193, 194
  post-crop vignetting, 151
curves control. See **Tone Curve**
  panel
custom text, 298, 303
customizing
  background color, 110
  filmstrip, 120
  Grid view, 106–109
  Loupe view, 104–105
  panel end marks, 123–125
  slide shows, 298–305, 314
  Web galleries, 362–365

D

Darken slider, 204
Darks slider, 147
database backups, 95–96
date information
  file naming with, 23–24
  organizing photos by, 9–10
  searching for photos by, 77–78
Defringe pop-up menu, 212
deleting
  collections, 99
  folders, 84
  keywords, 99
  old backups, 126
  PSD files, 268
  rejected photos, 44, 380
  user presets, 161
  virtual copies, 155
  See also **removing**
Density slider, 177
Detail panel
  Chromatic Aberration sliders, 212
  Noise Reduction sliders, 190, 217

Detail panel (*continued*)
    preview window, 165, 207, 217
    sharpening sliders, 207–210
Detail slider, 208
Develop module, 129–166
    Adjustment Brush, 170–181, 217
    Auto Sync mode, 158
    Basic panel, 130–142
    before-and-after views, 140
    black-and-white conversions, 274–277
    Camera Calibration panel, 213, 215–216
    contrast controls, 143–147
    copying-and-pasting settings, 156–157
    Crop Overlay tool, 192–194, 195, 196, 197
    Detail panel, 165, 190, 207–211, 212, 217
    editing multiple images, 156–157
    exposure controls, 135–140
    Fill Light slider, 205–206
    Gradient Filter, 182–183
    Histogram panel, 139
    History panel, 188–189, 217
    HSL panel, 148–149
    keyboard shortcut, 130
    local adjustments, 169–184
    preset creation, 159–162
    quick tips about, 165–166, 184, 217
    Red Eye Correction tool, 203–204
    Reset button, 148, 177, 217
    split screen views, 140
    Spot Removal tool, 198, 200–202
    Tone Curve panel, 143–147
    Vignettes panel, 150–151, 166, 191
    virtual copies, 154–155, 217
    white balance controls, 130–134
Develop Settings pop-up menu, 216
digital photos. *See* **photos**
dimmed mode, 40
disclosure triangles, 82
DNG (Digital Negative) format, 7
    advantages of, 29
    converting photos into, 8, 32
    exporting files in, 220
dodging and burning, 170–177

Doty, Kim, 209
double-processing photos, 253–258
Draft Mode Printing option, 340, 347, 353
drop shadows, 301, 302
droplets, 250–251
Dual Display feature, 112–115
duotone effect, 286–287, 288
duplicate photos, 32
dust removal, 198, 405
DVDs, burning photos to, 393

E

edge frame borders, 349–352
edge vignetting
    creating, 150–151, 166
    fixing, 191
Edit Color Label Set dialog, 121–122
Edit Photo with Adobe Photoshop dialog, 239
editing
    History feature for, 188–189
    multiple images, 156–157
    photos in Photoshop, 240–244
    portrait workflow for, 381–384, 387–392
    travel workflow for, 404–409
    undoing edits, 188–189
Effect pop-up menu, 170, 173, 175
effects
    Adjustment Brush, 170–181, 184
    Gradient Filter, 182–183, 184
email
    PDF slide shows via, 312–313
    sending photos via, 226–229, 393–394
    Web gallery links to, 360–361
Embedded & Sidecar preview, 17, 19
embedded metadata, 67–71
end marks for panels, 123–125
Engine panel, 368–369
Erase button, 174
EXIF information, 67, 68
Export Actions folder, 228, 252
Export as Catalog dialog, 93
Export button, 220

Export dialog, 220–225, 232
    For E-Mail preset, 226, 228, 234, 393
    Format pop-up menu, 222
    Post-Processing section, 228, 251, 252
    RAW image settings, 232
Export Slideshow to PDF dialog, 312
exporting
    actions for, 226, 227–229, 252, 268
    catalogs, 92–94, 234
    emailing after, 226–229, 393–394
    keywords, 99
    photos as JPEGs, 220–225, 393
    plug-ins for, 230–231, 234
    presets for, 221, 224–225, 234
    quick tips about, 234
    RAW images, 232–233
    slide shows, 312–313
    Smart Collection settings, 99
    Web galleries, 370
Exposure slider, 135–140, 278, 382
External Editor options, 238
external hard drives
    backing up photos to, 11–12
    space remaining on, 100

F

Fades slider, 311
Feather slider, 176
File Handling pop-up menu, 7
File Naming templates, 14, 22–25, 81
Filename Template Editor, 22–24
Fill Light slider, 205–206
filmstrip, 36, 37
    customizing display of, 120
    filtering Picks from, 100
filters
    filmstrip, 100
    Library Filter bar, 74, 288, 380, 403
    turning on/off, 99
finding
    missing files/folders, 97–98
    photos, 74–79
Fine Art Mat template, 321, 324, 326
Fit in Window view, 38

fixing problem photos, 187–217
artifact removal, 199–202
backlit subjects, 205–206
camera calibration issues, 215–216
chromatic aberrations, 212
cropping images, 192–195
dust spot removal, 198
edge vignetting, 191
noise reduction, 190
RAW images, 213–214
red eye removal, 203–204
retouching portraits, 180–181
sharpening images, 207–211
straightening images, 196–197
undoing edits, 188–189
flagging photos, 43–44, 100
Flash-based templates, 358–359, 368–369, 370
Flatten Image option (Photoshop), 258, 260
Flickr Export plug-in, 230–231
Flow slider, 176
folders
deleting, 84
exporting as catalogs, 92–94
importing photos into, 8–10
missing, 98
moving photos between, 82–83
organizing photos in, 3–4, 8–10
renaming, 84
subfolders in, 84
watched, 20, 21
Folders panel, 82–85, 267, 379
Font Size pop-up menu, 117
Format pop-up menu, 222
frame borders, 349–352
Friedl, Jeffrey, 230
FTP uploader, 371, 372
full-screen slide show, 295, 312

G

Google Maps, 73
GPS data, 72–73
Gradient Filter tool, 182–183, 184

gradients
applying, 182–183
background, 305
inverting, 184
Grayscale button, 274, 279, 288
grayscale conversions. *See* **black-and-white conversions**
Grayscale Mix sliders, 279
Grid view, 39
customizing, 106–109
keyboard shortcut, 39
grouping photos, 86–88
Guides panel, 325

H

Hamburg, Mark, 198
hard drives. *See* **external hard drives**
HDR Conversion dialog, 263–264
HDR (High Dynamic Range) images, 262–267, 268
Heal option, 200
hiding
menu bar, 41
panels, 36–37, 111
toolbar, 39
window title bar, 41
High-Contrast Portrait Effect action, 247–252
highlights
adjusting, 135–137
clipping warning, 135, 136, 137, 381
color picker, 283, 286
Highlights slider, 147
Histogram panel, 139
History panel, 188–189, 217
HSL panel, 148–149
HSL/Color/Grayscale panel, 148, 274, 279, 288
HTML templates, 356, 358, 372
Hue sliders
Camera Calibration panel, 216
Split Toning panel, 283, 284, 285

I

ICC color profiles, 342
Identity Plate, 116–119
copyright watermark, 314
frame borders saved as, 352
graphical, 118–119, 362
printing photos with, 326–327, 353
resizing, 297, 308, 314
rotating, 352
saving, 117
slide shows and, 296–297, 300, 301, 314
text for, 126, 296–297, 301, 327
Web galleries and, 362–363
Identity Plate Editor, 116–119, 296, 350, 362
Image Info panel, 364
Image Pages slider, 372
Image Settings panel, 318, 322, 332, 336
images. *See* **photos**
Import button, 90
Import from Lightroom Catalog dialog, 94
Import Photos dialog, 5–6, 32, 162
importing photos, 5–19
automated, 21
backup process, 11–12
canceling imports, 5
develop settings, 15
file handling options, 7
folder organization, 3–4, 8–10
keyword assignments, 16
located on your computer, 12
metadata options, 15, 28, 30–31
naming/renaming options, 13–14, 22–25
preference settings, 26–28
previewing images, 16–19
quick tips about, 32–33
shooting tethered and, 20–21
storage location for, 2
travel workflow and, 401
importing presets, 162
impromptu slide shows, 59, 295
interactive adjustments, 174
interface tips, 36–37
IPTC metadata, 67, 68
iTunes, 309

J

JPEGs
contrast added to, 288
editing in Photoshop, 239, 246
exporting, 220–225
printing to, 347–348
saving images as, 220

K

Keep Square checkbox, 334, 335
keyboard shortcuts
before-and-after views, 140
cell views, 39
Grid view, 39
Loupe view, 38, 126
panel navigation, 160
show/hide options, 37
zooming in/out, 100, 199
Keyword List panel, 63
keyword sets, 62
Keyword Suggestions feature, 61
Keywording panel, 60, 61
keywords, 60–66
assigning, 16, 60–66, 99
deleting unused, 99
exporting, 99
Painter tool, 65–66
removing from photos, 63
sets of, 62
sub-keywords and, 64, 99
suggested, 61
Kloskowski, Matt, 307, 417

L

labels. *See* **color labels**
landscape orientation, 334, 335
Lasso tool (Photoshop), 240
Layers panel (Photoshop), 248–249,
256, 350
Layout Engine panel, 328, 333
Layout panel
Print module, 321, 322, 323, 324,
334
Slideshow module, 299
layouts
multi-photo, 328–335

print, 321–325, 328–338
slide show, 292–295, 298–306
Web gallery, 356–359, 362–365
Lens Correction sliders, 150, 191
lenses
correcting vignetting from, 191
filtering photos by, 78
Library Filter bar, 74, 288, 380, 403
Library module, 35–100
catalogs, 89–96
collections, 45–59, 292, 356
Compare view, 51–53
database backup, 95–96
exporting photos from, 220
filmstrip, 36, 37, 100, 120
finding photos in, 74–79
Folders panel, 82–85
GPS data in, 72–73
grayscale conversions in, 272–273
Grid view, 39, 106–109
keywords used in, 60–66
Loupe view, 38, 104–105
metadata options, 67–71
moving photos in, 82–83
Quick Collections, 58–59
Quick Develop panel, 163–164, 273
quick tips about, 99
relinking missing photos in, 97–98
renaming photos in, 80–81
Smart Collections, 56–57
sorting photos in, 42–59, 379–380
stacking photos in, 86–88
Survey view, 47–49
view options, 38–41
Library View Options dialog, 104,
106
Lightroom
background color, 110
dual-monitor setup, 112–115
interface tips, 36–37
Photoshop integration, 239–246,
389–390
resources for learning about,
417–418
upgrading from earlier versions of, 6
Lightroom LIVE! Seminar Tour, 418
Lights Dim mode, 40
Lights Out mode, 40–41
controlling, 41
cropping photos in, 195

Lights slider, 147
local adjustments, 169–184
creative effects, 178–179
deleting, 173
dodging and burning, 170–174
gradient filter effects, 182–183
painting with effects, 175–177
quick tips about, 184
Locate dialog, 98
Loupe view, 38
customizing, 104–105
keyboard shortcuts, 38, 126
LRCAT files, 94, 96
Luminance sliders, 149, 190
Luminosity blend mode, 258, 261

M

Macintosh users, 355
Magic Wand tool (Photoshop), 349
Make Select button, 52
margins sliders
Print module, 321, 322, 323, 351,
353
Slideshow module, 299
Masking slider, 209, 210
master photos, 77
Match Total Exposures option, 166
Maximum Size template, 318
memory cards, 5–19
menu bar, 41
**Merge to HDR in Photoshop
command,** 262
**Merge to Panorama in Photoshop
command,** 234
metadata
copying, 71
embedded, 67–71
finding photos using, 77–79
GPS data, 72–73
preferences, 28
slide shows and, 303–304
synchronizing, 71
templates, 15, 30–31, 69
XMP sidecar files, 28, 69–70
Metadata filter, 77
Metadata panel, 67–69, 72
Metadata pop-up menu, 15
Metadata Presets folder, 31

Minimal preview, 17, 19
missing files/folders, 97–98
monitors
    calibration of, 342
    Dual Display feature, 112–115
moving photos, 82–83
MP3 music files, 310
music in slide shows, 308–310, 413
My Lightroom Photos folder, 3, 7, 8
My Pictures folder, 3

N

naming/renaming
    collections, 99
    color labels, 121–122
    exported photos, 222
    folders, 84
    imported photos, 13–14, 32
    photos in Lightroom, 80–81
    Photoshop edited files, 268
    presets, 161
    template for, 14, 22–25
National Association of Photoshop
    Professionals (NAPP), 417, 418
Navigator panel
    history states in, 188
    viewing photos in, 38–39
    white balance adjustments and, 134
New Action dialog, 247
New Develop Preset dialog, 161,
    216, 285
New Metadata Preset dialog, 30–31
New Preset dialog, 224
New Smart Object via Copy
    option, 254–255
New Template dialog, 302, 324
Noise Reduction sliders, 190, 217
Noiseware Professional, 217
numbering photos, 14, 24

O

Opacity setting
    Background Image, 307
    Identity Plate, 301, 314
Organize pop-up menu, 8

organizing photos
    collections for, 45–59
    date feature for, 9–10
    folders for, 3–4, 8–10
    importing and, 8–10
    keywords for, 60–66
    stacking and, 86–88
    See also **sorting photos**
Output Settings panel, 364, 414
output sharpening, 223
Overlays panel
    Print module, 325, 326, 327, 350
    Slideshow module, 298, 300, 301,
    314

P

Page Setup dialog, 320, 321
Painter tool, 65–66, 99
panels
    end marks, 123–125
    expanding all, 126
    hiding, 36–37, 111
    keyboard shortcuts, 160
    linking, 126
    opening, 165
    resizing, 99
    Solo mode, 111
    See also **specific panels**
panorama stitching, 259–261
paper selection options, 320
paper/printer profiles, 342–343
PDF slide shows, 312–313
Perceptual Rendering Intent, 344
Photo menu, 234, 239
Photomatix Pro, 268
Photomerge feature, 234, 259–261
photos
    background, 306–307
    backing up, 11–12
    comparing, 47–49, 51–53
    cropping, 192–195
    deleting, 44, 380
    duplicate, 32
    editing multiple, 156–157
    emailing, 226–229
    exporting, 220–225
    finding, 74–79
    flagging, 43–44, 100

    importing, 5–19
    missing, 97–98
    moving, 82–83
    numbering, 14, 24
    organizing, 3–4, 8–10
    previewing, 16–19
    printing, 317–353
    rating, 42–43
    renaming, 13–14, 80–81
    resizing, 324
    sharpening, 207–211
    sorting, 42–53
    stacking, 86–88
    straightening, 196–197, 404–405
    viewing, 38–39
photosharing plug-ins, 230–231,
    234
Photoshop
    color space in, 238, 268
    creating actions in, 247–252
    double-processing photos in,
    253–258
    edge border preparation in,
    349–350
    editing photos in, 240–244
    jumping to/from Lightroom,
    239–246, 389–390
    merging HDR images in, 262–267
    Photomerge feature, 234, 259–261
    preparing files for, 238
    quick tips on using, 268
    saving edits in, 245
    sharpening images in, 258, 261
    Smart Object feature, 253–258
Photoshop Elements, 33
Photoshop Lightroom. *See*
    Lightroom
Photoshop User **magazine,** 417
Photoshop World Conference &
    Expo, 418
Picks
    collections from, 45–46
    filtering, 100, 380
    flagging photos as, 43–44, 100, 379
    Survey view of, 49
Picture Package feature, 328–335
Pictures folder, 3
pixel Loupe, 133
Playback panel, 308, 310, 311

playing slide shows, 295, 305
Plug-in Manager, 230
plug-ins, Export, 230–231, 234
plus sign (+) button, 54, 56, 57, 97
PNG file format, 350
Point Curve presets, 143, 279
portrait orientation, 335
portrait workflow, 375–396
    backing up the photos, 378
    client proofing via Web gallery,
        385–386
    creating collections of photos, 380
    delivering final photos, 393–396
    editing for initial presentation,
        381–384
    emailing the photos, 393–394
    final editing process, 387–392
    printing the photos, 394–396
    shooting the photos, 376–377
    sorting the photos, 379–380
portraits
    retouching, 180–181
    sharpening, 211
    trendy effect, 152–153, 247
    workflow for, 375–396
post-crop vignetting, 150, 151
Post-Processing section, Export
    dialog, 228, 251, 252
Preferences dialog, 26–27
presets
    built-in, 159–160
    camera calibration, 216
    creating your own, 161–162
    Develop module, 159–162
    duotone, 287
    export, 221, 224–225, 234
    File Naming, 14, 22–25, 81
    importing, 162
    metadata, 30–31, 69
    previewing, 159, 162
    saving, 25, 161
    sharpening, 211
    split toning effect, 285
    updating, 166
Presets panel, 159, 161, 211
Preview in Browser button, 359,
    415
previewing
    grayscale conversions, 165, 288
    imported photos, 16–19

presets, 159, 162
second monitor, 115
slide shows, 294, 310, 314
time required for, 19
Web galleries, 359, 415
zoom ratios for, 165
Print button, 344, 396
Print dialog, 344–346, 395–396
Print Job panel, 325, 339–344,
    347–348
Print module, 317–353
    Cells panel, 329
    Collections panel, 336, 337
    Guides panel, 325, 326
    Image Settings panel, 318, 322, 332,
        336
    Layout Engine panel, 328, 333
    Layout panel, 321, 322, 323, 324, 334
    Overlays panel, 325, 326, 327, 350
    Preview area, 319, 328, 353
    Print Job panel, 325, 339–344,
        347–348
    Template Browser, 319, 321, 324,
        328, 333
print queue, 353
Print Settings options, 346
Print Setup dialog, 320, 321
printer/paper profiles, 342–343
printing, 317–353
    16-bit, 341, 353
    collections, 336–338
    color profiles for, 342–343
    edge frame borders, 349–352
    Identity Plate, 326–327, 353
    image orientation for, 320
    to JPEG files, 347–348
    multiple photos per page, 319–320,
        328–335
    page layouts for, 321–325, 328–338
    paper selection for, 320
    printer selection for, 320
    quality settings for, 340, 346, 348
    Rendering Intent options for, 344
    resizing photos for, 324
    resolution settings for, 340, 347
    saving custom layouts for, 324,
        347–348
    selecting photos for, 318, 319
    setting options for, 339–346

sharpening photos for, 341, 348
templates for, 318, 319, 324
text in photo layouts, 326–327
workflow for, 394–396
problem photos. *See* **fixing
    problem photos**
Profile pop-up menu, 343
profiles
    camera, 213–214
    paper/printer, 342–343
ProPhoto RGB color space, 238, 268
PSD files, 220, 268
Pupil Size slider, 203
Put in Subfolder checkbox, 8

Q

Quality slider, 222, 228, 312
Quick Collections, 58–59
    adding photos to, 58
    markers for, 107
    removing photos from, 59
    saving as permanent collections, 59
Quick Develop panel, 163–164, 273

R

Radius slider, 208
Random Order checkbox, 295, 311
Range sliders, 147
rating photos. *See* **star ratings**
RAW photos
    camera profiles for, 213–214
    contrast applied to, 288
    converting to DNG format, 8
    editing in Photoshop, 239, 246,
        389–390
    exporting, 232–233
    metadata info in, 69–70
Record button, 247
Recovery slider, 136, 137, 275, 381
**Rectangular Marquee tool
    (Photoshop),** 349, 391
Red Eye Correction tool, 203–204
Red Primary slider, 216
Red/Cyan slider, 212
Red-labeled images, 53
Region sliders, 146

Rejects
    deleting, 44, 380
    flagging, 43–44, 379
Relative Rendering Intent, 344
relinking missing photos, 97–98
removing
    artifacts from photos, 199–202
    dust spots from photos, 198
    keywords from photos, 63
    photos from Survey View, 100
    red eye from photos, 203–204
    slide show photos, 294
    Web gallery photos, 357
    See also **deleting**
Rename Photos dialog, 81
renaming. *See* **naming/renaming**
Rendering Intent options, 344
Repeat One Photo Per Page
    checkbox, 320, 333–334
Reset button, 148, 177, 217
resizing. *See* **sizing/resizing**
resolution settings, 225, 238, 340
retouching photos
    Adjustment Brush for, 180–181
    See also **fixing problem photos**
rotating
    Identity Plate, 352
    text, 301, 314
"rule of thirds" grid, 192, 193
rulers, 321, 353

S

Saturation sliders
    Basic panel, 142
    Camera Calibration panel, 216
    HSL/Color/Grayscale panel,
        148–149
    Split Toning panel, 283, 284, 285,
        287
saving
    photos as JPEGs, 220–225
    Photoshop edits, 245
    presets, 25, 161
    print layouts, 324, 347–348
    slide shows, 302
    templates, 25, 302, 324
    Web galleries, 370, 372
Scale slider, 297, 308, 314, 351

searching photos, 74–79
Select Catalog dialog, 91
Select image, 52
shadows
    adjusting, 138
    clipping warning, 138
    color picker, 283, 287
    drop, 301, 302
sharpening images, 207–211
    Adjustment Brush for, 175
    exporting and, 223, 234
    output sharpening, 223
    Photoshop used for, 258, 261
    presets for, 211
    print settings for, 341
shooting tethered, 20–21, 32, 376
shortcut icon, 227–228
Show Cell Numbers checkbox, 365
Show Guides checkbox, 325, 326
Show Info Overlay checkbox, 104
Show Preview checkbox, 6
Site Info panel, 360–361, 372
Size slider, 176, 200
sizing/resizing
    brushes, 172, 176, 200, 217
    frame borders, 351
    Identity Plate, 297, 308
    panels, 99
    photos for printing, 324
    slideshow photos, 299
    thumbnails, 38, 126, 372
sky darkening technique, 182–183
slide shows, 291–314
    backgrounds for, 305, 306–307
    creating collections for, 292, 314,
        410–411
    customizing slides for, 298–305, 314
    duration options, 311
    emailing, 312–313
    exporting, 312–313
    full-screen, 295, 312
    Identity Plate in, 296–297, 300, 301,
        314
    impromptu, 59, 295
    layouts for, 292–295, 298–306
    metadata in, 303–304
    music added to, 308–310, 413
    ordering photos for, 293
    PDF format, 312–313

    playing, 295, 305
    previewing, 294, 310, 314
    random order option, 295, 311
    removing photos from, 294
    resizing photos in, 299
    selecting photos for, 292
    templates for, 293, 294, 298, 302
    text used in, 303–304
    title slides for, 296–297, 314, 413
    transitions for, 311
    travel photography, 410–413
sliders
    navigation shortcuts, 165
    resetting, 140, 165
    See also **specific sliders**
Slideshow module, 291–314
    Backdrop panel, 305
    Collections panel, 292, 314
    Layout panel, 299
    Options panel, 300, 302
    Overlays panel, 298, 300, 301, 314
    Playback panel, 308, 310, 311
    Preview area, 293, 294, 310, 314
    Template Browser, 293, 294, 298,
        302, 412
    Titles panel, 296–297
Smart Collections, 56–57, 99, 100
Smart Objects, 253–258
snapshots, 166, 189, 288
Snapshots panel, 166, 189, 288
Solo mode, 111
sorting photos, 42–59
    collections for, 45–59
    color labels for, 53, 121–122
    keywords for, 60–66
    Pick flags for, 43–45
    Quick Collections for, 58–59
    Smart Collections for, 56–57
    star ratings for, 42–43
    workflow for, 379–380
    See also **organizing photos**
sound options, 27
Soundtrack checkbox, 308, 310
Split Toning panel
    duotone creation, 286–287
    split-tone effect, 282–285
split-screen views, 140
spot removal
    artifact removal, 199–202
    dust removal, 198, 405

Spot Removal tool, 198, 200–202, 405

sRGB color space, 222, 234

stacked photos, 86–88

Standard preview, 17, 19

star ratings, 42–43, 76

stitching panoramas, 259–261

Stolzenbach, Issac, 152

Straighten tool, 196–197

straightening photos, 196–197, 404–405

Stroke Border checkbox, 336

subcollections, 55

subfolders, 84

sub-keywords, 64, 99

Survey view, 47–49

  Pick flags used in, 49

  removing photos from, 48, 100

  reordering photos in, 48

Swap button, 52

Synchronize button, 164

Synchronize Folder dialog, 267

Synchronize Metadata dialog, 71

Synchronize Settings dialog, 164

synchronizing

  catalogs, 92–94, 267

  Develop settings, 164

  metadata, 71

T

Targeted Adjustment tool (TAT)

  Grayscale panel, 279–281, 288

  HSL panel, 149

  Tone Curve panel, 145

Temp slider, 132

Template Browser

  Print module, 319, 321, 324, 328, 333

  Slideshow module, 293, 294, 298, 302, 412

  Web module, 358

templates

  file naming, 14, 22–25

  metadata, 15, 30–31, 69

  print, 318, 319, 324

  saving, 25, 302, 324

slide show, 293, 294, 298, 302

Web gallery, 356, 358–359, 368–369

tethered shooting, 20–21, 32, 376

text

  Identity Plate, 126, 296–297, 300, 301, 327

  Photoshop, 244

  print layout, 326–327

  slide show, 298, 301, 303–304, 314

  Web gallery, 357, 358, 364, 367

Text Overlays checkbox, 298

Text Template Editor, 304, 327

thumbnails

  badges in, 107

  preview, 16–19

  resizing, 38, 126, 372

  Web gallery, 357, 363, 372

Thumbnails slider, 38

TIFF files, 220, 239, 246, 265

Tint slider

  Basic panel, 132

  Camera Calibration panel, 215

title slides, 296–297, 314, 413

Titles panel, 296–297, 413

Tone Curve panel, 143–147

  contrast adjustments, 143–146, 276, 279

  keyboard shortcuts, 144, 145

  Point Curve presets, 143

  Range sliders, 147

  Region sliders, 146

  Targeted Adjustment tool, 145

toolbar

  display options, 99

  hiding, 39

travel workflow, 399–418

  backing up the photos, 401, 403

  creating collections of photos, 402–403

  editing the photos, 404–409

  flagging the photos, 402, 403

  importing the photos, 401, 403

  slide show creation, 410–413

  Web gallery creation, 414–415

type. *See* **text**

Type tool (Photoshop), 244, 389

U

Uncheck All button, 6

underexposed photos, 166

undoing

  edits, 188–189

  moves, 83

Unsharp Mask filter (Photoshop), 258, 261, 266

Upload Settings panel, 371, 372

uploading Web galleries, 370–371

V

Versace, Vincent, 317

Vibrance slider, 142

viewing photos, 38–39

  blackout modes, 40–41

  Compare view, 51–53

  Grid view, 39, 106–109

  Loupe view, 38, 104–105

  Survey view, 47–49

  zooming in/out, 100

Vignettes panel, 150–151, 166, 191, 382

vignetting

  creating, 150–151, 166, 382

  fixing, 191

virtual copies, 154–155

  filtering for, 77

  grayscale conversions and, 272–273, 274, 278, 288

  resetting, 217

Volume Browser, 97

W

Waitt, Ted, 79

warning triangles, 165

watched folders, 20, 21

watermarks, 314, 364

WB pop-up menu, 130

Web galleries, 355–372

  captions in, 364

  cell numbers in, 365

  client proofing via, 364, 385–386

  collections for, 356, 372

color options, 366–367, 372
customizing, 362–365
downloadable, 370
email links in, 360–361
exporting, 370
Identity Plate in, 362–363
layouts for, 356–359, 362–365
previewing, 359, 415
removing photos from, 357
saving, 370, 372
selecting photos for, 356
site titles in, 357, 362–363
templates for, 356, 358–359,
   368–369
text in, 357, 358, 364
thumbnails in, 357, 363, 372
travel photos in, 414–415
uploading, 370–371
Web links in, 360–361

Web module, 355–372
   Appearance panel, 357, 359, 362,
      363, 365, 368, 369
   Collections panel, 372, 385
   Color Palette panel, 366–367, 368,
      369, 372
   Engine panel, 368–369
   Image Info panel, 364
   Output Settings panel, 364, 414
   Site Info panel, 360–361, 372
   Template Browser, 358
   Upload Settings panel, 371
wedding photography workflow,
   416
white balance controls
   Develop module, 130–134, 381
   resetting, 165
   shooting tethered and, 32
White Balance Selector tool, 126,
   133–134, 381

window title bar, 41
workflows
   portrait photography, 375–396
   travel photography, 399–418
   wedding photography, 416

X

XMP sidecar files, 28, 29, 69–70, 232,
   233

Z

zoom ratios, 165
Zoom to Fill checkbox, 322, 323,
   328, 332
Zoom to Fill Frame checkbox, 300,
   306
zooming in/out, 100, 126, 199

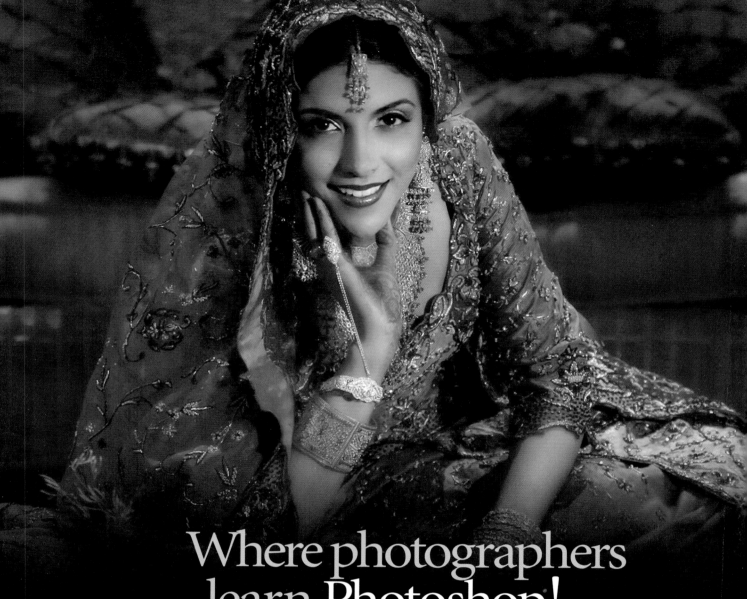

Where photographers learn Photoshop!

Every day, the National Association of Photoshop Professionals teaches photographers from around the world how to turn ordinary into extraordinary and memories into masterpieces. We're your ultimate resource for Adobe® Photoshop® training, education, and news.

Join today and receive...

- *Photoshop User* magazine
- 24-7 Online tech support
- Exclusive member discounts
- Unlimited video tutorials

And, as a bonus, you'll get "The Best of *Photoshop User*: The 10th Year" DVD

One-Year Membership $99* • **Two-Year Membership $179***
Use code NAPM-1UM for your bonus gift.

 National Association of Photoshop Professionals
Photography by David Ziser, Professional Photographer and Photoshop World Instructor ©2007